Manifesting

the Life of

JESUS

Practical Daily
Thoughts on the Christ-life

Jim Fowler

C.I.Y. Publishing
17102 Blanco Trail
San Antonio, Texas 78248
www.Christinyou.net

Manifesting the Life of JESUS

Practical Daily Thoughts on the Christ-life

© 2021 by Jim Fowler

Published by
C.I.Y. Publishing
17102 Blanco Trail
San Antonio, Texas 78248

ISBN 13 digit – 1-978-929541-63-8

Scripture quotations are from the New American
Standard Bible, Copyright © 1960, 1962, 1963, 1968,
1971, 1972, 1973, 1975 by The Lockman Foundation,
La Habra, California.

Printed in the United States of America

FOREWORD

The "word of the day" that my wife and I were considering that morning was "opuscule." It is a word rarely used in contemporary English, though it was more frequently used in English in the eighteenth century. Trying to figure the word out from its constituent parts, I knew that *"opus"* was Latin for "a work," particularly a literary work; and we still use it when we refer to an author's *magnum opus*, the largest and most popular work an author has written. The second part of the word, *scul*, is also Latin, referring to something that is small, little, brief, or minor. We still use that suffix in the word "miniscule." So, *opuscule* is used to refer to a small literary or musical work, and is the opposite of a *magnum opus*. My wife suggested that my one-page daily readings were just that – brief written works – an *opuscule* every day.

This present volume is the third volume of daily readings that I have written, compiled and published. In doing so, I have completed my objective of a trilogy of short daily readings on various Christian topics. The first volume (2017) is entitled, *The Issue is Jesus*. The second volume (2019) is entitled, *Focusing on Jesus*. And this, the third volume (2021) is entitled, *Manifesting the Life of Jesus*. The combination of the three titles will be entitled, *The Jesus Trilogy*.

There was no predetermined organizational agenda, no rhyme nor reason for the ordering of these daily readings. I was desirous of allowing the Spirit of the Lord to bring ideas to my mind, and these often came around 4:00 a.m. in the morning as I was awakening. I would take those half-baked ideas with me to the recliner where I write, and see how they developed and took form. When I completed sufficient articles to be used every day for an entire year, I did rearrange a few of the articles to correspond with the Advent season and the Easter season of the Church calendar.

There may be subjects or themes in this volume that are presented differently than you have heard before. Don't let that throw you; keep reading, and let the Spirit guide your thoughts. Don't accept something just because Jim Fowler wrote it and put it into print.

Every writer is in large part a compiler of ideas that have been accumulated along the way and over the years of the author's journey. The manner in which those ideas have been expressed in writing may be original and unique, but the ideas have often been trafficked over many years. I have often found inspiration for ideas by listening to the sermons of our pastor, Jerome Marroquin, at Sonrise Christian Fellowship in Fallbrook, California. Many ideas have been gleaned and developed from a lifetime of reading, especially favorite authors such as Soren Kierkegaard, Jacques Ellul, W. Ian Thomas, and others. As I live life and read from a variety of sources including digital blogs and social media posts, I try to stay attuned for germinal ideas that might be developed into a daily reading *opuscule*.

It is my expectant hope that this collection of writings will be used by God to reveal and suggest concepts to Christian readers that will enhance the development of their Christian lives and understanding for many years to come.

Jim Fowler
October, 2021

Table of Contents

Foreword..iii

Table of Contents..v

Words of Appreciation.. vi

Daily Readings 1-366

Indices..367

    Scriptural Index...369
    Topical Index...373

Words of Appreciation

As these daily readings were originally posted sporadically on Facebook over a period of almost two years (2020 and 2021), there are many who have responded with "likes" and made comments of appreciation for the content of the readings during that period. Thank you to all of you for your words of encouragement and challenge. I am unsure whether the confinement and quarantine of the global coronavirus pandemic during those years allowed for additional readership, or whether the backlash against Facebook during the 2020 election year caused some to back away from the social media platform altogether. God knows, and my responsibility has simply been to share what came to my mind. I have taken those Facebook posts and formatted them for this book of daily readings.

In particular, I will mention the following persons, knowing that I run the risk of leaving out some who should probably be mentioned. Regular responses to the readings were made by Matthew and Michelle Morizio, Don Burzynski, Gloria Jeannie Woods Grief, Diana Busby, Janet Bobrow, Chris Moore, Steve and Nancy Talbot, Muriel Ruppert, and many others.

Special thanks to Diana Busby for taking the time (it took a month) to read through the entire manuscript and make general editing suggestions concerning grammar, punctuation and acceptability of content. The readability of this book is due to her diligent editing.

Thank you to all who have assisted in the development of this volume of readings.

Jim Fowler

NO MORE PROMISES

I made a promise – both to God and to myself. I promised myself that I would not make any more promises to God. You see, I have made many promises to God over the years. I have promised NOT TO DO this or that; not to sin in a certain manner, not to have pride about what I have done. I have made promises TO DO this or that; to spend more time in fellowship with Christian brethren, to be more loving towards my wife. But I must confess that my track record on keeping promises is abysmal. Is that what Paul meant when he wrote, "The good that I would, I do not do; and the good that I would not, that I do" (Rom. 7:19)?

Solomon in his wisdom wrote, "It is better to not vow, than to vow and not pay" (Eccl. 5:5). Based on such wise advice, I have made a promise to make no more promises to God. Yet, I know that this might create a vicious cycle of continued failure. I have a sneaking suspicion that I will not be any more successful in keeping my promise to make no more promises to God than I have been with my promise-keeping in the past. I am admittedly a fickle and fallible specimen of humanity. My good intentions far outrun the consistency of my follow-through. "Woe is me; I am a man of unclean lips" (Isa. 6:5), with no integrity.

My only feasible recourse is to throw myself upon God's grace, and to recognize that any good that I might manifest must derive from the inherent and intrinsic goodness of God's character. "Not that I am adequate to consider anything as coming from myself (my own ability to keep my promises), but my adequacy is derived from God (His grace to effect anything and everything He desires to be and do in me)" (II Cor. 3:5). The issue is not what I promise to do or not do, but what God wants to do and not do in and through me that is of any lasting consequence in my human life. So, I am not making any promises to God disguised as "new year's resolutions" as I begin this, another year.

JANUARY 2

UNREALISTIC EXPECTATIONS

"I think I have a right to expect that my children should make me feel loved." Those were the words of an older mother estranged from her grown children, and thus cut off from involvement in her grandchildren's lives also. The words were uttered through much pain and exasperation, unaware of what caused the alienation with her children. She blamed the children for being insensitive and unloving, without realizing that it was she who had a most inadequate understanding of love. Love flows out of God through us to others. Such love has no expectations of response or reciprocation – no strings attached!

Even God, who is the ultimate essence of love, cannot make anyone "feel loved." "God so loved the world that He gave His only begotten Son" (Jn. 3:16), but every person must individually receive that love gift. Then, in the process of a love relationship, each person must determine to grow deeper in God's love and thereby experientially "feel loved" by God sensing His loving arms around them, and His guidance in every circumstance of life. "Feeling loved" is not an emotion that others are responsible to grant. "Feeling loved" is a decision to accept and appreciate the sentiment and actions of another (God or other people).

It is a most unrealistic expectation to think that others should "make us feel" one way or another. It sets up a "performance trap" that will inevitably create alienation when other people are unable to effect the emotional state such a person might expect or desire. Such unrealistic expectations become a form of "emotional blackmail," that expects another person to be responsible for your feelings. No one can make another person "feel loved." No one can make another "feel happy." Our feelings are a result of our own choices. We choose to be the conduits of God's one-way unconditional love, and we choose to let God alone fulfill our human needs and desires.

2

HIDE AND SEEK

Almost everyone has played the childhood game of "hide and seek." One person hides their eyes, while everyone else runs to find a hiding place, and the seeker attempts to find the others in their hiding places until everyone is found. A reverse variation on the game is called "sardines;" everyone in the group hides their eyes while one person runs to find a hiding place. The entire group seeks the one who is hiding; and when found each seeker quietly joins the hidden one in the hiding place until they are packed into the hiding place like "sardines." The difficult part of this variation is to remain quiet without giggling.

Have your ever thought of playing "hide and seek" with God? Since God is all-knowing, He has an advantage when we seek to hide. Adam and Eve played such a game in the Garden of Eden, attempting to hide from God after they had sinned. They were soon found. But, to reverse the roles, does God ever hide from us? Yes, He does! Not desiring to look at our sin, He graciously "hides His face" (Deut. 31:18; Ps. 30:7; Isa. 54:8; 59:2). Beyond that, He purposefully hides and remains a mystery to our finite understanding, in order that we might seek Him. God sometimes hides from our awareness to reveal Himself to our needs.

The hidden God was historically revealed in His Son, Jesus. "No one knows the Son except the Father; nor does anyone know the Father except the Son, and anyone to whom the Son wills to reveal Him" (Matt. 11:27). Jesus said, "He who has seen Me has seen the Father" (Jn. 6:46; 14:7,9). Experientially, however, His presence and activity ever remain an infinite, hidden mystery. He hides Himself from our full awareness; and at the right time, He surprises us with the revelation of His grace and character. God hides Himself in the marginalized people of our society where we least expect to find Him. Jesus said, "As you have done it unto the least of these, you have done it unto Me" (Matt. 25:40,45).

JANUARY 4

THINGS WORK TOGETHER FOR GOOD

Paul's statement has once again proven its practical value. "All things work together for good for those who love God and are called according to His purpose" (Rom. 8:28). The "good" (here used generously; i.e. the best outcome) of the Trump presidency is that his shenanigans and shifty double-talk have caused the world to hate religion. Identifying, as he has, with evangelical religion, he has exposed religious sentiment for the fraud that it so often is. The world has observed that the "Trump card" for religion is nothing but a sham – just a "joker" whose value will always be questionable and variable.

As the circumstances of national politics and international collusion work themselves out in history, we are all rather befuddled how any "good" can result from such shady conspiracies and cover-ups. It is, however, a "good" that serves God's purposes to be aware that religion is the absolute obverse of the dynamic grace-operative of the Spirit of the living Lord Jesus that forms the impetus of Christian faith. Genuine Christians are Christ-ones, identified in spirit-union with the living Lord Jesus (cf. I Cor. 6:17).

The need of the hour is now to explain that Christianity (Christ-in-you-ity) is not religion. Nor is it some superficial "relationship" with the socio-religious image of Jesus. Christ-in-you-ity is the reality of the indwelling Spirit of the living Lord Jesus (cf. Rom. 8:9; II Cor. 13:5) dwelling within and living out from the spirit-core of one who has received the Spirit of Christ within his/her spirit. The Spirit of Christ within such a Christ-one will of necessity manifest the spirit-character of Jesus in Christian behavior (II Cor. 4:10,11; Gal 5:22,23). It is by that means, and that only, that the world will see the love of Jesus Christ in our social relationships, in the fellowship of our churches, and in the discourse of our national and international politics.

REAL FREEDOM

People in the United States of America pride themselves as being persons who enjoy the freedoms afforded them in the Constitution of the United States. At the same time, many in this country are not experiencing real freedom. In the hustle and bustle of modern life, the performance expectations of "being the best you can be" and maintaining a certain "standard of living" to keep up with one's peer group keep many people exhausted in never-ending performance. The added religious burdens of do, do, do, and go, go, go to please God only intensify the pressures to perform and diminish the enjoyment of real freedom.

Real freedom is only experienced in the personal knowing of God's grace in Jesus Christ. Grace is the provision and resource for living that God has made available in His Son, Jesus (cf. Jn. 1:17). It is totally antithetical to all mandated expectations of human activity. Grace is the divine dynamic whereby any/all performance expected of us is accomplished through us. This is not a passivism wherein we have no responsibility, but our God-given freedom of human choice is repeatedly given the opportunity to respond in faith to God's willingness to freely give us all things – to exercise receptivity to Gods activity of Grace.

Jesus told those listening to Him, "You will know the Truth, and the Truth shall set you free" (Jn. 8:32). Identifying Himself as the personified Truth (Jn. 14:6), Jesus proceeded to say, "If the Son sets you free, you will be free indeed" (Jn. 8:36), i.e, experiencing real freedom. Real freedom – freedom from all performance expectations and freedom to be the completely fulfilled person that God intends you to be by His provision of grace – can only be experienced in union with the divine and living Lord Jesus. "It was for freedom that Christ set us free; do not be subjected to the enslaving performance expectations" (Gal. 5:1). There are many pseudo-freedoms, but Christ is the real freedom.

JANUARY 6

FROM THE INSIDE OUT

Christians have long misunderstood how Christian behavior functions. The common misconception is that Christians behave in conformity with the behavioral admonitions of "thou shalt…" and "thou shalt not…" That may have been true in the law structure of the old Jewish covenant but fails to understand the glorious reality of God's grace provision in the new covenant. Christian behavior is not facilitated by external behavior modification, but by the internal process of "the Spirit of Christ" (Rom. 8:9) indwelling the human spirit, energizing divine character to be manifested in our physical behavior.

When we receive the "Spirit of the living God" (II Cor. 3:3) within our spirit, it is like having an artesian well of godliness deep within us, available to produce "springs of living water" (Jn. 4:14). Jesus said, "He who believes in Me, as the scripture said, 'From his innermost being will flow rivers of living water'" (Jn. 7:38). That is what the grace-provision of the new covenant is comprised of the dynamic enabling of everything God the Father, Son, and Holy Spirit desires to manifest and exhibit in and through us as Christians. "His divine power has granted to us everything pertaining to life and godliness" (II Pet. 1:3).

Christians function behaviorally from the inside out. Within our spirit dwells the Spirit of the living Lord Jesus, complete with the divine character of God. The character of God in our spirit is meant to influence the attitudes of our mind, the affections of our emotions, and the volitional determinations of our will, thus actuating human behavior in our soul, while preserving our created human freedom of choice. The choices we make in our soul are behaviorally implemented in our bodies as the Christian "manifests the life of Jesus" (II Cor. 4:10,11) via "the fruit of the Spirit" (Gal. 5;22,23). Christian behavior functions from the inside out, from spirit to soul to body.

THE CABOOSE AT THE END OF THE TRAIN

While visiting a railroad museum recently, I was particularly interested to observe the numerous caboose cars and to determine their purpose at the tail-end of early North American trains. A caboose was originally a "cabin-house" (*cabhoose*) mounted on a flatcar, where the rail crew could assemble and even cook a meal. Later, the cupola on the top of the cabin allowed the crew to look forward the length of the train and observe whether the loads on the various cars were stable, and also to check for overheated bearings on the cars ahead. The conductor in the caboose would jump down to set the track switches in early models of American train cabooses.

Some have noted that in likeness to the caboose at the end of the train, our human feelings are to be the trailing end of our behavioral conveyance in the Christian life. When we arrive at a conclusion in our mind, and a determination to act in our will, our emotions should fall into line as we move forward. Just as the caboose does not have a power-source to pull the train, human emotions are not adequate to be the driving force of behavior in our human lives. When we attempt to allow our human feelings to serve as the engine that drives our train, we will usually discover that our train is rolling backwards and our relationships with others are suffering greatly.

We have all observed that some people seem to be driven by their emotions, and these can often be quite erratic. When fickle feelings are allowed to lead our train, our self-oriented emotions and affectations can cause us to jump track and have a disastrous train wreck. Our human emotions must follow where our reasoned thoughts and carefully determined choices lead, and that in accord with the planned track that God has laid for our particular lives. We must intentionally determine to keep our emotions as the caboose at the end of the train.

JANUARY 8

ALLOWING FOR DIFFERENT IDEAS

When speaking at a conference or seminar, listeners in the audience often approach me to explain that another speaker thinks or teaches something different than I am teaching. My response: "Isn't that great! You get a variety, rather than the same ol' diet or data." Why is it that religious people think that everyone who is a Christian should think the same way as every other Christian? Religious people have such a quest for conformity of thought and action. They have a difficult time learning to agree to disagree agreeably and allowing for diversity of opinions and interpretations within their group.

This is likely due to the fundamentalist tendency that projects the idea that there is only one proper Christian way to think and act. Everyone should carve their religious totem-pole in the same manner, with the same fundamental ideas. On the contrary, there is only one Person central to Christian being and understanding, and the living Lord Jesus expresses His mind (I Cor. 2:16) and lives His life (Jn. 14:6) uniquely in every Christ-one, allowing for the plurality and diversity of the Body of Christ. We do not seek cookie-cutter uniformity of thought and action, but the unity wherein Christ in every Christian loves the other.

Christian congregations misrepresent the Lord they claim to believe when they engage in the vociferous clamoring of various individuals attempting to defend their position by proving that their interpretation is the correct Christian expression. Christians must cease their internecine strife and back away from the argumentation whereby they attempt to absolutize their interpretations and opinions. In such process, they become an idol-factory producing packaged ideas, doctrines and strictures of moral propriety. Such idolatrous deification of our human ideas is totally contrary to the purpose and function of the living and loving Body of Christ.

RELIGIOUS QUANTIFICATION

Religion is the natural tendency of fallen man to establish external criteria to quantify their performance, and thereby evaluate how they are doing or not doing in their self-evaluated relation to God as they might perceive Him. Via self-determined categorizations and classifications, religionists employ numerical assessments and statistical percentages in their attempt to quantify and measure ecclesiastical and behavioral growth. Such quantification over-simplifies reality into objective mathematical data categories, and fails to account for God's divine action and His spiritual objectives in individual lives.

Such objective mathematical quantification is becoming the standard of categorizing and calculating human knowledge in every field of human thought and study today. Indicative of the naturalistic approach of human calculation, such an approach disallows for the subjective and meta-empirical approaches to human knowledge. A fair approach to knowledge (Latin *scientia*) necessitates an even playing field that does not insist on solely naturalistic data to the exclusion of spiritual and supernatural phenomena – a willingness to consider the mysteries that defy reason and quantification, such as interpersonal love, relational oneness, and heavenly sublime experience.

Genuine spirituality, comprised of spiritual oneness with the living Lord Jesus, is beyond religious quantification. How does one quantify the depth of one's relationship with God? How does one quantify character and subsequent behavioral outcomes? Yes, Jesus said, "By their fruit you shall know them" (Matt. 7:16,20); but human determination and evaluation of either the quality or quantity of "the fruit of the Spirit" (Gal. 5:22,23) will inevitably be tainted by human perspective. Only God in Christ by the Spirit knows the extent of the manifestation of divine character in our human behavior.

JANUARY 10

PROGRESS IN THE CHRISTIAN LIFE

Recently I read a quote from Thomas Merton that was used as a meme on Facebook. It was a statement that makes a person stop and think. It went like this: "If the 'you' of five years ago doesn't consider the 'you' of today a heretic, you are likely not growing spiritually." The import of this statement is that there is a necessary progress and growth in the Christian life. If we are not learning and growing in our faith and understanding, then we soon become a stagnant Christian who is sliding backwards rather than moving forward as a disciple (learner, follower) of Jesus. We are intended to "grow in the grace and knowledge of our Lord and Savior Jesus Christ" (II Pet. 3:18).

Most Christians can look back over their Christian life and realize that their beliefs and practices have changed over time. What they once thought to be correct biblical interpretation and proper behavioral disposition has changed as they continue to study the ways of God and deal with the practicum of Christian life. This is to be expected because the Christian life is not a static parking spot of thought, but a dynamic process of advancing toward maturity. We are to be growing in awareness of the ways of God which are beyond our understanding (Isa. 55:8,9) and past finding out with finite knowledge (Rom. 11:33).

Progression toward maturity in the Christian life is not to be evaluated by acquisition of knowledge or by placement of function in the institutional church. Our growth, progression and forward movement in Christian faith is attributable to what we are allowing God to do in our lives. "For it is God who works in you, both to will and to work for His good pleasure" (Phil. 2:13). "He who began a good work in you will perfect it until the day of Christ Jesus" (Phil 1:6). As we listen in obedience and are receptive by faith to the daily revelation that God speaks to our hearts, we continue to grow as God intends.

"SEND A LITTLE LOVE MY WAY"

Some readers may remember the song, "Send a Little Love My Way," when it was being played on the radio in the 1970s and 80s. The catchy tune and meaningful words caught my attention. The song was written by Henry Mancini and Hal David, and first released in 1973. Anne Murray sang the song with the Henry Mancini orchestra in the movie, "Oklahoma Crude;" and it was nominated for the Golden Globe Original Song of 1973. These repeated words resonated with my thinking:

"Everyone needs to be loved, and I'm no exception;
I was born to reject rejection."

God created us as social interpersonal persons who need other persons to be and to function as the human beings He created us to be. As John Donne wrote, "No man is an island." In other words, there is a basic human need for love and social acceptance from and with others. As the song states, "Everyone needs to be loved, and I'm no exception." Every person is created with a basic need to love and be loved. We are social beings and need the acceptance of others and, most of all, the acceptance of God's love (I Jn. 4:8,16), whereby He can love others through us.

Fallen human beings so often fail to function as conduits of God's love, and instead reject other people in order to pursue their own selfish purposes. Such selfish social rejection can be very damaging as parents reject children, husbands reject wives, friends reject friends, etc. Such rejection, the opposite of the love and acceptance we all need, is inspired by the Evil One, and is only transcended when Jesus, the divine Lover, comes to inhabit our spirit. "The love of God is shed abroad in our hearts by the Holy Spirit who is given to us" (Rom. 5:5), and "The fruit of the Spirit is love..." (Gal. 5:22). As we allow such divine love to be manifest through us, we do indeed "reject rejection."

JANUARY 12

MAKE THE MOST OF THE "NOW"

The created order that we live in is a transitory world. It was not intended to endure forever. There has been change throughout the ages, and there will be constant change as long as time remains. Such constantly changing realities should not lead us to fatalism, but to an awareness and appreciation for the transcience of the moment. "Everything comes to pass; nothing comes to stay" was the comment of a seasoned missionary. Life goes on, and we must learn to enjoy each moment. Make the most of the "NOW"; it is as fleeting as the beauty of a rosebud, the ecstasy of young love, or the exhilaration of a new experience.

James wrote, "You do not know what your life will be like tomorrow. You are a vapor that appears for a little while and then vanishes away" (James 4:14). A cloud in the sky appears in varied forms and soon drifts by and dissipates. *Carpe Diem* ("seize the day"), wrote the Roman poet, Horace, knowing that it will vanish just as quickly as it came into being. The issues of each day come and go, and the brevity of each moment demands that whatever we hold, we must hold most lightly. Appreciation of the ephemeral, the short-lived glimpses of reality beyond the present, is what keeps us hungering and thirsting for more.

The transcience of this worldly sphere draws our attention to the eternal realm of unchanging permanence in the reality of the Triune God. Jesus said, "Heaven and earth will pass away, but My words will not pass away" (Lk. 21:22). Christians are convinced that they are progressing toward a "new heaven and new earth" (Rev. 21:1), where transcience is superseded by eternality. "This slight momentary affliction is preparing for us an eternal weight of glory beyond all comparison, because we look not to the things that are seen but to the things that are unseen; for the things that are seen are transient, but the things that are unseen are eternal" (II Cor. 4:17,18).

ATTITUDES TOWARD RELIGION

The general attitude of those in Western society is that religion serves a good purpose in its advocacy of moral and civil behavior, and as a social rallying point for those like-minded persons who need a sense of belonging to a group with a cause. Religion may indeed serve such a purpose, but the damage caused by institutional religion is far more comprehensive than those who are sympathetic to religion are aware. Religion can be an innocuous assembly of unthinking persons centralized around historical events and belief-tenets, but unscrupulous leaders often find a sense of power in such religious groups whereby they attempt to manipulate adherents, enslave them, and mobilize them for self-determined social and political agendas.

Under the guise of "freedom of religion," religion has become a cover for the most heinous activities. Religion provides a blurred perspective of the most diabolic self-serving actions of human-kind; cf. clergy abuse of women and children. Religion has been a driving force for a large percentage of the wars and human conflicts throughout human history, including murderous inquisitions, crusades, pogroms, and genocidal exterminations. Religion is an abomination to God, and God hates religion.

There should be no sympathy or resistance among Christian people when they hear or view the assault upon religion and the inevitable decimation of religion. The problem comes when those who have the authority to enact such a war on religion have no spiritual understanding (cf. I Cor. 2:14) and are unable to differentiate between abusive corporate religion and the legitimate devotion of Christian people who have received the Spirit of Christ in their spirit to be their life and character. Genuine Christianity – Christ-in-you-ity – is not religion and is to be differentiated from the perversion of faith called "Christian religion" – an abomination that God cannot help but hate.

JANUARY 14 ·

THE FOUNDATION OF FREEDOM

Human freedoms within every social group must be established on a firm foundation. Jesus warned about those who build upon sand that can be washed away in a storm, rather than on solid rock that can withstand the assaults of the weather (Matt. 7:24-27). The national and personal freedoms enjoyed in the United States of America have a baseline foundation on what was intended to be a fixed constitutional document of a law-based republic. But our nation's Constitution is being assaulted today by those who desire fluid interpretation and the shifting sand variability that corresponds to the prevailing agenda.

If the people of this great nation do not stand up and demand adherence to the Constitution that our founding fathers established, then the foundation of our freedoms will be eroded; and this great experiment in democratic governance "of the people, by the people, and for the people" will crumble like a house of cards. How do we forestall such and preserve our freedoms that have stood for two and a half centuries? By utilizing our representative form of government, we are obliged to vote for candidates who promise to conserve constitutional law in this country.

In addition, as Christ-ones living within this great country, we should desire to preserve our freedom of the worship of God afforded by the Constitution, and appreciate even more the foundation of the spiritual freedom that was purchased for us by the death of Jesus Christ. Our firm foundation is Jesus. "It was for freedom that Christ set us free; stand firm an do not be subject to a yoke of slavery" (Gal. 5:1). "You were called to freedom" (Gal. 5:13). Christ-ones are free to be all that God intends us to be, and free to manifest the character of God (Gal. 5:22,23) in civil, loving relation with others, that by the dynamic provision of God's enabling grace.

SUGAR-COATING OUR JUDGMENTALISM

Not wanting to admit to their judgmentalism, some people will recognize their tendency to be opinionated and outspoken as they express their observations of what they perceive to be true and accurate, but those same people may not want to admit that they are being judgmental. Being judgmental is often defined by such people as being condemnatory, and they do not consider themselves to be engaging in condemnation of other people, despite their condescending remarks about the thoughts or actions of other persons. Such "opinionated and outspoken" persons are adjudged by many in our society to simply be exercising their constitutional "right of free speech."

Such judgmentalism is often not appreciated, especially by those persons about whom these observations and opinions are being made, or when they are challenging or criticizing the value-system or ideology that those listening might believe and ascribe to. Yes, the Constitution of the United States allows for freedom of thought and expression in a pluralistic society; but, within interpersonal relationships, one must consider whether such outspoken comments are kind, constructive, and sensitive to the feelings of other people. Going beyond legal rights, we must act in love that seeks the highest good of other people.

Interpersonal relationships among Christians are not best served by critical, outspoken personal opinions. It is possible to have spiritual discernment without being judgmental. "There is a time to speak, and a time to be silent" (Eccl. 3:7). Every thought we might have does not have to be verbalized. There is a time to bridle our tongues (James 1:26; 3:2) and keep our opinions to ourselves. It is best that we take "the log out of our own eye" (Lk. 6:42), view others with compassionate forgiveness, and seek to build them up. Failing to do so, Christians will continue to be adjudged by the world around us as intolerant and judgmental.

JANUARY 16

THE COVENANTAL METANARRATIVE

In order to grasp the storyline of Biblical history, the overarching metanarrative of God's dealings with His people, one needs to be aware of the structural scaffolding of the concept of covenantal agreements and arrangements between God and His people. The Hebrew word for "covenant" is *berith;* whereas the Greek word for "covenant," used within the New Testament, is *diatheke.* The Greek word implies that the superior party, God, "puts through" an arrangement in the best interest of mankind.

God stepped into the quagmire of human sin and corruption to deliver the family of Noah (Gen. 6:18; 9:9), and gave the covenant sign of the rainbow as surety that such a catastrophic flood would not need to be repeated, because He had a plan to deliver mankind in the life and death of His Son, Jesus.

The covenantal promises of God to Abraham (Gen. 12-22), with promises of descendants, land, nation and blessings, were fulfilled physically for the Israelite people, but had a larger scope of spiritual fulfillment through the Person and work of Jesus and the Christian community. Christians are the primary intended recipients of the promises of God to Abraham (Gal. 3:14, 29).

The ultimate and "eternal" covenant (Heb. 9:15; 13:20), referred to as the "new" covenant (Jere. 31:31; Heb. 8:10,13), is the Jesus covenant, the arrangement that was implemented and ratified in the life, death, resurrection and Pentecostal outpouring of the Son of God. The Jesus covenant is *autodiatheke*, meaning that Jesus is the covenant in Himself. Jesus was explaining such when He said to the disciples, "This cup is the new covenant in My blood" (Lk. 22:20; I Cor. 11:25). God's eternal covenant arrangement is that the risen and living Lord Jesus is, in Himself, the grace-dynamic of God's provision whereby He fulfills all of God's intentions for mankind.

YOU CAN'T BE A "BETTER CHRISTIAN"

Over and over again, I have heard people lamenting the fact that they need "to be a better Christian." The means by which they mistakenly believe they can become such a "better Christian" are the incentives to performance that have been proffered by their religious instructors. Did those religious performance incentives serve to cause one to BE a Christian? NO! We are "saved by grace through faith," and that salvation is not of ourselves and our performance "works," but what God has done and is doing by His grace-activity to form the very life and character of the living Lord Jesus within our spirits and lives.

When a person quits focusing on trying to be a "better Christian," only then will they be available to become what they were trying to become, and that without any effort or undue concern on their part. They will be submitting to God in Christ that He might BE and DO whatever HE might desire to do to form them into the unique Christ-one they are meant to be. As long as one is striving to become a "better Christian," by means of religious activities, they will struggle to become what God never intended them to be. When we receive the living Lord Jesus, we are "complete in Christ" (Col. 1:28), "His divine power has granted us all things pertaining to life and godliness" (II Pet. 1:3).

Our regenerated spiritual condition is one of fullness (Eph. 3:19), perfection (Phil. 3:15), righteousness (Eph. 4:24), and holiness (Eph. 1:4), and one cannot get any "better" than that! But when it comes to our behavioral expression, there is always room for growth and advancement. We can progress in sanctification as Christ is "formed in us (Gal. 4:19). We can allow for a more authentic and representative expression of the Christ-life to be manifested in our physical behavior (II Cor. 4:10,11), and externally that will appear to others as a "better Christian," even though our spiritual condition can't be any "better."

JANUARY 18

CONSTANT AND CONSISTENT RECEIVING

"As many as received Him, to them He gave the right to become children of God, to those who believe in His name, who were born not of blood, nor of the will of the flesh, nor of the will of man, but of God (Jn. 1:12,13). John implies that "receiving is believing," and *vice versa*, "believing is receiving." Saving faith is more than mere mental assent to the historicity of the physical personage of the Jesus who walked around Judea as an itinerant teacher two thousand years ago. Rather, saving faith is the spiritual receptivity of the very Being and activity of the risen and living Lord Jesus who desires to be our entire life.

Paul henceforth wrote, "For by grace you have been saved through faith; and that not of yourselves, *for salvation is* the gift of God; not as a result of works, so that anyone may boast" (Eph. 2:8,9). Earlier Paul had asked this question of the Galatian Christians, "This is the only thing I want to find out from you: did you receive the Spirit *(of the living Jesus)* by the *performance* works of the Law, or by hearing with faith?' (Gal. 3:2). It is foolishness to think that it was our performance (Gal. 3:1,3). To become a Christ-one, we have all received the Spirit of Christ into our spirit by faith; otherwise we do not belong to Christ as a Christian (Rom. 8:9).

To the Colossians Paul wrote, "As you received Christ Jesus, so walk in Him" (Col. 2:6). How did we receive Christ Jesus? As John explained, we did so by faith-receptivity (Jn. 1:11,12). How do we walk out, live out, the Christ-life? By faith, the receptivity of the manifestation of the Christ-life in every moment and action of our lives (cf. II Cor. 4:10,11). It is not the result of what we do, but what He does; not our production of "Christian living," but His out-living of His Christ-life. Faith is "our receptivity of His activity" (initially and continuously). We receive Jesus and His activity in constant and consistent faith.

JESUS PLUS NOTHING

Why is it that Christian people in general have such a propensity to seek to add other criteria to the simplicity of receiving Jesus as their Life? Whenever we try to add something to the simplicity and singularity of Jesus, we diminish Him; we make Him less than He is, indicating that He is not enough in Himself. Jesus is not just part of the equation of salvific life, requiring an additional element to make Jesus more effective. Jesus is "in Himself" everything that God has to give to restore human beings to the intent that God had in creating mankind to be the unique expression of His life and character in His creation.

The message we Christians have to share with the world is simply Jesus – Jesus plus nothing!

Not Jesus plus baptism (baptismal regenerationism)
Not Jesus plus speaking in tongues (glossalalism)
Not Jesus plus a "second work of grace" (supplementalism)
Not Jesus plus election/predestination system (determinism)
Not Jesus plus "once saved always saved" (closed system)
Not Jesus plus eschatological perspective (futurism)
Not Jesus plus sexually straight/not gay (sexism)
Not Jesus plus specified moral behavior (moralism)
Not Jesus plus keeping the rules (legalism)
Not Jesus plus our accepted belief system (fideism)
Not Jesus plus church membership (ecclesiasticsm)
Not Jesus plus religious expectations of activity (religionism)

Jesus is everything any human being requires to be all that God intends us to be to His glory. Jesus is enough, and those who are satisfied with Him will not seek something else to supplement Him. Jesus explained to the Philippians, "For me to live is Christ" (Phil. 1:21), and to the Colossians, he wrote, "Christ is our life," everything we need!

JANUARY 20

A VISIT TO THE BOOKSTORE

There was a time in my life when an opportunity to go into a
bookstore was like putting a kid in a candy store. I spent more
days and hours than I would care to calculate perusing the
shelves of both new and used bookstores. Books were my best
friends. I had an idolatrous obsession with books and the
knowledge to be gained from books. It may seem somewhat
oxymoronic, then, that a bibliophile ("lover of books") like me
should declare that I find modern bookstores to be extremely
depressive. Overall, I avoid general bookstores these days and
seldom visit a bookstore except to grab a cup of coffee.

The books that are popular in general bookstores today are
overwhelmingly written from a humanistic perspective that
encourages readers to operate independently to better
themselves and achieve self-chosen goals. There are always a few
books on Christianity and Christian living that are sprinkled
throughout the "religion" section of bookstores, but most of these
are just as humanistic in philosophical orientation as the secular
volumes. The Christian community has shot itself in the leg by
misrepresenting the Christian life as a never-ending sequence of
performance activities to be better Christians, rather than
appreciating and being receptive to the grace of God in Christ.

The Christian life is not a "how-to," self-help endeavor. Any book
on Christian living should be as far removed from the "self-help"
section of any bookstore, as a science textbook should be
removed from the magic and witchcraft section. The "religion"
section of general bookstores is an abominable amalgamation of
disparate world religion texts, obscure spirituality volumes, and
self-identified Christian religion screeds. Unknowing readers fail
to realize that humanistic religion is essentially antichristian, and
they will not come to know the grace of God in Jesus Christ in
most of the books of the general bookstore.

JESUS IN HIMSELF

Religious people commonly attempt to detach Jesus from the blessings He came to bring. They refer to the "benefits" that Jesus bestows, and fail to realize all that Jesus came to provide is "in Himself." All the benefits and blessings of Jesus are inherent in the personal Being of Jesus.

Jesus is the grace of God in Himself. Grace is a Person.
Jesus is the gospel in Himself. The "good news" is a Person.
Jesus is the kingdom in Himself. The kingdom is a Person.
Jesus is the covenant in Himself. The covenant is a Person.
Jesus is the Torah in Himself – the law written on our hearts
Jesus is the New Creation in Himself. He makes all things new.
Jesus is salvation in Himself. Salvation is a Person.
Jesus is heaven in Himself. Heaven is a Person.
Jesus is the blessing of God in Himself. The blessing is a Person.
Jesus is life in Himself. Eternal Life is a Person. (cf. Jn. 14:6)
Jesus is righteousness in Himself. Righteousness is a Person.
Jesus is sanctification in Himself. Holiness is a Person.
Jesus is freedom in Himself. Freedom is a Person

Jesus is ALL things of God, all divine reality, in Himself. He is "Him who fills all in all" (Eph. 1:23). Ultimate reality is a Person. Everything that has to do with Christianity must be viewed through the reality of Jesus, inherent and intrinsic in Himself. All that Jesus came to bring to mankind, He brings in Himself – not distinct and separated from Himself. Christians must avoid separating Jesus from what He conveys.

There is *NOTHING* Jesus came to bring other than Himself. *EVERYTHING* that is made available by God's Grace is encompassed in the Personal Being of the Living Lord Jesus. Jesus is the only gift of God to mankind. Everything that comprises Christian living is inherent in the very Being of Jesus.

JANUARY 22

HOW SHALL WE THEN LIVE?

The preacher was expounding on the scripture text for the day. He had done his homework in the biblical dictionaries and commentaries and was explaining the cultural background of the narrative and referred to the meaning of some of the words in the original language (Hebrew or Greek) to amplify the meaning of the text. He was to be commended for staying true to the text in its original cultural and textual context and to the foundational hermeneutic principle that a biblical text cannot mean now what it did not mean then, else it can mean anything to anyone, in which case it does not mean anything to anyone.

But, I suspect that there were other parishioners present on that Lord's Day who may have been asking the question that I was asking at the end of the preacher's talk. The question was posed in a book title written by Francis A. Schaeffer, first published in 1976, *How Should We Then Live?* Historical and cultural data pertaining to an ancient text does not in itself constitute Christian preaching and proclamation. The congregants had taken a respite from their busy lives on this first day of the week and were facing another week of challenges of how to allow the Christ-life to be lived out, and they did not receive any instruction as to how to allow such life to be lived out by faith.

Was this really an example of Christian preaching and proclamation? Information about the cultural setting of the text and data dissemination of details about words in the text do not, in themselves, constitute Christian preaching. Greeks who had come to the Jewish Passover came to Philip and said, "We would see Jesus" (John 12:20,21). That is still the need and the cry of people in every age. What we have to share with people is Jesus – how the dynamic life of the living Lord Jesus dwelling in those who have received Him by faith provides the grace-dynamic of the life and character of Jesus in our daily lives.

FEAR ... FACTS ... FAITH

Fear is a natural human response to unexpected and uncertain situations of life. When walking through the woods and you spot a black bear on the path ahead, it is a natural response to react with fear and apprehension for your own well-being. Unexpected social phenomena, like the recent coronavirus pandemic can create individual and social fear. Fear is not wrong in itself; but, if it becomes an overwhelming and paralyzing psychological fixation not based on factual data, fear can become an unfounded neurotic overreaction. We want our mental and emotional expressions of fear and hope to have a foundation in factual data.

Accurate factual data can serve as the valid explanation for our fear, or it can serve as the antidote to dispel unfounded fear. Inadequate factual data may produce a fear of the unknown. The factual data that governs our fear may be comprised of physical and naturalistic information, or it may be divine data and supernatural phenomenal expectation without naturalistic explanation. We must allow for a latitude in the means of human knowing (*scientia*).

Thus, we recognize that even our faith must be founded on factual data. Faith not based on facts degenerates into mere wishful thinking and false hope – a mental creation of unreality. Perhaps you have heard of the cultic groups who encourage the handling of venomous snakes as a sign of one's salvation or holiness. Such so-called "faith," ends up merely as "faith in one's own faith," rather than faith in an object or person that can reasonably be expected to act on our behalf. Christian faith believes that "perfect love casts our fear" (I Jn.4:18), and recognizes that "perfect love" is a personal object – "God is love" (I Jn. 4:8,16), capable of controlling whatever situation we might confront. Faith is receptivity of God's activity, and hope is the reasonable expectation of God's continuing activity on our behalf.

JANUARY 24

THE AUTOMOBILE

Why is your automobile referred to as an "automobile"? In the late nineteenth century many inventors were attempting to produce a self-propelled vehicle for personal travel. The horse-drawn carriage required the care and feeding of horses to pull the carriage, so there was a quest to produce a vehicle that would propel itself. In the Greek language, the word for "self" is *auto* or *autos* (by, in, of, from, out of itself or one's self), so a vehicle that could mobilize itself by means of an onboard propulsion engine was called an "automobile."

The same prefix can be transferred to the understanding of the work of Jesus Christ. Jesus is everything Christian "in Himself." The Christian gospel is simply and only the message of Jesus – *Solus Christus*, as the sixteenth century reformers used to say, without fully understanding the import of that phrase. Everything that Christians think Jesus provides or produces for us is in, by, out of Himself – Self-energized by the divine-human Savior – and never to be considered separate from Him.

> *autobasileia* .. Jesus is the kingdom in Himself
> *autodiatheke* .. Jesus is the covenant in Himself
> *autosoterion* .. Jesus is salvation in Himself
> *autocharis* .. Jesus is grace in Himself (Jn. 1:17)
> *autoeuangellion* .. Jesus is the gospel in Himself
> *autonomos* .. Jesus is the law in Himself
> *autoeulogia* .. Jesus is the blessing in Himself
> *autozoe* .. Jesus is spiritual life in Himself
> *autodikaiosune* .. Jesus is righteousness in Himself
> *autohagios* .. Jesus is holiness in Himself
> *autoagape* .. Jesus is love in Himself
> *autokalos* .. Jesus is goodness in Himself

Jesus is, in Himself, everything God desires for mankind.

HAILING A CAB

When moving around in a large city anywhere in the world, it is usually relatively easy to wave your arm and hail a cab to seek transportation to another location. Derived from the type of horse-drawn wagon known as a *cab*riolet, often used to taxi people and goods to various locations in a city, the word was abbreviated as "cab" (or "taxi") in modern motorized times. In this article, we will be using **CAB** as an acrostic to refer to the progression of human behavior derived from the spiritual **C**haracter of a spirit-source in the human spirit, to **A**ttitudes and **A**ffections in the soul, and hence to the expression of **B**ehavior in the physical body.

This is the progression of all human behavior. Contrary to popular humanistic opinion, our behavior is not simply a matter of deciding to do one thing and not do another by human will-power, regulated by the social pressure of behavior modification or social religious moralism. Whether our behavior is good or evil, socially acceptable or unapproved, politically correct or incorrect, our human behavior finds it origin in a spiritual source of character – the character of the spirit-source that dwells in the spiritual core of our being.

From that inner core of spiritual nature and spiritual identity, we must intentionally choose to draw from and be receptive to (the choice of faith) the character of the spiritual personage that dwells within us. It is, of course, possible for Christ-ones to go outside of themselves (cf. I Jn. 4:4), and "hail a CAB" that will cause us to misrepresent who we are in our spiritual identity. Yes, the spirit-source within a human individual may have a character of either good or evil, for all human beings are indwelt by either God or Satan. Spiritual conversion is the exchange of spirit-source from Satan to the Spirit of God in Jesus Christ (cf. Acts 26:18), and from there we "hail the CAB."

JANUARY 26

DEAR CHRISTIAN FAMILY

Whenever there was a snag, i.e. a problem in the interactive dynamics of our family, I would exercise my prerogative and responsibility as father and often write a letter to the person(s) involved. It would be very direct, focusing on the problem at hand, sharing my perspective, and proposing a solution. Though not the Father of the Christian family (He has that job well under control), I am taking this opportunity to write an open letter to my Christian family, to those "called out" to be Christ-ones in the Body of Christ, and that in order to express my perspective and concerns, as well as a suggested solution to our problems.

The history of the Christian religion reveals that most of the conflicts, the doctrinal disputes, the policy procedures, the arguments about who is right and who is wron – they inevitably occurred in the context of non-essential peripherals when Christ-ones began to argue about something other than Jesus. Such issues are largely insignificant and certainly not of sufficient import to cause a rift in our Christian unity and fellowship. Does the person who thinks different than me believe in Jesus as their Lord and Savior and Life? Then Jesus in me will undoubtedly get along with Jesus in them. And if there is a conflict between us, it will **not** be the expression of the living Lord Jesus but will be an expression of the "flesh," that diabolic patterning in our human desires that seeks to express our sinful selfish opinions.

Dear Christian brothers and sisters: our singular and sole message that we should desire to share with the world and with one another is **JESUS**. Anything beyond Jesus is superfluous and not of ultimate importance. When we have spiritual union with the living Lord Jesus who has become our life (Col. 3:4), there should be no explanation of us and our actions apart from Him. Our only responsibility is to manifest the life and character of Jesus (II Cor. 4:10,11) and exhibit our single truth – **JESUS**.

JESUS – FILLS ALL IN ALL

In his epistle to the Ephesians, Paul wrote, "He (*God the Father*) gave Him (*Jesus the Son*) as head over all things to the church, which is His body, the fullness of Him who *fills all in all*" (Eph. 1:22,23). The implications of what Paul meant by Jesus being "Him who fills all in all" have been much debated in Christian history. Some pushed this phrase into a generalized philosophical premise of monistic pantheism, indicating that God in the Spirit of the Son fills and occupies all people and all things universally with all the complete totality of His own Being. Such monistic universalism corresponds with Eastern philosophy.

General Christian hermeneutics through the centuries of Christian history have sought an explanation and clarification of what Paul meant by the "all in all" that Jesus is said to fill. Many commentators have noted that later in this same epistle, Paul refers to the risen Christ ascending far above the heavens, "so that He might *fill all things*" (Eph. 4:10). Others have also cited Paul's words in I Cor. 15:28, "When all things are subjected to Him, then the Son Himself also will be subjected to the One who subjected all things to Him, so that God may *be all in all*," seeming to refer to the consummation of all things in the future.

In Ephesians chapter one, the immediate context of 1:23 is that of the *ecclesia*, the Body of Christ, (what in modern English, we refer to as "the Church," though contemporary usage can lead us astray). As the Head of the assembly of the saints, Jesus fills every spiritual need and blessing in every receptive Christian individual – every Christ-one. Jesus fulfills everything that humanity needs in spiritual union with and derived out from Himself. Swiss theologian, Karl Barth, so emphasized Jesus as the reality of everything "Christian," he was charged with "Christomonism" – despite the fact his thesis was simply the extension of the reformation motto, *Solus Christus*.

JANUARY 28

THE INTEGRITY OF GOD

A brief, but valid, definition of "integrity" is "the integral oneness between what one *says* and what one *does*." Notice that "integral" and "integrity" derive from the same root source of "integer." The whole number of one (an integer) is the unifying factor between statement and action, between essential character and consistent expression. Fractional division destroys the oneness of the integer and leads to the misrepresentative action of hypocrisy. When what one *says* and what one *does* are at odds with one another, this often leads to the observation, "What you *do* speaks so loud, I cannot hear what you *say*" – a fractured witness.

The integrity of God points to an integral oneness between what He *says* and what He *does*. There is no dis-integration in God. God does not say one thing,and then do another. Yet, the forensic and juridical orientation of much reformed theology has explained that God declares or pronounces a person justified (righteous) but does not actually make a person righteous; it remains but a legal fiction or a speculative projection. The integrity of God is maligned and sacrificed when men claim that God declares something that He does not do. God cannot/does not make fallacious statements. "God cannot lie" (Tit. 1:2; Heb. 6:18). Justification is not an ethereal "legal fiction" of make-believe that God declares but does not enact.

What God declares He does. When God pronounces something to be so, He has made it to be so. When God states His intentions, one can be sure that He will deliberately act in faithful integration with His intent. The integrity of God is the essential integration of God's character of consistent faithfulness and the expressions of His grace-activity in total consistency with His character. Integrity has its epitome in the consistent character of God, evidenced in the faithfulness of God to His covenant promises God is a faithful promise-keeping God (II Cor. 1:20-22).

THE THREAT OF DYING

My friend, Bob, barely survived an event of cardiac arrest and was diagnosed with congestive heart failure. Later, he chose to enter hospice care. The doctor came in one day and diagnosed him with stage-four pancreatic cancer. Bob's response was, "Oh well, I'm going to die anyway. It doesn't matter if it occurs sooner than expected." Two weeks later Bob died.

I share this recent occurrence to emphasize that physical death is inevitable among human beings. "It is appointed that man should die, and then comes judgment" (Heb. 9:27). But when faced with the personal threat of dying physically, even those who have eternal life in Jesus Christ often lose their perspective of God's power and promises and begin to panic.

The recent threat of the SARS-Cov-2 virus (coronavirus 2) with its COVID-19 disease capable of causing a pandemic of global death is the most recent "threat of dying" we have encountered. Prior situations throughout history include bubonic plague, influenza epidemics, Viking raiders, bombing raids in war, cancer, etc. Threats of death, visible or invisible, armies or microorganisms, are to be expected while living in this world.

C.S. Lewis wrote, "Do not let us begin by exaggerating the novelty of our situation. We are all sentenced to death prior to the present situation, and a high percentage of us are likely to die in unpleasant ways. Death is not a chance we might encounter but a certainty" that will transpire for all of us.

When threatened with death by the Roman authorities, Peter and John declared, "Now, Lord, take note of their *threats* and grant that Your bond-servants may speak Your word with all confidence" (Acts 4:29). Now is the time to counter the "threat of dying" with the good news of eternal life in Jesus Christ.

JANUARY 30

"THE REST OF THE GOSPEL"

In the year 2000, Greg Smith published a book entitled *The Rest of the Gospel*, subtitled *"When the Partial Gospel has Worn You Out."* The text of the book is a compilation of transcribed taped messages by Baptist pastor, Dan Stone, during the latter years of the twentieth century. The title seems to be a double entendre, referring both to the promised "rest" of the Christian when living by the dynamic of God's grace, as well as the "remainder" of the gospel that most Christians have not heard because their pastors have emphasized a gospel of performance works rather than the gospel of God's grace in Jesus Christ.

Dan had a unique way of sharing his faith in a casual and personal manner, speaking primarily in small home-groups rather than with large audiences from a pulpit. The message of our spiritual "union with Christ" and the grace dynamic by which Christ's indwelling life is manifested in us, through us, and as us was shared by means of many practical anecdotes from his own life. Dan had learned through many trials and tribulations what Jesus meant when He said, "Come unto Me, all who are weary and heavy-laden, and I will give you *rest*" (Matt. 11:28). Such "rest" was not the rocking-chair relaxation of leaning back and twiddling one's thumbs, but the laying aside of all labors of human performance, our works of self-effort, in order to *rest* in the sufficiency of God's activity of grace.

Such is consistent with Paul's message to the Hebrews (4:1-11), where he indicates that those who have received Jesus have entered the *rest* of God's sufficient grace. Many Christians, however, have come short of experiencing this grace-*rest* because they are unwilling to *rest* from their human works (as God did from His creation-work on the seventh day of Sabbath-*rest*), persisting in their disobedience of faithlessness. We *rest* as we are obediently receptive to the activity of God's grace.

WHAT IS THE WORLD GOING TO DO?

"The world is going to do what the world is going to do" is a motto I have used since the passenger planes were flown into the World Trade Center by Al-Qaeda operatives on September 11, 2001. There was no doubt in my mind that the tactics of the world would demand that retaliation be meted out upon those who "did it." There would be a war against this elusive ideological army, and such has been the case for many years. The world engages in disputes, dissensions, factions, strife, enmities, outbursts of anger, impurity, and sensuality – "the "works of the flesh" (Gal. 5:19-21) leading to conflict and war.

Satan is the "ruler of this world" (Jn. 12:31; 16:11), and his character is always selfish, sinful and evil. All that he engenders and energizes in all of fallen mankind will express his diabolic character (cf. Eph. 2:2; I Jn. 3:8) as the Evil One (Matt. 13:19,38; II Thess. 3:3; I Jn. 5:19). All of the expressions of the world-system will exhibit the character of the spirit-source that energizes them. French author, Jacques Ellul, identifies these world-expressions as *The New Demons* in a book by that title published in 1975, identifying such as politics, education, science, government, institutions, business, media, and of course religion.

Religion is of the world, and religion is going to do what religion is going to do, as it has done for millennia. We can expect religion to continue to pursue its own selfish ends. Religion, like the world-system, is so predictable, so inevitable, so true to its source, so infested with the character of selfishness, so focused on power and might (Zech. 4:6), so engaged in the posturing of using people rather than loving people. The living Lord Jesus and the Christ-ones who are spiritually united with Him are "not of this world" (Jn. 18:36) and stand counter-intuitively against the character of the world, evidencing "love, joy, peace, patience, kindness, goodness, faithfulness, gentleness..." (Gal. 5:22,23).

FEBRUARY 1

ARE BABIES BORN GOOD OR BAD?

Your theological upbringing will likely determine how you answer this question. If you grew up in a church that subscribed to Pelagian and/or Arminian theology, you are likely to believe that babies are born innocent and only later, at "the age of accountability," decide to opt for sin and become "sinners," or opt for Jesus. If you grew up in a church that subscribed to Augustinian and/or Calvinistic theology, you are likely to believe that all human beings are born sinful because of Adam's sin, and this character is ingrained and infused into every child from the moment of their human conception, never to be overcome.

Have I complicated the issue, or do you have a settled answer to the question posed? What if someone (like me) were to suggest that babies are not born good or bad, evil or innocent? ... that babies are born amoral ... that the humanness of every new-born child carries with it no sinfulness and no righteousness ... and there is no inherent or intrinsic character to be imputed to any human child at the time of their birth? Uh oh, where did this form of theological thought come from? Is there a label to be applied to such thought? Simply put: No original sin, no original goodness, no original innocence, no inherent character attribution.

Yes, I am proposing that babies are just born as physical human babies, and they have been born like this ever since Adam and Eve bore their children. They are derivative human beings with freedom of choice and will derive spiritual character from one spiritual source or the other – from Satan or God. The effect of Adam's sin on the entirety of the human race (cf. Rom. 5) is that the spirit of the Evil One indwells the spirit of every child born (cf. Eph. 2:2), and they will inevitably draw from such as "slaves of sin" (Rom. 6:6-20) and "children of disobedience." Every human being has the option, though, of exchanging the spirit of Satan for the Spirit of Christ (Acts 2:18) in spiritual regeneration.

LOVE: THE COUNTERACTION TO REJECTION

We have all experienced personal rejection from other people, and often from family and friends who we considered to "have our back." The world we live in is a rejective world. The character of the "ruler of this world" (Jn. 12:31; 14:30; 16:11) is rejective. Lucifer was from his commencement, a selfish and egotistical being, declaring, "I will be like the Most-High God" (Isa. 14:14; Ezek. 28:14), and his first temptation of mankind was, "You, too, can be like God" (Gen. 3:5). Self-absorbed persons are preoccupied with themselves and what they want and will inevitably reject others in order to get what they want.

The world system is a rejective system, and all who live within it have experienced rejection. It is a "dog eat dog" world wherein most people are looking out for their own interests and rejecting others in the process. Personal rejection causes hurt and pain that often lasts for a long time, creating wounded psyches and alienated relationships. The humanistic solution offered to our rejected society is simply that of "one reject consoling other rejects" with the platitude of "I know how you feel; find someone who will accept you." Often misinterpreted as "find a lover," this often leads to continued rejection.

The counteraction to personal rejection is unselfish love. "God is love" (I Jn. 4:8,16). God's love always flows outward in concern for others, causing Him to "so love the world of humanity that He gave His only begotten Son" (Jn. 3:16), who "loved us and gave Himself for us" (Gal. 2:20). Those who receive God's love in Jesus Christ are identified as Christ-ones, "accepted in the Beloved" (Eph. 1:6), and the "love of God is shed abroad in their hearts by the Holy Spirit who is given to them" (Rom. 5:5). Such divine love seeks the highest good of others, without considering what we get out of it. Love accepts others and their fallibilities, fully aware that "no one is perfect" (Rom. 3:23).

FEBRUARY 3

THE ABSURDITY OF REVERSION

In light of all the spiritual riches that we have received in Jesus Christ, how could we even consider reverting back to the religious law? How could we even entertain the idea of re-engaging in the performance rules and regulations of religion, thinking that they have any value in the sight of God? Over and over, in every one of Paul's epistles, he is combatting the tendency of Christians in the various locations where he had preached the gospel of grace via "the finished work" of Christ – the absurd tendency to go back to the enslaving legalism of "keeping the rules" and thinking that God is pleased with what they are doing for Him, rather than all that Jesus Christ has done and continues to do for us by His grace.

Every one of Paul's epistles carries this theme – from Galatians to Hebrews (probably chronologically the first and the last of Paul's epistles in our New Testaments) – we observe Paul's caution of "making the gospel of grace of no effect" by failure to appreciate the all-sufficient grace of God in the living Lord Jesus, for the manifestation of His life (II Cor. 4:10,11). Failure to manifest the life of Christ is to engage in the misrepresentation of sin.

If you are living in Grace-land, why would someone go back to muddling in the Law paradigm? If one is living in the Promised Land, why would they go back to wandering in the wilderness of insufficiency? If a Christ-one is enjoying abundant Life, it is absurd to return to the death-valley of the dry bones. If we are enjoying the intimacy of union with Jesus, the bridegroom, dalliance with the Law is adultery (cf. Rom. 7:1-7). If we are the free children of Sarah, why would we revert to being the slave children of Hagar (Gal. 4:22-31)? If God dwells in the temple of our body (I Cor. 6:15-19), why should we be concerned with rebuilding a physical temple in Jerusalem with all of its sacrifices and required observances? Oh, the absurdity of reversion!

JESUS IS EVERYTHING

EVERYTHING that God has to give is **JESUS.**
EVERYTHING that mankind needs is **JESUS.**
EVERYTHING that has saving significance is **JESUS.**
EVERYTHING that is rightfully called "Christian" is **JESUS.**
EVERYTHING that makes me a new person is **JESUS.**
EVERYTHING that comprises righteousness is **JESUS.**
EVERYTHING that constitutes holiness is **JESUS.**
EVERYTHING that expresses the love of God is **JESUS.**
EVERYTHING that provides stability in our life is **JESUS.**
EVERYTHING that gives life ultimate meaning is **JESUS.**
EVERYTHING that brings peace to our lives is **JESUS.**
EVERYTHING that brings joy to our lives is **JESUS.**
EVERYTHING that directs us to worship is **JESUS.**
EVERYTHING that transports us to heaven is **JESUS.**
EVERYTHING that is God in my life is **JESUS.**
EVERYTHING that is of eternal value is **JESUS.**
EVERYTHING that glorifies God the Father is **JESUS.**
EVERYTHING that drives us to prayer is **JESUS.**
EVERYTHING that brings beauty to life is **JESUS.**
EVERYTHING that brings unity among men is **JESUS.**
EVERYTHING that fills our need for friendship is **JESUS.**
EVERYTHING that overcomes sinfulness is **JESUS.**
EVERYTHING that enlightens my way is **JESUS.**
EVERYTHING that makes life fruitful is **JESUS.**
EVERYTHING that makes my heart sing is **JESUS.**
EVERYTHING that is real truth is **JESUS.**
EVERYTHING that fulfills God's promises is **JESUS.**
EVERYTHING that sets us free is **JESUS.**
EVERYTHING that makes me sufficient is **JESUS.**
EVERYTHING that gives me strength is **JESUS.**
EVERYTHING that brings satisfaction to life is **JESUS.**
EVERYTHING that allows us to do "good works" is **JESUS.**
EVERYTHING that makes life worth living is **JESUS.**

FEBRUARY 5

"IT IS NO LONGER I WHO LIVES"

In that classic verse of Galatians 2:20, Paul declares, "I have been crucified with Christ. It is no longer I who lives, but Christ lives in me; and the life that I now live, I live by faith in the Son of God who loved me and gave Himself for me (*on the cross*)." For centuries now, Christians have struggled to understand what Paul meant by, "I have been crucified with Christ. It is no longer I who lives..." And tragically, Christian teachers have not been able to explain the meaning. Even *The Message Bible* states, "Christ's life showed me how, and enabled me to do it (*please God*). I identified myself completely with him" (Gal. 2:19).

The use of the pronoun "I" in Galatians 2:20 does not always refer to the same "I" identity. This seems to be the cause of so much confusion. The "I" that was crucified and "no longer lives" is the spiritual "I" of the Satan-life identity that was not understood, because the *natural* man does not understand spiritual things (I Cor 2:14). It was the "I" that was controlled by "the spirit that works in the sons of disobedience" (Eph. 2:2). Not understanding the spiritual "I" we could only surmise that it was the "I" of "independent self," as humanism fallaciously posits to camouflage the work of the Evil One in the unregenerate. The "I" now lived by faith is the "new I" of spiritual identity in Christ – the Christ-life living in us. The Christ-one has become a "new creature in Christ" (II Cor. 5:17), wherein the risen and living Lord Jesus has become our life" (Col. 3:4) and identity.

So many people have been deceived. The "I" who no longer lives is the false "I" identity that I thought I was living by my own means; the humanistic self-potential, "I can do it!"; the "I" that thought he was living independently self-generatively, self-sufficiently, quite capable to pull off a life pleasing to God. That false sense of identity died with Christ when I became a "new man" (Eph. 4:24; Col. 3:10) living in union-identity with Christ.

FEBRUARY 6

THE MYSTERY OF WORSHIP

We don't know how to worship as we ought any more than we know how to pray as we should (Rom. 8:36). That is why worship is such an enigma to many Christ-ones, as they seek ways to orchestrate the mystery of worship. Patterns of public worship vary so greatly in Christian circles around the world (liturgical, charismatic, etc.). Often worship is made into a "production," men seeking to orchestrate for others what cannot be orchestrated. Church leaders try to manufacture "worship" by setting the mood with lighting, music, etc. One pastor referred to worship in his church as "programmed spontaneity" (*oxymoron*).

Every activity in the Christian life must begin with God, be received by man, and return to God in man's response of faith. God reveals Himself as singularly worthy of worship. He has done so historically in the incarnation, crucifixion and resurrection of the Son, and does so individually in personal revelation. Recognizing such, those who "know" God in Christ through the Spirit respond with Spirit-prompted and Spirit-led personal appreciation, affection and adoration, praising God for who He is and what He has done, expressing their love for the Lord. Jesus becomes both the subject and object of our worship.

Christian worship is more than just a "happy-clappy" frenzy of working an audience up to a certain level of excitement. Rather, it should be the spontaneity of the Spirit (Jn. 4:24), directing us to appreciation and adoration for the worthy character of God. God invites us into the fellowship of experiential participation with Himself. How do you express your personal greeting for one you love, for example, when your spouse comes out of the air terminal? That likely will dictate your style of worship as you worship God. Our worship should be our particular manner of "practicing the presence of God" (cf. Brother Lawrence), focusing on Jesus, and taking us beyond our mundane daily thoughts.

FEBRUARY 7

"THAT I MAY KNOW HIM"

Having had his fill of religion, the apostle Paul wrote to the Philippian Christians. He had all the credentials that Jewish religion required, and his Law-keeping performance was the envy of the pious elite. Yet, Paul writes, "I count all things to be loss in view of the surpassing value of knowing Christ Jesus my Lord, for whom I have suffered the loss of all things" (3:8). He expresses the real desire of his heart – "to know Him" (Jesus) in an ever deeper and intimate way, "the dynamic power of His resurrection-life," "the (common) fellowship of His sufferings, being conformed (experientially) to His death" (Phil. 3:10).

Paul's desire to "know Jesus" goes far beyond "knowing about" the details of His life, or the message that He taught, or the data-knowledge of the historical Jesus; but neither was it a mystical or gnostic "special knowing" that Paul sought. Paul already knew Jesus in a personal and experiential knowing of spiritual relationship and union as a regenerate Christian, but his quest was to "know Him" in a deeper and more intimate way. Relationships can always be stronger and tighter as persons spend time with and communicate with one another to know the heart and desires of the other person.

Paul's desire was, and our desire should be, to know Jesus in an ever-deeper, experiential relationship. This is the kind of relational knowing that bears life – "Adam knew Eve, and she conceived and bore a son" (Gen. 4:1). This kind of knowing commences with the desire to "be known by God" (Gal. 4:9). Can we say with Paul that we desire to know how the living Jesus thinks and feels; that His thoughts might be our thoughts; that His concerns might be our concerns; that His heartbeat might be our heartbeat? Do we desire to know Jesus in a manner whereby He functions as our LIFE (Col. 3:4); His life is experientially manifested through us and "as us" (cf. II Cor. 4:10,11)?

"THE POWER OF HIS RESURRECTION"

Having abandoned religion and all of its performance-expectations, Paul expresses the desire of his heart to "know Jesus" in an ever-deeper intimacy and explains that such desire will involve experiencing "the power of His resurrection." Paul had received the resurrection-life of the risen Lord Jesus when he was regenerated – spiritually "united with Christ in resurrection, and raised to newness of life" (Rom. 6:4). But Paul yearned for an experiential awareness of the dynamic (Greek word for "power" is *dunamis*, from which we get the English "dynamite") activity of God exhibited in raising Jesus from the dead (cf. Phil. 3:10).

Paul's quest was not necessarily to participate in a power-theology, to engage in the miracle-working exhibitions of Jesus, but to experience the silent dynamic of Christ's resurrection life that manifests itself in the "fruit of the Spirit" (Gal. 5:22,23). We are "joined to Jesus who was raised from the dead, in order that we might bear fruit for God" (Rom. 7:4). Paul desired "the surpassing greatness of God's divine power (*dunamis*), the working of the strength of His might which He brought about in Christ, when He raised Him from the dead and seated Him at His right hand in the heavenly places" (Eph. 1:19,20).

Jesus "was declared the Son of God with power by the resurrection from the dead, according to the Spirit of holiness" (Rom. 1:4). So, "if the Spirit of Him who raised Jesus from the dead dwells in you, He who raised Jesus from the dead will also give life to your mortal bodies through His Spirit who dwells in you" (Rom. 8:11). The power of the Holy Spirit is the "power of Jesus' resurrection-life." It can also be identified as the Grace of God, the dynamic of God in action in loving concern for our highest good. The "power of His resurrection" is the dynamic by which every Christ-one is empowered to live the Christian life, which is simply the manifestation of the Christ-life.

FEBRUARY 9

"THE FELLOWSHIP OF HIS SUFFERINGS"

Paul was aware that to "know Jesus" in relational intimacy would involve not only the knowing of "the power of His resurrection," but simultaneously knowing "the fellowship of His sufferings" (Phil. 3:10). Previously in this very sentence, Paul had indicated all that he thought was gain in his religious career he now counted as loss (as rubbish), compared to the surpassing value or knowing Christ, for whom he had "suffered the loss of all things" (3:8). All of his ambitions for position and prestige in the Jewish religion – all that he had thought was important – was wiped out. What, then, did he mean by "the fellowship of His sufferings?

Paul was not desiring some form of masochistic pain, nor was he thinking of some blessing to be received by self-inflicted flagellation, but he knew that there was something to be gained by participating in the pathos of Jesus (Greek word for "suffering" is *patheo*). He had experienced his share of physical sufferings (Acts 26:9-15; II Cor. 1:8-11), but he still wanted to partake and participate (Greek *koinonia*, fellowship, from *koine*, common) in the commonality of Christ's sufferings – *His* sufferings. The greatest of sufferings is not physical pain but the internal pain that grieves and breaks one's heart.

Paul wanted to experientially empathize with the broken-heartedness of Jesus, to feel what causes Him pain, causes Him to weep and breaks His heart. Such identification with Christ in bearing the burdens of a fallen world is a partnership in laying down our lives in intercession for others; suffering for the sake of righteousness (I Pet. 3:14) is not suffering for our own stupidity, but suffering because the living Lord Jesus lives in us, and the world hates the risen Lord Jesus – always has; always will. Paul also wrote, "Now I rejoice in my sufferings, and in my flesh I do my share on behalf of His body, which is the church, in filling up what is lacking in Christ's afflictions" (Col. 1:24).

"CONFORMED TO HIS DEATH"

In his personal explanation of his highest spiritual aspirations, Paul's desire to know the living Lord Jesus included his desire of "being conformed to His death" (Phil. 3:10). This was not a suicidal death wish, but a desire to experience what led Jesus to voluntarily give His life as a substitutionary sacrifice for mankind's sin, despite having no sin in His own life (II Cor. 5:21). This phrase is likely an expansion of the previous phrase of experiencing the "fellowship of His sufferings" and articulates his willingness to sacrifice and give up everything for others as an intercessory witness (Greek word *mature*, "martyr") of Jesus.

Every Christ-one has already been crucified with Jesus (Gal. 2:20), has "died to sin to live to Christ" (Rom. 6:2,10) in their spiritual regeneration; but Paul is referring to an experiential sanctification process ("being conformed" is a present tense participial verb that is an on-going action), whereby we are willing to die to, set aside, and sacrifice everything we previously thought meaningful: our reputation, our educational pedigree, our pastoral placement, our ambitions to advance, our regular salary and retirement benefits, and any concern for a legacy – everything the religious system indicated was important.

This radical repudiation of all selfish aspirations is similar to the attitude that Jesus was referring to when he spoke of "denying oneself and taking up one's cross daily to engage in following Him" (Lk. 9:23). It may be what Paul mentioned when he wrote of "constantly being delivered over to death for Jesus' sake, so that the life of Jesus also may be manifested in our mortal flesh" (II Cor. 4:11), or what some have termed "the mortification of the flesh" in order to be led by the Spirit. The Christ-life is always a cruciform (cross-shaped) experience, for such dying is the prerequisite to experiencing the resurrection life of Jesus – dying to anything that is not Him in order to exhibit Him alone.

FEBRUARY 11

NARCISSISTIC CHRISTIAN RELIGION

Those who constantly think that "It's all about me" – how and whether I am doing, or not doing enough to please God are engaging in narcissistic Christian religion, a form of religious spirituo-mental illness. The Christ-life is not about us; it's about HIM (Jesus) and whether the Christ-one, a Christian, is allowing HIM (Jesus) to be lived out and manifested (II Cor. 4:10,11) in our human behavior to the glory of God the Father. We are to "fix our eyes on Jesus, the author and perfecter of our faith" (Heb. 11:2), and, when we fail to focus on Him, we inevitably begin to fixate on ourselves with narcissistic ideas of spiritual progress.

The question, "How am I doing?" evidences that we are thinking of the Christian life as a religious performance process that we must enact. Far too many Christians are engaged in spiritual navel-gazing, attempting to evaluate their progress at "getting better" by looking in the hole. This is a morbidly introspective trait of self-absorbed religious neurosis – attempting to calculate one's successes and brood over one's failures – all the while wondering why I'm not getting better, just getting more neurotic. When the Christian life becomes all about me, how I'm doing and what I need, it is but neurotic religious narcissism.

The more I focus on me and my performance to "do things right," the less I focus on the living lord Jesus – what He has done for me and what He is doing in and through me. Fixating on ourselves, we fail to "fix our eyes on Jesus, the Author and Perfecter of our faith (Heb. 12:2). The sad fact is that the Christian religion has so acculturated itself to the "try harder, do more" narcissism of self-salvation, many religious people think that is Christianity. We must eschew our self-consciousness and self-focus and self-ability in order to focus on Jesus and be conscious of what He is doing in our lives, faithfully allowing for our availability to His Grace ability.

FROM SELFISHNESS TO LOVING OTHERS

An author once stated that "The essence of Christian conversion is the spiritual transformation of an individual from the character disposition of selfishness to the character disposition of loving other people." That statement pretty well sums up what is the objective of Christian conversion/ transformation. All human beings enter into life with a nascent character disposition of selfishness — they want what they want when they want it. The infant wants nourishment and a diaper change and cries until such is provided. The adult business-person wants more assets in his/her portfolio and strives to acquire such.

The natural character disposition of every human being is selfishness. Such a dispositional nature is not essentially innate in human persons but is necessarily derived from the character of the spirit-being who occupies and resides in the spirit-core of every human-being based on the first sin of Adam. "In Adam" all mankind became "sinners" (Rom. 5:19) and suffered the consequences of spiritual death (cf. Eph. 2:1,5; Heb. 2:14) and the spiritual character expressions of "the spirit that dwells in the sons of disobedience" (Eph. 2:2) as "slaves of sin" (Rom. 6:6,16-20). Sin and selfishness are the character of Satan, the Evil One.

Christian conversion/transformation is clearly explained by the apostle Paul as "turning from deriving out of the character-being (Greek *exousias*) of Satan to deriving out of the character-being of God" (Acts 26:18). All humans are spiritually derivative beings and derive all character from either Satan or God. The character of God is love (I Jn. 4:8,16) that seeks the highest good of others in contrast to all diabolic selfishness. The need of mankind is not behavioral modification or moral values education, but a spiritual exchange from the spiritual presence and behavioral expression of the selfish character of Satan to the spiritual presence and behavioral expression of God's love for others.

FEBRUARY 13

GRACE: THE BASIS OF CHRISTIAN FREEDOM

The misconception of God's grace and its accompanying Christian freedom causes many who call themselves "Christians" to think that they are absolutely free to do anything they want to please themselves. That is not the intended outcome of grace. Christian freedom is not libertinism or the freedom to engage in illicit and licentious behavior. Divine grace is God's activity of manifesting His character in human creatures unto His own glory (Isa. 43:7). He does so by means of His Son, the living Lord Jesus, and by the empowerment of His Holy Spirit (I Thess. 1:5), thus acting in the fullness of His triune Being.

God's grace was introduced and inaugurated specifically in the incarnation of the Son of God made flesh (Jn. 1:17). God's grace in the *general* sense has always been the expression of His character of compassionate giving and loving-kindness that seeks the highest good of His creation, but the *specific* redemptive expression of God's grace is always Christological. From the occasion of the Son being incarnated in human flesh in the person of Jesus through to His being obedient unto death in the crucifixion (Phil. 2:8) and paying the redemptive price of death for the sins of all men, we observe the active grace of God.

Such divine grace-action frees mankind from all attempts to save himself and earn favor with God in the human performance of good works. God, by His grace, has done all that needs doing to redeem, regenerate, and restore humanity to function as God intended from the beginning. Grace, however, is not merely an historical event or action. God's grace-action is the eternal dynamic provision by which every Christ-one lives the Christ-life, thus freeing us from all religious acts of legalistic performance to please or appease God. Grace is the action of God as He continues to do all that needs doing in the Christian life. His grace-provision allow us the freedom to simply BE who we are in Christ.

44

FREE TO BE

Most American people seem to think of freedom as freedom *from* something. It may be freedom *from* tyranny or oppression, be it foreign armies or local police. It may even be freedom *from* being told what to do by authorities.

Freedom *from* consequently allows for the obverse of the freedom *to* be or do something. The freedoms guaranteed by the constitution include the freedom *to* speak openly, *to* protest, *to* participate in religion, *to* have a vote in our democratic republic, etc. But such freedom *to* is not freedom *to* do anything a person desires, particularly when such impinges on the freedom of others. We are social creatures, requiring the limitations of some personal freedoms in order to respect the freedoms of others.

Transitioning now to Christian freedom, there is also freedom *from* and freedom *to*. The Christian, by participation in the Person and work of Jesus Christ, has freedom *from* the law performance requirements, freedom *from* sin, freedom *from* the fear of God's judgment, etc.

The consequent obverse of freedom *from* is the freedom *to* be and/or do. We must be cautious and aware that the freedom *to* do can easily degenerate into a form of oppression when religious leaders assume the authority to tell the followers what is expected of them. Freedom *to* do can result in another form of enslavement, wherein many Christians are enslaved in the programs' religious performance expectations.

Our primary Christian freedom is the freedom *to* be or behave as the Christ-one we have become, the freedom to live out of the Life of the One who is Life within us by loving concern for others. Christians are free to live by the grace provision of the indwelling Christ-life (cf. Gal. 2:20).

FEBRUARY 15

THE PURPOSE OF THE CHRISTIAN FAITH?

Let's go back to some Christian basics.

If you were asked to explain the purpose or objective of the Christian faith, how would you answer that question? Perhaps these options can assist in formulating your answer:

> To overcome our selfishness and give us the power to LOVE.
> To change our identity from a "sinner" to a "saint."
> To turn us from deriving from Satan to deriving from Jesus.
> To allow us to avoid hell and spend eternity in heaven.
> To let Jesus provide for us an eternal assurance.
> To bring glory to God.
> All of the above.

The next question may be just as difficult:

How does a human individual enact and participate in this purpose? Here are some options to consider:

> A person has to "get saved."
> A person has to believe that Jesus died and rose again.
> A person must be receptive to the grace of God in their life.
> A person must receive the Spirit of Christ into their spirit.
> A person must feel the presence and power of God within.
> All of the above.

Have you formulated your answers to the foregoing questions?

Can you provide scripture reference for the answers given?

Consider these verses: Jn. 3:7,16,36; 5:24; 6:40; 10:28; Acts 16:31; 26:18; Eph. 2:8,9; Jn. 1:12; Jn. 20:22; Col. 2:6; Rev. 3:20; Eph. 1:18; Rom. 1:16; 8:9,16; 6:23; Gal. 2:20; James 4:8.

FEBRUARY 16

OUR RAISON D'ETRE

Periodically it is instructive to stop, evaluate, and ask ourselves if our lives, overall, are satisfying, fulfilling, pleasurable, and worth living. Or, on the contrary, is the experience of our life dissatisfying, discouraging, and a drudgery of monotonous repetitive activities that do not seem to be moving toward anything meaningful. Every once in a while, everyone needs to take a self-assessment of their *raison d'etre*, their reason for being, and whether there is an intentional and purposeful progression in their lives toward what they regard to be of value. Am I engaged in a life worth living, and will I be able to look back on such and consider it to have been "a life well lived"?

A person identified with the living Lord Jesus, a Christ-one, must first consider the "reason for being" of a Christian. What do we exist for? Surely, we are more than random rational beings thrust upon planet earth to amuse ourselves, try to make a few social changes for the good of mankind, and climb the alleged ladder of success as the collective of humanity might evaluate such. The words of God through the prophet Isaiah speak to the purpose of our existence: "Everyone who is called by My name, and whom I have created for My glory, whom I have formed, even whom I have made" (Isa. 43:7). "How can My name be profaned? My glory I will not give to another" (Isa. 48:11).

The Christ-one (Christian) lives here on earth to "bring glory to God." We must ask ourselves whether the trajectory of our lives is bringing glory to God. What is happening in our lives may not be enjoyable, pleasurable or self-satisfying, but to the extent that we are available to the expression of God's character in the midst of our circumstances, we can allow God to glorify Himself by manifesting His character. Our part in the process is the personal availability and receptivity to what God might want to do. That is what we call "faith" – our receptivity of God's activity.

FEBRUARY 17

SELFISHNESS

The other day I was asked to identify the one thing that I dislike (actually, they used the word "hate") more than anything else. A short list of dislikes went through my mind (falsehood, disregard for others, pretense, etc.), but I settled on what seemed to me to be the most comprehensive and pervasive characteristic that seemed to encompass all of the others. My answer to the inquirer was, "I think the thing I hate more than anything else is selfishness." When subsequently asked to explain my answer, I indicated that selfishness seems to be the summarization of the contra-God character of the Evil One, Satan.

My thoughts went to the narrative of Isaiah 14, where "the star of the morning, son of dawn" (Lucifer?) is said to have "fallen from heaven, been cut down to the earth, and weakened the nations." But the selfish character of his heart continued to assert, "I will ascend to heaven, raise my throne above the stars of God, and make myself like the Most High (God)." God speaks through the prophet, "Nevertheless, you will be thrust down to Sheol, to the recesses of the pit." This pericope seems to reveal the origin of selfish egoism that denies the intended derivativeness of all creatures from the character of their Creator God.

The selfish "I" problem among mankind (Greek word for "I" is *ego*) seems to have originated when the Evil One in the form of a serpent suggested to the original couple, "You, too, can be like God" (Gen. 3:5), introducing the selfish aspiration of ego-centricity. When I want to be my own self-center of self-determination and self-generation (diabolic fallacy of humanism) of "good and evil" (Gen. 2:17; 3:5,22), then I have necessarily rejected God's intent that I derive from His character of love (cf. 1 Jn. 4:8,16) by seeking the highest good of others. Narcissistic selfishness that thinks "it's all about me," indicates that we have succumbed to deriving from the character of the Evil One.

48

FEBRUARY 18

CONCRETE OR SILLY-PUTTY?

It is instructive to ask ourselves whether our human belief might best be compared to concrete or *Silly-Putty*? Many people's belief-tenets are more like the rigid, unbending characteristic of concrete, a firmly formed composite of thoughts bound together with a religious compound into a fixed form of solidity that often takes the form of fideism – a form of idolatry wherein our thoughts and beliefs become a god for which we will live or die and defend at all costs.

Now, I agree that there is nothing wrong with having a fixed, solid foundation of thought and belief. Jesus did mention the necessity of not building on shifting sand, but building on a solid rock foundation. The question must be asked, however: Is the solid rock foundation to be the formation of our personally constructed belief-system, or is the foundation to be personal connectivity with the living Spirit of Christ? The danger of fundamentalism results when our thought-doctrines are formed into static and immovable deification forms.

Some may object to living faith being compared to *Silly Putty*, but let me explain why I would choose such over concrete. *Silly Putty*, originally created by the United States military as a rubber substitute in WWII, is composed of silicone polymers that allows it to have elasticity. It can bounce like a ball, flow like a liquid, and shatter if given a sharp blow. Such pliability and flexibility has similarity to the living faith we are to have in relationship with the living Lord Jesus. Isaiah states, "O Lord, we are the clay; You are the potter. All of us are the work of Your hand" (Isa. 64:8). The clay used in ancient times could dry up if not formed and fired in the kiln. Many an idol was formed out of such clay. *Silly Putty*, on the other hand, remains malleable, ready to be formed into multiple shapes day after day, just as we must be receptive by faith to the formation of God's character in our lives.

FEBRUARY 19

ALL FREEDOM IS CONTEXTUALIZED

Freedom has its limits. There is no such thing as absolute freedom. Some will react by attempting to argue that "God has absolute freedom." Really? Then, why is it that God "cannot lie" (Titus 1:2)? God's freedom is contextualized and limited by His character. God does what He does only because He is who He is! He always acts in accord with His character, and cannot do otherwise. For example, "God is love" (I Jn. 4:8,16) and always seeks the highest good of others. The context of His character does not allow Him to be tempted with evil, to exhibit evil character, or even to tempt people with evil intent (James 1:13).

Increasingly, we have observed generations of people who fail to understand that all freedom has its limits. When children from infancy have no authoritative limits placed on their desires to do anything they selfishly please, they grow up with a skewed sense of unlimited freedom and a false identity of being an "independent self" (a god unto themselves). As they grow toward adulthood, they often defy all authority, with a false sense of freedom that entitles them to live without limitations in all spheres of life. Recent protestors yelling about freedom from police abuse and defunding the police, along with ordinarily civil people hollering that their freedom is being impinged by having to wear masks or maintain social distancing due to the coronavirus are evidence of this false sense of freedom.

As Christians, the limitation of our freedom is always contextualized by the character of the God who lives within us. The love of God compels us (II Cor. 5:14) to limit our freedoms and avoid seeking freedoms that impinge upon others, including the possibility of endangering their health. Divine love for others should establish the limiting parameters of our personal freedoms, willing to defer to legitimate authorities and to the opportunities to allow God to love others through us.

THE GOSPEL ACCORDING TO ABRAHAM

No, this is not some questionable apocryphal book, or a recently excavated document of historic Jewish importance. Writing to the Galatian Christians, the apostle Paul wrote, "The scripture, foreseeing that God would justify the Gentiles by faith, preached the gospel beforehand to Abraham, saying, 'All the nations will be blessed in you.'" (Galatians 3:8). The "good news" revealed to Abraham was couched in outstanding promises (Gen. 12-21) of all that God intended to make available in His Son, Jesus Christ, allowing people of every nation and race to be made righteous simply by receiving the risen Son of God by faith.

The "gospel according to Abraham" is the proclamation of all the promises of God that find their ultimate fulfillment in God's Son, Jesus Christ. Yes, many of the pictorial images are initially shrouded in the religious history of Judaism and the Jewish peoples, but careful observation reveals that they point to the full-orbed gospel: (1) universal for all people of all races and genders; (2) the dynamic grace-provision of God's supply of action; (3) the internal vitality of Jesus' indwelling presence by the Spirit; (4) the relational presence of God in His people; and (5) a unique, one of a kind, and eternal covenant relationship. The essentials of the gospel were all revealed to Abraham.

It is a sad indictment upon the teachers of the church today that the majority of those who identify with Jesus Christ today as "Christ-ones" do not fully understand "the gospel according to Abraham," and thus fail to make the connection with the thread of redemption that is woven through the metanarrative of God's actions from Genesis to Revelation. The promises of God to Abraham are all fulfilled in Jesus. Those who are of faith (the receptivity of God's activity in Christ) are the children of Abraham (Gal. 3:7) who are blessed (Gal. 3:9) with the fulfillment of all God's promises (cf. I Cor. 1:20) in Jesus Christ.

FEBRUARY 21

MARRIAGE

Marriage is the union of two quite often very disparate people with diverse personalities. There is truth in the saying, "opposites attract!" But there is also truth in the awareness that opposites often clash and grind against one another. The process of accepting those differences and functioning together despite those differences will inevitably have its friction points and conflicts, hopefully leading to understanding of one another's peculiarities in order to enjoy times of smooth interaction and mutually satisfying love. Anyone who thinks marriage is easy has likely never been involved in a marriage relationship.

I used to pontificate and proclaim that the two major detriments to an enjoyable and workable marriage were "selfishness" and "lack of communication." I have since reduced the niggling irritations of marriage to the single cause of selfishness. The opposite of love that seeks the highest good of the other is simply selfishness. Even failure to communicate is often attributable to the selfishness that does not think the other person worth the effort of taking the time and effort to clarify the issues and hammer out the differences of opinions and values in interactive communication leading to the agreement to love one another.

There may also be truth in the saying that "some people are impossible to live with." I have much sympathy for those married to spouses having deep-seated personality disorders, often displaying addictive fixations or other forms of mental illness not evident prior to the commitment of marriage. The common marriage vow is the promise to love the other person "for better or for worse, until death do us part." But realism demands that we admit that the "worse" of marriage can become so destructive to the parties involved as to necessitate separation or divorce. Divorce is not the unforgivable sin! The dissolution of a marriage can sometimes be the most loving thing to do.

THE LAW AS A SIDELINE

The Mosaic Law and its performance requirements has become equivalent with the Jewish religion of the Old Testament, in the minds of many people. I am suggesting that we take another look at the old covenant record to see if the Law was really the focal point of God's dealings with the Hebrew people. The apostle Paul seems to explain that the Mosaic Law was a secondary sidetrack to what God intended through the fulfillment of His Messianic promises to Abraham: "the Law, which came four hundred and thirty years later, does not invalidate a covenant previously ratified by God, so as to nullify the promise" (Gal. 3:16,17).

God made promises to Abraham within a covenant agreement that he (Abraham) and his progeny would be blessed in their own land as a great nation (Gen. 12-21). The Jewish people focused on the physical dimension of the promises, which God fulfilled; but the long-term projection of the promises was to be fulfilled spiritually in Jesus Christ and those who would be "in Him" by faith. This was the mainline track of God's trajectory – promises fulfilled – but due to the egotism and exclusivism of the Israelites, God later made an off-ramp, a side-line, a spurt, a side-track, i.e. the Mosaic Law, which they eagerly embraced, thinking they could facilitate the fulfillment of God's promises by their human performance. The Law was designed to make evident the human inability to implement the objectives of God.

The Law was an add-on, a go-nowhere performance trap, never intended to fulfill God's promises. The Jews did not understand that! Christians have not understood that! Those who consider the contrast between law and grace to be the focal point of the Christian gospel presentation (dispensational fundamentalism) are utilizing a secondary and peripheral springboard (the Law) as a platform to build a shaky construct of contrast with the divine focal point of God's grace in Jesus Christ.

FEBRUARY 23

IN-BETWEENNESS

Some might think of "in-betweenness" somewhat like being caught "between a rock and a hard place," struggling to find a way to escape. Or perhaps a social situation, like being caught in a corporate power-play between two equally powerful career climbers – are you with us or against us? The majority of people likely find "in-betweenness" to be quite uncomfortable, and that is the case with Western thinking processes in general. People don't like to be left "hanging in the middle" and would rather stand on a solid place on one side or the other. I am going to suggest that the highest form of human experience occurs when abiding in the in-betweenness of contrasting opposites.

In previous discussion of such "in-betweenness," I have referred to the "tensioned balance" of thought in the form of dialectic – the willingness to remain in-between opposing concepts that are so incongruent as to be incapable of being brought together, yet accepting both as valid. Some call it "paradox." Some refer to such as relativism that will not posit an absolute of either/or. The Greek philosopher, Plato, called this *metaxy,* living in a space in-between the tensions of human existence. To make sense of life, we must learn to live with apparent contradictions that cannot be resolved into definitive absolutes of logic.

The Lord Jesus Christ might be seen as the Master of the tensioned simultaneity of "in-betweenness." He understood Himself to be the *theanthropos* – the God-man – deity and humanity in the one Person of the Messiah/Savior. Jesus was quite aware of the incongruous juxtapositions of divine sovereignty functioning simultaneously with human responsibility – God's actions of grace received by the human response-ability of faith. Christians must learn to live in the tensioned "in-betweenness" of redemption already accomplished and the "not yet" expectation of heavenly existence.

MY WEAKNESS; HIS STRENGTH

Most people do not want to emphasize their weaknesses, their inabilities, or their flaws. Our natural tendency is to try to cover-up, and present ourselves as strong and competent, having our every thought and action under control. I want to be very personal with you: The other day I physically collapsed and had to be taken out by ambulance to the hospital, diagnosed with a complete depletion of magnesium and diminished levels of other minerals. In addition, my blood sugars were all out of whack. After four days, I was released, though still very weak.

Of more consequence was the "dark night of the soul" that I experienced the last night of my hospitalization. Feeling alone, my mind went places it had never gone before. Thinking the world would be better off without me, I began to meticulously consider the manner and means by which I could facilitate my own demise – manually by knife, gunshot, or overdose of drugs; the timing required to throw oneself off of a bridge, under a train, a bus, or a semi-truck. It was only the revealing of the morning sunlight that collapsed the vortex of darkness that had enveloped me. I was immediately aware that the diabolic death-dealer (Heb. 2:14) has been wreaking havoc in my weakened body and mind. I knew I had to share what I experienced with others, family members, personal friends, doctors, pastor friends, etc., not to seek counsel, *per se*, but to be honest and upfront with all who might be concerned – hiding nothing.

There will be some who might think that I should conceal these negative thoughts of weakness, so as not to unduly influence others or cast aspersions upon myself. Rather, I take the apostle Paul's approach when he notes that God's power is evidenced and brought to fruition in our weakness. His conclusion was, "I will rather boast about my weaknesses, so that the power of Christ may dwell in me" (II Corinthians 12:9).

FEBRUARY 25

CRUCIFORMITY

This word was originally an architectural term. It was used of a building that was formed in the shape of a cross. Many of the medieval cathedrals were constructed in a cruciform shape. Worshippers entered into the narthex and then into the nave, where most were seated. If they continued to the crossing of the perpendicular arms of the cross, they could enter into one of the transepts. To proceed farther would be to enter into the chancel area and then into the sanctuary toward the apse. The purpose of this reading is not to discuss ecclesial architecture, but to consider how "cruciform" can be used to refer to a cross-shaped life that allows the cross of Christ to shape our lives.

Though the life of a Christian, a Christ-one, is to be the out-living of the indwelling presence of the risen Lord Jesus, it is important to recognize that there is always a preceding process by which resurrection-life is realized. Resurrection to life presupposes the death of the one resurrected. We must beware of the emphasis of triumphalism that so focuses on the end of the process that it fails to explain the necessity of cross-life in order to fully appreciate resurrection-life. It is only in the process of death – our dying to our self-concerns – that we can experience the resurrection-life of Jesus, focusing on loving concern for others.

"Cruciformity" is the process of self-denial that every Christ-one must participate in to fully enter into the experience of resurrection-life. "Jesus said to His disciples, 'If anyone wishes to come after Me, he must *deny* himself, and take up his cross and follow Me'." (Matt. 16:24). Paul subsequently explained, Tthe grace of God has appeared, bringing salvation to all men, instructing us to *deny* ungodliness and worldly desires..." (Titus 1:11,12). The dying process of the termination and negation of selfishness is the necessary precursor to the process of allowing Jesus to live out His resurrection-life in our behavior.

THE GLORY OF THE CROSS

If you were attempting to enumerate the characteristics of the character of the triune God, would you include the explanation that "sacrificial dying" is at the heart of God? Most Christians would rather emphasize that the Living God is about abundant (cf. Jn. 10:10) and triumphant life made available to and in His followers by Jesus the Savior (cf. Jn. 3:16). The counterintuitive concept of Christian thought is that dying is essential to living. This is self-evident in the historical narrative of Jesus' life wherein the execution instrument of the cross is the prerequisite to the triumph of the resurrection of Jesus on Easter morning.

It seems extremely difficult for many contemporary Christians to understand the "glory of the cross" (Gal. 6:14). It was even more difficult for those in the first century, who knew well the gory public reality of a criminal's death on the execution instrument of a Roman cross. It was almost inconceivable that the gory could be transformed into glory. It requires an understanding of what was happening on the cross – that Jesus was voluntarily taking the death He did not deserve on behalf of all sinful humanity who did deserve the death consequence of their sin. It is a glorious reality indeed that "He who knew no sin (Jesus) became sin in our place, that we might be graced with His righteous" (II Cor. 5:21) presence in our spirit.

Such self-sacrificing death and denial to all our selfish concerns and interests must be played out in every Christian's life, allowing for Christ's glorious life to be expressed. Jesus explained that "the grain of wheat must fall into the ground and die, in order to being forth life" (John 12:24). In like manner, "the one who loses his life (even hates it) shall have life eternal" (Jn. 12:25). The glory of the cross is evidenced when we willingly choose death to our self-concerns, and these are exchanged for Christ's loving concern for others through us.

FEBRUARY 27

FALSE ALLIANCES

The Christian gospel is not to be identified with any cultural phenomena. Christianity is not culture or enculturation. It is not to be identified with such ever-changing ideations of collective social thought and action. Christians must beware of adopting any false alliances with organizations, nations, governments, political groups, or ideological movements, including ecclesiastical organizations that tout themselves as being acceptably aligned as "Christian." It is through such false alliances that Christians are often misidentified by the world around them and "pegged" by their false alliances and agendas.

When people develop the idea that their patriotic nationalism or social concern identifies them as a "Christian," or at least evidences that they are a more "spiritual" and enlightened Christian, they are on a crash-course to disappointment and disaster. Jesus refused to affiliate or align Himself with the issues and parties of His day. He exposed the Pharisees, Sadducees, and Zealots – the Jewish special interest groups of the day. He would not allow Himself to be grouped with the anti-Roman sentiment that wanted to set Him up as a king to challenge the emperor of Rome and overcome their national oppression.

The Christian gospel stands alone in its singular uniqueness. It is the "good news" (Greek *euangellion*) of the restorative indwelling presence of the living Lord Jesus in the spirit of a regenerated individual, who has received Jesus as life and Lord by the receptivity of faith. That spiritual phenomenon can take place in individuals from any nation, religion or ideology – from any race, class, gender, or political persuasion. How unfortunate that the word "evangelical" has been politicized and bastardized to the point that it is devoid of legitimate meaning. Unless and until its biblical meaning is restored, we are better off without such a moniker that can be adopted as a "false alliance."

THE LIE

The first falsehood that any human ever heard was straight from "the father of lies" (Jn. 8:44) himself, when in the midst of the perfection of the garden, the serpent, representing Satan (Rev. 12:9) defied the truth statement of God (Gen. 2:17) and said to the first couple, "You will not die; you will become like God, knowing good and evil" (Gen. 3:4,5). That was the first diabolic lie invested with the humanistic premise of self-potential that denies the created necessity of derivativeness and dependence of humanity upon the Creator God. The "father of lies" would have us to believe "derivativeness is tyranny," contrary to the functional purpose of our creation to derive character from God.

The Satanic lie remains dominant among humanity today in the humanistic inculcations to act out of our own alleged self-potential and "be all you can be." Derivativeness is not tyranny, as the humanists would tell us. Derivativeness is the freely chosen unhindered free-flow of God's character and empowering in a human life, allowing us to be godly people. No one can be godly apart from the presence of God's character and action, despite all the religious humanism that encourages self-generated enterprises and constantly mandates performance exercises that will allegedly make us more like God.

The most deceiving part of the devil's lie of human self-potential is that it is based on the impossible premise that human beings can self-generate and actuate their own character. As derivative creatures, humans are incapable of such god-like self-origination and will inevitably derive from a spirit-source – God or Satan. God is His own center-of-reference. All that is consistent with who He is will be good; all that is not consistent with who He is will be evil. Such self-centered reference is a fallacious impossibility for mankind. Instead of self-derivation, man found himself deriving from the character of Satan as a "sinner."

FEBRUARY 29

WE ARE NOT "INDEPENDENT CREATURES"

Let's get technical. The Creator God – Father, Son, and Holy Spirit – did not create human beings to be "little gods" who could draw from their own self-resource for their human existence and function. Human beings were not designed by the Divine Designer to be "independent selves" drawing *ek autos*, "out of themselves" to develop their own nature and identity, to self-generate their own character and behavioral expressions thereof, or to have the intrinsic and innate self-potential to independently derive from inside of themselves the necessary ontological being and empowering for their own human actions.

This does not necessarily mean that humans are not choosing creatures with "freedom of choice" and response-ability to self-determine their personal choices. But, as dependent and derivative creatures, human choices will involve a binary option of derivation either from Satan or from God, choosing to draw character *ek diabolos* (out of the devil – I Jn. 3:8) or *ek Theos* (out of God – II Cor. 3:5). These are the only two choices of spiritual source for human being and action. Yes, such options are antithetical to all the world's humanistic assertions of unlimited human potential to "be all you can be" and "to do great things in this world." Such incentives should cause us to recall the false assertion, "you can be like God" (Gen. 3:5).

We cannot "be like God," for we are not "independent beings" with intrinsic character of goodness or holiness (nor the diabolic character of selfishness or sinfulness). All humans are derivative creatures, deriving their nature (either as children of wrath – Eph. 2:2; or as "partakers of the divine nature" – II Pet. 1:4), their identity (either as children of the devil – Jn. 8:44; or as "children of God" – Gal. 2:26), and character (either as "sinners" – Rom. 5:19; or as "righteous" – Rom. 5:19), either from the spirit-source of God or Satan – not established independently, *ek autos*.

MARCH 1

"NOW IS THE DAY OF SALVATION"

In recent conversations with several Christian brothers, I have been chagrined that they wanted to spend the time discussing what is going on in the world (the pandemic or the political turmoil concerning such), or they wanted to discuss their speculations about what they projected would take place in the future (the judgment of God or the second coming of Christ). I hung up the phone rather disappointed after such conversations, repeating to myself, "The issue is JESUS, and how He is being allowed to manifest His character and life in my behavior" – the rest is simply peripheral background noise – buzz and fuzz!

It is so easy to let our minds get caught up in contemporary events of the present or projected events of the future. Paul wrote to the Corinthians, saying "Now is the day of salvation" (I Cor. 6:2). We must learn to live in the NOW, not distracted by the world's attempts to turn our attention to what is regarded as essential current news, or by religion's attempts to occupy our minds with hypotheses of speculation about what God might do in the future. Jesus said, "Do not worry about tomorrow; for tomorrow will care for itself. Each day has enough trouble of its own" (Matt. 6:34).

"Now is the day of salvation" (I Cor. 6:2), and the issue of the day is JESUS. Salvation will never come through the political pseudo-saviors who are constantly haranguing us with their claims that they will "save the day" for our country and make the future bright if we will cast our vote for them and allow them to lead the country. Jesus is our only Savior, and our salvation is securely settled by our spiritual union with Him. Having been "joined in one spirit" (I Cor. 6:17) with the living Lord Jesus at regeneration, we can NOW allow the "saving life of Christ" (Rom. 5:10) to function in our lives as Christ-ones, manifesting His life and character in all that we do, to the glory of God.

MARCH 2

WHAT GOES AROUND, COMES AROUND

We have all heard (and perhaps used) the phrase, "What goes around, comes around." It implies a cyclical pattern that repeats itself over time. In the study of the natural world, we observe the rotation of the earth; and, because the axis of the earth's rotation changes throughout the year, we have the repetitive occurrence of seasons (more evident in some locations than others). The phrase is also used in reference to human behavior, to indicate that the consequences of one's choices will eventually have to be dealt with. Recall that Paul explained, "Do not be deceived; for whatever a man sows, this he will also reap" (Gal. 6:7).

This article attempts to consider the phrase, "What goes around, comes around" in the context of the cyclical pattern that can be observed in the realm of spiritual reality. Everything comes from God and returns to God; there is a divine source and divine purpose to all God's activity. Everything is *ek Theos* (out of God) and *eis Theos* (unto God). Paul states such: "for from (*ek*-out of) Him, and through (*dia*-by means of) Him, and to (*eis*-unto) Him are all things; to God be the glory forever" (Rom. 11:36). This is a denial of the "independent man" thesis and an affirmation of the "derivative man" reality. Everything that makes man "man as God intended" is derived from God and unto the glory of God.

"We do not know how to pray as we should" (Rom. 8:26), but the Spirit provides the impetus and the words, and thereby we communicate with God – we listen and allow Him to act; God is both the subject and object of our prayers. God actuates the expression of His glorious character within His creation and, when man recognizes such, he in turn praises and glorifies God for His character in worship. We are unable to convert anyone, but Jesus said, "Do not worry beforehand about what you are to say, but say whatever is given you in that hour; for it is not you who speaks, but it is the Holy Spirit" (Mk. 13:11).

"WE PREACH CHRIST CRUCIFIED"

Paul knew that the Corinthian Jews were obsessed with power, and the Corinthian Greeks were obsessed with philosophical wisdom. In the first chapter of first Corinthians, Paul tells the Christ-followers in Corinth that such were not the message he came to share. "For indeed Jews ask for signs and Greeks search for wisdom; but *we preach Christ crucified*, to Jews a stumbling block and to Gentiles foolishness, but to those who are the called, both Jews and Greeks, Christ the power of God and the wisdom of God. Because the foolishness of God is wiser than men, and the weakness of God is stronger than men" (I Cor. 1:22-25).

The message of a crucified Savior humiliated the Jewish desire for displays of God's power; it was a stumbling-block of failure. The message of the cross was just plain stupid and foolish to the Greeks; it humiliated their desire for lofty wisdom that could figure everything out. The cross wipes out all human expectations of what human success looks like. The message of the cross is the "wrecking ball" to all human pride. But simultaneously, with the aid of the Spirit, we come to understand God's power to destroy our selfishness, and God's wisdom in making beauty out of ashes.

Some, who want to emphasize the triumphal side of Christian thought, will argue that "we preach Jesus, risen from the dead." Yes, but there is no resurrection apart from the crucifixion. The cross of Christ continues to humiliate and humble our presuppositions that we are in control (power); that we have everything figured out (wisdom). The cross is not a summit that we can ascend, claim our victory, and say, "Look at me; I am King of the Mountain," Rather, it is a scandalous stumbling block and a revelation of foolishness to all human pride, revealing our inability to "make life work." It drives us to recognize that only the living Lord Jesus is sufficient to control our lives.

MARCH 4

THE EIGHTH DAY OF CREATION

Everyone with any biblical awareness is no doubt aware of the account of the seven days of creation in Genesis 1:1–2:3. There is active debate in both Jewish and Christian circles as to whether the "days" referred to are 24 hour days,or indefinite periods of time, as in "Moses' day," or the eons of scientific time calculation. There is no explicit reference to an "eighth day" in the Genesis narrative, but God did not cease to do His creative work after the seventh day. Mankind was to continue to live in the Sabbath Rest of the seventh day of creation; but on the eighth day (which may be the rest of our lives or longer), we are to live spontaneously in the manifestation of the divine life that has been breathed into our spirit.

The "eighth day" of creation may be what Paul was referring to when he declared, "Now is the *day* of salvation" (II Cor. 6:2). That would certainly align with Paul's references to our being "a new creation" in Christ (II Cor. 5:17; Gal. 6:16). Some have explained that the "eighth day" is "the promised new day of salvation in Christ." In the midst of Jesus' celebration of the Last Supper in the upper room, He said, "I will not drink of this fruit of the vine from now on until *that day* when I drink it new with you in My Father's kingdom" (Matt. 26:29; Mk. 14:25). "That day" could be another reference to what we are calling "the eighth day."

The "eighth day" is *the day* of realized fulfillment of all God intended for mankind. It may be viewed as the opportunity afforded to Christians to live "Life as God intended" in the spiritual condition of being "man as God intended"; *the day* of enjoying the grace provision of God in Jesus Christ; *the day* of abiding in the "saving life of Christ" (cf. Rom. 5:10); *the day* of appreciation and thanksgiving for all that God has made available in His Son, Jesus Christ. We can't be dogmatic about "the eighth day," but it has interesting allusions to all we have in Jesus.

PURITY

The concept of "purity" has become almost a laughing matter within our contemporary society. We still use the word in reference to "pure water," "pure gold," or "pure motives." But in reference to human thought or activity, many regard "purity" as an archaic concept. By definition, we often define "purity" by negation; ex. undefiled, untainted, uncorrupted, uncompromised, unmixed, or unadulterated. Few seem to be able to provide a positive definition of "purity" in the context of human condition, thought, or behavior. Those who do, often define "purity" by the prevailing cultural or religious morals of their time or place.

"Purity" requires a measuring standard on which to establish its meaning. The only appropriate standard of "purity" in terms of human behavior is the character of God. Purity is determined by the character of God in Christ; "He is pure" (I Jn. 3:3). God is pure because He is inherently within Himself undiluted and uncompromised, but positively He is the fullness of holiness and righteousness. It is possible, therefore, to indicate that every expression of sin is impurity (Prov. 20:9); impurity extends far beyond the parameters of sexual immorality. Purity is more than the retention of virginity or the practice of celibacy.

"Blessed are the pure in heart" (Matt. 5:8), Jesus said in the beatitudes. Purity is never a matter of human performance, whether restraint or effort. Purity is the unadulterated expression of God's character, and can only be derived from the presence of God in Christ by His Spirit dwelling in our human spirit/heart. God is at work in the Christ-one doing His purifying and sanctifying transformation of character to present His *ecclesia* as a "pure virgin" (II Cor. 11;2) before God the Father. In the meantime, we are to focus on God's character of purity (Phil. 4:8). "To the pure, all things are pure; but to those who are defiled and unbelieving, nothing is pure (Titus 1:15).

MARCH 6

DERIVED HUMILITY

The Christ-life is one of humility. When we look at the life of Jesus Christ on earth, we see it begins with a humble birth in a cattle-stall in Bethlehem and proceeds to a humiliating death on a Roman execution instrument reserved for criminals in Jerusalem. Humility is a defining feature of Jesus' life, and those who would be His followers must be willing to "take up their cross" (Matt. 16:24) and be willing to assume a similar character-disposition of selflessness, wherein they seek not their own personal and selfish interests "but with humility of mind regard one another as more important than yourselves, focusing on the interests and needs of others" (Phil. 2:3,4).

When Christ died, we died "in (union with) Him" (II Cor. 5:15; Col. 2:20; 3:3); and the remainder of the exchanged Christ-life lived out here on earth is occupied with implementing the implications of the cross, as well as the resurrection, in our Christian lives. Humility is the heart, the essence, of the cross-life experience which every legitimate Christ-one participates in – experiencing continual death to our selfishness, our self-preoccupation, even our self-consciousness. Christ's love for others necessarily overcomes our self-centeredness in the midst of its activation, and the resultant posture is that of humility, which can never be attained by our own self-effort.

It is impossible to attain or achieve humility. If it were possible, one would inevitably be proud of his performance and thereby negate all humility. In fact, the more one focuses on humility, the less likely such person is likely to participate in humility. Humility cannot be achieved but only received, because it is exclusively a gift of God's grace in the Son, Jesus Christ. A friend commented, "It wasn't until I received Christ and became a Christian that I could understand and experience humility." He was perfectly accurate and vulnerably honest. The character trait of humility must be derived as the life of the risen Lord Savior indwells us and is lived out in manifestation through us (II Cor. 4:11) to the glory of God and for others. Humility is the character of Christ, and it only exhibits itself supernaturally in our lives.

ACCEPTING INCONVENIENCES

Life is replete with inevitable inconveniences. Things don't always go our way, in a manner that we find comfortable, pleasant and convenient. Many people get very irritated when things don't go their way, when they encounter those annoying nuisances and hassles of daily life, when things don't go as expected or desired. Author Kristan Higgins wrote and published a novel in 2019 entitled, *Life and Other Inconveniences.* She seems to be saying that all of life is a sequence of inconveniences, and such a thesis does not seem to be at odds with Jesus' statement, "In this world you will have tribulation" (John 16:33).

Oscar Hammerstein's song, "Oh, What a Beautiful Mornin' ... Everything's Going My Way," just doesn't seem to be realistic. Life seems to be more like a series of unexpected trials that may be as minor as a paper cut, tangled bed sheets or tangled earphone cords, forgetting passwords (and getting locked out of your bank account because you forgot the password), being put "on hold" again and again, opening a page on your computer and the music starts blaring, losing the remote control, robocalls, having to wear face masks during the coronavirus pandemic – to name just a few! And then when you add in the effects of aging, where we drop things, knock things off the table, and are unable to find our glasses, such circumstances can cause irritation.

So, how do we respond to these inconveniences that can so easily become irritating? These constant situations should remind us there is so much of life that we cannot control, despite the fact that we are continuously inventing new equipment to make life more convenient. If we are truthful, we must all admit that we too often respond with irritation and anger – even expletives. A more constructive approach might be to say, "Okay, Lord, it appears that this is the next opportunity to allow You to manifest Your character in my attitudes and behavior!

MARCH 8

COMPLAINING

All of us have done our share of complaining when we've experienced inconveniences, when we react to the attitudes and actions of other people, and when things aren't going our way. The Israelite people murmured (grumbled, complained) to Moses about their plight in the wilderness, and God kept them there for forty years (cf. Numb. 11). Today, with our social media platforms, we voice our discontent and disgruntled attitudes for everyone to read. We complain about having to do the dishes, sweep the floor, rake the leaves, about colleagues at work, people at church, and about government officials, etc.

Some people's lives are glaringly epitomized by their complaints about the way things are happening around them. Often identified as "whiners," they express their negative gritching and grousing about everything that doesn't go their way, expressing their dissatisfaction with what is happening in their lives. They may even develop a critical spirit of discontent which does not appreciate anything that God is doing in their lives. They battle the circumstances, blame the situation for their miserable discontent, and have a bad attitude about everything that does not correspond with their selfish expectations.

Are such people enjoying all that God has blessed them with? Doesn't appear so. Jesus told His disciples, "Do not grumble among yourselves" (Jn. 6:43). Paul wrote, "Do everything without complaining or arguing" (Phil. 2:14,15). James wrote, "Do not complain, brethren, against one another, so that you yourselves may not be judged" (James 5:9). The antidote or solution to grumbling and complaining is found in Paul's admonition, "In everything give thanks (recognize God's good grace); for this is God's will for you in Christ Jesus" (I Thess. 5:18). On the other hand, the Psalmist writes, "I pour out my complaint before Him; I declare my trouble before Him" (Ps. 142:2).

DEMOCRACY

My wife and I enjoy learning a new word each morning while we are drinking our coffee. The word for the day was "adhocracy." I could not recall ever having heard the word, but I knew that the suffix at the end of the word (*-cracy*) was derived from the Greek word *kratos*, indicating power or strength. The god *Kratos* was so powerful, Greek mythology depicted him as killing fourteen other gods, including *Hercules*, *Hades* (underworld) and *Thanatos* (death), as well as *Ares* and *Athena* (the god and goddess of war). Having served on a couple of *ad hoc* committees, I knew that this Latin phrase meant "as needed or necessary" and often refers to a loosely structured meeting of people gathered for a particular purpose. So, the word adhocracy refers to the strength or power of such a loosely gathered group of people.

Let's change course and consider the word "democracy," which refers to the power of the people, from *demos* (the people of the village). Athens was the first city-state to implement direct democracy among its citizenry in the 5th century B.C., meaning that every person had the right to "have their say" directly on the issues of the city or state. This becomes impossible as the state or nation grows. What we have in the United States of America is a "representative democracy," where we elect leaders to represent us in the deliberation of issues affecting our community, state and nation. This means that every citizen has a responsibility to participate in the election of such representatives. In the Greek city-state of ancient Athens, the people were "called out" (*ek – kaleo*) for a meeting to make final determinations, and this gathering was referred to as the *ecclesia* (a word never intended to mean "church," though so translated throughout our Bibles). Citizens who did not exercise their responsibility in the "power of the people" were identified as the *idiotes* (yes, the idiots who did not care enough about the whole community or nation to show up and vote).

MARCH 10

GOD'S "NO" AND GOD'S "YES"

For every "yes," there is a "no." God introduced His definitive "yes" in the resurrection of Jesus from the dead. Yes, to man's restoration to participation with God with complete provision of God's grace for so doing. But the "yes" was preceded by a punctiliar "no" to the sinfulness of humanity at the cross of Calvary. The sin of mankind had to be taken care of by the substitutional death of Jesus in order that the life of Jesus might restore humanity to God's creative intent. From an historical perspective, the "no" of the cross preceded and facilitated the "yes" of the resurrection – no resurrection apart from the cross.

Experientially, the dialectic balance scale of God's affirmatives and negatives seems to tilt the other way. God's "yes" and "no" switch places, and we see that the positive swallows up the negative; the affirmative "yes" of God's grace overcomes the negative "no" to our ingrained patterns of sinfulness. We do not have to engage in the performance of "crucifying ourselves" in order to experience resurrection-life; we are simply receptive to the "yes" of Jesus' resurrection-life as He effects the "no" to our sinful propensities of fleshliness. God's grace actuates both the "yes" and the "no" simultaneously in the Christ-life.

Within the Christian life, there will be the ever-present counteraction of God's "yes" and God's "no." When people over-emphasize God's "no" to their sinful selfishness without the "yes" of God's grace provision, they end up with constant sin-consciousness, wallowing in defeatism as they focus on law-keeping and sinfulness. When Christians over-emphasis God's "yes" without awareness of God's "no," they end up with triumphalist revelry, failing to recognize God's rejection of the fundamental brokenness of humanity in sin and His intolerance of all that is contrary to His character. In (union with) Christ, God's "yes" always defeats the necessary "no."

70

CRUCIFORM LOVE

The world does not understand *agape* love, and neither does its religious handmaiden, "the church." Week after week the Christian religious teachers exhort their listeners, "God has loved you so much that He caused His only begotten Son to die for you; now go out and love others like God in Christ has loved you." It is an impossible ideal encouraging an impossible action of imitation. You can't love, nor can I love others as Christ loved us, because we do not have the essential character of love as He did and does. God *is* love (I Jn. 4:8,16), and that does not mean He *has* a quantity of love to spread around – some "love-potion #9" that can be sprinkled around like fairy dust.

Yes, there are numerous imperative commands in the Christian scriptures, indicating that we are to "love one another" (Jn. 13:34,35; 15:12,17; Rom. 13:8; I Jn. 3:11; 4:11) and "love our neighbor as ourselves" (Matt. 22:39; Rom. 13:9; Gal. 5:14), but in the new covenant of God's grace in Jesus Christ, all imperatives are based on indicatives of God's provision. "The love of God is poured out in our hearts by the Holy Spirit given to us" (Rom. 5:5). "The fruit of the Spirit is love... (Gal. 5:22). Agape love cannot be self-generated but must always be derived from the God who is Love, allowing Him to express His love through us.

Historically, the love of God for fallen humanity finds its epitome in the crucifixion of Jesus on the cross. I John 4:10 – "God loved us and sent His Son to be the satisfaction for our sins" (in dying on the cross). Gal. 2:20 – the Son of God loved me, and gave Himself up for me" (in dying on the cross). The same love that placed Jesus on the cross is the love that is available in (*union with*) Christ to flow through us to others. It is a sacrificial love willing to give up oneself for others in a total self-giving with no consideration of reciprocation. It is God's cruciform (cross-shaped) love that lays down its life in intercession for others.

MARCH 12

EVERYONE HAS SPIRITUAL BEING

In the evangelical realm of religion, a person is usually regarded as receiving spiritual existence and being when he/she is "born again" by believing in Jesus. It is time to challenge that supposition and explain that every human being has spiritual function. Every human person has spiritual function, psychological function, and physiological or bodily function. We all function within spirit and soul and body (cf. I Thess. 5:23). This tri-fold function is simply part of what it means to be human. It is not possible to be human without the distinctive triplicity of spiritual, psychological, and physiological function.

The common and popular teaching among evangelicals indicates that humans are born devoid of any spiritual being or function, and thus function self-generatively out of their own innate and independent being, often called "human nature." The spiritual function received in regeneration is thus viewed as an additive whereby they add a third level of function by receiving a "new spirit" (cf. Ezek. 11:19) or "new heart" (Ezek. 18:31; 36:31). Some teachers emphasized "exchanged life"; but there never was any spiritual exchange, for they only taught that regeneration was filling the spiritual gap or void in the natural man.

It seems far more biblical to assert that "everyone has spiritual being," and all humans are derivative beings deriving from the spirit-source of Satan or God. Because of Adam's fall into sin, all humans had the spiritual identity of being "sinners" (Rom. 5:19), functioning from "the spirit that works in the sons of disobedience" (Eph. 2:2), being "by nature children of wrath" (Eph. 2:3). When they express that spiritual being of Satan in sinful behavior, they derive spiritual character manifestation from the devil (cf. I Jn. 3:8). When a person is spiritually regenerated there is a spiritual exchange in our spiritual being whereby we now derive from the "Spirit of Christ" (Rom. 8:9).

LIVING BY THE LIFE OF ANOTHER

The naturalistic understanding of the humanistic philosophy that pervades the world of contemporary human thought has no comprehension of how one might "live by the life of another." Like Nicodemus, when told by Jesus that he needed to be "born again from above" (John 3:1-6), there is no understanding of spiritual things (I Cor. 2:14); for there is no distinguishing between the two planes of physical and spiritual life. Humanistic thought can only conceive of each person being given "one life to live" (a television show that ran from 1965 to 2012), and each person must do their best to make that physical life count in creating a better world in which all humanity is to live.

We only understand spiritual things when the Spirit of God (Father, Son, and Holy Spirit) comes to dwell in our spirit (cf. Rom. 8:9,11; Gal. 4:6; James 4:5) by the reception of faith. The presence of the Spirit of Christ in our spirit at spiritual regeneration gives us the necessary ability to appraise spiritual realities (I Cor. 2:12,14), particularly how receiving the spiritual life of Another, the living Lord Jesus, allows His life to become the controlling directive of our lives. We receive another life, the spiritual life of Jesus, in regeneration; and that life of Jesus living in us and being out-lived through us constitutes the Christ-life.

The apostle Paul wrote more explicitly of the indwelling and out-living of the life of Jesus Christ in the Christian than any other author. Noting that we are "partakers of Christ" (Heb. 3:14), he asked the Corinthian Christians, "Do you not recognize that Jesus Christ is in you? ...unless you believed in vain" (II Cor. 13:5). He explained to the Colossian Christians that the mystery of the gospel is "Christ in you, the hope of glory" (Col. 1:26,27) and later wrote, "Christ is our life" (Col. 3:4). To the Galatian Christians, Paul wrote, "It is no longer I who lives, but Christ lives in me" (Gal. 2:20). He lived by the life of Another, i.e., Jesus Christ.

MARCH 14

GOD IS ...

James Cleveland and the Southern California Community Choir
released a Christian gospel album in 1979 which included a song
entitled "God Is." The lyrics stated that "God is ...my light in time
of darkness; ...my joy in time of sorrow; ...my today and my
tomorrow" – each stanza concluding with "God is my all in all."
That song, "God Is," became a classic of gospel music.

Philosophers and theologians have been debating for centuries
what or who God is, asking themselves what constitutes,
comprises or characterizes God. Their philosophical and even
mystical musings about "the God beyond God" have created more
heat than light. There is a legitimate discipline of philosophical
theology that considers the existence and attributes of God. They
discuss what God is essentially, intrinsically, or inherently, and
often explain that God is *a se* (Latin for "of Himself, from Himself,
by Himself, in Himself), that God has an intrinsic character that is
Self-defined, Self-identified, Self-contained, and Self-generating.

These are mostly humanistic considerations of how fallible
human beings conceive of God. Who God is can only be rightfully
explained by God's Self-revelation of Himself in the Son, Jesus
Christ. God is unique in who He is – what God is only God is – "no
one is like Me" (Exod. 8:10; 9:14; Ps. 86:8; Isa. 46:9). God acts out
of His own being and character – God does what He does because
He is who He is. He never acts out of character.

God is Spirit (Jn. 4:24). God is true (Jn. 3:33). God is faithful (I Cor.
1:9; 10:13). God is light (I Jn. 1:5). God is a consuming fire (Heb.
12:29). God is love (I Jn. 4:8,16). These biblical expressions of
who God is are not contradictory to one another. God's wrath is
the necessary "no" to the "yes" of His inclusive love for mankind.
All of His attributes are necessarily non-transferrable, for His
character must be derived from Him in human behavior.

SEEING CHRIST IN EVERYTHING

Confession: In the past, when I heard people referring to "seeing God (or Christ) in everything," my philosophical and theological sensitivities would recoil in suspicious caution. It seemed to smack of a pantheistic worldview that regarded God or Christ to "be everything," or a panentheistic perspective that explained that God or Christ is "in everything." I agreed that we could see God at work in every situation, in accord with Paul's comment, "God causes all things to work together for good to those who love God, to those who are called according to His purpose" (Rom. 8:28); but I was leary of the "essentialist" interpretations that Christ *was* everything or *in* everything.

On a more subjective level, I began to accept that the Christ-one could and should "view everything around us with Christ-colored glasses, allowing His character and thinking to color our perspective of what we see." But, now with a bit more spiritual maturity and awareness, I think it is better to consider that as Christ lives within us as our life, we begin to see as He sees through His eyes; and we begin to see all people and situations from His loving perspective. This goes far beyond the natural, humanistic perspective of all people and circumstances viewed as expedient opportunities to use for our own advantage.

In the words of St. Patrick, the patron saint of Ireland, who died on March 17, A.D. 493.;"Christ be with me, Christ within me, Christ behind me, Christ before me, Christ beside me, Christ to win me, Christ to comfort me and restore me, Christ beneath me, Christ above me, Christ in quiet, Christ in danger, Christ in hearts of all that love me, Christ in the mouth of friend and stranger." On another occasion, Patrick explained His Christ-perspective in this way: "Christ in the heart of every man who thinks of me, Christ in the mouth of everyone who speaks of me, Christ in every eye that sees me, Christ in every ear that hears me."

MARCH 16

CRUCIFORM POWER

"All of life is an expression of power," wrote Reinhold Niebuhr. The quest for power is the driving force of the world, for the world-system is based on power-plays of success and achievement that elevate one person as superior to another. The world's sense of power is expressed through strength, knowledge, cleverness, performance, leverage, and the ability to destroy. They speak of a "higher power," political power, world powers, and abuse of power. Even Jesus' disciples fell prey to the lust for power, desiring to be on the right hand of Jesus when He rules the world (Matt. 20:20-23). Power is a seductive pursuit.

The power that the world seeks and wields is derived from the power-source of Satan. The power that the new covenant literature refers to is power derived from the Almighty and omnipotent God. This contrast of the spirit-source of power is evident in the exchange of power/authority in spiritual regeneration when a person is turned from "the power (Greek *exousia*, "deriving out of the being") of Satan to God" (Acts 26:18). The Christian sense of power recognizes that we derive power from Christ (I Cor. 1:24), and such power flows freely when we understand our identity and source of strength in Christ.

The apostle Paul gives us a practical sense of Christ's power when he writes, "The message of the cross is foolishness to those who are perishing, but to us who are being saved it is the power of God" (I Cor. 1:18). In II Corinthians 12:9,10, he goes on to explain that "such power is made perfect in weakness," the subversive power of humility, sacrifice and self-denial. Such cruciform (cross-shaped) power is so radically counter-intuitive to the world's sense of power that is regarded as ridiculously "foolish" by the world, to lay down and expend one's life for others. Paul boldly asserts, "When I am weak, then I am strong" in the derived strength and power of Christ to love others.

SELF-CONSCIOUSNESS

As a young man, I was very self-conscious. I was smaller than other students my age and not able to participate in the age-related competitive sports (certainly not football or basketball). Even in college I would sit on the back row behind the largest person I could find so I would not be noticed or called upon. Not until I was out of college and seminary did I read the verse Ephesians 1:3 in the King James Version about being "accepted in the beloved," i.e. accepted by God in (*union with*) Jesus Christ. My reasoning was, "If I am accepted by the living Lord Jesus, then no one else's opinion makes much difference; so, I am only responsible to be the Christ-one that I am 'in Christ Jesus'."

Self-consciousness is often due to an undue awareness of our own person and action, in perceived comparison and evaluation with that of others. It is usually a form of selfishness, especially when we believe that "everyone is looking at me, and thinking that I do not measure up to the norm." Someone might come along and ask, "Who do you think you are, thinking that everyone is looking at you; you must think that you are really important?" Such heightened awareness of oneself, often leading to inordinate preoccupation with oneself,when pushed to the extreme, can be a form of narcissism.

Among Christians there is a more subtle spiritual sense of self-consciousness. When Christians become overly occupied with how well they are doing in the Christian life; how they compare with other Christians and what other Christians think of them. "How does God think I am doing? I don't want to 'miss the mark.'" When we are self-conscious in the Christian life, it is a sign we are looking at the wrong person – looking at ourselves, instead of Jesus. Self-consciousness is one of the greatest sins of Christian people, because the Christian life is not what we are doing, but what Jesus is doing in and through us.

MARCH 18

SELF-DENIAL

Religion will inevitably turn every human action into a performance action that allegedly elicits meritorious credit toward ultimate salvation in the sight of God. Even such a benign action as self-denial, the willingness to forego self-concerns in order to engage in loving concern for others, has been contorted into a human performance action that religion encourages us to perform. Some of the self-diminishing admonitions that religion advises in restraining our desires in altruistic abstinence amount to masochistic self-beating akin to micro-suicide. It has been referred to as "self-mortification," "self-punishment" (self-flagellation), or "dying to self."

This is definitely not what Christ-ones are called to engage in. Self-reproach, self-condemnation, self-humiliation, self-debasement, self-abnegation, self-abstinence – the prefix self- in all of these words indicates that these are self-performed actions of ascetic renunciation of oneself. These amount to an absurd self-attempt to destroy oneself. Christ-ones who have already died to the old self (Rom. 6:8; Col. 2:20) in Christ's crucifixion, and have become a "new self" (II Cor. 5:17; Eph. 4:24; Col. 2:10) in union with Christ, most certainly do not seek to destroy the new spiritual creature they have become.

The Christian concept of self-denial (cf. Matt. 16:24; Mk. 8:34; Lk. 9:23) is an attitudinal orientation wherein we "do not just please ourselves" (Rom. 15:1), "do not merely look out for own personal interests, but also for the interests of others" (Phil. 2:4). Since selfishness is our natural default attitude, self-denial must be derived from God in Christ and might better be called God-induced reduction of our natural selfish desires, effected when the living and indwelling Lord Jesus is operative in our lives and we are allowing Christ's character of compassion and love to flow to others. Self-denial is derived from the character of Jesus.

WHAT IS GOOD?

Human beings have long debated the question, "What is good?"
Our problem seems to stem from an abundance of ambiguous
concepts of the meaning of "good." We speak of good credit, good
cholesterol, good coffee, good ideas, and good behavior. Is there a
difference in the way the adjective "good" is being used? Good is
regarded by many as what is pleasant and amenable to my
personal needs and pleasures. Evil, on the contrary, is regarded
as what one finds unpleasant in life. The child who gets a "good
spanking" probably doesn't find the experience pleasant and "for
his own good" as his parents might explain.

The English word "good" is not etymologically derived from the
word "God," as many have suggested. Believe it or not, I cannot
find a direct statement in scripture that states, "God is good."
Despite no direct references, the are many indirect references to
the "goodness" of God in action (cf. II Chron. 6:41; Ps. 68:10; Heb.
6:5). The first mention of "good" in the Bible is in Genesis when
God planted "the tree of the knowledge of *good* and evil" (Gen.
2:7) in the Garden of Eden. The "good" of that tree is but the
human concept of "good" relative to evil in the relativized human
preference of ego-centric determinations, self-determined
correctness of acceptable thought and action.

This exposes the necessity of differentiating between the human
"good" of relative evaluation, and the divine "good" of God's
character – relative human good and absolute divine "good."
When Jesus was called "good teacher," He responded by saying,
"No one is good, but God alone" (Mk. 10:18; Lk. 18:19). Goodness
can only be defined accurately in reference to God. 3 Jn. 1:11
reads, "The one who does good is of (Greek *ek* - derives what he
does "out of") God; the one who does evil has not seen God" (and
does not recognize that he is deriving evil character from, "out
of," the Evil One). Good and evil are always derived character.

MARCH 20

DO WE SEE GOD'S GOOD?

"God causes all things to work together for good to those who love God, to those who are called according to His purpose" (Rom. 8:28). If that be the case (and I believe that it is), the question might be asked, "Where is the 'good' in the coronavirus pandemic that has so affected the world during the past year?" Now, we must admit that all of God's good actions are not visible to human eyes. We cannot see everything that God is doing. To understand what God is doing requires His revealing Himself and His character in His actions.

We want to be "those who have eyes to see" God at work by His grace. Let us focus our attention on the "good" that can come to the Body of Christ in the midst of such a pandemic. The circumstances might cause the "Church," the people of God, to reacquaint themselves with what the Greek word *ecclesia* actually means. It means "to assemble, to gather, to congregate," referring to the dynamic interaction of people, not to a static building, not to an institution, and not to a programmed service. The curtailment of our gathering in loving consideration of others during the pandemic does not effect the shut-down of the Body of Christ. Instead, we intensify our recognition that the *ecclesia* is relational; we need each other; and we develop a greater desire to integrate, interact, and fellowship with our brothers and sisters in Christ in order to "encourage one another" (I Thess. 5:11).

The Body of Christ remains the Body of Christ whether it gathers collectively or not. French sociologist Jacques Ellul explained that Christianity only requires one person who will be the conduit of the Christ-life. *Ecclesia*, on the other hand, is comprised of multiple Christ-ones who gather and assemble together in a congregation. The living Lord Jesus can and will express Himself in every genuine Christian, individually and collectively.

THE CROSS AND POLITICS

What does the cross have to do with politics? EVERYTHING! It is an indictment on the way that the world of natural humanity conducts its politics. Jesus knew full well that He could have countered the crucifixion plan by sending twelve legions of angels (Matt. 26:53) to combat the effort to put Him to death. But, He did not choose the *modus operandi* of power-plays, the angry protests and violent confrontations of power-politics. Instead, He chose the counter-intuitive way of sacrificial love, laying down one's life for others. He chose the way of death by crucifixion rather than the battle of confrontation.

This does not mean that there was not an abundance of politicking going on surrounding the cross. Jesus' closest disciples failed to understand the ways and means of Jesus' kingdom. James and John sought to be seated at the right and the left of Jesus (Mk. 10:37) when He "came in glory," even getting their mother to lobby for such political favor (Matt. 20:21). Again, they did not understand that Jesus' "glory" was to die on the execution instrument of a Roman cross. Jesus asked the two disciples, "Can you drink from the cup that I am about to drink" (Matt. 20:22), the cup of suffering and death – that is My glory!

Pilate did not understand the ways of Jesus either. He asked Jesus, "Are you the King of the Jews?" (Matt. 27:11). Jesus explained, "I am, but My kingdom is not of this world" (Jn. 18:36); not meaning that His kingdom was abstract and projected into the heavenlies, but that His kingdom does not engage in political power-plays to one-up and conquer others like worldly kingdoms do. Jesus reigns via the cross! And as Christ-ones, if we desire to participate in His kingdom and His glory, we must live cruciform lives as the character and *modus operandi* of the crucified Christ is lived out through us, countering the ways of the world, laying down our lives in loving sacrifice for others.

MARCH 22

POLITICS

The word "politics" is based on the Greek word *politika*, first used by Aristotle as the title of one of his classic works. The Greek word for "city" is *polis*, so *politika* refers to the affairs and governance of the city (state, nation), inclusive of both conflict and cooperation in such determinations. Our nation has just observed a polarized animosity between political parties in the recent preparation for a national presidential election. It has been obvious that the political interactions of fallen men can be nasty and messy, full of subterfuge, selfishness, and sin, with abundant lies and false accusations hurled at their opponents.

It may never have crossed your mind that we might also consider the politics of God. Am I intimating that God is a politician? No, especially since that word is freighted with many negative connotations these days. But beyond the natural governance of physical cities, we might also consider what Augustine, in the fourth century, referred to as *The City of God*. He was referring to the community of God's people and how the governing affairs of God's community are so counter-intuitive and counter-productive to those practiced by the politics of man in the governance of our physical cities, states, and nations.

French sociologist Jacques Ellul's book, *The Politics of Man and the Politics of God*, was first published in English in 1972. It considers the political machinations of several personages in the seldom-studied biblical book of II Kings. Throughout the book, Ellul contrasts human governance with the divine governance of God over His people. The management of the *City of God* has no hierarchical power-plays and is not based on men's competitive achievements. In a final "Meditation on Inutility," Ellul compares the political contrasts in what I have reframed in an article, "The Usefulness of Uselessness, and the Uselessness of Usefulness" (1999), my take-off on Ellul's thesis.

USELESSNESS

Throughout the history of human thought many have questioned the *usefulness* of all the humanistic and religious exercises of men. By natural reasoning alone they have arrived at a broad philosophical perspective that recognizes the *uselessness* of all alleged humanistic *usefulness*. Often labeled as pessimists, negativists, passivists, or fatalists, they have nevertheless exposed the futility of man's repetitive endeavors of struggling and striving to be *useful*. Aristotle claimed that the supremely important activities in human life are those that are the most "useless," not leading to a greater external end for ourselves.

Jesus told a parable of a *useless* servant (Lk. 17:7-10). The point of the parable is that Christian servants are expected to spontaneously do what they are commanded to do. They "listen under" their Lord in obedience. Afterwards they do not expect time-off for an awards banquet to be praised for their productivity, their *usefulness*, or their indispensable value to God. The servant in Jesus' parable did not expect such. Rather, his self-declaration is, "We are *useless* slaves; we have done only that which we ought to have done."

The Christian servant recognizes that the dynamic of his action is indeed the grace-activity of God. Recognizing the *uselessness* of one's own endeavors of self-effort and "works," the Christian servant can declare, "It is not what I have done, but what Christ has accomplished in me and through me." "I do not presume to speak of anything except what Christ has accomplished through me," declares Paul (Rom. 15:18).

Someone reportedly asked Mother Theresa in Calcutta, India, "Why do you pick up all these pitiful people? They only die anyway! Isn't it all rather *useless*?" Her reply was, "God has not called me to be successful (*useful*); only to be faithful.

MARCH 24

PRIDE STINKS!

There has been a stench in the air during the past few months of the recent presidential election process. The foul, malodorous smell seems to have been emanating from a fractured attitude of incivility deep within the national psyche of the American people. Instead of the diverse opinions that must be tolerated in a modern representative democracy, we have stooped to the rancorous polarity of intolerance and personal pride. The partisan political pride of ideology among people of both parties is a national disgrace and must be overcome if the United States of America is to remain united and free.

The thoughts articulated by otherwise reasonable people are unbelievably haughty. Persons from both parties are guilty of political pride. One group thinks they are more intelligent, more astute, and have better understanding of what is going on in the world than the other group. One group thinks the others are going to destroy America. Then, there is the toxic mixture of religious pride and political pride: "I just can't go to church and worship God with people who support that candidate." Here we have the religious pride of thinking that my thoughts align with God's thought, my sympathies with God's sympathies.

The inspired scriptures have much to say about pride, especially in the wisdom of the proverbs: "When pride comes, then comes dishonor; but with the humble there is wisdom" (Prov. 11:2). "Pride goes before destruction, and a haughty spirit before stumbling" (Prov. 16:18). 'Proud, arrogant, scoffer' are his names, one who acts with insolent pride" (Prov. 21:24). "...the boastful pride of life is not from the Father, but from the world" – Satan (I Jn. 2:16). "God is opposed to the proud, but gives grace to the humble" (James 4:6; I Pet. 5:5). Pride stinks! and the sad fact is that the proud person struts on like a spunky skunk, oblivious to the stench that trails behind him; he can't smell it.

MAUNDY THURSDAY

Many churches around the world have special services on Maundy Thursday, and they often celebrate the Lord's Supper or Eucharist together on this occasion. Why? Because on the Thursday evening prior to Jesus' crucifixion on "Good Friday," Jesus met with His disciples in the upper room after sunset to partake of the Passover meal with them and to prepare them for what was to transpire in the coming days. What was going to happen? Jesus was going to die the next day (Friday), to be executed by Roman crucifixion, in order to be raised from the dead in resurrection on Sunday, the "first day of the week."

Some people think that "maundy" refers to foot-washing or to celebration of the Eucharist. During the Passover observance, Jesus said, "this cup is the new covenant in My blood"; the cup of the old covenant remembrance of blood on the doorpost to cause the death angel to "pass over" the home was to be transformed into a remembrance of the blood of the crucified Messiah, the Paschal Lamb, who shed His blood on the cross of Calvary for the exodus of all mankind from the tyranny of sin.

Why is this day called "Maundy Thursday"? What does "maundy" mean? The word "maundy" comes from the Latin, referring to a commandment, order or mandate. In the upper room, after Jesus had washed the disciples' feet and shared in the remembrance of the Passover with them and allowed Judas to exit the fellowship of the disciples, Jesus said to the remaining disciples, "A new commandment I give to you, that you love one another, as I have loved you" (Jn. 13:34). In the Latin Bible (*Biblia Sacra Vulgata*) this initial phrase reads, "*Mandatum novum do vobis...*" The word "maundy" is rooted in the word "mandate," referring to the new commandment of love given by Jesus. May Maundy Thursday celebration be a recognition of the mandate of Jesus that all of His disciples should "love one another, as He has loved us."

MARCH 26

THE DEATH OF DEATH IN THE DEATH OF JESUS

Some have wondered why this day is referred to as "Good Friday." Since it is the day when the Church commemorates and remembers the death of Jesus on the cross, why is it not called "Tragic Friday" or "the Friday of Lament, Grief or Sorrow?" This was, after all, the day when Jesus was led to Golgotha to be executed by means of Roman crucifixion, when the sun went dark (Matt. 27:45), the curtain of the temple was torn in two from top to bottom (Matt. 27:51). It only becomes "Good Friday" when it is revealed to us what God accomplished in the death of His Son, Jesus Christ, and the consequent resurrection from the dead wherein life could be restored to the fallen human race.

Death is the domain of the death-dealing devil – the "one having the power of death" (Heb. 2:14), who deceived mankind and energizes all sin that leads to death (Rom. 5:12; I Jn. 3:8). The death of Jesus, the One man who was without sin (II Cor. 5:12), was the defeat of "the one having the power of death, the devil" (Heb. 2:14). "The Son of God appeared to destroy the works of the devil" (I Jn. 3:8). He "disarmed the diabolic rulers and authorities, having triumphed over them" (Col. 2:15). But "death could not hold Him," and "God raised Him up again, putting an end to the agony of death" (Acts 2:24) – both Jesus' and ours.

It is important to understand that when Jesus died, we died. Where were we when Jesus died? In Him! "One died for all, therefore all died" (II Cor. 5:24). "He bore our sins in His body on the cross, so that we might die to sin and live to righteousness" (I Pet. 2:24). "You have died and your life is hidden with Christ in God" (Col. 3:3). "If we died with Him, we will also live with Him" (II Tim. 2:11). "I have been crucified with Christ; it is no longer I who live, but Christ lives in me" (Gal. 2:20). Jesus declared, "I am the resurrection and the life; everyone who believes in Me will never die" (Jn. 11:26). "The death of death in the death of Jesus."

RAISED UP WITH JESUS

Where were you when Jesus arose from the dead on that first Easter morning? Every Christ-one was objectively "in Him," joined "in union with Him" (I Cor. 6:17), being granted and endowed with the "power of resurrection-life" (cf. Rom. 1:4), the conquering life that overcomes death, the eternal life that bears and glorifies the character of Christ forevermore. Not only did we die with Christ in the crucifixion on the cross, but we were raised with Him in the resurrection. "God made us alive together with Christ, and *raised us up with Him*, and seated us with Him in the heavenlies in Christ Jesus" (Eph. 2:5,6).

It requires God's spiritual revelation for our "renewed minds" to understand and appreciate that we were "raised up with Jesus." We must move beyond mere historical chronology to grasp spiritual union with the eternal Savior that is beyond time or place. Vicariously representing every human being, Jesus took us all into His death – our pre-regenerate spiritual identity as an "old man/self" was "crucified with Christ" (Rom. 6:6; Eph. 4:22), – in order to take us into His resurrection and grant us His divine resurrection-life – the life of God once again dwelling in the spirit of individuals who are "new creatures in Christ" (II Cor. 5:17).

"Therefore, if you have been *raised up with Christ*, keep seeking the things above, where Christ is, seated at the right hand of God" (Col. 3:1). "If the Spirit of Him who raised Jesus from the dead dwells in you, He who raised Christ Jesus from the dead will also give life to your mortal bodies through His Spirit who dwells in you" (Rom. 8:11). "As Christ was raised from the dead through the glory of the Father, so we too might walk in newness of life" (Rom. 6:4). Personal, experiential participation in the resurrection-life of the risen Lord Jesus commences when one is spiritually reborn as a "new man/self" (Eph. 4:24). We were "raised up with Him through faith" (Col. 2:12).

MARCH 28

"YES, LORD!"

So many Christ-ones struggle and strive to understand and engage in meaningful times of prayer and worship. Much of their problem stems from the admonitions of religion advocating that these exercises must be done in a required procedure, at the right time, in the right place, and in the right way. Such attempts to perform and "do it right" lead only to frustrating failure. If you find a continuing quagmire concerning prayer and worship to be true in your life, you may still be suffering from the residuals of the "do right" religion. The spontaneous Christ-life is not complicated or demanding. However, religion always is!

Prayer should be personal conversation with the personal triune God of Father, Son, and Holy Spirit. It should not be a contrived procedure with regulated vocabulary that conforms to religion's expectations. My personal prayer vocabulary is quite limited; limited to a spontaneous "Yes, Lord!" At first, I didn't even realize I was praying. When reading a book or an article that resonates with my Spirit-filled spirit, that glorifies God and articulates the presence and activity of Jesus in my life, I will often clench my fist and spontaneously exclaim, "Yes, Lord!" It took me a long while (years) to realize that in that moment I am praying and worshipping God (without all the trappings religion requires).

This "Yes, Lord" exclamation of prayer and worship is juxtaposed with the apostle Peter's response when he was on the rooftop at the home of Simon the Tanner in Joppa. When a voice from heaven told him to take some of the non-kosher animals from the sheet and eat them, Peter replied, "Not so, Lord" (Acts 10:14). Peter's "do right" religion of Judaism would not allow that kind of freedom from the dietary rules and regulations. Such ritualistic attitudes and acts of defiance and rebellion should never be part of our prayer and worship. In compliance and surrender, we submit ourselves to God's direction, saying, "Yes, Lord!"

PATIENCE

How often have you heard someone say, "God is teaching me patience in this troubling situation"? Or perhaps you have heard people say, "What I need is more patience; I am praying for God to give me more patience." I am inclined (and have done so) to ask these people, "Do you know the living Lord Jesus? Because if you have received Jesus as your Lord and Savior, He came complete with His character when He came to live in you, and within His divine character is the ability to manifest patience." Patience is part of the "fruit of the Spirit" (Gal. 5:22,23), and we must not be self-selective fruit-pickers, but utilize the full cluster of His divine character-fruit.

We must admit that some personalities have more natural forbearance and exhibit a calm composure to a greater extent than others. They don't seem to get ruffled and upset so easily. They let the water of circumstances roll off their backs, have a "come what may" attitude, and are laid back, sometimes even passive; but that is not the supernatural character of patience that is derived only from the Spirit of Christ within. Our natural personality traits must not be mistaken for spiritual character.

Patience is not a lesson that is taught nor a human attitude to be sought. Patience is not a natural personality trait – some have it; some do not. No, patience is in the cluster of the "fruit of the Spirit" (Gal. 5:22,23); not something we can produce or manufacture. Patience is the character of God (cf. II Pet. 3:9) and must be derived from Christ within. When we receive Jesus to become a Christ-one, Jesus comes to dwell in us with the full character of God. Every Christian has a full complement of patience, waiting to be exhibited as we allow the living Lord Jesus to be manifested in our behavior as we love others (I Cor. 13:4). Thereby, we can "encourage the fainthearted, help the weak, and be patient with everyone" (I Thess. 5:14).

MARCH 30

ENDURING PAIN

We are not called to be stoics, who advised that we "bite the bullet," "just hang in there and tough it out" when facing pain. What virtue is there in being able to suppress our feelings in some form of alleged self-control? Those who advocate "no pain, no gain" often move beyond the realm of physical exercise to the philosophical idea that pain builds character. If character has a spiritual source, then how can physical pain build spiritual character? Whether one's pain is acute or chronic, if medicine can alleviate the pain, then it seems reasonable to take such. There does not seem to be inherent value in enduring pain.

Many have turned to the book of Job to consider how he endured pain and suffering. Job's friends believed that personal sin was the cause of all pain and suffering, but the narrative of Job seems to deny such, reminding us of human finitude, the fragility of life, and the necessity of trusting that God cares for us and seeks our highest good. Through his ordeal, Job does seem to have developed an expanded perspective and appreciation of God's grace and love. Thomas Merton wrote, "If we love God for something less than Himself, we cherish a desire that can fail; we run the risk of hating Him if we don't get what we hope for."

In the new covenant literature, it is Paul's painful ordeal with a "thorn in the flesh" (II Cor. 12:7-10) that people consult to understand how he endured the pain. Paul sought relief in his prayers, but the only answer was God's response, "My grace is sufficient for you, for power is perfected in weakness." There are no easy answers or formulas for the problem of pain; it does no good to try to figure it out. We keep our eyes on Jesus and not on ourselves and our pain, believing that God's grace seeks our highest good; and He will not allow us to be tried beyond what we are able (cf. I Cor. 10:13). In the midst of pain, we are to allow the character of Christ to be exhibited in attitude and behavior.

THE CROSS-LIFE

Some may consider the combination of "cross-life" to be oxymoronic. The cross was a Roman execution instrument leading to a gruesome death for criminals and traitors of the Roman empire. Where's the life in that? Only Jesus could turn the death-intent of the cross to the means of life; and that He did being unjustly crucified on a Roman cross, rising from the dead after three days, and making His resurrection-life available to all who would receive Him in order to be joined with Him spiritually (I Cor. 6:17), allowing His life to be their life (Gal. 2:20, and expressing the sacrificial Christ-life lovingly laid down for others.

The resurrection-life of Jesus that every Christ-one receives necessarily involves the continuing cross-life of Jesus. The cross-life is embedded in the resurrection-life; yea, it is the integral character of the resurrection-life. The "Yes" of God's positive action of grace in the Christ-life must necessarily involve the "No" of God's continuing work in dealing with the residual patterns of sinfulness and selfishness in the fleshly desires of our Christian soul. This has nothing to do with any religious striving or performance. The positive swallows up the negative as the positive function of divine grace in Jesus continues to put to death that which is misrepresentative of His character.

Yes, the living Lord Jesus lives in every Christian, but His intent is not to make us more spiritual or a "better Christian" (those are not possible); however, His indwelling presence and function does express His character of self-denial, humiliation, and self-giving – all of these being features of His willingness to experience the cross. "Christ in us" is always "Christ in us for others!" The living Lord Jesus continues to sacrificially lay down His life for others "as us." That is the "cross-life" within the Christ-life, as we avail ourselves by faith to present ourselves as a living sacrifice (Rom. 12:2) to God and for others.

APRIL 1

CHRISTIAN MINISTRY

The Greek word translated "ministry" throughout the New Testament is *diakonos*. The word was used to refer to a "servant" in biblical times, one who executes the commands of others, probably derived from *diako*, meaning "to run errands." The same word, *diakonos*, is used to designate "ministry" as well as "service"– "to serve" is "to minister" to another. Paul used this word to recommend that certain persons be designated to "serve tables" in the early *ecclesia* so the apostles would have time to engage in preaching (cf. Acts 6:2), and the word was transliterated into a designation of "deacons" (I Tim. 3:8,10,12,13) rather than simply "Christian servants."

Christian service or Christian ministry has unfortunately been professionalized in the church for many centuries. It was never intended to be a profession requiring seminary training with a degree in ministry to become a "minister," "priest," or "pastor." One of the emphases of the sixteenth century Protestant Reformation was to explain the "priesthood of all believers," not requiring a professional intermediary priest between Christ and the Christian. The Baptists expanded the concept to the "ministry of all believers," calling all Christians to be priests unto God (I Pet. 2:9), ministering to and serving others.

Christian ministry occurs when the life of Jesus Christ living within a Christ-one fills us up and spontaneously overflows in service for the lives of others. What is within (for the Christian, the person and character of Christ) spills over for others, and they often become like the one who ministered or served them. Today, we often refer to leaders in the various levels of government,as "public servants," though this has also been perverted by professionalism. Whether their character, attitudes and behavior might be admirable or despicable, it spills over into those with whom they work.

THE NECESSARY SEQUENCE

Only ... if Jesus were born as He was born, conceived of the Holy Spirit (Matt. 1;20), called Emmanuel, "God with us" (Matt. 1;23), the Word become flesh (Jn. 1:14), the God-man "in the form of a man" (Phil. 2:8), could He have lived as He lived.

Only ... if Jesus lived as He lived, without sin (II Cor. 5:21), the perfect man in being and action, doing nothing from His own initiative, allowing the Father abiding in Him to do His works (Jn. 14:10), speaking what the Father was speaking (Jn. 8:28), could He have died as He died, the sinless sacrifice.

Only ... if Jesus died as He died, "obedient unto death, even death on a cross" (Phil. 2:8), the vicarious sacrifice for the sins of humanity in our place (II Cor. 5:21), taking the death consequences for men's sin, paying the price (I Cor. 6:20; 7:23) to redeem and reconcile all mankind, could He have risen from the dead as He did on the third day.

Only ... if Jesus rose from the dead in resurrection, victorious over death (I Cor. 15:57), could He be the firstborn among many brethren (Rom. 8:29), experiencing life out of death (I Jn. 3:14), and ascending into the heavenly presence of God.

Only ... if Jesus ascended to the Father, having accomplished His redemptive mission (Jn. 17:4), sitting down on the right hand of God the Father, could He consequently be poured out in Spirit-form on the Day of Pentecost.

Only ... if Jesus were poured out in Spirit-form on Pentecost (Acts 2:1-36), the last Adam becoming life-giving Spirit (I Cor. 15:45), by the Lord, the Spirit (II Cor. 3:7) indwelling our spirit (Rom. 8:16), can we be birthed by the Spirit.

Only ... if we are born of the Spirit from above (Jn. 3:3-6), with the Spirit of Christ in us (Rom. 8:9), united with Christ (I Cor. 6:1), partakers of the divine nature (II Pet. 1:4), complete in Christ (Col. 1:28; 2;10), can we be the redeemed and restored humanity whereby the living Lord Jesus re-presents His life in and through us to the glory of God.

APRIL 3

THE WAY GOD MADE US

Many people are unaware of how God created human beings to function. The apostle Paul wrote, "May the God of peace Himself set you apart to function as intended; may your **SPIRIT** and **SOUL** and **BODY** function in maturity until the coming of our Lord Jesus Christ" (I Thess. 5:23). Spiritual function, psychological function, and physiological function are the three levels of human function.

SPIRIT – *pneuma* - makes us unique as human beings, allowing us to enter into spiritual union with the Triune God. The human spirit has no independent function; it is simply the capacity to be occupied and indwelt by Spirit-personage (the spiritual presence and function of God or Satan). The spirit-being in our human spirit is the basis of each individual's spiritual nature, identity, character, and life/death. God's intent is that the Spirit of Christ (Rom. 8:9) should occupy our spirit, as we become Christ-ones.

SOUL – *psyche* – is where, like other created animals, human beings exercise psychological function that leads to individual behavior. The mental function of the human mind is superior to all other creatures. The emotional function of our human emotions is extremely complex. The volitional function of the human will exercises freedom of choice (not free-will which is God's prerogative alone). The "flesh" – *sarx* – is our unique combination of selfish and sinful patterns in the desires of our human soul, developed when "the spirit that works in the sons of disobedience" (Eph. 2:2) embedded his character in our desires.

BODY – *soma* – is the external instrument by which we exhibit physiological behavioral function. The derived character of the spirit-being within influences the attitudes in our soul, and for the Christian, the life of Jesus is to be manifested in our physical bodies (II Cor. 4;10,11), to the glory of God.

KNOWING OUR IDENTITY – WHO WE ARE

Humans have more than one level of being/function from which they have attempted to attribute their identity:

Spiritual identity – A person's deepest identity is in the core of our being, in our spirit. We are who we are on the basis of the spirit-being who indwells our spirit. This is a derived identity (corresponding to derived nature, character, and life or death – derived from either God or Satan. Our derived identity is either that of "sinners" (Rom. 5:19) or "saints" (Rom. 8:27). The identity of a Christian is that of a Christ-one, and His presence and function in us identifies us as "holy ones," righteous, and perfect.

Soulish sense of identity – based on the camouflage that Satan foisted on the human race to disguise the fact that he was "the spirit working in the sons of disobedience" (Eph. 2:2) i.e. all unregenerate, natural human beings from the time they were born. Having bought into the humanistic fallacy that we were an "independent self" (that it wasn't really Satan working in us), we think we are in charge, that we can "do our own thing," that we can be anything we want to be and do anything we want to do, that we can be our own center of reference, that we can "be like God" (Gen. 3:5) with self-potential to generate our own actions and base our identity on those actions that express our selfish fleshliness. The minds of men have been blinded (II Cor. 4:4) by Satan to think that derivation from God is tyranny.

Physical sense of identity – This external sense of identity posits that "I am who I am because of my physical prowess, my athletic abilities, my buff body; or for the female, an hour-glass body, attractiveness, business acumen, etc." What I am in and of myself: "I am somebody because I am a doctor, lawyer, pastor, or star athlete, or because I associate with important people, or belong to the right organization (Baptist, Episcopalian, etc.).

APRIL 5

THE UNITY BRIDGE

On numerous occasions throughout human history after two regions or countries have engaged in warfare against each other, when the conflict has subsided the two sides determine to build a "unity bridge" across the river that divides them. A modern example is "The Unity Bridge" mutually constructed by the countries of Tanzania and Mozambique across the Rovuma river, inaugurated in May, 2010. Another example of such a unity bridge might be the Széchenyi Chain Bridge connecting Buda and Pest across the Danube River, reconstructed on more than one occasion after skirmishes in the region.

In like manner, to reunite estranged and alienated people, God arranged for the cross of Calvary on which His Son Jesus died in our place to be a unity bridge, a bridge to bring sinful and fallen mankind together with Himself in reconciliation and peace, as well as to unify peoples and nations from around the globe in recognition of their oneness in a new humanity in Jesus Christ. In their natural fallen spiritual condition, selfish and sinful human beings emphasize and magnify their differences, claiming superiority of being, thought, prowess, etc. The cross was the bridge of unity where the Son of God laid down His life to bring people together in oneness, once and for all.

The cruciform "unity bridge" is still functioning in our estranged and embittered society today. In Paul's day, it was Jews and Gentiles who were divided (Eph. 2:11-22), seemingly unable to be reconciled. Today we still have the residuals of slavery in the conflict of black and white. Many nations of the world hold long-term animosities and acrimony. We have even had leaders in our own country who have fostered division instead of unity. The churches have been no help for the most part, arguing and dividing about doctrine and worship practices. The "union bridge" of the cross of Christ is our only hope.

"TO LIVE IS CHRIST; TO DIE IS GAIN"

The apostle Paul and Silas had been beaten with rods and thrown into the inner prison while in Philippi, all based on false charges of sedition against the Roman government (Acts 16:22-40). Their reception in Laodicea and Berea was equally as hostile as they were chased out of town. Writing to the Philippian Christians, Paul does not bemoan his treatment but encourages his readers to participate in the joy that is theirs in Christ Jesus. What a joyous life of glory we have in understanding that it is no longer we who live, but Christ lives in us. It is not us that enemies seek to persecute, but the Jesus who lives in us.

In light of his narrow escapes from death, Paul explains to the Philippians his perspective that whether he continues physical life or dies physically, he desires that Jesus Christ should be exalted. Contemplating the either/or of life and death, Paul writes, "To live is Christ; to die is gain!" (Phil. 1:21). Since the living Christ lives in the Christ-one (Rom 8:9), Christ is our life (Col. 3:4) and physical death cannot separate us from Christ (Rom. 8:38,39), then we can approach physical death with a "nothing to lose; everything to gain" attitude. But the question must still be asked, "What is the gain in physical death?"

In this ironic case, the gain is not in acquiring something more than Jesus, but the gain is in the loss of the problematic hindrances that fetter the free-flow of the Christ-life. In physical death the Christ-one retains everything of eternal value in Christ Jesus, but we jettison all of the picayune bothers, the petty and pesky problems, the flak, the "body-fuss" as Norman Grubb used to say, the hecklers, the persecutors, the false-accusers, the back-biters, the detriments. In heaven, we still have the eternal, pure and unadulterated presence and life of Jesus; there is no loss of Jesus, but there is the gain of losing all of the detrimental detractions that seek to limit the enjoyment of His life in the now.

APRIL 7

ARE YOU A GOOD LISTENER?

In social situations, we often observe people who are not good listeners. They are often quite proud, wanting to make their opinions known, and they like to hear themselves talk. One of Job's counsellors, Elihu, said, "Listen to me, I too will tell you what I think" (Job 32:10). There are many like him to this day! Yet, the Bible admonishes us not to listen to the wrong people who are not speaking words from God.

The primary listening referred to in the scriptures is the conversation between God and His people. God repeatedly asks His people to listen to Him, and the people of God are keen to believe that God is listening to their prayers. David, for example, writes, "Listen to my prayers, God; and do not hide Yourself from my pleading" (Ps. 55:1; cf. 39:12). Listening to God should not be construed as physical hearing an audible voice (though this is possible) but often involves an inner realization and prompting from God, with the spiritual awareness that God is attempting to send you a message in one way or another.

Our listening to God is the essence of obedience. "If you *listen obediently* to my commandments which I am commanding you today, to love the Lord your God and to serve Him with all your heart and all your soul, He will provide for you" (Deut. 11:13). To "listen obediently" becomes the essence of our relationship with God in the new covenant. The Greek word translated "obedience" is *hupakouo*, meaning "to listen under." Obedience is not a matter of keeping rules but is the relational communication whereby we "listen under" God to ascertain what He desires to do next in our lives, in order that we might respond with the receptivity of faith that allows Him to do so. Jesus said, "My sheep listen to My voice, and I know them, and they follow Me" (Jn. 10:27). We must be quick to hear, and slow to speak" (James 1:19). Thereby, we become a good listener.

THANKSGIVING

Thanksgiving, i.e. "giving thanks" as an expression of gratitude, goes back much farther than the attribution of the Thanksgiving holiday to a 1621 harvest feast shared by the English colonists (Pilgrims) of Plymouth and the native Mashpee Wampanoag people of Massachusetts and Rhode Island. George Washington proclaimed the first national day of thanksgiving on Nov. 26, 1789. "as a day of public thanksgiving and prayer, to be observed by acknowledging with grateful hearts the many and signal favours of Almighty God." In the midst of the Civil War (1863), Abraham Lincoln declared an annual Thanksgiving Day celebration to be observed by all the states of the union on the final Thursday of November every calendar year.

When Jesus "gave thanks" prior to feeding the multitude on the far side of the Sea of Galilee (Matt. 15:36; Mk. 8:6; Jn. 6:11) the original Greek word used is *eucharistesas*. Likewise, when He shared the cup of wine with His disciples at the last supper, saying "This is My blood," He "gave thanks" (*eucharistesas*) (I Cor. 11:24). That is why many Christians call the remembrance of the communion celebration the Eucharist. The Greek word is a combination of two words, *eu* = good and *charis* = grace. So, to "give thanks" is to recognize the "good grace" of God and express appreciation for such grace in an attitude of gratitude.

We do not just "give thanks" before eating, however. There are many scripture references to recognizing the "good grace" of God in all situations. We are to be "always giving thanks for all things in the name of our Lord Jesus Christ to *our* God and Father" (Eph. 5:20). "Do everything in the name of the Lord Jesus, giving thanks through Him to God the Father" (Col. 3:17). "In everything by prayer and supplication with thanksgiving let your requests be made known to God" (Phil. 4:6). We recognize the "good grace" of God in all that He is and for all He does, because He is who He is.

APRIL 9

SPIRITUAL DEATH

Death is not merely the absence of life, as popularly defined by many Christian teachers. Such definition by privation, i.e. something is dead if deprived of life, is not always a valid argument. If something is defined by what it is not, then the absence of positive assertion, ends up being nothing. So, if we were to define "sin" as the absence of righteousness, then sin has no real definitive existence – sin is nothing and does not require justification. Recognizing this, we do not want to assert that "spiritual death is nothing," for that would imply that there is no need of any redemptive or saving action on behalf of humanity.

We must recognize that there is more than one plane of life. On the physical plane, the death of a living body does create a static corpse, having no life. The paramedic checks for "signs of life" and finding none declares the person dead. This is a conclusion based on the deprivation or absence of life. Conversely, spiritual death is very active, full of motion and action. Spiritual death is energized by "the spirit that works in the sons of disobedience" (Eph. 2:2), causing natural human beings to be "dead in trespasses and sins" (Eph. 2:1,5). There is an ontological dynamic to spiritual death, and Jesus was born and crucified "to destroy the one having the power of death, that is the devil" (Heb. 2:14).

Spiritual death is the consequence of sin. "The wages of sin is death" (Rom. 6:23). "Death spread to all mankind, because all sinned" (Rom. 5:12), and "sin reigned in death" (Rom. 5:21). "Any person manifesting sin derives such character expression out of (*ek*) the devil, but the Son of God appeared to destroy the works of the devil" (I Jn. 3:8). By means of the incarnation, crucifixion, resurrection, ascension, and Pentecostal outpouring of the Spirit, the Last Adam (Jesus) became the life-giving Spirit" (I Cor. 15:45), whereby "the law of the Spirit of life in Christ Jesus has set you free from the law of sin and of death" (Rom. 8:2).

CHRISTOLOGY

Theology is the study of God – Who He is and what He does. Within the broad study of theology are many specific subsets of study including Christology (Christ), pneumatology (Spirit), theological anthropology (human beings in relation to God), hamartiology (sin), soteriology (salvation), hagiology (holiness), ecclesiology (church), eschatology (last things), etc. There is, however, a sense in which Christology comprehensively encompasses all the other theological categories. Jesus said, "If you have seen Me, you have seen the Father" (Jn. 14:7,9). "If you have known Me, you have known the Father" (Jn. 8:19). Christology is central. The issue is Jesus!

Christological studies throughout the history of the Christian faith have often concerned themselves with debate of how Jesus could logically be the God-man (Greek *theanthropos*), fully god and fully man simultaneously, in order to be "the one mediator between God and man (I Tim. 2:5). At the Council of Nicea in A.D. 325, Athanasius prevailed in asserting that God the Father and God the Son were of same being (Greek *homoousios*). The Council of Chalcedon in A.D. 451 clarified that the natures of deity and humanity were brought together (*hypostasis*) in the one Person, Jesus Christ, without sacrificing the distinction of the two.

It is important that Christology be expanded beyond the objective and historical factors of the God-man union, to consider the subjective implications of the post-Easter resurrection-life of the risen and living Lord Jesus, dynamically alive by the Spirit in the lives of faithfully receptive individuals in every age. Some have termed this "Spirit-Christology," recognizing that "the last Adam (Jesus) became life-giving Spirit" (I Cor. 15:45); so "now the Lord is the Spirit" (II Cor. 3:17), and "if anyone does not have the Spirit of Christ, he is none of His" (Rom. 8:9). The hymn asks, "You ask me how I know He lives? He lives within my heart."

APRIL 11

VIA NEGATIVA – WHAT'S GOING ON INSIDE?

Via Negativa is Latin for "the way of the negative." The Christian life is not just "sugar and spice; ain't it fun being nice?" If we are honest, we know that there is an on-going process of allowing the cross-work of Christ to work in our lives and "put to death" or "put an end to" our old ways of thinking and action. This has been termed by some as "the way of the cross." The first thing we must admit is that the "negative way" can only be understood if an individual is engaged in the "positive way" (*via positiva*) of participating in the Christ-life, allowing the Christ-life dwelling within our spirit to negate all that is not His character in the mind, emotion and will of our soul and our bodily behavior.

Some have presented the experiential Christ-life in a triumphalist manner that emphasizes only the "positive" victory that belongs to the Christian in Christ. (I Cor. 15:57; I John 5:4). Yes, we do want to focus on the positive,and rest in all that is ours in Christ Jesus, but a complete presentation of the gospel demands that we explain what is taking place in the Christian's soul as the divine life engages in the process of dealing with the residual sin and selfishness patterns that remain in the soul of a regenerate person, a born-again believer. These fleshly patterns formed in the thoughts, affections and volition of our soul, that "wage war against the Spirit" (Gal. 5:17,18) are the source of the psychological conflict within the Christian.

Via negativa has often been characterized as an effort and performance that the Christ-one must engage in order to excise the residual sin-tendencies in the soul of the Christian. Not so! Human performance is out – the dynamic grace of God is in as the generator of the Christ-life. The *via negativa* process is accomplished, not by our efforts, but by allowing the Positive One, Jesus Christ, to swallow up the remaining negatives of sinful fleshliness by overcoming all that is not of Him.

THE FALLACY OF TRYING TO "DIE TO SELF"

Though the *via negativa* process is sometimes called the "way of the cross," this must not be extended to the fallacy of trying to "die to self." Trying to "die to self" becomes another performance effort of trying to "become more spiritual" in the Christian life – a totally fallacious attempt. Christians are not to be trying to root out "fleshly" patterns of selfishness and sinfulness by their own doing via avoidance, abstinence or self-flagellation. Some forms of religion specialize in such masochistic exercises of so-called "self-mortification" or "self-crucifixion." It is impossible to crucify oneself; it always required executioners.

Religion has misused several biblical statements attempting to justify the encouragement to "die to self." Paul wrote, "I die daily" (I Cor. 15:31); "we are being put to death all day long" (Rom. 8:36); "constantly delivered over to death for Jesus' sake" (II Cor. 4:11). These refer to Paul's physical persecution of being beaten almost to death but do not refer to a continuing crucifixion within the Christian. Which "self" is religion attempting to assassinate? If it be the physical-self, that is suicide. If it be their soulish self, that is personality annihilation. If it be their spiritual-self, they will never achieve self-regeneration and surely do not want to destroy the spiritual "new self" that they have become as Christ-ones – that is apostasy.

The "old man" has already been put to death in Christ's death. "You have died and your life is hidden with Christ in God" (Col. 3:3). "I have been crucified with Christ; it is no longer I who live, but Christ lives in me" (Gal. 2:20). The only one who can deal with and overcome ongoing sin is Jesus. The positive swallows up the negative; the "fruit of the Spirit" (Gal. 5:22,23) swallows up the "deeds of the flesh" (Gal. 5:19-21). When a Christian "submits himself to God" (James 4:7), the devil is resisted by the only One competent to resist him – JESUS.

APRIL 13

TEMPTED TO THE OLD WAY OF THINKING

It's time to be honest and engage in a little time of confession. I know who I am in Christ, the many blessings that are mine in Christ Jesus, and that I live the Christ-life only by the grace of God. But in times of tiredness or weakness, I am still susceptible to the tendency to revert to that old religious default concept of thinking that God is judging me on my performance, that God is not going to be happy with me because of what I have done, or conversely that God is going to be "pleased as punch" with how I have performed. Or I think that what is happening in my life must be a punishment for something I have done, or conversely that I am being rewarded by God for what a good Christian I have been.

Every Christian has to be "on guard" (I Pet. 5:8; II Pet. 3:17); for Satan, the tempter, knows right where to cause us to revert to the old religious and humanistic mind-set (this reveals the need for the renewing of the mind – Eph. 4:23; Rom. 12:2). Satan hates the grace of God and tempts us to go back to that religious law-keeping performance paradigm of thought. We know that is not the way that God works or views us. The grace of God was the only means by which we became a Christian; and by His grace in the work of the Holy Spirit He continues to empower us to function as a Christian. But the tempter keeps introducing the thought that our Christian living is a matter of what we must do to stay on the "right side of God" and in His "good graces."

Has this been true in your Christian life also? Have you been tempted to go back to the old way of thinking? This "fleshly" way of thinking is deeply embedded in the thought-patterns of the "flesh" that still reside within the soul of every Christian. No Christian will never reach a point of maturity where he can cut Galatians 5:17 out of his bible, claiming that the truth of that verse is no longer applicable to him, that there is no inner conflict of "flesh" and Spirit within him.

OBLIVIOUS TO OTHERS' TRIALS

We often generalize and pontificate judgmentally about others' behavior, when we do not have a clue what problems they are facing, or what trials are on their plate. Beyond our awareness, there are many people who are dealing with personal and private struggles, moral binds, marital conflicts, etc. Surely, we have enough compassion to give them the benefit of the doubt, and then step forward to consider how we might come alongside and assist them in their unseen difficulties. Shame on us for being so quick to judge a person prior to knowing all that is going on in their life – which we never do. The old American Indian proverb says, "Don't criticize, until you have walked a mile in the other's moccasins."

Mary T. Lathrap (1828-1895) wrote a poem entitled "Judge Softly"; but it became better known by her use of that Indian proverb, "Walk a Mile in His Moccasins."

"Pray, don't find fault with the man that limps, or stumbles along the road.
Unless you've worn his moccasins, or stumbled beneath the same load.

There may be tears in his soles that hurt, though hidden away from view.
The burden he bears if on your back, may cause you to stumble, too.

Judge lightly the man who sins, don't pelt him with words, stones, disdain.
Unless you have no sins, and only wisdom and love your heart contains.

Just walk a mile in his moccasins before you abuse, criticize and accuse.
Try to find a way to see through his eyes, instead of your own muse."

The words of our Lord Jesus were, "Judge not, that you be not judged. Why do you look at the speck that is in your brother's eye, but do not notice the log that is in your own eye? Or how can you say to your brother, 'Let me take the speck out of your eye,' and forget the log is in your own eye? Hypocrisy!" (Matt. 7:1-5).

APRIL 15

RELIGION HAS TO GO!

Religion should be conquered, smothered, outlawed, and otherwise rendered extinct. But that will never occur, because natural, fallen human beings are continuously inventing another form of religion – another system of human performance wherein they hope to please and appease the false deities they have constructed in their minds. The demise of all religion would require the demise of Satan, who is the spirit source of all religion. As the ruler of this world (Jn. 16:11; Eph. 6:12), Satan has been overcome in God's grand scheme of spiritual realities, but not rendered inoperative in the present world-system.

Twentieth century Swiss theologian Karl Barth wrote, "The revelation of God (*in the Son, Jesus Christ*) is the end of all religion." The ultimate reality of God's restoration for mankind arrived in this world in the incarnation of Jesus. Religion in its myriad forms (including Judaic and Christian religions) has been exposed as a bankrupt sham, unable to be of any real and eternal benefit for human beings (cf. Col. 2:20-23). The apostle John explained that when "the Word became flesh" (Jn. 1:14), the new covenant reality of "grace and truth" was inaugurated, made available, and realized (Jn. 1:17) for the restoration of humanity.

Though religion, energized as it is by the "ruler of this world," Satan, was overcome at the cross (Col. 2:15), the adversary continues to roam around like a chained roaring lion (I Pet. 5:8), seeking to devour unsuspecting persons who fail to recognize the difference between religion and the reality of God's salvation in the Son Jesus Christ. There is such a great need, even among those who call themselves "Christian," to realize that Christianity is not religion and must be distinguished from the ideological systems and programs conceived by the institutional forms of religion. Christianity is the living Lord Jesus Christ living within and through those who receive Him by faith.

FREEDOM IS NOT FREE

If freedom isn't sought for and fought for, then some form of enslavement will likely be the default condition. This is a general truism when it relates to social freedoms from government intrusion or freedom from oppressive policies and practices of those in control. It was true for the freedoms won in the formation of the United States of America. Our freedoms had to be fought for in the Revolutionary War to avoid the slavish taxation imposed by Great Britain – taxation without representation. There is always a price to be paid for freedom. Freedom is not free!

The seeking of human freedom never ends. The destroyer (I Cor. 10:10) and diabolic death-dealer (Heb. 2:14) will remain active until he is eventually thrown into the pit of fire (Rev. 20:10). Those acting in the power of the Evil One (I Jn. 5:19) in this world will continue to oppress and abuse others until that time. The quest for freedom and the delimitation of human injustices is a constant battle. Cries for freedom resonate throughout our society: issues of sexual slavery, spousal and child abuse, unfair discriminatory practices, excessive power and control, systemic racism in law enforcement and employment opportunity, etc.

There is another kind of freedom that also came at a cost. All of humanity was enslaved in sin, being "slaves of sin" (Rom. 6:6,17,20), "held captive by the snare of the devil to do his will" (II Tim. 2:26). No human effort, performance or payment could gain our freedom. Only the free grace of God in the Son, Jesus Christ, could provide the price necessary for spiritual freedom; we were "bought with a price (I Cor. 6:20; 7:23). As the lyrics of the hymn state, "He sought me and He bought me with His redeeming blood." Freedom was not free, but the price was paid by Jesus. "It was for freedom that Christ set us free" (Gal. 5:1), and His grace allows us to continue to live in that freedom.

APRIL 17

YOU MEANT IT AS EVIL; GOD MEANT IT AS GOOD

Li'l Joe was the youngest of twelve brothers. Being the "baby" of the family, his mother favored and coddled him; and this led to no little resentment among the other brothers especially when his father made him a coat of many colors that set him apart. The disdain of the other brothers became apparent on an occasion when L'il Joe was sent out on expedition with his older brothers, and they conspired to throw him into a well, putting blood on his coat to make it look like a wild animal had killed him. Unbeknownst to the brothers, a slave trader found Joe in the well and carted him off to Egypt to be sold as a slave.

As a slave to Pharoah's body-guard, Potiphar, Joseph acted with utmost integrity, and found favor with the Pharoah for his God-given ability to interpret dreams. Utilizing the interpretation, Pharoah was able to plan for the future and made Joseph head of the Ministry of Agriculture. Famines came upon the land, but the reserves were sufficient; and people from surrounding areas came to get grain, including Joseph's brothers. When they recognized Li'l Joe in charge of distribution, they were afraid he would act with revenge against them. He assured them he would not: "You meant it for evil; God meant it for good!" (Gen. 50:20).

God can take the worst of circumstances, even a sinful conniving situation, and cause such to work for His good. "God causes all things to work together for good to those who love God, to those who are called according to His purpose" (Rom. 8:28). The one who does the evil is no less accountable for what they have done. The phrase, "God meant it for good," has become theologically problematic. Did God purpose or permit the situation? Did He orchestrate or allow the situation? Can God permit something He did not purpose? God is the essential cause of all things, but He is not the culpable or blameworthy cause of evil, even while allowing for such by the creatures' freedom of choice.

PERSONIFIED GRACE

When I graduated from Bible College more than fifty years ago, I did not have a clear understanding of grace, and the only definition I could have mustered was that "grace is the undeserved favor of God." In the tradition in which I was trained, grace was regarded as a dubious theological emphasis of the Baptists, who allegedly thought that a person could slide into heaven on the grease of God's gratuity by simply believing, i.e., assenting to the historical death of Jesus on a cross. What a tragic misrepresentation of the grace of the gospel of Jesus Christ and an unfair caricature of the teaching of our Baptist brethren.

Tragically, many contemporary Christians have similar rote and milquetoast explanations of God's grace. In its lowest common denominator, grace is "God at work." In the early church, grace was regarded as a commodity dispensed in the Eucharist. God's grace could be leveraged by human performance. The ecclesiastics were deemed to have the power to dispense or withhold God's grace via various techniques and procedures. Grace became an operative principle that could be employed and manipulated for the purposes of the power-structure of the institutional church. Grace in the hands of man becomes tyranny!

Dietrich Bonhoeffer referred to "cheap grace" comprised of mere easy-believism without discipleship. More recently, some have advocated "hyper grace," the subsumption of all humanity into the life and redemptive work of Jesus, so there is not response-ability for individuals to respond in faith to engage in an intimate personal relationship. The apostle John gives us a key to understanding God's grace: "Grace and truth were realized (made known, revealed, inaugurated) in Jesus Christ" (Jn. 1:17). "The Word became flesh" (1:14); grace became personified in Jesus Christ (1:17). The divine grace-action of God is always by means of His Son Jesus Christ and the power of the Spirit.

APRIL 19

RELIGION AND LAW

Religion is always based on the performance of some kind of law-keeping that demands observing behavioral rules and regulations to please a perceived deity. Law-based belief-systems will inevitably construct a religious structure to regulate acceptable performance of the law. Religion and the law are mutually dependent on each other. Where there is one, you will find the other; where one is missing, you will not find the other. Since "Christ is the end of the law" (Rom. 10:4), we can conclude that Christianity is not religion. There is no law-structure to hold such religion together. "We have been released from the Law (Rom. 7:6), and therefore from all religious requirement."

Some Christians recognize that they are not obliged to keep the old covenant Mosaic Law with its "big ten" commandments; but they so readily accept and submit to the performance requirements of their particular ecclesiastical group, whether they be written or unwritten expectations. This kind of legalism (aka *nomism*, from the Greek word *nomos* meaning "law") is the subtle work of religion to bind people to keeping the rules and regulations expected by the church leaders. It should be noted that the Latin base-word for "religion" is *religare* and means "to tie or bind up" (ex. a ligament binds bones or cartilage).

If you are a Christ-one, joined to the living Lord Jesus (I Cor. 6:16), then you are "dead to the Law" (Rom. 7:4). Your only connection to the old covenant Law is that its intent "has been put into your mind and heart" (Heb. 8:10: 10:16) by the presence of the Spirit of Christ. The living Lord Jesus is the Living Torah, the internal reality of the character of God, the dynamic expression of "the perfect law, the law of freedom (James 1:25), the "law of love" (James 2:8) whereby we bear the burdens of others (Gal. 6:2). Christ living in the Christ-one should never submit to the Law (Gal. 5:18) but live by His grace (Rom. 6:14).

A BAG OF BAUBLES

The two girls, Sally and Nancy, had been friends since they were young children. They enjoyed the same toys, games, and activities. At every opportunity, they could be found playing together, giggling in the midst of their make-believe charades, and imagining grandiose scenarios of being princesses in a magical kingdom. One of their more quiet, indoor activities, usually reserved for rainy days, was to compare the contents of their bulging bags of baubles. They each had a purse into which they had placed small items they thought were interesting: It might be a shiny rock, a marble, a trinket, a charm, a key, a memento from a previous trip, a piece of jewelry they found on the playground, or any other small item that caught their eye.

These bags of baubles were regarded as very valuable in the friendship of Sally and Nancy. Periodically, they would bring out their collection to compare their treasures and in the process share their memories of how they acquired the various pieces. When each item was pulled out, they would "ooh" and "aah" in appreciation for what the other had acquired.

Such child's play allows for creative imagination and interaction within child development. The apostle Paul wrote, "When I was a child, I used to speak like a child, think like a child, reason like a child; when I became a man, I did away with childish things" (I Cor. 13:11). The problem comes when immature adults continue to engage in the religious practices of comparing their bags of baubles. "My rock shines brighter than your rock." "My trinket is more valuable than your token." "My church is bigger than your church." "My church believes the Bible word-for-word." "I go to a more spiritual church." "Our preacher is on television every week." "We have the biggest youth program in town." "We believe in eternal security." It is time to put away childish things, and look only to JESUS in love for others.

APRIL 21

THAT'S WHAT IT'S ALL ABOUT

As a young person back in the 1960s, I can recall regularly going to the roller-skating rink. We rented skates (usually came home with blisters) and attempted to learn new tricks as we went 'round and 'round the floor. The music was blaring and the lights were flashing. Beginners were learning how to stand up on wheels, while the show-offs were zipping around the rink, often without concern about who they were knocking down. The boys and the girls were eyeing one another to determine who they might ask to join them on the "couple's skate." All in all, it was only one step above organized chaos.

At about intermission time the public address announcer would holler, "It's time to do the hokey-pokey," and with a roar of excitement the skaters would make a big circle around the rink, leaving enough room for movement. The music would begin, "You put your right foot in; you take your right foot out; you put your right foot in, and you shake it all about. You do the hokey pokey and you turn yourself around – that's what it's all about." The right foot was followed by the left foot, the right hand, the left hand, and finally with putting one's whole self in and whole self out, shaking it all about. That's what it's all about!

In one sense, we are all involved in the "hokey-pokey" of life with things shaking all about, and many are not able to stand up in the midst of the shaking. But what is the "jeopardy" question that finds its answer in "that's what it's all about"? Is this just a general humanistic question about those who have the skill to remain upright on their skates after all the shaking? Or can we broaden the circle of the question to consider what the meaning and objective of all of life is about. From a Christian perspective, the "ins" and "outs" of all the hokey-pokey of living in this world only find meaning when we understand that Jesus is our life – "That's what it's all about!"

THE OBJECTIVE IS NOT TO ACT LIKE A CHRISTIAN

A sincere soul hears the sharing of the gospel of Christ and responds by receiving Jesus into their spirit by faith. An equally sincere (but misguided) Christian witness then advises this new spiritually reborn Christian, "Now the objective is to go and act like a Christian." "Now that you have become a Christian, you must commit yourself to behave like a Christian." An abundance of behavioral principles is subsequently suggested: read the bible every day; pray every day; go to church every week; give ten percent of your gross income; tell others how much joy you are experiencing in being a Christian.

Is it any wonder that we do not see a line of interested people waiting and wanting to know what it means to become a Christian or "act like a Christian"? Religious treadmills are not very exciting and not highly sought after. Trying to "act like a Christian" is perhaps the most frustrating activity any person has ever engaged in. It is rather like running a one- hundred-yard sprint toward an imaginary line and running full-speed into a brick wall. After regaining consciousness, the dopey religious runner might ask, "How well did I do?" "Well you gave it your best effort, but I hope you learned the futility of that exercise.

Let's get this perfectly straight – no human person can ever "act like a Christian." It is an absolute impossibility, a sheer oxymoronic absurdity. When out of touch with reality, someone might attempt to act like their self-chosen make-believe avatar representation or icon-caricature. Utter craziness! A Christ-filled Christian is not intended to "act like a Christian." The only one who can act like Jesus Christ, or accurately present himself as Christ, is the living Lord Jesus Himself. Only the living Lord Jesus Christ can live and manifest the Christ-life in our mortal bodies (II Cor. 4:10,11), living out His divine life and character in our human behavior to the glory of God.

APRIL 23

CHRISTIANITY IS NOT ROLE-PLAYIING

The young Christian girl was an aspiring actress, always on the lookout for roles she might play in upcoming plays or movies. She could sing. She could dance. She could act. She could morph into whatever person or situation she was asked to assume. But the time eventually came when she became increasingly aware that in showcasing her talents as an actress, she was not being real to herself. She was always a counterfeit, faking the *persona* of a variety of characters; but few people (even her friends) knew the person she really was, i.e. her real identity, her true values, her deep-down desires, her eternal purpose in life.

In his play, *As You Like It*, William Shakespeare wrote, "All the world's a stage, and all the men and women merely players. They have their exits and their entrances; and one man, in his time, plays many parts." But to regard Christianity as play-acting or role-playing is a denial of the reality that Jesus came to bring in Himself. The English word "role" implies acting as someone you are not, to masquerade by assuming a *persona* that is not real, to perform a charade. Such simulation of "faking it," by means of a ruse or "putting on a show" is indeed a counterfeit, engaging in a *false persona* by means of the "father of lies" (Jn. 8:44).

One man, a pastor, was aghast that I should suggest that Christianity is not role-playing. "Of course, it is; that is exactly what Christianity is – our attempt to 'live like Jesus'," he adamantly affirmed. He was well entrenched in the "Religious Acting Company" wherein religion is the ultimate stage for role-playing. "Put on your mask, assume your place, the show (performance, production) must go on!" But, Christianity is not a charade show, the fiction of a simulated experience of virtual reality. Christianity is not a stage-show wherein we act like someone we are not. Christianity is the living Lord Jesus Christ, not representing, but re-presenting His life and character as us.

DESERT! – GO A.W.O.L.

Many of the early Christians were pacifists, refusing to join the army and engage in the warfare of killing others. They took seriously such words as, "My kingdom is not of this world. If My kingdom were of this world, My servants would be fighting" (Jn. 18:36). After Emperor Constantine (AD 325) joined the Roman empire with the church, such attitudes diminished. Paul's admonition to "endure hardness, as a good soldier of Jesus Christ (II Tim. 2:3; cf. Phil. 2:25; Phlm. 1:2) convinced other Christians to see themselves as soldiers engaged in a spiritual army (cf. Rev. 19:19) and fighting against evil.

In the hymnody of the church, we observe numerous references to Christians being soldiers in an army. It was in AD 1865 that Sabine Baring-Gould wrote, "Onward, Christian soldiers! Marching as to war, With the cross of Jesus, Going on before." Prior to that, in 1707, Isaac Watts wrote, "We're marching to Zion, beautiful, beautiful Zion; we're marching upward to Zion, the beautiful city of God." The problem with such a concept of storming Zion is, "You have come to Mount Zion and to the city of the living God, the heavenly Jerusalem" (Heb. 12:22); "The Jerusalem above is free; she is our mother" (Gal. 4:26). The heavenly city of God is already made available to us in Jesus.

If we choose to use the imagery of the church as an army of soldiers fighting a war against evil, it can be easily demonstrated that whoever is in charge of military strategy is choosing the wrong battles, making disastrous alliances, and quite unaware of how the enemy operates. When fighting Goliath, David said, "The battle is the Lord's" (I Sam. 17:47). The battle against Satan and evil was won on the cross (Col. 2:15; I Jn. 3:8), so our efforts to fight such are futile. If you see yourself as a soldier in God's army fighting evil, you are fighting a battle already won; and you might consider deserting and going A.W.O.L. from the pseudo militia.

APRIL 25

ONENESS WITH GOD IN CHRIST

From the earliest stated aspirations of humanity, there has been a desire to be "like God" (Gen. 3:5). The Satanically inspired humanistic approach posits that each human being is an "independent self," who becomes his own center of reference, with the potential and capability to self-determine as well as self-implement the objectives that he or she self-postulates and pursues. Little does the majority of humanity realize that this popular humanistic theory is a falsified cover-up to conceal the spiritual reality that fallen humanity (cf. I Jn. 4:7) is indwelt by (Eph. 2:2) and held captive to do the devil's will (II Tim. 2:26).

How does religion suggest that human beings should seek to be "like God"? Employing some of the same humanistic premises, both Western and Eastern Christian religion suggest that human beings need to engage in the self-effort of varying human performances to achieve a condition of "oneness with God in Christ" whereby they are "like God." The Western church is more blatant about its "works theology," with a litany of prescribed legalisms for conformity to God. The Eastern church is more abstract in encouraging the process of *theosis* wherein one achieves purification, illumination and transformation into holy oneness of likeness to God (but not technically deification).

Biblical explanation seems to indicate that such oneness with God in Christ is granted to every Christ-one when that person receives the living Lord Jesus by faith. "He who is joined to the Lord is one Spirit with Him" (I Cor.6:17), "having become partakers of the divine nature" (II Pet. 1:4). The presence and function of the Father, Son, and Holy Spirit within the spirit of the Christ-one constitutes spiritual union, participation and intimacy with God in His fullness. The human aspiration to be "like God" is ontologically and dynamically impossible. We are derivative beings who choose by faith to allow God's character expression.

TRAINED TO PERFORM

Those who would engage in training others to perform must themselves be trained to perform such. Some seek to train their dog to perform at the dog show. Others train horses and elephants to perform in the circus. Seals, dolphins, and whales are trained to perform at the water park. The organ-grinder must train his monkey to perform for the audience on the street. Teachers serve as performance trainers, instructing children to perform to standards in mathematics, languages, science, etc. We send our children to those who can train them to perform in sports, dance, music, etc., for the enjoyment of an audience.

The business world is constantly training workers to perform and produce for the company. An employee is trained to set goals for achievement with performance outcomes calculated by percentages and quotas. The humanistic premises of the world system, orchestrated and engineered by the "ruler of this world" (Jn. 12:31; 16:11), always demand responsibility for human performance in order to succeed, to "climb the ladder" of advancement, and enhance the organization as well as one's placement therein. The world's performance expectations are the means by which progress is evaluated.

As an integral part of that humanistic world system, religion has readily adopted such a system of performance training, utilizing such behavior modification to train people to behave in accord with the "thou shalt" and "thou shalt not" expectations of laws. Christianity, however, is totally antithetical to the world's agenda of being trained to perform. The Christ-life is energized by the dynamic grace of God in Jesus Christ – not by what we are trained to perform. Grace is God doing what we are incapable of being trained to perform and what only He is capable of doing. "We are not adequate to consider anything as coming from ourselves, but our adequacy is from God" (II Cor. 3:5).

APRIL 27

WE SERVE A GOD WE CANNOT CONTROL

God is God! Man is man! It is imperative that we recognize and respect the difference. God is not a marionette that we can control by pulling the strings to make Him dance. On the other hand, neither are human beings merely marionettes that God controls by pulling the strings in a deterministic manner. In the religions of fallen mankind, there seems to be a constant quest to control God in one way or another. Religious leaders craft their so-called worship services to orchestrate how they want to project God's alleged action and to manipulate people in the pew to respond in accord with the programmed objective.

God is not a trained monkey who will do whatever we might bid. Prayer is not a human leveraging whereby we provide the "work order" for God's performance. Fallen mankind has always attempted to "get a handle on God," to get God and His ways figured out in order to control and manipulate His action. Some religionists think they know the *modus operandi* of God, that God acts immutably and unchangingly in a systematized and deterministic course of action. Having prescribed the parameters of God's being and action by human reasoning, they then declare that God will always act in a certain way, if human beings will just respond to him as prescribed.

God is HOLY – singularly set apart from all that is not of Him. God does what He does, because He is who He is. He will always do things uniquely His way, in accord with His own character;, and created humans will never be able to change or control such. A true perspective of our human inability to be God, or to "play God," or control God should cause us to bow down and worship God by submitting (James 4:7) to Him and His ways. God is a personal God, the Great "I AM" (Exod. 3:14); and human beings were created as personal beings, allowing for a personal relationship between humanity and the Almighty God.

WHAT IN THE WORLD IS GOING ON?

Perhaps you have noticed that many people around us are discouraged, thinking that our government, our nation, our morality, our values, our rights are deteriorating; and it appears that our society is "going to hell in a handbasket." This pessimistic perspective of what is happening in the world in which we live is likely built upon false presuppositions of humanistic possibility for world betterment. If we had any hope for human world betterment, then such humanistic hopes may have been dashed by recent circumstances; but it just reveals that we were attempting to build on quicksand.

The world is going to do what the world is going to do, always consistent with the character of the one who is "ruler of this world" (Jn. 12:31; 16:11), the Evil One. The "spirit of this world" (I Cor. 2:12) is fixed in the character of iniquity and the anti-Christ, the negative of God's positive. Christians should have no expectations for human or world bettermen, and recognize that the world is not going to get better. It will remain uncivil, non-cooperative and mean-spirited, muddling along in the pragmatic expedience of "whatever works," as it seeks to "put band-aids on cancer" to coverup whatever social problems might arise.

Yes, the world is a cesspool; and even religion (regarded by many as the best form of worldliness) was regarded by Paul as but a dung pile (Phil. 3:8). Those identified as "conservatives" have been attempting to conserve and preserve all the wrong things. We should be focused, instead, on the progressive action of God's grace, whereby He always acts in accord with His character. God intervened in the world by sending His Son, Jesus Christ (Jn. 3:16) who conquered the world forces (Heb. 2:14; I Jn. 3:8; Col. 2:15). The responsibility of Christians is not to make the world better, but simply to be and to do what God in Christ wants to be and do in us today in the midst of the world in which we live.

APRIL 29

LOOKING BACK – LOOKING FORWARD

When we come to a new year, it is a time to look back to review and evaluate how the previous year played out, and also to look forward to the opportunities that may present themselves in the upcoming new year. Since we in the West use the Gregorian calendar, we begin the new year on January 1 each year. Unlike other dates, this is not determined by lunar or solar phenomena, but was somewhat arbitrarily selected as far back as 153 B.C. Various other days have been designated for the Chinese New Year, the Japanese New Year, the Islamic New Year, and the Jewish New Year; but January 1 has now been universally recognized as the start of the global civil calendar year.

The month of January is named after Janus, the god of change, beginnings and transitions in Roman mythology, the god of doors and gateways. When depicted graphically, Janus was a two-faced god, with a face looking backwards and a face looking forward. How appropriate then that the first month of the new year in Gregorian and Julian calendars should be named January, with the opportunity to look back in recollection of the previous year and also look forward to what the new year might bring.

When we look back to the past, we should learn from mistakes and failures; but we must be cautious about inordinate focus on what is behind us. The past is past – water under the bridge – and we must proceed to move forward. Paul's words are appropriate: "Forgetting what lies behind, we press forward to what lies ahead" (Phil. 3:13). In considering the opportunities of the future, we must "count the cost" (cf. Lk. 14:18) of engaging in the endeavor we might be planning to participate. Dietrich Bonhoeffer, in his classic book, *The Cost of Discipleship*, cautioned Christians about the easy-believism of religious secularism that fails to recognize the "costly grace" of following Jesus by carrying one's cross even unto death – dying as a precursor of life.

OBEDIENCE

Most Christians are familiar with the hymn "Trust and Obey," written by John H. Sammis in 1887. The difficulty comes in explaining the meaning of those terms. The dictionary meaning of "obedience" is "yielding in compliance and conformity to orders or authority; keeping the rules." If we use that definition in reference to new covenant obedience, it results in a very skewed understanding that is not consistent with God's grace in Jesus Christ (cf. Jn. 1:17). Properly performing the rules and regulations is the basis of religious expectations of obedience, but this is counter to the relational obedience of the Christ-life.

Conversely, there are some Christians who believe that faith and obedience are not their responsibility as Christians. Such thinking is usually based on a deterministic paradigm of theology that views God as sovereignly responsible for everything in the Christian life, including faith and obedience – His grace provides for everything. Such thought relieves Christians from all responsibility often leading to passivism or acquiescence. Recent theological explanation refers to the vicarious and substitutional life of Jesus into which all Christians are subsumed, thus denying the faith-love response that is at the heart of real personal relationship between the Christ-one and the divine Trinity.

The Greek word used for "obedience" in the New Testament is *hupakouo*, a compound of *hupo* = under (cf. hypodermic) and *akouo* = to listen or hear (cf. acoustics). New covenant obedience is to "listen under" the divine voice in order to ascertain what it is that He wants to be and to do next in our lives. "My sheep hear My voice" (Jn. 10:27), Jesus said. Instead of a responsibility to perform, God created us with response-ability via freedom of choice to respond to God's promptings by means of the "obedience of faith" (Rom. 1:5; 16:26), our receptivity of Christ's activity, submitting to His dynamic grace-work in our lives.

MAY 1

PERICHORESIS

Have you ever taken ballroom dancing lessons? I have not, but my daughter and granddaughter enjoy ballroom dancing and having attended some of their events and observed their smooth and graceful dancing, I have come to appreciate the complexity of the various dance styles. As they move in unison with one another, I have expressed my amazement of having never seen anyone step on their partner's toes. My daughter explained that if a dancer gets their feet stepped on by their partner, it is not the partner's fault, but the fault of the dancer who failed to move correctly and get their feet out of the way of their dance partner.

To dance around the floor together in such close choreographed moves brings to mind the Greek word *perichoresis*, used for centuries in Christian theological thought. The preposition *peri* = around, and *chora* = space; so *perichoresis* refers to moving around in the same space. Early Christian writers used the term to explain that the Father and the Son, Jesus Christ, were ontologically one in the *homoousion* of "one being"; and in the operation of their dynamic function they always act as one – where one is acting, the other is also acting, moving around inseparably as one in the same space. They also used the word *perichoresis* in reference to the hypostatic union of deity and humanity functioning singularly in the one Person of Jesus Christ.

The Christ-one (Christian), joined in spiritual union with the living Lord Jesus (I Cor. 6:17) as a "partaker of the divine nature" (II Pet. 1:4), has the privilege of participating in the divine dance of the functional dynamic of the triune God. The Christian does not become Christ, for we are personally distinct as participants in our relationship with one another; but there is an interactive symmetry that expresses oneness, unity and intimacy as Christ and the Christian dance in the same space *perichoretically*, with no one stepping on the other's toes.

A NARCISISSTIC MAN

He had a brilliant mind and was driven to be a success in life by the world's standards. As a natural "man of the world," he was unaware of spiritual realities (I Cor. 2:14). His objective was to rise to the top, to be "king of the mountain" in every endeavor he engaged. He succeeded in his quest and rose to a high position in the company where he worked, which brought wealth and prestige. People took notice of him and kowtowed to him as if he were a god. He came to believe their accolades, to the extent he thought the world revolved around him – "I am the center of my universe; It's all about me!"

Convinced of his own self-importance, his self-assurance allowed him to convince others of the same (even his children). He had an excessive need for admiration and did not handle criticism well. Wearing expensive suits and ties, he was often asking, "How do I look?" Pragmatic expedience was his operative principle; truth was relative. Paul seems to have written about such a man when he referred to "lovers of self, lovers of money, proud, arrogant, abusive, ungrateful, and unholy" (II Tim. 3:2). "Love does not envy or boast; it is not arrogant or rude; it does not insist on its own way; it is not irritable or resentful" (I Cor. 13:4,5).

Such men seem incapable of expressing genuine love for others; their self-love leaves no room for loving others, and they often have no empathy or sensitivity for others. They usually love things (mammon) more than people. What relationships they might have are usually superficial, because they steamroll over other people and leave a debris field of hurt and bewilderment behind them wherever they go. The man I am thinking of divorced his wife, whom he once told, "I am never wrong; don't blame me for any of the problems." It is a sad indictment on our society when we are forced to admit that many successful men are very similar to this narcissistic man.

MAY 3

A NARCISSISTIC WOMAN

She was regarded by many people who knew her as a very self-absorbed individual, concerned more about her own desires and conveniences than other's interests or needs. Many people attempted to avoid her, not willing to engage in anything other than superficial small talk with her, because they were quite aware that she did not really care about anything they were doing or had to say. She had few close friends. Her favorite pronouns were "I," "me" "my"; and it was quite obvious that in her mind everything revolved around her preferences and activities. In the performing world, she was regarded as a "diva," always wanting to be in the spotlight – "Look at me!"

There are two kinds of such narcissistic women. Some are *overtly* narcissistic, usually exhibiting a loud-mouthed, "in your face" manner of "look at me; I demand your attention." They are easily identified as the attention-seekers that they are. Others, however, are *covert* narcissists who engage in more subtle, under-handed expressions of manipulative self-concern. They are just as self-absorbed, having little empathy for the needs or feelings of others, because they do not care about you or your problems, only their own. "It's all about me!" is the underlying mantra of all such narcissistic women. Their self-absorption and personal attention-seeking are often evident in how they dress and present themselves to the public in order to be the "show-offs" they are.

The inordinate selfishness of narcissistic women often causes them to be demanding and contentious, not easy to live with or even to interact with. The poet who wrote the Proverbs seems to have been quite aware of such women. He writes, "It is better to live in the corner of a roof than in a house shared with a contentious woman" (Prov. 21:9; 25:24). "It is better to live in a desert than with a contentious and vexing woman" (Prov. 21:19).

MAY 4

SEXUAL SELF-STIMULATION

Religions and cultures often have some taboo subjects that are *verboten* for public discussion. Sexual self-stimulation, aka masturbation, is often one of those subjects. But if the Christ-life permeates every facet of our lives on earth, then this subject is certainly not off-limits. The subject of sexuality is dealt with extensively in the Bible, in both old and new testaments; but interestingly the sexual act of auto-stimulation, aka masturbation, is not mentioned in the Christian scriptures. The Bible is silent on this subject. If an interpretive principle were applied: "Where the Bible speaks, we speak; where the Bible is silent, we are silent," much controversy would be avoided.

Surveys indicate that a large percentage of both males and females in our society engage in sexual self-stimulation. Due to religious and cultural admonitions, many of these people have felt guilty about such activity. If the Bible does not say this activity is wrong, then on what basis do people feel guilty of wrong-doing? It can only be false-guilt. If one attempts to confess (agree with God; *homologeo* = "to say the same thing") concerning sexual self-stimulation, it cannot be confessed as sin, because there is no basis for identifying masturbation as transgression of God's character or violation of God's intent. Yes, cultural mores can be very restrictive and oppressive. If sexual self-stimulation is not morally right or wrong, then it becomes a simple choice of "shall I or shall I not" so engage.

Since we are derivative beings, and we make choices to derive from either the character of Satan or God, Christian persons will have to discern whether the personal activity of sexual self-stimulation should be engaged in in a manner that is expressive of the Christ-life and is glorifying to God as we appreciate how He created us. Some will so engage, and others will abstain – let all be done to the glory of God!

MAY 5

SHALOM!

If you have spent time among Hebrew-speaking people, you have heard them greet one another with "Shalom"; and the person greeted responds with "Shalom." The word means "peace be with you," but it is used casually as "hello" and "goodbye." The Hebrew word, *Shalom*, has a depth of meaning that includes "the God of peace" (I Thess. 3:16; 5:23; Heb. 13:20) creating a garden of peace for the first created couple and the condition of a peaceful relationship with God. Human rebellion and rejection of deriving *shalom* from God led to the expulsion of mankind from the garden and the absence of God's inner peace in man's spirit.

God promised to restore *shalom* to mankind: "To us a child is born, Mighty God, Everlasting Father, the Prince of Peace" (Isa. 9:6). The first announcement of His birth by the angels to the shepherds was, "Glory to God in the highest, and on earth, peace (*shalom*) among men" (Lk. 2:14). The means of the restoration of God's *shalom* required that God's Son be "pierced, crushed, and the chastening of our lost *shalom* fell upon Him" (Isa. 53:6). Knowing what was coming, Jesus could say to His disciples, "My *shalom* I give to you; not as the world gives, give I to you. Don't let your heart be troubled, nor fearful" (John 14:27).

For the Christ-one, "having been justified through faith, we have peace (*shalom*) with God" (Rom. 5:1); and "the peace (*shalom*) of God, which transcends all understanding, guards our hearts and minds in Christ Jesus" (Phil. 4:7). The gospel and kingdom of *shalom* peace (cf. Eph. 6:15; Rom. 14:17) are ours as we participate in the *shalom* presence of God in Christ. This is not just a static absence of conflict or problems (as the world defines peace), but it is the dynamic *shalom* of deriving from the Prince of Peace (*shalom*) for the inner peace of His function in our soul and the external peace evidenced in our relationships with others as He manifests His character of *shalom* through us.

126

"ALL FLESH IS NOT THE SAME FLESH"

This phrase is a quote from Paul's first epistle to the Corinthians. Paul wrote, "All flesh is not the same flesh, but there is one flesh of mankind, another flesh of animals, another flesh of birds, and another of fish" (I Corinthians 15:39). Paul was pointing out that among the varying species and classes of biological animals, including human beings, there is a variety of anatomical and muscular differences. The Greek word *sarx*, translated as "flesh" throughout the New Testament, initially referred to the muscle or the meat of an animal, sometimes referring to the entire flesh carcass of a biological animal.

In third and fourth century B.C. the Greek philosophers were instrumental in applying another dimension to the Greek word *sarx*. Epicurus, in particular, added a more psychological dimension that joined *sarx* to the desires of mankind. This natural evolution of the word *sarx*, which happens in all languages over time, led to the new covenant writers' usage of the phrases, "the desires of the flesh" (Gal. 5:17,24; Eph. 2:3) and "fleshly desires" (II Pet. 2:10,18). This allows us to understand the inner conflict that Paul referred to,: "the flesh sets its desires against the Spirit, and the Spirit against the flesh" (Gal. 5:16,17).

God gave every one of us a full set of God-given desires in our soul; but these became uniquely warped with selfishness and sin (the character of Satan), creating flesh patterns in our desires. Your flesh patterns are not the same as my flesh patterns – we each have our unique propensities to sin and selfishness. When we became a Christ-one, with the Spirit of living Lord Jesus dwelling in our spirt, those fleshly desires did not disappear and are in conflict with the desires of the Spirit. It is not our responsibility to fight against our flesh-patterns, however; for "the Spirit sets its desires against the flesh" (Gal. 5:17), and we live in the victory that is ours in Christ Jesus.

MAY 7

CHRISTIANITY DOESN'T WORK!

If we are talking about making our Christian endeavors work successfully as the world system calculates success, then it is indisputable that "Christianity doesn't work" to achieve the end that the world calls "success." Christianity is not a workable system of techniques and procedures of behavior and productivity that can be implemented in a social experiment to create ideal human behavior and social functionality in the world in which we live. Christianity was never meant to work by the initiative of human performance, nor in conjunction with the objectives of the world-system for the betterment of mankind.

From the humanistic world perspective of human performance to better oneself and the world around you, Christianity doesn't work because the objective of Christianity is not seeking such betterment. The objective of Christianity is to allow the indwelling life of the living Lord Jesus to manifest His life and character in our behavior to the glory of God. The Christ-life will never serve as a leverage to seek the fulfillment of our own selfish desires, or to accomplish the desires to make the world a better place. If and when the world observes the manifestation of the Christ-life, the world will exclaim, "It just doesn't work to achieve our self-determined goals and objectives."

The inner spiritual dynamic of the living Lord Jesus is required in order to function as a Christian. "The mystery is Christ in you, the hope of glory" (Col. 1:27). "Do you not recognize that Christ is in you?" (II Cor. 13:5). By means of that divine presence and nature, "God is at work in you, both to will and to work for His good pleasure" (Phil. 2:13). "Our adequacy is derived from God" (II Cor. 3:5). Paul wrote, "I do not presume to speak of anything except what Christ has accomplished through me" (Rom. 15:18). Such expression of the Christ-life is counter-intuitive and contrary to the world's productivity expectations.

DIVINE DETERMINISM OR HUMAN FREE-WILL?

In most philosophical and theological discussions on the subject at hand there is an either/or dichotomy that either affirms divine determinism and rejects human free-will, or accepts human free-will and denies divine determinism. The label of Augustinian-Calvinism is often affixed to the former of the two views, and the label of Pelagian-Arminianism is often attributed to the latter of the two alternatives. What if a human thinker does not subscribe to the divine determinism that posits that God's omniscience and omnipotence demand that He has predestined all circumstances to occur, nor to the human free-will thesis that humans freely choose to determine their actions and have the innate and intrinsic power to implement those decisions?

Is it possible that the Creator God Self-limited (as only He could do) His omnipotence and omniscience to create human beings with freedom of choice (not free-will) to exercise response-ability (receptivity of faith) to the grace-activity of God in a true personal relationship and also limited the human potential of mankind by creating them as choosing derivative creatures who necessarily derive and receive from a spirit-source (either God or Satan) to manifest action and character? Such a position denies the causal necessity of divine predeterminism (predestination), as well as the human potential of humanistic free-will.

This explanation seems to me to be biblically-sound, and does justice to the attributes of God (God alone has free-will) and the constitutional function of human beings (derivative choosing creatures). At the same time, it circumvents the pitfalls of Calvinistic determinism as well as those of Arminian free-will, and denies the prevailing philosophical humanism so widely accepted today. It is not a compromise but a clearly delineated explanation that God is God, and man is man. Does this position have a label? Let's call it "Theological Anthropology."

MAY 9

ARE YOU WILLING TO BE A MARTYR?

On the Mount of Transfiguration, just prior to His ascension, Jesus told His disciples, "You shall be My witnesses both in Jerusalem, and in all Judea and Samaria, and to the remotest part of the earth" (Acts 1:8). The Greek word translated "witnesses" is *martures*, the word transliterated into English as "martyr." There is more to being a Christian witness than just bearing verbal testimony. It involves the willingness to give up everything for what one believes,;for, if it is just a belief-system that one is advocating, it is unlikely they will be willing to die for such. If a person is participating in the eternal life of Jesus, then he will be more likely to give up everything, including his life, for Jesus.

If the situation were to arise; and all Christians were being rounded up, interrogated, and killed if they would not renounce their faith in Jesus, how many of the Christians you know would likely stand up for their faith and submit to martyrdom? How many of the Christians you associate with would likely "have your back" and refuse to report you for being a Christian? Only by the grace of God would any of us be able to stand up willing to be a martyr in such a situation, willing to "stand the line" for our brothers and sisters in Christ, even it meant that our own lives were jeopardized by so doing.

Dietrich Bonhoeffer called it *The Cost of Discipleship* and was willing to lay down his own life for what he believed (i.e., what he had received). The cost of discipleship is that the believer is "all in," willing to lay it all on the table, and willing to die in order to take a stand for Jesus. That's what it means to be a martyr-witness. I have to wonder how many contemporary Christians are so united to Christ (cf. I Cor. 6:17) that they know He alone is their life (Col. 1:4), and they know that even in physical death they cannot be separated (Rom. 8:38,39) from the One who is Life Eternal, the One who is the Son of the Living God.

RELIGION IS NOT CHRISTIAN BEHAVIOR

Religion does not create, does not encourage, does not foster, and does not inspire Christian behavior. In fact, the greatest detriment and deterrent to Christian behavior may be religion and its falsely incentivized behavioral admonitions. Do recall that the English word "religion" comes from the Latin word *religare* which means "to bind up" or "to tie together." Religion tends "to bind us up in rules and regulations of behavior" of "thou shalt" and "thou shalt not" and "to tie us together with others who will likewise conform" to such socio-behavioral standards, and thereby join a community of behavioral conformists.

Writing to the Christians in Colossae, Paul asks, "If you have died with Christ to the elementary principles of the world, why, as if you were living in the world, do you submit yourself to decrees, such as, "Do not handle, do not taste, do not touch!" (which all *refer to* things destined to perish with use)—in accordance with the commandments and teachings of men? These are matters which have, to be sure, the appearance of wisdom in self-made religion and self-abasement and severe treatment of the body, *but are* of no value against fleshly indulgence" (Col. 2:20-23). Notice that "what appears to be wise and moral in self-made religion is of NO VALUE to counter human sin.

Religion fosters mimicry, monkey see/monkey do, hypocrisy, putting on a show, play-acting, rule-keeping, rote actions of going through the motions. Religion fosters people-pleasing, pleas to keep the programs going, berating those who do not conform; but this is not Christian behavior. Christian behavior is only the outcome of the Christ-life in the Christ-one (Christian) as He (JESUS) manifests His life and character in the unique manner that He wishes to express Himself in each Christian person. It cannot be proceduralized or formularized in moral codes of defined conduct encouraged by religious instruction.

MAY 11

LIVE AND LET LIVE

A popular phrase in our culture is "live and let live," often referring to neutrality and tolerant non-interference in another's life. The phrase was included in a book of English proverbs collected by John Ray in 1678, and is today often associated with libertarianism. In contemporary usage, the phrase is used similarly to the phrase, "do your own thing," recognizing the value of diversity and the avoidance of any moral judgments. But non-judgmentalism can, and has been, pushed by some, to the point of total relativism, implying the absence of any absolute standards of human and social moral behavior.

When used in the liberalized and humanistic manner just described, the phrase would appear to be contrary to any Christian understanding. To turn a blind eye of personal disregard, for example, to those caught in the clutches of sin, "ensnared by the devil and held captive to do his will" (II Tim. 2:26), is not the character of Christ's loving concern for others. But consider with me whether a positive interpretation of the phrase "live and let live" might be appropriate.

A Christ-one, living by the spiritual Life of Another (the Life of Jesus Christ), is to allow the Christ-life to be lived-out spontaneously in their behavior in every situation. We are to live as who we are "in Christ," concerned primarily with our BEING in union with the living Lord Jesus, rather than the contrived agenda of religious DOING to achieve or accomplish their pre-set goals and establish our religious identity thereby. We simply allow Christ to live "as us," not preoccupied with attempting to cause other people to live in the same manner as we live, having no judgmentalism or extended expectations, willing to agree to disagree in open-minded discussion, and avoiding attempts to take a speck out of another's eye when we may have a log in our own perspective (Matt. 7:3-5). Live by letting Him live in us!

UP AND DOWN – FASTER, FASTER

The religious activities of many church people are akin to railroad workers using a hand-car to travel to their job-site. One worker stood on each end of the hand-car, pushing up and down on the see-saw "walking bar" to propel the cart forward. Also known as a "hand-trolley" or "jigger," there were thousands of these human-propelled carts on the rails until gas-powered engines were installed on many of the work-carts in the early 20th century. The operation of the railway hand-car was very exhausting hard work, especially when loaded with supplies and tools to be transported to where the work was to be performed.

To add to the imagery, let me suggest that in common with the old covenant religion of the Law, much of the work being attempted by means of hand-car self-exertion was on a side-track of the mainline railroad. Such a "spur" was a by-pass that ended in a dead-end against a "bumper block." All of the energy expended to accomplish transportation to the site and the labor required to repair the rails was involvement in a task that was ultimately going nowhere and could never achieve the objective intended. What a waste of human energy and performance in the efforts of attempting to fulfil legalistic requirements.

The exhausting performance-works of most forms of religion amount to the false hope of propelling a "hand-car to heaven." Up and down they go, with the mistaken idea that the faster they go, the sooner they will collect the rewards of their labor. All the while, they are on a side-track that goes nowhere; it just ends in a dead-end with no real destination. It is time to yield to progress and allow the grace-dynamic of God in Jesus Christ to provide the complete propulsion necessary to propel us down the mainline of God's fulfillment of all His promises in His Son, Jesus Christ (cf. II Cor. 1:20). "God is at work in us, both to will and to work for His good pleasure" (Phil. 2:13).

THE APOCALYPSE

After explaining the genre of apocalyptic literature to a group of young people, one young man came back the following day inquiring about what he referred to as "apicaloptic" writings. His transposing of the vowel sounds was a perfect *faux pas*, for the cryptic pictorial images of apocalyptic literature can create a "pickle of an optic," difficult to decipher. The Greek word *apocalypse* means "to unveil or reveal," thus we use the word "revelation." The apostle John clearly states in the opening verse that the vision he saw was "the revelation of Jesus Christ," not the revelation of calculable future events.

This last book in our Christian bibles epitomizes and summarizes the message of the new covenant literature, *The New Testament*. From the four gospel records through to "The Revelation," we observe what Karl Barth referred to as "the revelation of Jesus Christ – the end of religion." The parabolic picture-stories that Jesus told were primarily exposés of the prevailing Jewish religion, and the Jewish leaders listening finally realized such (Matt. 21:45). Paul's epistles were constantly combatting the Judaizing religionists who sought to undermine the gospel of grace. In the *Apocalypse*, the apostle John records a series of images that picture the victory of Jesus over religion.

John, who describes himself as "the disciple whom Jesus loved" (Jn. 13:23; 19:26; 20:2; 21:7), because he couldn't fathom being loved like Jesus loved, seems to have been a person who was relationally subjective and had a propensity to enjoy pictorial analogies such as "the light of the world" (Jn. 8:12; 9:5) and the "good shepherd" (Jn. 10:11,14). In conjunction with the other disciples, he saw the radical contrast between the character of Jesus and the characteristics of religion. Describing the apocalyptic vision, he used imagery that leaves the reader with a series of pictorial ponderables that defy precise explanation.

GOD DOESN'T WANT TO BE YOUR HELPER

Many have prayed in their time of trouble, "Lord, help us through this situation." God seems to be perceived as the Divine Assister in times of need. There is no doubt that such a detached perspective of God prevailed in the old covenant religion. We read the words of the psalmist, "In my distress I called upon the Lord, and cried to my God for help; He heard my voice from His temple, and my cry for help before Him came into His ears" (Ps. 18:6). But the new covenant realization of God's indwelling grace should take us beyond the concept of an external God throwing us a life-line when we are floundering to the recognition that the triune God is our life within us.

Miles J. Stanford, best known for his *Green Letters*, wrote: "God doesn't intend to help us live the Christian life. Immaturity considers the Lord Jesus a Helper. Maturity knows Him to be life itself." When God is regarded as one's helper, the implication is that you are in charge; but God will come alongside as your apprentice, assistant, or servant when you can't quite pull-off what you have set your mind to do. God is demoted and diminished to serving as a "come-along" tool to pull you out of your troubles. This coincides with the humanistic motto, "Do your best, and God will do the rest," but it is not Christian.

Notice that Stanford wrote, "God doesn't intend to help us live the Christian life." He doesn't want to serve as our helper; He wants to be the fullness of His own life in every Christ-one (cf. Col. 3:4). Jesus intends to be the "all in all" (cf. Eph. 1:23) in us – our life, our righteousness, our holiness, our wisdom, etc. But we must not forget that Jesus does refer to the Holy Spirit as "our Helper" (Jn. 14:16,17,26; 15:26; 16:7), indicating that He, the living Jesus in Spirit-form, provides everything necessary to enter into communion-prayer (Rom. 8:26), wherein we will find all-sufficient "grace for help in time of need" (Heb. 4:16).

MAY 15

MINDFULNESS OR "THE MIND OF CHRIST"?

Have you noticed the emphasis on "mindfulness" that is pervading all fields of contemporary thought, including science and education in recent years? What is behind all this push for "mindfulness?" Is it similar to "positive thinking" (Norman V. Peale) or "possibility thinking" (Robert Schuller)? Is it connected to the "science of the mind" and the Divine Mind theories of Ernest Holmes that were the foundation of Christian Science and Religious Science? Does it have any ties to the Transcendentalism of the 19th century via Emanuel Swedenborg,\ or to the mysticism of Jacob Boehme in the 16th and 17th centuries?

Yes, in part, there are connections to these schools of thought; but the original emphasis on mindfulness can be traced back to the Buddhist concept of *sati*, often translated "mindfulness," which involves meditative techniques that allow the human mind to enter into an existential present-moment awareness of self-knowledge that suspends all moral judgment concerning right or wrong, allowing freedom of thought and feelings to flow through the mind. In the 1970s, clinical psychology and psychiatry began to experiment with "mindfulness" in therapeutic treatments of addiction, depression, anxiety, and other behavioral issues.

Particularly and increasingly, we are seeing what has been termed "a contemplative turn" in the field of education, employing "mindfulness" as a form of altered consciousness that promotes non-judgmentalism among modern students. The Christian should recognize that humanistic and Eastern religious thought "does not understand spiritual things" (I Cor. 2:14) as they pertain to the ultimate spiritual reality to be discovered only by means of the Spirit of Jesus Christ (cf. I Cor. 3:1). By the spiritual presence of Jesus, the Christ-one (Christian) has the spiritual "mind of Christ" (I Cor. 2:16), which is far superior to any performance procedures of humanistic "mindfulness."

RELIGION IS MIDDLE CLASS

In a sermon by Timothy Keller, entitled "Blessed Are the Poor," a particular statement caught my attention: "Religion is middle class. Religion appeals to those who say: 'I can do it, if I work hard enough.'" It was an interesting combining of economic class-structure and gradation of spiritual development.

The materially wealthy, the upper class, are on the other side of "the eye of the needle" (Matt. 19:24; Mk. 10:25; Lk. 18:25), looking longingly through the narrow opening at the Kingdom of God, but not willing to surrender the hold they have on their material goods (or should we say the hold that their material goods have upon them). They are seldom able to make the hard choice to choose spiritual richness over material riches.

The restless middle class are attracted to religious participation and performance. They are striving to reach the level of those who have wealth and privilege and willing to do almost anything necessary to reach that level. When an opportunity is presented to advance themselves by the self-effort of religious performance, they are the first to sign-up and volunteer, thinking that such religious involvement will get them closer to God, being awarded greater rewards in heaven.

The "poor in spirit" (Matt. 5:3) are receptive and available to anything and everything that God has for them in Jesus Christ, humbly recognizing that they have nothing of value to bring to the table to exchange for their neediness. They readily respond to the gospel of grace as impoverished recipients willing to "deny themselves" (Matt. 16:24) as they participate in the "kingdom of heaven." Their spiritual maturity is obvious as they acknowledge their weakness and inability, saying with Paul, "When I am weak, then I am strong in His strength" (II Cor. 12:10); "my sufficiency is derived only from Christ" (II Cor. 3:5).

MAY 17

INTERPRETING THE SCRIPTURES

The Bible is the only book in the world that requires the reader to know the author of the text in order to understand the text. Without knowing God relationally through the revelation of His Son Jesus Christ and the personal regeneration of the Spirit, a reader of the biblical text is just reading someone else's mail and will never fully understand what the author intended to convey. The Jewish people of the first century regarded themselves as "the people of the book"; but Jesus responded to their religious misconceptions, saying, "You are mistaken, not understanding the Scriptures nor the power of God" (Matt. 22:29).

A text inspired by the Spirit (II Tim. 3:16) exists not as a literary work to be analyzed by minds "blinded by the god of this world" (II Cor. 4:4) but to mold souls that have received the Spirit as their teacher (Jn. 14:26) and have submitted to be led by the Spirit (Rom. 8:16). Not only is such spiritual appraisal (II Cor. 2:10-15) required, but the Christ-one must recognize that a text apart from its context, will usually become a pretext to assert any opinion one might have, leaving the reader or listener completely perplexed. We must beware of *eisegesis* (reading our preconceived meaning into the text), rather than legitimate *exegesis* (drawing the meaning out of the text): e*x* = out of; *hēgeisthai* = 'to guide, lead, or draw." Legitimate interpretation of the biblical text will allow the Spirit to "draw out" the meaning intended by the author of the text to the heart of the believer.

Jesus chastised the Jewish leaders, "You examine the Scriptures because you think that in them you have eternal life; and it is those very Scriptures that testify about Me; and yet you are unwilling to come to Me so that you may have life" (Jn. 5:39,40). "Now in Jesus Christ and by the scriptures of the prophets, the intent of the eternal God has been made known to all the nations, leading to obedience of faith" (Rom. 16:26).

138

PERTURBATION

What does it take to make you perturbed? For many of us, our response to the slightest aggravation, irritation or inconvenience can cause us to "go off course" in perturbation. Any little disturbance or interruption in our status-quo can "set us off," ruffle our feathers, cause us to "get our panties in a bunch," and break out in vocabulary laced with expletives. It takes so little to perturb some of us – the door doesn't open as expected, the drawer sticks, the button doesn't go through button-hole easily, our colleague doesn't follow through – and we are quickly agitated, flustered, upset, and sometimes "boil over" in anger.

Did the earthly Jesus ever get perturbed? His twelve disciples surely gave Him occasions to be agitated, upset, or perturbed. On one occasion, when He finally arrived in Bethany after the death of His friend, Lazarus, it is recorded that "Jesus wept" (Jn. 11:35); but this appears to be loving empathy over the loss of a friend, rather than being troubled or upset. Mary and Martha, on the other hand, were perturbed that Jesus had remained on the other side of the Jordan River (Jn. 11:6) and failed to return immediately to heal their brother. They exclaimed, "If you would have been here, my brother would not have died" (Jn. 11:21,32). Jesus appears to have been panic-proof and perturbation-free.

How can the Christian, living in this world, remain unperturbed? "In this world you will have tribulation" (Jn. 16:33), Jesus promised. This includes the turbulence of trials that might cause one to be disturbed or perturbed. Jesus told His disciples, "My peace I give to you" (Jn. 14:7), "the peace that surpasses comprehension" (Phil. 4:7). The peace of Christ within and the acceptance of circumstances without allow the Christian to be unperturbed. When the apostle Paul was dealing with his "thorn in the flesh," God's answer to his prayer for deliverance was, "My grace is sufficient for you" (II Cor. 12:9).

MAY 19

CHRISTIANITY IS NOT DISSEMINATION OF DATA

Data and facts cannot save anyone. Accurate theological propositions formulated in a systematic corpus of doctrinal creed, though believed adamantly and held sincerely, will never be the basis of becoming a Christ-one. Christianity is not a believe-right religion, nor is it a didactic teaching institution with the objective of disseminating accurate doctrinal data. No one can be educated into being a Christian, nor instructed into being a better Christian. Christian maturity is not a matter of what you know cerebrally. The accumulation of knowledge, despite its biblical accuracy, tends only to create arrogant ideologues.

Yet, the people who comprise the *ecclesia* assemblies of what we call "churches," seem to have been misinformed concerning the objectives of Christian faith and the purpose of Christian gatherings. Much of the preaching and teaching from the pulpits of the churches seems to be the dissemination of informational data. People in the pews have concluded that the accumulation of biblical and theological information is the objective of Christian maturity in order to be knowledgeable and mature Christians. And to achieve that end, pastors must be knowledgeable teachers with the most advanced seminary degrees.

Christianity is not knowledge acquisition or dogmatic data dissemination. Christianity commences when individuals have an experiential encounter with the risen and living Lord Jesus, receiving His presence into their spirit to be their life and their Lord. Knowing Jesus in such a personal relationship is far more fulfilling than knowing doctrinal information. Christianity is not a matter of knowing "this" or "that," historic doctrinal positions or theological theories, but a personal knowing of the living Lord JESUS that can mature and advance as we "grow in the grace and knowledge of our Lord and Savior Jesus Christ" (II Pet. 3:18). We desire to know HIM, not data-facts.

WE SHOULD NOT BE SURPRISED

God foreknew it would be this way. It didn't take God by surprise that the wisdom of this world would view Christians as fools. Through the prophet Isaiah, God explained, "For My thoughts are not your thoughts, nor are your ways My ways," declares the Lord. "For as the heavens are higher than the earth, so are My ways higher than your ways and My thoughts than your thoughts" (Isa. 55:8,9). Natural mankind does not understand either the thinking or the actions of God, and it should not cause consternation among Christians that the thinking of the world regards them to be imbeciles.

Writing to the Corinthian Christians, the apostle Paul explained that the Greeks considered the ways of God in orchestrating a crucified Savior to be "moronic," while the Jewish thinkers considered a crucified Messiah to be an unsurmountable stumbling-block (I Cor. 1:20-30) because Jehovah had indicated that "cursed is anyone who hangs on a tree" (Deut. 21:23). He went on to say, "We speak God's wisdom in a mystery, the hidden wisdom which God predestined before the ages to our glory; the wisdom which none of the rulers of this age has understood" (I Cor. 2:7). And they still don't!

The late United States Supreme Court Justice, Antonin Scalia, a fervent advocate of the gospel of Jesus Christ, is quoted as saying to Christians: "Have the courage to have your wisdom regarded as stupidity. Be fools for Christ. And have the courage to suffer the contempt of the sophisticated world." Christians should not be surprised that the wisdom of the world cannot comprehend the spiritual realities of the gospel (I Cor. 2:14), will always regard the gospel as an absurdity, and will constantly endeavor to make it difficult for Christians to freely worship and share their faith openly. We should expect such from the world around us and allow the Spirit of Christ within to respond with grace.

MAY 21

THE NEED OF MANKIND IS LIFE

For so long, we've encouraged unbelievers to "invite Jesus into your life." But, Jesus doesn't want to be an invited guest in your mixed-up and messed-up life. Jesus wants to bring His Life into your life. What you presently have is death, a miserable existence of selfishness and sinfulness wherein you think you are in control and mistakenly exclaim, "This is the life!" All the while, you are a "slave to sin," to "the spirit that works in the sons of disobedience" (Eph. 2:3). Oh yes, you exclaim, "I am free to do as I please"; but, in that pseudo-freedom, you are deceived by the Deceiver into thinking that you are an independent being.

"The one having the power of death is the devil" (Heb. 2:14), and the natural man is "dead in trespasses and sins" (Eph. 2:1,5). As the source of all sin and selfishness (I Jn. 3:8), being the manifestation of His evil character, Satan has deceived the minds of fallen mankind (II Cor. 4:4) into believing that they are "going it alone" and "doing their own thing" to be the best that they can be. Those who have subscribed to his deceptive religious thinking, think they are the source of all their own sin, that their humanness was corrupted by Adam's initial sin with the consequence of "original sin" being transmitted to all humanity.

Jesus does not want to be an add-on glommed on to your counterfeit existence and enhancing your fake self-sufficiency. Jesus has no interest in participating in your religious silliness of going through the liturgical motions and regarding such as having eternal significance. The risen and living Lord Jesus desires to be received by faith to occupy your human spirit. The Life that He wants to supply to you is Himself. He is the Life mankind needs (Jn. 14:6). This Life is the spiritual Life of God, for Jesus is the divine "life-giving Spirit" (I Cor. 15:45). Rather than being an invited guest, Jesus desires to be your all-in-all, all of Him in all of you, totally sufficient (II Cor. 3:5).

WHAT MAKES SIN SIN?

When most people think of "sin," they think of certain actions that can be specified in the behavioral commands of "thou shalt" or "thou shalt not" engage in these actions. If that be true, then behavior modification, as suggested by the humanistic psychologists, should be enough to change the actions and remedy the problem. Those seeking to identify sin beyond the external actions of sin may proceed to consider internal psychological factors, and may identify "sin" in human weaknesses, temperaments, or personality disorders; or they may conclude that sin emanates from some so-called "old nature" in the human or from the "old man." Some forms of religion identify sin in the corruption of humanness effected at the Fall of mankind and indicate that such "original sin" corruption is forever inescapable since it is innate to all human beings.

The Greek word for "sin" is *hamartia*, which means "to miss the mark," as in archery. What is the mark or the target? Not the keeping of legalistic rules or commandments. The objective is the character of God manifested in human behavior; sin is anything contrary to the character of God. But even this is another definition by privation; i.e., sin is that which is not the character of God. The explanation of "sin" must affirm the presence of features and qualities, rather than their absence.

Sin, as well as righteousness, is derived from spiritual character and not to be identified in specified actions or psychological propensities. Righteousness is the character of God, and sin is the character of the Evil One. Neither is intrinsic to or inherent within created humanity; both are derived from a spirit-source – God or Satan respectively. Righteousness is derived from Jesus Christ, the "Righteous One" (Acts 3:14; 7:52; 22:14) "The one doing sin derives what he does (*ek* – "out of") the devil (I Jn. 3:8). The character of the Evil One – that is what makes sin sin!

MAY 23

EASTERN RELIGION IN WESTERN THOUGHT

Most people in the western world have been trained to reject the Christian worldview that the God of the universe has revealed Himself in His Son, Jesus Christ. But, they are amazingly open and susceptible to eastern religious concepts. Why is this so? Since the middle of the 19th century, eastern thought has transferred ideas, concepts and practices into the thinking of the western world by adapting and packaging such thought in syncretistic psychologized humanism. Neither the humanistic western worldview or the more mystical eastern religion presuppositions understands or accepts genuine spiritual things (I Cor. 2:14).

People in both east and west often view Christianity as a religion offering a "ticket to heaven" in the future. Eastern religion, on the other hand, seems to be more concerned with offering people personal betterment and has packaged their concepts in psychological practices offering such. Stressed out from trying to handle life in a complex world while having no spiritual discernment, westerners are keen to accept practices offering stress-reduction, relaxation, tranquility, serenity, good vibes, positive energy, wholeness, enlightenment, mental focus, higher consciousness, inner awareness, well-being, and the like.

Eastern religious thought packaged in such practices as mindfulness, biofeedback, transcendental meditation, yoga, *tai chi*, hypnosis, *feng shui*, repetition of mantras, acupuncture, self-understanding via the enneagram, etc. are accepted by westerners despite their having no supportive scientific data as to their effectiveness. Much of this focus on trying to fix me and make me feel better is but a form of spiritual narcissism. Eastern religious practices do have a spiritual component, but people must be discerning about which spirit is functioning: Is it the "spirit of error" (I Jn. 4:6), i.e. the "spirit of this world" (I Cor. 2:12), or the Spirit of the Living God manifested in Jesus Christ?

LIVING IN GRACE, YOU WILL ...

Have nothing to hide; nothing to boast about
Have nothing to prove; nothing to be ashamed of
Have nothing to gain; nothing to lose
Have no need to seek approval; no need to seek followers
Have no one to convince; no one to impress
Have no need to seek a title or position in the church
Have no obligation to support the institution

Not be preoccupied with sin
Not be concerned about perfunctory performance
Not be concerned that others think differently than you
Not be concerned about what others think of you
Not be afraid to share your failures
Not be worried about what you should DO for the Lord
Not be self-conscious about how well you are doing
Not feel wounded when you are rejected by the faithful

Be free to hear the voice of God
Be free to love the unlovable
Be free to BE the saint God has made you in Christ.
Be free to avoid the trappings of religion
Be free to serve others as the Spirit leads
Be free to give as prompted by the Lord
Be free to minister according to your spiritual giftedness
Be free to view all of life as opportunity to worship

Enjoy the total provision of God's dynamic grace action
Enjoy the adequacy and sufficiency for living the Christ-life
Enjoy Jesus as your closest friend
Enjoy freedom from the constraint of the Law
Enjoy being the vessel of the "fruit of the Spirit"
Enjoy participating in the fellowship of the Trinity
Enjoy the fellowship of those who know grace in JESUS

MAY 25

PROCLAIMING THE GOSPEL

Contemporary Christianity has often cheapened and diminished
the meaning of "proclaiming the gospel." Gospel proclamation
has been reduced to bumper-sticker and t-shirt logos that
amount to nothing more than slogan-shouting, often with no
more relevance than the person on the street-corner shouting
bible verses or dooms-day denunciations to the passers-by. The
anonymous dropping of tracts in public places and the plethora
of memes containing cutesy statements on internet social media
are cheap substitutes for proclamation. The emphasis on
evangelistic witnessing by some likewise often degenerates into
propagation of propaganda instead of Spirit-filled proclamation.

The Greek words for "proclamation" (*kerygma* – noun; *kerysso* –
verb) are invested with meaning that goes beyond mere
recitation or broadcasting of information. Genuine proclamation
or preaching of the gospel involves the action of the Holy Spirit to
implement the dynamic implications of the Person and events of
Jesus Christ being heralded. Such proclamation is much more
than simply "how to get saved" or "please come join our church."
It is proclamation of the kingdom-reign of Christ (Lk. 9:2,60),
based on the historical events of the crucifixion (I Cor. 1:23) and
the resurrection (I Cor. 15:11,12) of Jesus. This is why Paul
explains that in partaking of the Lord's Supper, we "proclaim the
Lord's death until He comes again" (I Cor. 11:26). Paul advised
Timothy to "proclaim/preach the Word (*logos* – Jesus, Jn. 1:1,14).

Kerygmatic theologians of the twentieth-century emphasized
that when the content of the *kerygma* is preached (i.e. Jesus'
death and resurrection), it is understood that God calls upon the
hearers to believe in God's redemptive action in Christ,
recognizing the need for repentance of sin (Matt. 3:2; Lk. 24:47)
and receiving God's grace in Jesus. The "proclaimed word" enacts
an existential encounter with Jesus and His "saving life."

MAY 26

PERSONAL SECURITY

Personal security has a wide variety of meanings. Some people find personal security in knowing self-defense procedures, in carrying pepper-spray or guns, in having alarms in their home, in having enough insurance to make sure their physical assets are protected. Some religious people find personal security in the theological doctrine of "eternal security" and knowing their ultimate destiny when they die. But the objective of this article is to consider the subjective sense of security about one's personal and spiritual identity and relationship with God and with others.

Are you secure enough in your relationship with God to believe and know that there is not anything you could do to cause God to cease loving you, or cause God to reject you?

Are you secure enough in your marital relationship to believe that there is not anything you could do or tell your spouse that would cause your spouse to quit loving you, to think less of you, or to reject you

Are you secure enough in knowing who you are, that if someone you trust were to reject you, it would not affect your opinion or view of yourself or of them, but only reveal the character (and perhaps insecurity) of the one who rejected you?

Are you secure enough to withstand someone making false accusations about you, with the awareness that such falsity and fallacy need not affect your well-being or thoughts?

Are you secure enough to recognize that someone's perception of you doesn't say anything about you but is only a projection of them, so use it to attempt to understand them and their needs? Know your identity in Christ as a Christ-one and the vital security of your relationship with the living Lord Jesus.

MAY 27

EMPATHY

Many are unable to differentiate between sympathy and empathy. Both words utilize the Greek word *pathos* which refers to emotional suffering. Sympathy uses the preposition *syn* (together with) suggesting understanding of and identification with another's pain and suffering; whereas empathy uses the preposition *em* (in) suggesting that one person can feel the pain and suffering of another to the extent that they enter into such pain and suffering and make it their own in an intercessory manner. Obviously, empathy involves a selflessness and love that requires a person to come out of their self-absorbed orientation and enter into the *pathos* of the pain and suffering of another.

In 2004 the film, "The Passion of the Christ," co-written and produced by Mel Gibson, was released. It graphically portrayed the *pathos* of suffering and emotion that Jesus endured as He was vicariously crucified for the sin of mankind. Pathos has long been used in rhetoric and dramatic communication as a technique to draw the audience into the emotional passion of the subject at hand. Preachers have been trained to use this technique in their attempts to persuade the audience to respond as they intend. Another English word derived from *pathos* is "pathetic," which might refer a person's miserable condition or to a speaker's pathetic. self-serving use of the technique of *pathos*.

Given the narcissism of our contemporary culture, fueled as it is by humanistic premises of the self-absorption of orienting all things around ourselves which doesn't foster or leave room for empathy, we see fewer and fewer examples of empathy. When a person is only concerned for themselves, their myopic perspective does not allow for the concern and *pathos* for others. Narcissistic people are incapable of feeling empathy for others. The Spirit of Christ in the Christ-one will lead Christian persons to enter into the experience of real empathy for others.

THE RELIGIOUS ZOO

My visit to the religious zoo was a bizarre experience. The sign outside of the entrance did not advertise a zoological collection. It simply pointed to a "fellowship gathering" place – diversity without discrimination. The greeters at the entry made it a pleasant enough experience, welcoming every guest with a big smile and a verbal "Welcome. Come on in and have a seat." Eventually, the person in charge, the zoo-keeper I presumed, stood up amidst some musical fanfare and began to explain what the zoological experience was about. I soon sensed that the objective being encouraged was that everyone present was being called to imitate an historical character whose name was Jesus.

In fact, I had read a sign in the vestibule which explicitly stated, "Our mission is to call people to be like Jesus." Having attended a zoological exhibit previously, I had observed the other attendees mimicking the chimpanzees, jumping up and down and screeching – aping the apes. Farther down in the primate enclosure were many varieties of monkeys; and, once again, the attendees were attempting to imitate in a "monkey see, monkey do" ritual. In the aviary there were many who attempted to parrot the parrots with the phrase, "Polly want a cracker!" Special exhibits showcased animals taught to perform actions that were not instinctual to the natural behaviors of their species.

Allow me to share with you my reaction to the religious zoo experience. I must confess that I am not really interested in the pretentious imitation that causes people to make fools of themselves in behaviors that are not instinctual to their species, to their humanity and the intended relationships thereof – their relationships with God and with others. I am interested in seeing human beings function in authentic manifestations that exhibit the character of the One Who created them and redeemed them through His Son, Jesus Christ.

MAY 29

RIGHTEOUSNESS REALIGNED

The foundation and source of all rightness, righteousness and justice is the Triune God. Therefore, to begin to understand righteousness, humans must commence their study with the character of God. Human thought about righteousness went awry when humans began to think of rightness in the context of law rather than God. The Greek goddess of justice and moral order was *dike*, and Christian thought began to use the Greek word *dikaiosune* to refer to the justice and righteousness of God. Jesus was referred to as *dikaion*, "the Righteous One" (Acts 3:14; 7:52; 22:14), who came to bring *dikaiosune* to all humanity.

Even more confusion resulted when the Protestant reformers began to emphasize *dikaiosune* as a major theme of the Reformation, but were couching the theme of righteousness in the legal paradigm of juridical rightness and forensic justification. Conceiving of God as the Judge in the cosmic legal courtroom, the reformers regarded those elected to be Christ-ones as having been pronounced or declared right before God – not made righteous in any way but regarded to be so in sort of a legal-fiction. The corruption that "original sin" had inflicted on humanness could only be put aside and overlooked by imputing or attributing righteousness to those not made righteous.

The Protestant readjustment of the theme of righteousness was a fiasco, as they failed to realign righteousness with the character of God in Jesus Christ. Jesus, the Perfect Man, the "Righteous One," submitted Himself to the "righteous act" (Rom. 5:18) of vicarious death on a cross for the sins of all humanity. He did so to forgive our sins (as only God could do) and to make available to receptive persons the "gift of righteousness" (Rom. 5:17). By His indwelling presence in our spirit, the Christ-one is "made righteous" (Rom. 5:19) and "becomes the righteousness of God in Him" (II Cor. 5:21); righteous as He is righteous (I Jn. 3:7).

1 CORINTHIANS 13 – FOR HUSBANDS

If I speak with the authority of the head of the house,
  but do not have love, I am just blowing off steam.
If I claim to know the mysteries of marriage
  and to have knowledge of gender distinctions,
  but do not have love, I am just an arrogant theorist.
If I provide enough money for my wife's every need
  and sacrifice myself on the altar of marital success,
  but do not have love,
I am just another bankrupt marital casualty.

A husband's love is patient when she is never ready on time,
Kind even when she is in "one of her moods,"
And not jealous of her social skills and friends.

A loving husband is not provoked when she
  does not think or act as he expects
And does not keep a list of when she has hurt or wronged him.
The love of a husband bears all the misunderstandings,
Believes that God is sufficient to make the marriage work,
Hopes that the relationship will glorify God
  and endure all the inevitable difficulties.

If there be marriage seminars, they will be forgotten.
If there are books on marriage, they will be destroyed.
If there are theories of gender distinctions and marital roles,
  they will fade away.

But there now abides in the Christian husband
Faith that God was right in creating us male and female,
Hope that the marriage union
  will represent the union of Christ and the Christian.
But the greatest is Love by which we seek the highest good of the
  other without selfishly considering what we get out of it.

MAY 31

1 CORINTHIANS 13 – FOR WIVES

If I exercise my freedom to speak my mind and say what I think,
    but do not have love, I am just a dripping faucet.
If I know the mysteries of how to please a man
    and the guidelines of a Proverbs 31 wife, but do not have love,
    I am just going through the motions.
If I submit myself to my husband in total availability,
    and do not give myself in love,
I am but a pitiful marital martyr.

A wife's love is patient with all her husband's "big ideas,"
adaptable to his preferences, and supportive of his leadership.
The love of a Christian wife does not nag,
Does not keep a running list of all the times he hurt her feelings.
Is not provoked when he does not pick up his own things,
    does not come home when he says he will,
    or wants to do something at inconvenient times.

In love for her husband a wife will keep herself attractive,
    join him in his recreational pursuits,
    and express her admiration for him often.
A wife's love bears all the insensitivities,
Believes that God will mold the marriage and the man,
Hopes that God will be glorified in what they do,
    and endures the inevitable marital conflicts.

All the feminist propaganda will disappear.
All the latest fashion styles will soon be old-fashioned.
All the material things will break down and deteriorate.

But now abides faith in God's sufficiency,
Hope for a marriage that glorifies God,
But the greatest of these is the Love that puts the other first
    so as to enjoy God's intent for marriage.

1 CORINTHIANS 13 – FOR COUPLES

If I have read all the marriage manuals,
  attended all the seminars and weekend encounters,
  but do not have love, I am just a knowledge-laden partner.
If I set aside time in my calendar to spend meaningful time
  with my spouse on date-nights and vacations,
  but do not have love, I am just an over-scheduled participant.
If I have exhausted my resources trying to juggle a career,
  marital relationship, and a family,
  but do not have time to love my spouse, I am a marital failure.

Love is more than the ooey-gooey, touchy-feely,
  heart-fluttering, temperature-raising, goose-pimpling,
  infatuation that the world advertises as ultimate love.
Love always has a spiritual component
  that connects us down to the core of our being.

Love is readily available to the other
  (love takes time and energy);
Love is always open to creative novelty
  (not just the same ol' same ol');
Love involves transparent visibility
  ("they were naked and not ashamed" – Gen. 2:25)

Love is tender, thoughtful, and romantic.
Love is attentive, complimentary, and giving.
Love is persistent, endearing, and enduring.

Now there abides in our relationship:
  the receptivity of faith, willing to derive from the divine source;
  the expectancy of hope that things will get better and better;
  and the perfect love that is the "fruit of the Spirit" (Gal. 5:23);
But the greatest of these is LOVE that unconditionally seeks the
  highest good of the other with no thought of what I get out of it.

JUNE 2

FIXER-UPPER

Most are acquainted with the popular reality television show called "Fixer Upper." Chip and Joanna Gaines own and operate Magnolia Homes, a remodeling and design business in Waco, Texas, and "Fixer Upper" films the process by which the couple turns dilapidated houses into showcase homes.

Many have mistakenly approached the maintenance of their Christian lives as a fixer-upper project. They may know they were "saved by grace" (Acts 15:11; Eph. 2:5,8) in the redemptive action of Jesus Christ, but they seem to think that the "finishing touches" of the conversion process are their responsibility to fix-up. Not so! When Jesus exclaimed from the cross "It is finished!" (Jn. 19:30), He was indicating that He had set in motion everything necessary for mankind to be restored to God's intent. Yes, we still have sinful and selfish misrepresentative patterns in our fleshly desires (II Pet. 2:10,18), but "the Spirit sets its desires against the flesh" (Gal. 5:17) to overcome such and manifest the character of Christ. "He who began a good work in you will perfect it until the day of Christ Jesus" (Phil.1:6). "Faithful is He who calls you, He also will bring it to pass" (I Thess. 5:24).

When Christians realize the dynamic grace of God is the actuator of the continuing Christ-life, that the Christian life is not a fixer-upper project to make ourselves better and renovate our imperfections, then we can cease trying to serve as the fixer-upper in the lives of others also. We can cease trying to "play Holy Spirit" by offering corrective procedures in the lives of fellow-Christians. Richard J. Foster wrote, "When we genuinely believe that inner transformation is God's work and not ours, we can put to rest our passion to set others straight." When we understand the spiritual exchange from "the spirit of this world" to "the spirit of God" (I Cor. 2:12), we can forego the fixer-upper changes in ourselves and others.

WHEN YOUR TANK IS EMPTY

Some people tend to panic when they look down at the instrument panel of their automobile and the fuel gauge reads "EMPTY." Everyone knows that you cannot go anywhere when the tank is empty and you are out of fuel – but then again, is that totally true? In a figurative sense, when our tank of emotional energy and creative ideas seems to have run dry or we have "run out of steam" for cranking out those perfunctory activities that we regarded as essential to getting us somewhere in life; when our religious efforts of performing for God are not getting us anywhere, and we feel sidelined or stuck in a cul-de-sac of go-nowhere inability – what will our response be?

The responses are varied in such a situation: some may panic, others may fume with anger, while others may back-off in disgust, but God rejoices when your tank is empty! He then knows that you are not going to proceed by your own effort, and you are likely to be ready and willing to draw from His infinite supply of grace by the activity of the Spirit of Jesus Christ. Our awareness of emptiness can be a wake-up call to ascertain the dynamic ability of God. When we recognize our inability to crank out the Christian life, we often come in honesty before God and say, "I can't; only You can, and I am willing to let You do so." God is delighted when we come to such a point of need.

Our emptiness is an opportunity for His fullness to fill full our need. We might reword the lesson that Paul learned, "When I am empty, then I am full with the fullness of His all-sufficient grace" (cf. II Cor. 12:10). As Christ-ones we must recognize that "of His fullness we have received, grace upon grace" (Jn. 1:16). God's grace is God in action in total consistency with His character. His grace is expressed operatively by the power of the Holy Spirit in our lives, and by the empowering means of the Holy Spirit He can take us wherever we need to go, and use us as He desires.

JUNE 4

"YOU DO YOU"

The first time I heard this phrase was from the mouth of a rude twenty-something young man who used it dismissively, revealing his aggravation with or unconcern for what we were doing. I really wasn't sure whether the phrase was used derogatively, or perhaps even with sexual overtones, as in "Go .... yourself!" Upon further reflection, I chose to give the young man the benefit of the doubt and believe that he was using a contemporary slang phrase used in the youth culture, which means, "Do what you have to do," "Do your own thing," "Do whatever allows you to accomplish your agenda." It is a phrase that has become popular among the youth in the early decades of the twenty-first century.

The phrase does reveal, however, the narcissistic egoism of so many contemporary young people. "You do you, and I'll do me. Don't bother me, and I won't be concerned with you." While such a self-absorbed perspective does allow another the freedom to be and do whatever they choose to be and do, the factor which is missing in such an attitude and comment is the relational interaction and involvement with another person. "You do what you want, and I'll do whatever I want," cuts one off from the basic God-given need for sociability and reveals why so many contemporary young people tend to be loners.

Human beings were created with a social need to be involved with other human beings. John Donne was correct in noting that "No man is an island," existing isolated and alone. We need each other. "Do not merely look out for your own personal interests, but also for the interests of others" (Phil. 2:4). That reveals the importance of the *ecclesia* (what we call the Church), the gathering of Christ-ones around the One they have in common. "Do not neglect the gathering of yourselves together, as is the habit of some, but gather to encourage one another" (Heb. 10:25). Rather than "you do you," it might be "we do us" in Him.

OVERWHELMED

Most people have had the sensation of being overwhelmed. But, since there are many ways to be overwhelmed, we must clarify whether we have been physically overwhelmed, emotionally overwhelmed, or spiritually overwhelmed (or all at the same time). The English word *overwhelmen* has been used since the mid-fourteenth century, and meant "to turn upside down." By the fifteenth century the word meant "to submerge, to inundate, to overcome" (physically or figuratively). Modern usage continues to bear the meaning of "inundate, submerge, overcome, bury or drown, defeat or overpower."

The Greek verb *baptizo* has overlapping meanings with the English word "overwhelm." *Baptizo* can also refer to being overwhelmed, overcome, submerged, immersed, buried, or inundated. *Baptizo* can also have reference to physical action, to emotional action, and to spiritual action. The physical action of being overwhelmed is evidenced in the Jewish and Christian practices of submerging an individual in water. Jesus was submerged in the Jordan River by John the Baptist (Mk. 1:19), to "fulfill all righteousness" (Matt. 3:15). Reference is also made in scripture to the Israelites being overwhelmed (*baptizo*) by the cloud as they crossed the Red Sea in the Exodus (I Cor. 10:2).

The emotional sense of being overwhelmed (*baptizo*) by anguish is seen in Jesus' comment to Peter that He had an overwhelming (*baptizma*) that Peter could not participate in, i.e. the redemptive sacrifice for humankind. John the Baptist was aware that Jesus would also extend a spiritual overwhelming: "I baptize you with water; but One is coming who is mightier than I, He will overwhelm (*baptizo*) you with the Holy Spirit and fire" (Lk. 3:16; Acts 11:16). Paul explained, "by one Spirit we were all baptized into one body..." (I Cor. 12:13); our human spirits were overwhelmed by the Spirit of Christ.

JUNE 6

"I DON'T DO THIS; I DON'T DO THAT!"

The gravel-voiced preacher, J. Vernon McGee, once said: "When I hear Christians say, 'I don't do this, and I don't do that; I am following God's set of rules,' I immediately recognize that they know very little about the grace of God. They are trying to live the Christian life in their own strength. But Paul says, 'Be strong in the grace that is in Christ Jesus'" (II Tim. 2:1). The preacher clearly understood that there is a clear-cut dichotomy between what we do or don't do, our performance of commission or omission, and the grace dynamic of God's action whereby He does everything that needs doing in our lives.

Christianity is NOT what I don't do! "I don't gossip; I don't tell lies; I don't steal; I don't bear false witness; I don't murder; I don't get drunk; I don't watch porn; I don't make love with my neighbor's spouse..." Preacher McGee would likely have said, "Big Deal! Neither does the bronze statue in the city park. Does that make the bronze statue virtuous, righteous, godly, holy, Spirit-filled, a good Christian? No! The statue just stands there in solid rigidity and doesn't do anything constructive or destructive, but no moralistic attributes can be assigned to it. It simply serves as a bird perch with the accompanying excrement thereof.

Definition by absence, negation, or privation does not prove anything. Yet, that has long been how Christian thinkers have attempted to define "evil" as the absence of good. Augustine of Hippo (354-430) wrote, "For what is that which we call evil but the absence of good" (*Endiridon*). This led Boethius in the sixth century to conclude, "Evil is nothing." Our definitions must have positive substantiation. Attempting to define righteousness by what you don't do is somewhat like attempting to define gold by explaining it is not excrement. Just because it is not excrement doesn't make it gold! The positive substantiation of righteousness is God's character manifested in Jesus Christ.

ELECTROMAGNETISM

James Clerk Maxwell (1831-1879) was a Scottish scientist in the field of mathematical physics. His most notable achievement was to formulate the classical theory of electromagnetic radiation, bringing together for the first-time electricity, magnetism, and light as different manifestations of the same phenomenon – a unification of nature's basic forces. Albert Einstein built upon the findings of Maxwell and sought to develop a "unified field theory." Maxwell's observations and conclusions were the basis for a new branch of physics called "electromagnetism" with continued study of electromagnetic forces.

Electromagnets are different than permanent magnets. Permanent magnets are made up of material that has been magnetized and has developed its own magnetic field. Electromagnets are made of coils of wire with electricity passing through them. Moving charges create magnetic fields; so, when the coils of wire in an electromagnet have an electric current passing through them, the coils behave like a magnet. In the home, by far the most common use of electromagnets is in electric motors. As long as a current is flowing through the coil, it creates a dynamic magnetic attraction; but when the current is not flowing the attraction that pulls the objects together ceases.

Here's a question: Is our spiritual connection with God more like a permanent magnet or an electromagnet? I suggest it is more like an electromagnetic attraction-connection. As long as the dynamic current is flowing, the electromagnetic field holds the objects together; but without the dynamic current the object returns to its inert state. As long as the dynamic grace of God is flowing between God and the receptive human being there is an unbroken connection of grace-faith, held firm as the flow of God's grace creates a field that pulls and bonds us in the tightest possible union. God's grace never fails – we are safe in His action.

159

JUNE 8

THAT'S YOUR RELIGION TALKING

Most of us have known some very brilliant people – people who could think logically for themselves and draw their own conclusions. Many such brilliant people are Christians, but often times they have not thought through their Christian faith in a reasoned manner. They and others, regardless of their mental acumen, have heard many clichés from the pulpit that sounded very valid and religious, which they have thoughtlessly incorporated into the formulation of their faith-talk without analyzing what they are saying. One's religious thinking is inevitably reflected in one's conversation about life in general.

"Yes, that person's behavior is not representative of the character of Christ, but we cannot question whether he is a Christian, because a Christian is 'once saved, always saved,' eternally secure in Christ." "We must be careful about making moral judgments about people's actions or events that transpire, because 'God is the cause of all things,' and it is not for us to question what God is doing." "It is not right or fair to question another person's faith, because 'we are not responsible for our faith; it is given to us by God,' and to question such would impinge upon God's attribution of faith in another person."

The foregoing comments, and others such as "all things are predestined by God," "Prayer changes things," "Faith moves mountains," "God blesses those who tithe," "Do your best and God will do the rest," are clichés of unthinking Christians parroting what they have heard the preacher say from the pulpit. When we hear such comments, we can safely conclude "that's your religion talking," and it would be beneficial if some people would give more serious thought to what they are saying in reference to God. Better yet, it would be useful if more people could differentiate between religion and the true reality of what it means to be a Christ-one in union with the living Lord Jesus.

160

JUNE 9

"GOD'S WAYS ARE ALWAYS RIGHT"

We are not saying that God's ways are always easy ... or pleasant ... or most expedient to our plans and purposes ... or always turn out the way we want them to transpire. We are quoting from the prophet Hosea, who in following God's way for him was led into very trying times of trial. Hosea was instructed to marry an unfaithful whore, illustrating the unfaithfulness of God's people, Israel (and us). Time and time again, he sought her out and brought her home to show his love for her. Yet, he wrote, "For the ways of the Lord are right, and the righteous will walk in them, But, transgressors will stumble in them" (Hosea 14:9).

God does what He does because He IS who He IS. He never acts out of character. That is why His ways are always right and righteous. His ways are expressive of His character of righteousness and justice. What a contrast, then, with fallen and sinful mankind, among whom "there is none righteous, no not one" (Rom. 3:10). However, "if Christ is in you, though the body is dead because of sin, yet the spirit is alive because of righteousness" (Rom. 8:10). "...made righteous in Him" (II Cor. 5:21).

Those who delight in and are desirous of God's righteousness will determine the righteous way of God in obedience (*hupakouo* – "to listen under") and walk in that way by faithfully deriving the righteous character of God from the "Righteous One" (Acts 3:14; 7:51; 22:14) dwelling in their spirit, receiving and manifesting His righteous character in their human behavior. "The righteous man shall live by faith" – (Hab. 2:4; Rom. 1:17; Gal. 3:11; Heb. 10:38), "filled with the fruit of righteousness, which comes through Jesus Christ, to the glory and praise of God" (Phil. 1:11). God's ways are always right because they serve God's intentional purpose of love for us. He seeks our highest good in everything He leads us into (cf. Rom. 8:14) – always for His righteous and loving purposes.

161

JUNE 10

THE MOMENT OF AWARENESS

Have you ever experienced a point or moment of revelation and awareness when your eyes were opened to a reality of which you were previously unaware? These times of realization or recognition often enlighten us to something that is not as it ought to be in our lives, or to the awareness of a previously unknown or unnoticed truth of which we should avail ourselves. Whether it is an awareness of what is wrong or the awareness of an opportunity to make right, both can evoke strong feelings. Our English language has at least two words to describe these moments of eye-opening awareness: anagnorisis and epiphany.

Anagnorisis is often used in the literary context of tragedies and times of sorrow when a character recognizes the horrible life-changing truth about themselves or their situation. Anagnorisis derives from a Greek word (*ana* = again; *gnorisis* = to make known) and means "recognition." It often refers to the moment of awareness or recognition of something terrible or disturbing. For example, in order to become a Christ-one, an individual must come to the awareness of his own sinfulness. "All have sinned, and come short of the glory of God" (Rom. 3:23). This point of revealing or awareness of sin is an example of anagnorisis.

The other English word, "epiphany," is better known, especially among Christian believers. Epiphany is also derived from Greek (*epi* = upon; *phanein* = to appear) and was used in the Christian calendar to refer to the appearance of the Magi in Jerusalem, commemorated on January 6 each year. In general usage, the word "epiphany" has come to mean the moment of awareness when something is manifested to one's consciousness, particularly the appearance of something of spiritual significance. Many Christians have experienced an epiphany awareness in the spiritual exchange of receiving the Spirit of Christ in the regeneration of their spirit (cf. Rom. 8:9).

WHAT IF ...

Despite the realization that "what ifs" are hypotheticals, the speculative and theoretical "maybes" of human thought and conversation, they allow us to propose some conjectures that will hopefully not undermine your faith. Hypotheticals can be utilized to examine the hypotheses (*hypo* = under; *thesis* = to place) of the foundations that underlie the conclusions of our thought-structures – of what we believe.

What if I could convince you that ...
... Jesus never turned water into wine?
... Jesus never walked on water?
... Jesus never healed any physical infirmities?
... Jesus never performed any miracles?

What if I were to present evidences that ...
... there was no star that shown over Bethlehem?
... there were no magi that came from the East?
... Jesus never went to Egypt with His parents?
... there was no threat on Jesus' life by Herod?

What if I could make a logical case ...
... that there is no reason to expect a rapture?
... that there is no compelling evidence for a second coming?
... that there is no cosmological evidence for heaven?
... that there is no cosmological evidence for hell?

Are you so thoroughly convinced that the living Lord Jesus is the life-giving Spirit (I Cor. 15:45) who has come to live in your spirit (Rom. 8:9) and has become your LIFE (Col. 3:4) – that the love, and joy and peace that you presently experience are so intrinsically valid, that such hypothetical questions would not impinge on your faith in Christ? I hope so, for the issue is JESUS, and everything else is but peripheral detail.

JUNE 12

THE USE AND ABUSE OF ALCOHOL

The Bible is not against the use of alcohol. Paul urges Timothy to "use a little wine for his stomach and ailments" (I Tim. 5:23), but cautions about being "addicted to wine" (I Tim. 3:3-8). The Psalmist refers to God providing "the wine which makes man's heart glad" (Ps. 104:15), while Solomon wrote, "Wine is a mocker, strong drink a brawler, and whoever is intoxicated by it is not wise" (Prov. 20:1). As with all things available to God's people, "all things are lawful, but not all things are expedient, and we must not come under the power of any" (I Cor. 6:12; 10:23). "Let your moderation be made known to all" (Phil. 4:5).

Why are people in our culture and around the world so drawn to the use and abuse of alcohol and drugs? This is not something new, but the consequences have such a high cost (financially and relationally). Some say that there are some people who are genetically predisposed to the use and abuse of alcohol. It's in their genes! I don't know, but there does seem to be a predispositional propensity for such among those who have grown up in families of users and abusers of alcohol. The old covenant seems to indicate that "the sins of the father can be passed on to future generations" (Exod. 34:7; I Kgs. 15:3).

Some began to use and abuse alcohol due to the peer pressure of image or personal experimentation. In the process, some acquired a taste for such and found it relaxing, while others found that alcohol made them less inhibited or socially intimidated. Some use and abuse alcohol for the sake of excitement, the stimulating feeling of getting "buzzed," while others use alcohol to escape and relieve the stressful problems of life. Some, in rebellion, have used alcohol with a false sense of being "in control" of their lives by being "out of control." Those who are Christ-ones must beware of becoming dependent on alcohol, rather than dependent on the Lord Jesus Christ.

WHY PRAY?

If the omniscient, all-knowing God knows all things, even our thoughts, then why do we pray? Not to give God information. Not to make God pleased that we are "checking in." The primary purpose for prayer is not for the benefit of God, but because it is beneficial to our own spiritual growth as a Christ-one. I do not direct my prayers to God because He needs me to do so or even tells me to do so, but because in prayer I am aligning my thoughts and feelings and determinations with the purposes of God. To ask the question, "Why pray?" is akin to asking, "Why communicate with your spouse?" Because in the process, we understand and align ourselves with the other.

The Danish thinker, Soren Kierkegaard, wrote, "Prayer does not change God, but it changes the one who prays." The French thinker, Jacques Ellul, wrote similarly, "Prayer is a mirror in which we are called to contemplate our spiritual state. Since it is a real encounter with God, we can in prayer see ourselves as God sees us." Prayer is beyond language and verbal communication (cf. Rom. 8:26,27); it is the intimacy of relationship. To pray is to obey, but that must be understood in the new covenant context of "listening under" (Gk. *hupakouo*) God in order to know His heart and to respond with the affirmation, "Yes, Lord!"

In John Bunyan's words, "Prayer opens the heart to God, and is the means by which the soul is filled by God." Charles Bent explained, "The real end of prayer is not so much to get this or that desire granted by God, as to put our human lives into full and joyful conformity with the will of God." The English preacher, F.W. Robertson, further suggested, "Pray 'till prayer causes you to forget your own desire, and allow it to merge into God's will." Yes, "prayer is aligning ourselves with the purposes of God," said E. Stanley Jones. In prayer, we submit and surrender ourselves to God. Why pray? To enter into and know God and ourselves.

JUNE 14

FEELING GUILTY

Do you have someone in your life that always seems to make you feel guilty? They may be purposely attempting to cause you to feel guilty by their judgmental attitude, or they may inadvertently cause you to feel guilty because of your own perceived sense of inadequacy or responsibility when you compare yourself to that person. Paul makes an interesting comment about self-comparison: "For we do not presume to rank or compare ourselves with some of those who commend themselves; but when they measure themselves by themselves and compare themselves with themselves, they have no understanding" (II Cor. 10:12)

It needs to be clearly stated, "Feeling guilty is not the same as being guilty!" Who are you trying to please? Whose standards are you trying to live up to and perform? I remember one fellow in college who delighted in making people feel guilty by asking, "Are you still doing it?" People would question themselves, "What am I doing that this person thinks is wrong?" He just seemed to enjoy "getting under people's skin," watching people squirm by asking his irritating questions and attempting to send them on a guilt-trip. People eventually learned to dismiss him as irrelevant.

Religion specializes in making people feel guilty. The mere sight of a pastor or preacher or priest or parishioner makes some people feel guilty. Much of this is false-guilt, because one cannot be genuinely guilty before God if God has not indicated that what you are involved in is wrong or sinful. Just because the religious folk think some action is wrong doesn't make it wrong. For a Christ-one participating in new covenant Christianity, "there is now no condemnation for those who are in Christ Jesus" (Rom. 8:1). This would speak to the Christian who engages in the self-condemnation of feeling guilty when not really guilty before God for trespassing against His character.

RELATIONAL TRANSPARENCY

The honesty of transparency necessarily allows for the vulnerability that is required for intimacy and close connectedness in any relationship, whether with God, friends, or in marriage. At the heart of all genuine love is personal vulnerability. To love unconditionally always allows for the vulnerable possibility of being hurt, of having your deepest feelings or even your past history exposed in a manner that disturbs you. The mutuality of love is willing to risk such vulnerability, knowing that love will always be superficial, if not hypocritical, if we do not "open up" transparently to the other.

Genuine love will always seek the depth of union-intimacy, despite the cost of vulnerability, because anything less is simply the play-acting of hypocrisy. The depth of intimacy in our relationship with God (and with spouse) will be directly proportionate to the openness of our transparency. Transparency is the foundation of trust, and this requires honest communication. It requires the recognition that this relationship is NOT just about YOU; a relationship requires at least two parties. To the extent that the other does not know you fully, you (and they) cannot really participate in a relationship of intimacy.

As long as we are attempting to keep secrets from the other, we will never experience the deepening intimacy of a oneness in mind, heart, and spirit. Selfish secrecy is deadly to the necessary intimacy of deep relationships. We need to be an "open book," willing to share everything: our flaws, faults, failures, mistakes, sins, and aspirations, everything that is meaningful to know us and our past. There is a security in realizing that rejection is less likely to occur when there is a trusting relationship of transparency. On the other hand, we do not want our transparency to wound the other party. Some people are not emotionally mature enough to engage in relational transparency.

JUNE 16

"WHAT A CHARACTER!"

The exclamation, "What a character!" often refers to someone unique and eccentric, one-of-a-kind, like Rodney Dangerfield or Dennis Rodman. It can also be used to describe the character development of a personal figure in a book or dramatic production. The predominant modern use of the idea of "character" is built upon humanistic and psychological characteristics of personality and/or behavior. Some would indicate that our character is determined innately by our unique combination of genetics (it's in our genes), while others advocate that we should help people to develop their character through classes in "character education."

The Greek word *charakteras,* from which we get the English word "character," is only used once in the New Testament (Heb. 1:3). There it refers to Jesus, the Son of God, being of the exact character, or the essential nature or divine being of God the Father. When Christ-ones become partakers of the "divine nature" (II Pet. 1:4) of the living Lord in spiritual regeneration, we receive the essential being and character of the triune God into our human spirit as the basis of our new identity as a "new creature" (II Cor. 5:17) in Christ. This is the spiritual component and reality that is missing in all humanistic concepts of character.

All correct theological thinking begins and ends with the character of God. We must commence our concepts of God by considering who God IS in Himself (*a se*). His character is the nature of His Being, revealed in His Son, Jesus (cf. Heb. 1:3). God does what He does because He IS who He IS. He desires to manifest His character in His creation to His own glory (Ps. 72:19; Isa. 43:7; 48:11). Jesus Christ revealed the character of God in a man (Jn. 14:7,9). The character of God in Christ manifested in the behavior of Christ-ones in whom the living Jesus lives is God's objective in His creation of humanity.

THE RADICAL EXCHANGE

So many Christians are self-absorbed in the questioning of what God wants them to do for Him. Some are even on the verge of a paranoid questioning whether they are performing correctly or doing enough to please the Lord. These poor souls have been propagandized by the religion of performance and have been deliberately denied the gospel message of the grace provision of God in Jesus Christ and the awareness of the radical spiritual transference or exchange that occurred in their human spirit at regeneration, whereby they have been provided with everything necessary to be and to do what God desires.

God is not asking you to change anything about who you are or what you do, but simply to understand, affirm and settle-in to the radical exchange that has taken place in your spirit in spiritual regeneration. God simply wants us to recognize (re-cognize: perceive, become aware) of what He has done for us and in us in the finished work of Jesus (cf. Jn. 19:30) and embrace the radical new reality of who we are and all we have been given as a "new creature" (II Cor. 5:17) in Jesus Christ – all that God has caused us to become in Jesus Christ as a re-created Christ-one, wherein the living Lord Jesus indwells us to become our life (Col. 3:4).

What happened in the radical exchange within us? The "spirit of error" was exchanged for the "spirit of truth" (I Jn. 4:6; Jn. 16:13). "The spirit of this world" was exchanged for "the spirit of the living God" (I Cor. 2:12). "The spirit that works in the sons of disobedience" (Eph. 2:2) was exchanged for "the Spirit of God at work in you" (Rom. 8:9; Phil. 2:13). The "spirit of antichrist" (I Jn. 4:3) was exchanged for the "Spirit of Jesus" (Acts 16:7; Phil. 1:19), "the Spirit of Christ" (Rom. 8:9; I Pet. 1:11). The "spirit of stupor" (Rom. 11:8) was exchanged for the "Spirit of Wisdom" (Eph. 1:17); "the spirit of fear" was exchanged for "the Spirit of power and love" (II Tim. 1:7), the "Spirit of grace" (Heb. 10:29).

JUNE 18

THE ULTIMATE TRANSFER

If you have served in the national military or in a career with a major corporation, you are probably quite familiar with the concept of being transferred from one location to another to serve the needs of your employer. In many cases the transfer involves a complete transplanting from one state to another, even from one country to another. But there is an ultimate personal transference that occurs within a person's human spirit when they become a Christ-one, a Christian. God "rescued us from the domain of darkness, and transferred us to the kingdom of His beloved Son" (Col. 1:13,14).

This ultimate spiritual transfer is what the risen and living Lord Jesus was referring to when He told Saul on the Road to Damascus, he would be engaged in when he was sent to proclaim the gospel to the Gentiles, "to open their eyes so that they may turn from darkness to light, and from the power of Satan to God, that they may receive forgiveness of sins and an inheritance among those sanctified by faith in Me" (Acts 26:18). It is the transfer from the domain or dominion or power (Greek – *exousia*, "out of the being of") of Satan's spiritual darkness to the regenerated spiritual kingdom of the light and life of Jesus.

This transfer from Satan's domain to the Kingdom of Christ is also explained by the apostle Paul again in his epistle to the Ephesian Christians. He challenges them to remember their previous spiritual condition, when they "walked according to the course of this world, according to the prince of the power of the air (*Satan*), of the spirit that is now working in the sons of disobedience," and their "being by nature children of wrath," like all sinful and fallen mankind; but God "made them alive together with Christ," for "by grace we have been saved" through the finished work of Christ, "raised up with Him and seated with Him in the heavenly places in Christ Jesus."

YOUR IDENTITY IS NOT IN YOUR ACTIONS

The following quotation is from Helmut Thielicke, the German pastor/theologian used by God to minister to the German people during the Nazi regime. Read it and ponder its significance: "Jesus did not identify the person with his sin, but rather saw in this sin something alien, something that really did not belong to him, something that merely chained and mastered him and from which he could be freed and restored to his real self. Jesus was able to love men because He loved them right through the layers of mud." What conclusions do you draw from what Pastor Thielicke wrote during a difficult time in history?

The world and its subsidiary, religion, has programmed us to believe, "you are what you do." If you do carpentry, you are a carpenter. If you do teaching, you are a teacher. If you do sin, you are a sinner (cf. Rom. 3:23). If this be true, humanity is hopelessly locked in sinfulness, from which there is no salvation. God forbid! Our natural tendency is to identify a person with their sinful actions: that person is a murderer, a thief, an adulterer, a liar, a narcissist, a philanderer; but, in I Cor. 6:9-11, Paul mentions such activities and exclaims, "Such were some of you" (I Cor. 6:11) in the past. Their identity had been exchanged from being a "sinner" to a "saint" in spiritual regeneration.

Our deepest sense of identity is in the spiritual core of our being. We started out as a "sinner" (Rom. 5:19), and in receiving Jesus by faith we became a "saint" (Eph. 1:1; 2:19), a "holy one." As a "sinner" our deeper spiritual source was Satan (Eph. 2:2; I Jn. 3:8; II Tim. 2:16), but as a "saint" our inner spiritual source is Jesus Christ (I Cor. 1:30; II Cor. 5:21; Col. 1:22). This is why Thielicke indicated that sin (and he would have included righteousness) is "alien" to who we really are, for it is the character of a spirit-source that inhabits our human spirit, even though we can misrepresent our spirit-identity in our actions.

171

JUNE 20

WHY THE RESISTANCE TO JESUS OR SATAN?

Religion has traditionally and historically specialized in creating either/or alternatives: either this extreme or that extreme with no in-between – Catholicism or Protestantism, Calvinism or Arminianism, conservatism or progressivism; but, when presented with the ultimate spiritual either/or between Satan's action and Christ's action operating in human beings, they scream "foul." Why the reaction of repudiation, resistance, or rejection of this dichotomy of spiritual source, especially when there is adequate biblical statement of such? Is it because Satan does not want people to realize that everything contrary to God is derived from (Greek *ek* – out of) him, the Evil One?

"The natural man does not understand spiritual things" (I Cor. 2:14). "Satan has blinded the minds of unbelievers" (II Cor. 4:4). This deception of spiritual realities in the humanistic world- view carries over into Christian thinking in the denial of the either/or alternatives of spiritual source, spiritual nature, spiritual identity, spiritual character, etc. When one declares that human beings are spiritually indwelt by either Satan or Jesus, that every person is dependent upon and controlled by either Satan or Jesus, there is an adamant denial of such among evangelicals. They remain deceived by the Deceiver.

Evangelicals have so bought into the humanistic premise that man is an independent self, that when God is not working in a human being, said human being is independent and operating from "self" resource, from self-sufficiency, as his/her own center of reference. They adamantly insist on believing that every human being has the god-like free-will to choose to enact their own salvation by their own belief-choice, or to choose to go their own way, do their own thing, and make of themselves anything that they want to be. They reject the either/or of Jesus or Satan, choosing instead their own self-potential of self-governance.

DIFFERENTIATION MUST BE MADE

Many, perhaps the majority of people in the Western world today, confuse and meld together morality, religion, and Christianity; they cannot clearly differentiate between these realities nor determine what authority they may contain.

Morality is discovering the bounds of the social mores and social boundaries the social community you are a part of espouses and accepts. Even the law courts of the U.K., Canada, and the U.S.A. have indicated that the "community standards" tolerated in any given community are the basis of determining moral bounds and social mores for that particular community, as distinct from national legislation of morality laws, though calculation of harm to individuals in the community must be given consideration.

Religion involves ascribing to and usually legalistically adhering to the behavioral regulations of acceptable behavior in the religious community in which any given individual is participating. The basis of these regulations may be objectively determined by a book of ethical prescriptions of right or wrong, acceptable or unacceptable behaviors. Otherwise, the determination of acceptable standards of behavior may be made subjectively by the standing leadership and authorities of the particular religious community of which one is a part.

Christianity, on the other hand, is allowing the living Lord Jesus who dwells within receptive Christ-ones to provide His impetus and affirmation of behavioral expressions that are manifestations of His character. The Spirit of Christ dwelling in the receptive human spirit (cf. Rom. 8:9,16) of an individual Christian will spontaneously prompt and lead (Rom. 8:14) that person to uniquely express His character in behavior and ministry. The authority for such is not in codified laws of behavior, but in the dynamic Lordship of Jesus in each Christian's life.

JUNE 22

"TAUGHT BY THE SPIRIT"

The Church of Jesus Christ was never intended to be an educational institution. Yet, that seems to be the primary objective of the religious church organizations today. The history of this development goes back to 18th century England, when local churches set up Sunday schools for children who had to work during the week. After the Education Act of 1870 in Britain provided for universal elementary education, the role of Sunday schools changed. The local churches established instructional classes for catechesis of the dogma of their particular institution, either prior to or during the Sunday morning worship service.

The original purpose of the *ecclesia* assembly of those identified with Christ seems to have been a worship gathering which also included mutual sharing of what the Spirit of Christ was doing in or speaking to their individual lives. Yes, there was didactic teaching, but the acquisition of theological information and biblical knowledge does not seem to have been the objective. The early believers gathered together for mutual encouragement as they lived their lives in an antagonistic world, fellowship around the common provision of God's grace in the living Lord Jesus, and the opportunity to worship the living Lord together.

Instead of the idolatrous fetish for knowledge, worshipping at the altar of educational information, the early Christians emphasized the relational intimacy with the living Jesus as "taught by the Spirit" (cf. I Cor. 2:13). In His earthly ministry, Jesus had advised the first disciples that the Spirit would be their teacher (Jn. 14:26); and even as they shared the good news of the gospel, "the Holy Spirit would teach them in the moment what they ought to say" (Lk. 12:12). Such spiritual instruction needs to be emphasized today "that we may know the things freely given to us by God, and speak these things, not in words taught by human wisdom, but in those taught by the Spirit' (I Cor. 2:12,13).

174

RELIGION LEADS TO LAXITY ABOUT SIN

The young lady was brought up in a moralistic and legalistic local church. From the time she was a small girl she was taught that wearing lipstick, having one's ears pierced, cutting her long hair, shaving her legs, wearing skirts above her knees, and especially kissing a boy were all wrong and sinful activities. She struggled with all the rules but eventually decided that there was no real basis for the abundant prohibitions; that she didn't really need to keep all the negative prohibitions and the only real consequence of her violating the religious rules was that to do so produced false-guilt in her mind and emotions.

Jettisoning the legalistic morality of her religion, she became lax and promiscuous in her relationships, engaging in premarital sexual activity, as well as unlawful activities. The genuine guilt she felt under the conviction of the Holy Spirit "felt" the same as the false-guilt she experienced for the violation of the religious rules; so she learned to disregard those guilt feelings also and developed a calloused or seared conscience that minimized personal sin altogether. To this day the Holy Spirit periodically brings a twinge of guilt as she looks back at her life of sin; but, wanting to avoid the shame and guilt-feelings, she brushes them off by busying herself with other matters.

The pre-conditioning of how she dealt with the false-guilt feelings of violating religiously defined wrong-doing set her up for laxity about sin in general. What happened in the long-run was she, like many in her religious group, ended up repudiating the teaching and fellowship of the *ecclesia* altogether. This all-too-common scenario exposes how the religion of manufactured rules and regulations prepares people to treat sin nonchalantly, to fail to reckon on the seriousness of violating God's character, and to fail to appreciate the work of Jesus Christ in redeeming us from sin and renovating us to be "new creatures" in Christ.

JUNE 24

LIKE GOD?

More than once in scripture, we notice God stating, "There is *no one like Me*" (Exod. 9:14; Isa. 46:9). God is unique; He stands alone as the one God (Deut. 6:4; Exod. 8:10) of the universe, implying that what God is, only God is! Why, then, from the pulpits and Sunday School classrooms across our land do we hear week after week that the objective of Christian living is to "be like Jesus" or "be like God?" That is an impossible inculcation foisted upon Christian people, dooming them to failure by inability. Do we fail to remember that the first suggestion that we could "be like God" came from the devil (Gen. 3:8)?

What God is, only God is! What is attributed to God should not, and cannot legitimately, be attributed to human beings. The attributes of God are non-transferrable to anyone other than the Father, Son, and Holy Spirit. "God is Holy"; He is distinctly set apart from all creation as intrinsically and essentially Holy and sacred. John heard the angels singing, "You alone are Holy" (Rev. 15:4). It will always be an idolatrous attribution to say that we are holy in the same sense that God is Holy. We can never be essentially in ourselves "holy" in the same manner that God is uniquely and singularly Holy. Yet, Christians are referred to as being "holy ones" (Greek *hagioi*), saints (Rom. 1:7; 16:15; Eph. 1:1; 4:12) who are made "holy" (Eph. 5:27; Col. 1:22). We are made and identified as "holy" by the indwelling spiritual presence and function of the Holy One (Acts 2:27; 3:14; 13:35), i.e. Jesus Christ in us as Christ-ones. Thus, we can "be holy as God is holy" (I Pet.1:15,16) by manifesting God's holy character. Our attribution of being "holy ones," saints, is the derived presence and expression of God's holy character – derived holiness, not the essential holy character that is unique to God alone.

The same is true of the many admonitions we hear from Christian teachers encouraging us to "be like Jesus."

RELIGION KNOWS NOTHING OF GRACE

Consider these words from Steve McVey, "The old-time-religion and today's cutting-edge-religion have one thing in common – they are both religion. I want neither. Religion is the easy way out. All It requires is to learn the system, then practice and perfect your skills. Do it well enough and you will be rewarded by moving up to higher levels." McVey is correct. Religion is a matter of human skills at working the system. Learn the lingo, parrot the party-line, hobnob with the leaders, keep your nose clean; and it will be just a matter of time until you rise to the top. But who wants to be "king of the mountain" on the rubbish pile (Phil. 3:8)?

McVey went on to write, "Grace is different. It is courageous. It refuses to be diluted and polluted by conformity to convention. Grace loves those religion loathes. Grace is directed by relationship, not driven by rules. Grace cares, not controls. Grace serves others, and does not seek its own advantage." Grace is so far outside of the bounds of the operational apparatus of religion that it should be a crime for them to bastardize the word "grace" in their religious terminology. Grace and religion are one hundred eighty degrees opposite of one another. It is impossible for grace and religion to play together. God-given and God-energized grace is totally antithetical to man-made religion.

In his book, *What's so Amazing about Grace?*, Philip Yancey used the phrase, "grace is annoying." It is so because the human mind cannot pin it down in clever definitions and theological terminology. Grace allows for latitude of divine thought and action; religion wants to get it all figured out and buttoned up in precise categories and activities. Grace doesn't play by the religious rules. The human mind can't get grace figured out. It is impossible to package it up and market it in the religious market. It is the dynamic work of God which cannot be boxed up and sold. Grace is as unpredictable as the wind in Texas.

JUNE 26

A CHRISTIAN ATTITUDE TOWARD SCIENCE

Ralph Waldo Emerson wrote, "The religion that is afraid of science dishonors God and commits suicide." Allow me to reword and refine his comment: Christian faith that is afraid of science and its constant search to know (Latin *scientia* = "knowledge") how the cosmos functions, and the interaction of physical elements (including the transmission of viruses), inevitably veers off into religious superstition without the factual data necessary to address the contemporary world of human problems, or degenerates into collectively held nonsense, and will soon be regarded as irrelevant to contemporary conversation.

The widely-held thesis of inevitable antagonistic conflict between Christian thought and science is not necessarily true. There should be a positive attitude of compatibility between the two disciplines. A survey of twentieth-century Nobel Laureate recipients revealed that two-thirds of them claimed to be Christians. The alleged conflict is between ignorant religionists and ignorant scientists. Yes, there is much modern science that does not take God into account and operates with humanistic premises; but, for the most part, they still remain honest in their scientific observations because their observations must be reproducible by other scientists in order to remain valid.

Back to Emerson's statement: It is accurate that religion (as distinguished from Christianity) is often afraid of science. Why? Because religion claims to have everything figured out in an epistemological belief-system, allegedly derived from particular interpretations of a bible-book, and theological theories formulated by ecclesiastical authorities. Religion can, by its self-imposed ignorance, "commit suicide"; but genuine Christian faith comprised of participation in the eternal life (Jn. 14:6; I Jn. 5:12) of Jesus Christ is incapable of succumbing to self-willed repudiation of life, i.e. self-murder or suicide.

GRACE HAS NO CONTINGENCIES

I recently read this one-line "zinger" meme from Mike Q. Daniel: "God's activity *for you* is never contingent on your activity *for Him.*" That statement is worthy of pondering and amplification. Grace is God's activity – God in action in accord with His character. God's activity of grace toward us is never contingent on human action to please Him ... never contingent on our failure to act on His behalf ... never contingent on our accumulated acts of righteousness ... never contingent on our diminished sinning ... never contingent on our maturity level ... never contingent on our purity of love for Him or for others.

A contingency implies a necessary pre-condition to God's grace-action. God's love and grace are unconditioned. Any pre-existing necessary action by human beings alleged to serve as an exigency to incentivize or leverage God's grace-action is false. Nothing else must transpire or take place before God will act in grace. The "if ... then" contingency and exigency is invalid when applied to God's grace: IF this or that occurs; IF we do this or don't do that; THEN God will act in grace. NO! God's action will always and only be the action of grace. Nothing done by man will cause grace to happen, or keep such from flowing from God.

God does what He does in grace, because He is Who He is in His character, nature and Being. God's grace is never subject to chance or circumstance or subject to the doing or undoing of another. God will act as the God that He is despite whatever else might occur. God's grace was inaugurated and first manifested in the incarnation of His Son, Jesus Christ: "Grace and truth were realized through Jesus Christ" (Jn. 1:17). His grace continues to be enacted via His Son, Jesus, and empowered by the Holy Spirit. There is nothing that we can do, or not do, that will cause God to refrain from manifesting His grace action or to cause God to manifest His grace in greater measure.

JUNE 28

"BECAUSE I'M YOURS"

Daniel Montgomery and Timothy Paul Jones co-authored a book entitled, *PROOF: Finding Freedom Through the Intoxicating Joy of Irresistible Grace,* published in 2014. In the book, Timothy Jones tells the most captivating story of taking his eight-year old adopted daughter to Disney World in Orlando, Florida. The backstory is that her previous adoptive parents had not been equitable, and rejected her by refusing to let her go, even when the biological siblings went to the Magic Kingdom. Her personal understanding for the slight was that she had not been good enough to be given the privilege of taking such a vacation.

Made aware of this past slight, Timothy Paul Jones scheduled the time to take his entire family his wife and three daughters to Disney World. Anticipation ran high, especially since the other two daughters had been to the Magic Kingdom previously and had photographs of the oversized mouse and duck as memories. The unexpected reaction, however, came from the new adopted daughter. She began to "act out" in selfish and sinful ways: lying, stealing, insults meant to hurt her sisters. What was happening? Those who have experienced hurtful rejection, often attempt to set-up a situation for rejection because they know by experience how to deal with a rejective scenario.

Sitting his daughter down, Mr. Jones asked her why she was doing what she was doing. She immediately blurted out, "You're not going to take me to Disney World, are you?" He assured her that they were going to take a family vacation, and she was an important part of the family. When the time came, they all went to the Magic Kingdom and enjoyed the time together. At the end of the first day, Timothy Jones asked his thoroughly exhausted daughter, "So, how was your first day at Disney World?" Through tears she answered, "Daddy, I finally got to go to Disney World. But it wasn't because I was good; it's because I'm yours."

"IT'S ON THE HOUSE!"

There was always the din of loud and boisterous conversation in the neighborhood pub, and it tended to get louder as the evening wore on. One of the local yokels who often hung out in the pub was having a birthday; and, to celebrate such the pub-keeper raised a pint of lager and bellowed out an announcement in a loud voice for all to hear, "The next one's on the house, to celebrate Joe's birthday." The inn erupted with the noise of exuberance at the announcement that the next drink was free of charge, courtesy of the pub-keeper who would be "picking up the tab" and paying for a "round" for everyone in the establishment.

"On the house," is an idiomatic phrase, a metaphorical figure of speech, that became popular in the 1880s and means that the establishment owner or manager is extending the offer of food or drink at no cost to the customers, free of charge or payment to all designated recipients. Such an announced offer is usually well-received by those "in the house," those customers or patrons in the business or establishment on that occasion. Who doesn't want an offer of a free gift? Who would turn down a gratuitous opportunity to receive more of the product for which they came to the establishment.

The grace of God in Jesus Christ is "on the house," so to speak. It is free of charge and without possibility of effort or purchase. God has extended to all mankind – everyone "in the house" – the opportunity to participate in His intoxicating grace. "The free gift, the grace of God is through one Man, Jesus Christ, and has abounded to all men" (Rom. 5:15), unto justification of life" (Rom. 5:18). The price has been paid (cf. I Cor. 6:20; 7:23) by Jesus' death on the cross. Who would turn down such a gratuitous opportunity to receive everything necessary to be and function as the humanity God intended? But they do, because religion has illegitimately exacted "strings attached" contingency prices.

JUNE 30

GOD'S WAYS ARE NOT OUR WAYS

The world's ways are so antithetical to God's ways as to be regarded as lame and laughable by Christians, but the world will view God's ways in like manner – laughably absurd and inane. "The natural man does not understand spiritual things" (I Cor. 2:14), for "the minds of the unbelieving are blinded" (II Cor. 4:4). Man's way is the humanistic approach of seeing a problem and attempting to solve the problem by human ingenuity and invention. God's way for man is to see in every problem a possibility and opportunity of God's grace in action in ways beyond man's capability, as we allow Him to act on our behalf.

God speaks through the prophet Isaiah, "For My thoughts are not your thoughts, nor are your ways My ways," declares the Lord. "For as the heavens are higher than the earth, so are My ways higher than your ways and My thoughts than your thoughts" (Isa. 55:8,9). There is a definite operational dichotomy between the ways of man and the ways of God. Fallen human beings assume that they are "independent beings," sufficient for all their own needs and solutions by means of their own human effort and performance. "There is a way that seems right unto man, but the end thereof is death" (Prov. 14:12; 16:25).

God's way for mankind is that human beings might recognize they are derivative creatures meant to be dependent on God as they allow for the receptivity of God's activity through them, i.e., "by grace through faith" (cf. Eph. 2:8). It is not what we can do, but what we allow God to do. Human potential as contrasted with divine sufficiency (II Cor. 3:5). Christians must realize that it is an exercise in futility to attempt to impose God's ways upon the world and expect fallen humanity to perform the ways of God via religious rules and regulations of behavior modification, when they do not have the spiritual provision of the indwelling Christ and the dynamic of God's grace.

JULY 1

JUST BECAUSE YOU CAN, DOESN'T MEAN YOU SHOULD

Twice in his epistle to the Corinthians, Paul explains that just because something might be lawful or permissible doesn't mean that it is expedient or beneficial. The context of I Cor. 6:12 seems to indicate that "Just because it is not illegal to sue your neighbor doesn't mean that there are not good reasons to refrain from doing so" and "Just because it is not illegal to have sexual relationships outside of marriage doesn't mean that there are not consequences for so doing." The context of I Cor. 10:23 seems to indicate that "Just because it is lawful and permissible to eat meat sacrificed to idols doesn't mean you should flaunt your liberty when your freedom causes offence to your neighbor."

Just because an activity is permissible doesn't mean that it is the most loving thing to do, or that it expresses the character of God's Love in so doing. And even more so, just because it is a permissible activity as adjudged by the world, or even the church, doesn't mean that it is an activity God had purposed for you to engage in, that it is God's purposed and intended will to manifest Himself in that action through you, that Jesus desires to manifest Himself in you in that manner. Just because it is an open option doesn't mean you ought to do so, or that it would be God's *modus operandi* for you to be engaged in that activity.

After spending forty days fasting in the desert, Jesus was tempted by the devil. The temper said to the hungry Jesus, "Command these stones become bread" (Matt. 4:3). Jesus could have done so but knew His sustenance was from God, not bread. On the pinnacle of the temple, Satan tempted Jesus to throw Himself down as a publicity stunt. Jesus could have done so with no harm to Himself, but He was not out to put the Lord to the test. On a high mountain, the "ruler of the world" offered Jesus all the kingdoms of the world if He would but worship him. Knowing that was not what He should do, He commanded him to depart.

JULY 2

JESUS DID NOT CONFORM TO EXPECTATIONS

Most historians would agree that Jesus was a man who lived in the first century in the area of Palestine. It is well attested that Jesus was not well received by the Jewish leaders, who were allowed by the occupying Roman government to self-govern themselves in the area of Judea. They saw him as a threat to their religious system because He repeatedly challenged their religious rules and rituals and claimed to be the Son of God, even equal to God. Eventually, the Jewish religious leaders appealed to the hated Roman authorities to eliminate Jesus, using the trumped charge that Jesus claimed to be King, which wasn't all that offensive to the Jews because they were expecting a Messiah-King, but they knew it would incite the Romans who believed that Caesar alone was supreme King. Pilate, the Roman procurator, sentenced Jesus to death and retributively hung a sign over Jesus' head on the cross which read, "King of the Jews" (Matt. 27:37; Mk. 15:26; Lk. 23:38). In protest the Jews declared, "We have no king but Caesar" (Jn. 19:12-15), sucking up to the Roman government in their intense desire to get rid of Jesus, and preserve their religious enclave in Palestine.

After His resurrection from the dead, Jesus did nothing to usurp Roman governmental power; but the Christ-ones (Acts 11:26) who went forth and assembled as the *ecclesia* in Jesus' name continued without reservation to proclaim, "We have no King but Jesus!" and His kingdom is not of this world, for He reigns as Lord in us. They went on to exclaim, "This Jesus is risen from the dead and continues to live in Spirit-form" (cf. I Cor. 15:45). "He is the Christ, the Son of the living God" (Matt. 16:16), the Messiah expected by the Jews, and the divine Savior of all mankind by having taken the sins of all men and women of every race and nation. Much to the chagrin of the Jewish leaders, they had not rid the world of their nemesis, as Jesus continued to be lauded as the Messiah-King, and His life manifested in Christian followers.

A MAGIC BULLET

There are people who are always looking for a quick-fix "magic bullet" that will cure all of their problems. This catholicon quest for a cure-all remedy that provides a panacea for all of life's problems is hidden in plain sight. The term "magic bullet" was first used by German biochemist Paul Ehrlich (1854-1915), who received the Nobel Prize in physiology and medicine in 1908. Initially, he was using the term to describe an antibiotic drug to treat syphilis. Later, he used the term to explain the human body's immune response to various chemotherapy drugs in the treatment of carcinogenic diseases.

More generally, human beings have long sought solutions to previously unsolvable problems (physiological, social, and spiritual) by seeking a quick-fix "magic bullet" remedy without any deleterious side-effects. The Christian gospel explains that the cure for the deeper and more profound problems of humankind is to be found in the mystery of the Person of Jesus Christ, the Son of God, the God-man, the one mediator between God and man. The mystery (Greek *mysterion*) refers to something once hidden and unknown but now revealed and intended to be known by all, but not to be considered as "magical."

The apostle Paul wrote of "the mystery which has been kept secret for long ages past, but now is manifested" (Rom. 16:25,26); "God's wisdom in a mystery, the hidden wisdom which God predestined before the ages to our glory" (I Cor. 2:8); "the mystery which for ages has been hidden in God who created all things" (Eph. 3:9); "the mystery which has been hidden from the past ages and generations, but now has been manifested to the saints" (Col. 1:26). The content of the mystery "once concealed, now revealed" is "Christ Himself" (Col. 2:2; 4:3; Eph. 3:4), the good news of the gospel, "the riches of the glory of the mystery, which is Christ in you, the hope of glory" (Col. 1:27).

JULY 4

WHY DID JESUS HAVE TO DIE?

To attempt to explain the necessity and benefits of Jesus' death on a cross on Mt. Calvary has always proven a difficult subject to explain in human thought-categories. Christian thinkers through the history of Christianity have formulated numerous atonement theories, and unfortunately have often made those man-made theories into required acceptance for orthodox Christian belief. The theories that human theologians have devised to explain the whys and wherefores of "God's ways that are past finding out" (Rom. 11:33 KJV) should remain just what they are – theories of man, while we affirm the historical data that Jesus died on a cross for the sins of mankind.

What we want to avoid in trying to explain the death of Jesus is to indicate that the desires and objectives of God the Father and God the Son were "at odds" with one another. A popular theory explains that God the Father was full of wrath towards mankind because of human sin, and Jesus the Son volunteered to appease and satisfy the wrath of God the Father by dying as a human in the stead of all human beings, responding with grace instead of wrath. Such a theory must be questioned because it postulates a divide of mind and intent between God the Father and Son, and thus a disunity in the tri-unity of the Trinity.

It is clear that scripture indicates that human sin is connected with death in its various forms (spiritual, behavioral, physical) cf. Gen. 2:7; Rom 5:21; 6:10,23). There were death consequences of human sin that affected all of humanity (Rom. 5:12), and Jesus as the God-man was willing to die a human death to effect the remediation of those consequences. Having died, Jesus rose from the dead to restore divine life in the human spirits of receptive humanity. "By a man came death, and by a man came resurrection from the dead" (I Cor. 15:21). We are best to avoid human explanation beyond the basic facts that God has revealed.

186

GOSPEL SEQUITUR

The Latin word *sequitur* refers to how one thing follows after another, i.e., the logical sequence of statements or conclusions.

Jesus died on the cross to give Himself *FOR US*. Mankind was in the predicament of having rebelled against God, helplessly and hopelessly condemned to death by such transgression. Jesus Christ, the Son of God, operating in God's grace was willing to take the death consequence of sin for all mankind. "Christ died *for* sin once for all, the just *for* the unjust...." (I Pet. 3:18). "While we were yet sinners, Christ died *for* us" (Rom. 5:8).

Jesus rose from the dead to give Himself *TO US*. If Jesus simply paid the price of death for us and then said to mankind, "Now, do a better job next time," it would have been a terrible thing He did. By His resurrection, He gave us the provision of His life. "God has caused us to be born again to a living hope through the resurrection of Jesus Christ from the dead" (I Pet. 1:3). In the spiritual regeneration of being "born again" (Jn. 3:1-6), the very Life of the living Lord Jesus has come to live in us (Col. 1:27).

Jesus died on the cross to give Himself *AS US*. In His death, Jesus did more than simply give His life *for* us; He took us to the cross with Him. "The old man has been crucified with Christ" (Rom. 6:6). "You have died and your life is hid with Christ" (Col. 3:3). Along with Paul we can say, "I have been crucified with Christ; it is no longer I who lives, but Christ lives in me" (Gal. 2:20). "Reckon yourselves to be dead unto sin, but alive unto God in Christ Jesus" (Rom. 6:11).

Jesus rose from the dead to live His life *THROUGH US*. Jesus' death and resurrection were more than just a deposit for future benefits. The living Lord Jesus lives in us and *through* us as Christ-ones. "Christ lives in me" (Gal. 2:20). "For me to live is Christ" (Phil. 1:21). "Christ is my life" (Col. 3:4). "The Life of Jesus is manifested in our mortal bodies" (II Cor. 4:10,11). With Paul, we can say, "I do not presume to speak of anything, except what Christ has accomplished *through* me" (Rom. 15:18).

JULY 6

THE KING REIGNING IN HIS KINGDOM

When Jesus spoke about the kingdom, He wasn't talking about a geographical or ethereal location where people play harps all day and the angels surf on clouds! The three main words of the title are (1) king – Greek word *basileus*, meaning a person who reigns or rules. (2) reign – Greek word *basileuo*, meaning to reign or to rule. (3) kingdom – Greek word *basileion*, meaning where the king is reigning or ruling with royal authority – not the realm or the location of such rule; but the authoritative reign of the King. Where the King is reigning, there is the kingdom; for the King always reigns as Who He is whenever or wherever He is.

The kingdom of God in Jesus Christ is not an organization or institution, like what we call "church" today. It is not a geographic locality or a heavenly placement or even a far-off country in the Middle East, i.e. Israel. Early Christian writers referred to the *autobasileion*, meaning that Jesus is the kingdom "in Himself"; where Jesus (the King) is, there is the kingdom. We could also indicate that Jesus is *autochristianismos*, meaning that where Jesus is, there is Christianity. Christianity is Christ!

The prophetic announcement of the kingdom indicated that it would be "'Not by might nor by power, but by My Spirit,' says the Lord of hosts" (Zech. 4:6). Jesus explained "My kingdom is not of this world" (Jn. 18:26).. The kingdom of Jesus the King is promised to those who love Him (James 2:5), and thus have citizenship in heaven (Phil. 3:20). It has both "already" and "not yet" components: In His earthly ministry, Jesus said, The kingdom is at hand" (Matt. 3:2; 4:17), "The kingdom is in your midst" (Lk. 17:21). Paul said we presently "reign in His (Jesus') righteousness (Rom. 5:17) and life" (Rom. 5:17). There is yet to be the "handing over of the kingdom to God, the Father" (I Cor. 15:24,25), when the kingdom of Christ becomes all in all, and He will reign forever and ever" (Rev. 11:15).

FIELD OF VISION

I had a sudden diminishing of visibility. Therefore, I made an appointment and went to the ophthalmologist to have a series of tests to measure my vision. In the midst of those tests, the doctor got right in front of me and said, "Mr. Fowler, you have had a stroke! I want you to go immediately to the Emergency Room at the hospital down the street." I did so. They performed an MRI on my brain, and it showed two areas of blockage that indicated I had had two strokes. The primary effect of the strokes was the blurring of my peripheral vision. It was (is) like looking through a keyhole, a limited field of vision with fuzzy edges.

As I think about my present physical vision, what concerns me more is that so many people have a worldview that is just as restricted as my physical eyesight. They are looking at the world around them through a narrow tunnel that is framed by the blurred humanistic parameters of their own self-concerns. From this myopic field of vision, they are lacking a full-orbed perspective of all that is transpiring around them and are susceptible to what might enter from the edges of their frame of reference. They are spiritually "blinded" (II Cor. 4:4), so that they are unable to see the full picture of what God has done in Jesus.

We should seek a worldview that has the broadest possible viewpoint and perspective; I want to see the whole panoramic picture of life, to the extent that I am able to do so. If our worldview does not allow for divine action and eternal perspective, then we are seeing ourselves and life around us with a very self-limiting field of vision, failing to see the broad and infinite resources of relational interaction with God and His prepared *ecclesia* community. God's provision of His Son, Jesus Christ, is the corrective prism that provides a full-focused field of vision that gives us the perspective of where we stand in reference to the ultimate purposes and destiny of God.

JULY 8

PERIPATETIC OBVIATION

My pastor, Jerome Marroquin, and I were walking down the street in Istanbul, Turkey. A man came up behind us, wanting to engage us in conversation. He turned out to be a Turkish carpet salesman who wanted us to come into his storefront. His opening gambit was, "Are you an American?" I affirmed that I was an American, and asked him what caused him to question whether I was an American. His comment was, "By the way you walk." I wondered then, and pondered later, what characteristic about the manner in which I was ambulating made it obvious to the man that I might be an American?

Is there a particular way that an American tourist walks, as distinguished from other tourists? Do we amble, stroll, shuffle, push forward confidently to reach our goal? I knew that American tourists could be identified by their baseball caps, their running shoes, their bright clothing, their loud conversation, and their willingness to tip; but, by the way they walk? Transferring this question of "peripatetic obviation" to the way we walk and live as Christians, there are definitely certain traits that should be indicative and noticeable in our Christian behavior. John wrote, "The one who says he abides in Him (Jesus) ought himself to walk in the same manner as He walked" (I Jn. 2:6).

I think John is saying that the walking-behavior of a Christian should be the manifestation of the living Lord Jesus walking out His life and character in our peripatetic behavior. Peripatetic is derived from the Greek word *peripatein*, meaning "to walk around" – a word used almost 100 times in the New Testament. We are not meant to "walk in the darkness of sin and unbelief" (Jn. 8:12; 12:35), but "in the light, as He is in the light" (I Jn. 1:7). Christians are to "walk in newness of life" (Rom. 6:4); not "according to the flesh, but according to the Spirit" (Rom. 8:4; Gal. 5:16); "walking by faith, and not by sight" (II Cor. 5:7).

GRACE AND RELIGION ARE INCOMPATIBLE

Grace is God-given provision; religion is human performance.
Grace is new and original; religion is counterfeit and stale.
Grace is dynamic and alive; religion is static and dead.
Grace is joyously unpredictable; religion is boringly predictable.
Grace soars like an eagle; religion plummets like a rock.
Grace accepts people where they are; religion is judgmental.
Grace is free to go where He wills; religion is conformity.
Grace exhibits love to all; religion loathes what is different.
Grace always accentuates Jesus; religion uses the idea of Jesus.
Grace is above all systems; religion is always systematized.
Grace touches the eternal; religion is always here and now.
Grace is open freedom; religion is slavery to the mundane.
Grace is reality lived out; religion is hypocritical play-acting.
Grace is always relational; religion is rule-based.
Grace is concern for others; religion is control of others.
Grace exists to serve others; religion seeks its own advantage.
Grace unites us in loving fellowship; religion is divisive.
Grace frees us to be unique; religion demands we conform.
Grace is open-ended; religion is hierarchical and authoritative.
Grace is broad and universal; religion is narrow institutionalism.
Grace is inclusive and encompasses all; religion is exclusive.
Grace allows people to be themselves; religion boxes people up.
Grace is liberty to explore; religion binds people in ritual.
Grace appreciates diversity; religion demands distinctives.
Grace allows for new options; religion conserves the old ways.
Grace promotes unity and oneness; religion fosters conflict.
Grace encourages personal faith; religion quenches individuality.
Grace functions by God's giftedness; religion submits to leaders.
Grace brings one through suffering; religion seeks deliverance.
Grace encourages awe and reverence; religion desires ecstasy.
Grace generates righteousness; religion focuses on right belief.
Grace expresses God's character; religion is a façade of morality.
Grace is God in action; religion is the dysfunctionality of man.

JULY 10

GRACE: FOREIGN TO RELIGION

Grace is a Person; religion is principles and propositions
Grace is the living Lord Jesus; religion is legal justification
Grace is a relationship; religion is rules and regulations
Grace is relational community; religion is educational content
Grace is the saving life of Christ; religion is specified laws of conduct
Grace is liberating; religion is restrictive and oppressive
Grace has eternal purpose; religion is temporal utilitarianism
Grace seeks a person's highest good; religion uses and abuses people.
Grace is edifying growth in Christ; religion beats a person down
Grace is the dynamic activity of God; religion is the disciplines of man
Grace is divine energizing; religion is demanding effort
Grace is an adventure; religion is a dead-end venture.
Grace is God's doing; religion is man's doing and performance.
Grace is His exciting life; religion is the slow death of monotony.
Grace is moving through the trial; religion says "get me out of this!"
Grace is God's sufficiency; religion is man's best systems.
Grace is God's invitation; religion is human institution
Grace is spiritual empowerment; religion is human energy.
Grace is conjoined with truth; religion traffics in propaganda
Grace has a context of character; religion is characterized by power
Grace demonstrates God's love; religion desires man's esteem
Grace seeks an open conduit; religion demands commitment
Grace is open-ended; religion seeks prescribed parameters.
Grace is inexhaustible; religion will leave you exhausted.
Grace is Person to person; religion is participation in the organization
Grace is the loving heart of God; religion demands the loyalty of men.
Grace is "the hound of heaven"; religion hounds one to participate
Grace provides the resources of life; religion seeks your resources.
Grace is abundant supply; religion wants you to supply its needs.
Grace is individualized for you; religion is mass-produced conformity
Grace produces overcomers in Christ; religion produces burn-out.
Grace is God's productivity; religion is human programs
Grace is Jesus at work in you; religion is you working for Jesus.
Grace is unconditioned; religion motivates by obligations.
Grace is God's provision of empowerment; religion says, "Just do it!"
Grace is God's doing; religion is "go, go, go; do, do, do for Jesus."

FAITH DISTINCT FROM BELIEF

Quite aware that "faith" and "belief" are translated from the same Greek word *pistis* in the New Testament, it must be noted that they are linguistically differentiated. Latin differentiated between *fides* and *credo*; similar (but not the same) to the distinction being made here:

Faith is receptivity of God's activity; belief is assent to accuracies.
Faith is acceptance of God's grace; belief is adherence to the teaching.
Faith is dynamic dependency; belief is static dogmatization.
Faith accepts the unknown; belief wants precise explanation.
Faith is nourished by doubt; belief is averse to doubt.
Faith can coincide with unknowing; belief tries to have all the answers.
Faith can accept silence; belief talks and talks to convey its principles.
Faith is openness to the Person of Jesus; belief is "just the facts ma'am!"
Faith is relational bonding; belief is recitation of propositions.
Faith is a choice to be a conduit; belief is convinced of its correctness.
Faith says, "Yes, Lord! I accept Your way; belief argues, "yes, but....."
Faith takes formation as God's character; belief is formulated in dogma.
Faith is availability to God's ability; belief is affirmation of factual data.
Faith is individualized; belief demands corporate conformity.
Faith is a personal matter; belief can be capsulized in a creed.
Faith is between you and God; belief can be evaluated by commitment.
Faith hangs on for the ride; belief wants everything mapped out.
Faith is trusting the Truth; belief says, "tell me the truth."
Faith says "teach me Your ways"; belief wants systematic theology.
Faith is forever teachable; belief seeks to "get it all figured out."
Faith receives what God has for us: belief determines what is correct.
Faith allows for tolerant diversity; belief demands that all be the same.
Faith is focused on practical living; belief is assembled ideology.
Faith often resides in uncertainty; belief cannot tolerate uncertainty.
Faith allows God to be made real in men; belief finds reality in ideas.
Faith is not cause and effect; belief wants reasons and promises.
Faith knows it is beyond human logic; belief wants apologetic answers.
Faith is willing to take risks; belief wants guarantees of outcomes.
Faith lets God work supernaturally; belief looks to natural solutions.
Faith never seeks credit; belief wants recognition for what it has done.
Faith relies on God's righteousness; belief wants to know what is right.

JULY 12

HOW, THEN, DO WE SET OUR COURSE?

This question is not unlike the question that Francis Schaeffer posed in his popular book, *How Should We Then Live?* published in 1976. Our focus is simply to consider the choices a Christian has to orient their course of action in everyday life:

(1) We might choose in accord with our own want-to desires; these are the fleshly patterns of our selfish and sinful desires. This is what I want to do – what I find enjoyable and satisfying

(2) We might make a choice in accord with the best scientific evidence. When faced with the scientific data about the Corona-19 virus in 2020 many chose to disregard such and choose their own political inclinations.

(3) We might make a choice that is in accord with political pundits who are telling us what to do – those shouting the loudest with the biggest megaphone.

(4) Some will gauge their choices in accord with the morality standards of the community they are part of – this is what the majority of our community has determined to be right and wrong; just follow the moral majority.

(5) Some will attempt to choose in accord with their inner moral compass – the natural law of a built-in moral barometer. C.S. Lewis called this natural intuition or inclination of what is right, "the Tao," as in the Chinese religion of Taoism.

(6) There are always some who choose in accord with the religious persuasions of what they've been taught is "right," but the religious right sometimes has some very narrow and rigid restrictions of behavioral interpretation

(7) Our choice might be in accord with an emotional mob mentality. When correctness is determined by consensus, and everybody's doing it, the "might makes right" principle kicks in.

(8) A final option might be in accord with what we have heard from the inner voice of Jesus, the Shepherd. "My sheep hear My voice" (Jn. 10:16). This is the direction and leading of the Holy Spirit (Rom. 8:14), the Spirit of the indwelling Christ.

LOVING OTHERS AS OURSELVES

I read this statement in a church bulletin: "We intentionally love others as ourselves by social distancing and wearing masks." As far as it goes, the statement has a degree of truth within it, as we intentionally avoid transmission of the coronavirus by social distancing and wearing masks. But as it stands, there is a diminishing and weakening of the biblical instruction to "love others as ourselves" (Lk. 10:27) when it is framed in simple social graces and health decorum. Loving others is over-simplified when we view such as simply NOT doing something, refraining and avoiding action that would be harmful to another.

Many of the religions of the world have a negative form of the "golden rule" within their ethical admonitions. It goes like this: "Don't do to others what you do not want them to do to you." Such a call to avoidance of negative action, based on a concern for avoiding any adverse or harmful action coming upon oneself, certainly short-changes the positive and active reality of God's LOVE expressed to others for their sake.

The new covenant version of the "Golden Rule" necessarily involves the positive expression of God's *agape* love. "Do unto others as you would have them do unto you" (Matt. 7:12; Lk. 6;31). "The love of God has been poured out into our hearts by the Holy Spirit who has been given to us" (Rom. 5:5) and expressed via the "fruit of the Spirit" (Gal. 5:22). Such expression of divine love implies that loving action for others is only actuated by the grace of God. The "Golden Rule" does not inculcate more human performance effort, but is God's love expressed by God's grace – purposed love for others, with no thought of what I get out of it, no thought of self-concern or self-interest – what's in it for me, or how will it affect me. *Agape* love is concerned for others, not for ourselves, including the avoidance of negative effects coming our way.

JULY 14

"DON'T GO BACK!"

One of the predominant themes of the New Testament, of the new covenant paradigm, is that it tells us of all we have in Jesus that we didn't have previously and warns us not to revert, not to go back to the religious rule-keeping that kept us in the slavery of performance. Having been set free and given "rest" from all religious performance in Jesus' provision of grace, why would anyone consider returning to the back-breaking labor of chain-gang slavery. It is ridiculous to consider going from the superior to the inferior. Yet, many look back with the false memories of nostalgia, longing for "the good ol' days."

"The good ol' days" weren't as good as you might remember them to have been, despite the chorus on the side singing, "Gimme that ol'-time religion." What you thought you enjoyed about the past is no longer there. Law-based religion is *kaput*, done, ended, *fini* (Rom. 10:4). "Set your minds on things above; where you have died, and your life is hidden with Christ in God" (Col. 3:2). Now is the time to get to know Him, to "abide in Him" (Jn. 15:4), to settle-in, to make yourself at home in Him. Forget the miserable sand-storms of Egypt (or Oklahoma), and begin to enjoy "the riches you have in Christ Jesus" (Eph. 2:7; 3:8).

Rudyard Kipling once wrote, "There is no reason to look back when you have so much to look forward to." In like manner, C. S. Lewis wrote, "there are far better things ahead, than any we have left behind." The past is "water under the bridge." Paul spoke of "forgetting what lies behind, and pressing forward toward the goal of the prize of the upward call of God in Christ Jesus" (Phil. 3:13,14). Looking back, or dreaming of going back, is like grieving in the cemetery, in the "valley of the dry bones" (Ezek. 37:1-14) and is of no assistance in moving forward in the glorious land of God's grace. Looking back to the "has-been mirage" will only serve to cause you to drift backwards.

THE GLORY OF THE LORD

This biblical subject has been mangled by misunderstanding through the centuries of Jewish and Christian interpretation, and this is likely due to its being beyond human explanation, explication and description. In the Holy of Holies of the tabernacle and temple the glory of the Lord shown with the magnificence and splendor of God's divine presence – too bright for human eyes to appreciate. Not unlike the natural grandeur and beauty of a glorious sunrise or sunset, the glory of the Lord shines beyond human replication or explanation. The manifestation of the presence of the very Being, nature, and character of God leaves us overwhelmed in awe and reverence.

Because God's glory comes only from His own presence, the prophet tells us that "God does not give His glory to another" (Isa. 42:8; 48:11). God expresses His glory through His creation; "the heavens declare the glory of God" (Ps.19:1), and desires to express His glory more explicitly through His human creatures, "created for My glory" (Isa. 43:7); but it must be derived from Him. When we get a glimpse of the brightness of God's glory, we fall down in reverence and worship, sometimes bowled over by His awesomeness, singing "Worthy are you, our Lord and our God, to receive glory and honor and power" (Rev. 4:10,11).

For centuries God held back the full splendor and grandeur of His glory (though Moses caught a glimpse of it; cf. II Cor. 4:12-16) until He sent the full revelation of His Being in His Son, Jesus Christ. "God revealed the mystery (once concealed; now revealed), which is Christ in you, the hope of glory" (Col. 1:27). Jesus is not just the hope of going to heaven someday, but the expectation of our being the vessels of the glorious manifestation of God's glorious character when His very presence has entered our spirit and become our life as Christ-ones, able now to fulfill our destiny as human beings "created for His glory" (Isa. 43:7).

JULY 16

IT IS EASY TO "TALK THE TALK"

There are many who call themselves "Christians," who have walked the aisle of a church, or signed on a membership card, and enrolled as a "Christian" in the church. Many remain ignorant, however, of the essential internal spiritual reality of the living Lord Jesus dwelling in and living through a receptive individual. Many church members have, over time, learned enough of the Christian religious vocabulary, the distinctive "Christianese" chatter of their particular subset or denomination, to navigate the insider interactions and perhaps even to become a leader (a pastor, an elder, or a deacon) in their local church.

The average Christian (if there is such a creature) likely understands the basic historical background of Christian thought, that Jesus was born in Bethlehem, died on Calvary, and rose from the dead on that first Easter morning; but their practical Christian understanding is a mile wide and a quarter of an inch deep. They have learned how to be a religious chameleon, adapting their religious conversation to their surroundings. They have learned how to "talk the talk" of the group they are with, but all they have are multi-hued words about the real Word of God (Jn. 1:1,14) – Jesus-talk that is of no practical benefit.

The Christian gospel is not simply a belief-system framed in a *credo,* a statement of faith that one assents to, espouses, and discusses *ad nauseum.* The "good news" is the dynamic living reality of a Savior who died and rose three days later in resurrection, making Himself available to individuals who will receive Him by faith. The living Lord Jesus, the life-giving Spirit (I Cor. 15:45) becomes our very life, our *sola Christos* reason for being a Christ-one. The apostle Paul explained, "For me to live is Christ" (Phil. 1:21); "It is no longer I who lives, but Christ lives in me" (Gal. 2:20). A genuine Christ-one cannot just talk the talk but must allow for the out-living of the Christ-life.

WHY DO YOU GO TO CHURCH?

I am aware that there are many readers who do not attend the services of a particular local institutional church. But to those who do attend the assembly of the saints, regardless of the label on the sign outside, the question I am asking is "Why do you make the effort to attend the gathering of Christ-ones as they regularly assemble at a particular place and time?" The answers to such a question vary greatly. Some will admit that it is a habit that they have maintained since they were young. This is just something that Christians are supposed to do; there is a sense of "ought to" and necessity. "I've been a member there for many years; those are my people!"

Others may approach their answer to church involvement sociologically. God made all human beings as social creatures. "No man is an island" (John Donne). We all need the mutual interaction; we need each other. There is a God-given need among humans to belong to a group or a tribe. There's a sense of excitement in getting together with others of like-mind. Many people like to get "amped up" with the music, in which case church attendance is not unlike going to a music concert venue to hear the musicians. "There is a sense of excitement as everyone rocks and sways and claps together as they sing.

Some might be honest enough to admit that they assemble together because they want to be seen by others; they are there to maintain a social image as a respectable person in the community where they live. But I would hope that there are some who recognize they are part of something bigger than themselves in the "Body of Christ," the collective manifestation of the life and character of Jesus Christ on earth. In the process of assembling ourselves together, we also encourage each other (Heb. 3:12,13) to stand firm (Eph. 6:13,14) in the out-living of the Christ-life in the midst of the hostile world in which we all live.

JULY 18

FINISHING SCHOOL

The young girl was coming of age – that age when socially respectable parents of sufficient means send their children, especially young girls, to "finishing school" to learn to act socially respectable with proper cultural etiquette and social graces. Though they have been carefully trained in social manners within the instruction of their child-training, there are some "finishing touches" that need to be inculcated before these young ladies are sufficiently prepped to debut in fashionable society with the charm and gloss of proper socialites, ready to begin their social-climbing techniques of social betterment.

Some people seem to view the instruction of the church as a "finishing school" wherein we are learning the proprieties of Christian behavior and putting on the "finishing touches" of what it means to be a good respectable Christian. Their selection of a "finishing school" may have been done quite deliberately, with an eye to the level of social involvement they want to participate. Such perspective seems to overlook, however, the definitive comment of Jesus as He was dying on the cross, "It is finished!" "There is nothing more to be done! All is accomplished! The price has been paid for the redemption of mankind. A finished work!"

In His redemptive work on the cross, Jesus completed everything that needed to be accomplished *for* us objectively. Our response of faithful receptivity to His sufficient sacrifice is the invitation for Jesus to enter into our spirit in regeneration and commence His continuing work of grace *in* us, subjectively. The sanctification work of the Spirit of the living Lord Jesus, the process of allowing the holy character of the Holy One within to be manifested in our behavior, will come to fruition and maturity just as surely as did His redemptive work of dying in our place on the cross. "He who began a good work in you will perfect it until the day of Christ Jesus" (Phil. 1:6).

JESUS IS THE ONLY SIGNIFICANCE

Different people attach differing significance to different events and circumstances in their lives. What is important to one may be totally irrelevant and of no importance to another. These priorities of importance reveal that the meaning that we attach to differing circumstances of our lives establishes the significance that will determine our investiture of time and energy in those endeavors. Some people have determined that they themselves are of utmost significance, and they want to be seen as significant by others, "Look at me; I can do this; I can do that; I have accomplished great things." They come across as narcissistic!

From a spiritual perspective, there is nothing that will ever have the degree of significance in our life as does the reality of Jesus Christ and His work for us and in us. In comparison to the reality of Jesus, everything else is insignificant, because there is nothing else that has the eternal significance as does the only One who IS eternal life. 'I am the way, the truth, and the life" (Jn. 14:6), Jesus explained to His disciples, "no one comes to the Father, but by Me." "He that has the Son, has the Life; He that does not have the Son, does not have life," the apostle John wrote decades later (I John 5:12). The life of Jesus is my significance!

Let me declare unashamedly that Jesus is the only significance in my life. This is not because I have ascribed to Jesus a place of personal priority or significance. It is because Jesus IS my life (Gal. 2:20; Col. 3:4). Let everything else run through the sieve like water; Jesus is what remains when everything of considered significance has passed through and been found less important. Jesus should be the Christian's sole *raison d'etre* (reason for being). Paul explained "For me to live is Christ" (Phil. 1:21). "Christ is my life" (Col. 3:4). Paul declared without hesitation, "I am not ashamed of the gospel, for it is the power of God for salvation to everyone who believes" (Rom. 1:16).

JULY 20

ON BEING A WRITER

I did not aspire to be a writer. It was not a goal or career that I set out to engage in. For over fifty years, I did not think of myself as a writer or an author. Still don't! I have struggled with being a writer; it doesn't come easy; it is difficult and laborious; random ideas come to mind when I am awakening in the morning. I don't need an alarm clock; my thoughts awaken me. I pay attention to those initial thoughts. They often become the subject at hand for that day's writing. Do I know in advance what I am going to say in my writing? No, I let it flow together in accord with my mind's thinking. But this is not the same as *theopneustos* (II Tim. 3:16), God-breathed divine revelation of scripture; I do not have a clue how that works. Apparently, it is just listening to God in obedience – an example of "My sheep hear My voice" (Jn.10:3,4).

When I had more than thirty books commercially available, I was forced to admit, "I must qualify to be a writer". Throughout my fifty years as a local pastor preparing to share a message the following Sunday morning, I wrote out an outline of thoughts on what I was going to share. Writing out speaking notes to keep one's thoughts together in a sermon is far different than writing literary text meant to be printed and read as pertinent and informative by readers. In written materials, the grammar and punctuation must provide the pause in thought and change in direction, whereas speakers use a plethora of strange markings to remind themselves where they are going to pause and make emphasis. For me, writing is a combination of a creative art form, a personal discipline, a life-long development of vocabulary, constant learning of grammatical propriety, having a message of the indwelling Christ-life that burns on my heart, and the obedience of "listening under" God's direction of thought by the Holy Spirit. I can certainly appreciate the explanation of being a writer made by Flannery O'Connor, "I write because I don't know what I think until I read what I say."

A REASONED FAITH

If a person has been reasoned into Christian faith by the persuasion of logical human argumentation, some wise person may eventually come along and reason that person out of their reasoned faith by a more persuasive argument against Christ. If, however, a person has come to a personal relationship with the living Lord Jesus Christ by the convincing and convicting work of God's Holy Spirit (Jn. 16:8-11), employing the revelation-insight whereby "we know the things freely given to us by God, not in words taught by human wisdom, but in those taught by the Spirit, combining spiritual reality with spiritual words" (I Cor. 2:12,13), then we know that we know the living Triune God; and no one will ever be able to reason us out of such faith.

This is not to make an argument for unreasoned or irrational faith, for when we know that we know the living Lord Jesus, we should still "be ready to make a defense to everyone who asks you to give an account for the hope that is in you, yet with gentleness and reverence" (II Pet. 3:15). Apologetics, however, does not necessarily imply a rationalistic and epistemological-based argumentation of Bible proof-text evidences combined with human logic syllogisms supporting our argument. It will always come down to the necessity of the illuminating revelation of the Spirit drawing a prepared soul into union with Jesus.

Those who would argue for an anti-rational faith are ill-advised, because faith is not necessarily an enemy of human reason. The more we can learn about how the world formulates it arguments, the more we become discerning of how to differentiate between worldly thought and spiritual thinking. We can thereby formulate our gospel defense in a Spirit-empowered explanation of how the living Lord Jesus is the adequate answer to all the questions the world poses, but it is "God's wisdom in a mystery spiritually appraised" (I Cor. 2) by one in whom the Spirit of Christ lives.

JULY 22

JUST BECAUSE ...

... it is in print doesn't make it gospel.

... you can afford it doesn't mean you should purchase it.

... it is lawful,doesn't mean that it is expedient.

... you can doesn't mean you should.

... the preacher says it doesn't make it truth.

... you want something doesn't mean you need it.

... you're offered something doesn't mean you should take it.

... people are starving doesn't mean you can feed them all.

... there is a problem doesn't mean you have to solve it.

... he says he loves you doesn't mean he knows what love is.

... I say so doesn't make it so (unless you're the parent).

... it took you longer doesn't mean you failed.

... I disagree with you doesn't mean I don't like you.

... I'm not talking right now doesn't mean I'm angry with you.

... everything is different doesn't mean anything has changed.

... someone carries the burden well doesn't mean it isn't heavy.

... everybody else is doing it doesn't mean you should do it too.

... expedience is the world's way doesn't mean it should be ours

... something is free doesn't mean you should traffic on gratuity.

... her eyes don't tear doesn't mean her heart doesn't cry.

... it is doesn't mean it should be.

... your past was not perfect doesn't mean your future can't be.

... something ends doesn't mean it should not have been.

... you demand I do it doesn't mean I'm obliged to do so.

... I am controversial doesn't make me a disagreeable person.

... a person smiles all the time doesn't mean their life is perfect.

... God isn't visible doesn't mean His character isn't visible.

... Jesus is Lord DOES mean you can entrust your life to Him.

... Jesus is the Life DOES mean that there is life in nothing else.

... Jesus is the Savior,DOES mean that He is the remedy to sin.

... Jesus is the Light DOES mean that He exposes all darkness.

... Jesus is the Way DOES mean that other ways are dead-ends.

GOD'S ACTION – MAN'S ACTION

Many have noted that these daily readings have a repetitive emphasis on "what God does, as opposed to what man does" in the Christian life, i.e., God's action instead of man's action. Unashamedly and unabashedly, we emphasize God's grace-action in His Son, Jesus Christ, and repudiate the humanistic emphasis of human action and effort as being the means of human problem-solving and social betterment. Some have conjectured that such an emphasis is consistent with (or equivalent to) the Augustinian-Calvinist theological emphasis, which has a similar emphasis on God's action taking precedence over man's action.

But the deterministic paradigm of theology that is the foundation of Augustinian thinking (4th century), and later Calvinist formulation of theology (16th century), commences with different premises and proceeds with a different perspective than do these readings. Augustine speculated that the sin of Adam (Gen. 3) was seminally transmitted to every subsequent human generation by a process of "original sin" that postulated the core corruption of humanness involving the depravity of all human function and activity and the denial of the efficacy of any human freedom that might respond to God's grace-action.

These readings are not premised on such a deterministic paradigm, but commence with a theological perspective that human beings are spiritually derivative creatures, with the freedom to receptively derive either from "the spirit that works in the sons of disobedience" (Eph. 2:2) or the Spirit of the living Lord Jesus within the spirit of the human person (cf. Rom. 8:9). All humanity was negatively affected spiritually by the sin of Adam (Rom. 5:12-21) but have the response-ability to receive the living Lord Jesus made available to all mankind by the grace of God. By faith, the human choice of receptivity to God's grace-activity in Jesus Christ, we become Christ-ones.

JULY 24

"IF I PERISH, I PERISH"

Esther was a Jewish princess who won a beauty contest to become queen to Persian King Ahaseurus. Esther's uncle, Mordecai, was her guardian and advised her that Haman, the chief advisor, had asked the king to destroy all the Jews in the kingdom by genocide. Although required to seek permission to approach the king directly, Esther determined to enter his throne-room to plead for her people. "If I perish, I perish" (Esth. 4:16) was her resigned sigh. The king was appalled at the news of such a plot to kill her people and ordered the one who planned such be put to death on the gallows. The Jewish people celebrate their reprieve in the Feast of Purim every year.

Jesus was a unique person of history. The Son of God became a human man (Jn. 1:14), willing to forego the privilege and power of deity to live completely as a receptive human individual. "I do nothing of my own initiative," Jesus explained, "The Father abiding in Me does His works" (Jn. 14:10). When it was obvious that the Jewish leaders were conspiring with the Romans to put Him to death, He likened the situation to a seed being planted in the earth in order to later bring forth life (Jn. 12:24-26). "Like a lamb being led to slaughter" (Isa. 53:7), Jesus willingly submitted to wrongful death to serve as the Mashiach of mankind.

Dietrich Bonhoeffer was a German pastor when the Third Reich, the Nazis led by Adolf Hitler, assumed power in Germany. He was a vocal critic of the Nazi attempt to control the church, and their plans to exterminate the Jewish people across Europe. For his dissent, he was imprisoned by the Nazis; but such punishment gave him better access to assassinate Hitler. Joining others, they attempted to kill the Führer, but their attempt failed. For his part in the attempted assassination, Bonhoeffer was put to death in the Flossenburg concentration camp on April 9, 1945, just prior to the Allied liberation of the death camp fourteen days later.

YOUR CHRISTIAN RESPONSIBILITY

The world-system is always concerned about your performance responsibilities; i.e. what you do or don't do and how that fulfills the expectations that your authority figures have established for you. When you become part of the church, the Christian community that you identify with, there are still authority figures that have expectations of what you need to do (or refrain from doing) to fulfill your responsibilities as a Christian in that particular community. The do-right; do no wrong ethics of many religious communities can be very demanding as well as restrictive, to the point of being legalistic responsibilities.

Where is the freedom in all this – the advertised "freedom in Christ?" Is it simply freedom to conform or not to conform? If the gospel is the gospel of grace, where does responsibility fit into such? Christ-ones still have freedom of choice; and this entails a response-ability to what God is doing in our lives, but not necessarily the responsibility of performance as inculcated by religion. Many have been taught that it is their responsibility to share the gospel with the world, and they feel obligated to take the gospel to Africa. W. Ian Thomas explained that "Christians are not required to respond to the needs of the world around us, but only to respond to the Lordship of Jesus Christ in our lives."

Gregory A. Boyd noted, "Our central responsibility as Christians is not to solve the world's problems. Our job is to draw our entire life from Christ and manifest His life to others. Nothing could be simpler – and nothing could be more challenging." My morning prayer used to be, "I am only responsible to be and to do what Christ wants me to be and do today," but I realized this was a form of WWJD ("What Would Jesus Do") performance. A better prayer is: "I am only responsible to allow the living Lord Jesus to be and to do what He wants to be and do in me today, expressing Himself through me, as His Christ-one."

JULY 26

HOW DO YOU KNOW WHAT IS TRUE?

It is not human opinions that man needs; it is TRUTH that is personified in the risen Lord Jesus Christ (Jn. 14:6). It is not theology that man needs; it is the *Theos* (God) that the human ...ologies try inadequately to explain. It is not religion that man needs; it is the living Lord Jesus Christ who is far superior to all the man-made religions (Col. 2:23) that try to tie and bind people to a human conception of God. John Denver said, "The answers, my friend, are blowin' in the wind," but the divine answers to the spiritual needs of fallen humanity are "blowing in the wind" of the Holy Spirit (Jn. 3:8), directed at the hearts of mankind.

Mankind has sought knowledge since the first couple became enamored with "the tree of the knowledge of good and evil" in the garden (Gen. 2:9,17). It was a "pseudo-knowledge" suggested by the "father of lies" (Jn. 8:44), claiming that man could be his own center of reference and determine "good and evil" by his own whims. It was a lie! Humans only know true character of right and wrong, good and evil, when they know Him, Jesus. Everything consistent with God in Christ is good; everything not consistent with God in the Son is evil. The consequence of partaking of "the tree of the knowledge of good and evil" was disastrous submission to the "spirit of error" (I Jn. 4:6).

Fallen humanity never ceases to seek for knowledge of their own making and biting at the bubbles of unsubstantiated speculation. The early church had to weather the nascent, mystic truth-claims of the Gnostics (from *gnosis* = knowledge). This is evident in the writings of the apostle John (gospel, epistles, revelation). Both cerebral and ethereal knowledge of the so-called "mysteries of God" disintegrate into fairy dust in comparison to one's "knowing Him who is true, and knowing that we are in Him who is true" (I Jn. 5:20). Jesus is the Truth (Jn. 14:6), and by knowing Him we know the Truth that is eternal.

SCIENTIFIC PSEUDO-SAVIORS

Humans are constantly grabbing at straws, seeking ways and means to save them from their present predicament; and they are quite undiscerning as to whether what they choose really has the capability to resolve their problem, short-term or long-term. This has been particularly obvious in the field of environmental sciences, "environmentalism" so-called – for example, the "carbon credits" hoax touted a few years ago. Who was offering people the alleged line of credit for using less coal and petroleum fuels? Who else but the politicians, and their less-than-reliable promises to make good on their rat-hole investments.

The scientific pseudo-savior of renewable energy has been particularly evangelistic about their hope and expectations for wind and solar energy recently. Many have been quick to jump on the bandwagon of "faith in renewables." It is becoming increasingly evident to the scientific community that these "renewable energy" sources cannot save the planet earth. The trade-off of expense versus outcome is negligible. The cleanest and least expensive source of energy in the long-run remains nuclear energy, the "evil one" in the self-constructed pantheon of false-religious deities within the religion of scientism.

The God-sent Savior for the woes of mankind is Jesus Christ. Yes, we must continue to seek scientific solutions to the natural, physical problems that might arise during our brief occupancy on planet earth, but these are temporal compared to the big-picture of what Christ has accomplished. The sin of mankind affected even the cosmos we live in; "the creation was subjected to futility, but will be set free from its slavery to corruption into the freedom of the glory of the children of God" (Rom. 8:20-22). Our faith is not in "renewable energy" but in the One who has renewed all things in Himself and made us "new creatures" (II Cor. 5:17) to abide in the "new creation" (Gal. 6:15).

JULY 28

WHAT HAVE YOU LEARNED?

We do not cease being learners and students when we arrive at an arbitrarily established age. In fact, if you are not presently engaged in the process of learning, acquiring new understanding, attitudes and behaviors, then you are in the dying state of stagnation. It's a "go-nowhere" place to exist. There are many in our fellowships today who are not learning because they are unteachable. They are unwilling to learn, because they think they already know it all – the pride of thinking they have arrived at the summit of spiritual understanding. Learning requires humility, openness, and receptivity to what is being taught.

Learning is more than academic textbook learning acquired through educational discipline. Life-long learning means that every situation we encounter is an opportunity to learn. Every experience of life provides an opportunity to learn more about God and ourselves and the intended relationship we are meant to have. Every Christ-one is necessarily a learner. The word "disciple" (Greek *mathetes*) means "learner" or "follower." "The disciples were first called 'Christians' in Antioch" (Acts 11:26). To be a "disciple" is not an advanced level of Christian schooling, but simply means one who is learning from Jesus.

Jesus advised His disciples that the Holy Spirit would be their teacher in their learning process after He ascended to the Father (Jn. 14:26; cf. I Jn. 2:27). "Another" (Jn.14:18), just like Him because it would be Him in Spirit-form (cf. I Cor. 15:45), would "come-alongside" to be the Paraclete, teacher, helper and counsellor. Every Christian should be learning from the Spirit-teacher. What have you been learning during the recent difficult time of the health pandemic? Some have learned they had misplaced priorities, unrealized addictive tendencies, sensitive touch-points of perturbation, and socialization needs, as well as the sufficiency of the living Lord Jesus for all their needs.

CONTEMPORARY IDOLATRY

We read the biblical stories of the people of Israel and their repetitive return to idolatry. These were people who were "favored by God" to be His people, and yet they kept reverting to false-gods – to idols. The primary idolatrous god the nation of Israel kept going back to throughout the old covenant era was Ba'al, a polymorphic idol (both in image and ideology) which in its multifaceted forms was "the god of the land, earth, weather, fertility, etc." That's the way with idols – the fallen human mind is an idol-factory (Ezek. 14:3), manufacturing idolatrous false-gods to allegedly meet the needs of humans who have rejected God.

Before we swell up with pride, saying, "At least we are not like them. We do not keep returning to false-gods made of stone," which are not gods at all (Acts 19:26; Gal. 4:8), we probably should consider the forms of contemporary idolatry that exist in our day. On any given Sunday morning one can view acres and acres of mobile idols lined up in rows in the parking lots of local churches. Those church buildings can be idols of that group's success at attracting people, and the message board out front often touts the idolatry of denominationalism whereby people believe they are more right or more holy than others.

Nationalism can also be a form of idolatry. In the midst of WWII, Woody Guthrie wrote "This land is your land; this land is my land; this land was made for you and me." A popular motto during the Vietnam Conflict was, "our country, right or wrong." If Ba'al was the "land god" of Israel, does American nationalism verge on such idolatry? An idol can be anything that is so identified as a thing of worth, value or significance, even aligned with God, that it absorbs our hearts and minds. and becomes our primary hope, our savior. The assault on the U.S. Capital on Jan. 6, 2021 was made by an army of pseudo-evangelicals, some carrying religious flags with the fervor of nationalistic idolatry.

JULY 30

THE SIGNIFICANCE OF OUR EXISTENCE?

Some people do not want to explore "the significance of their existence." They would rather approach their existence like a pinball that bounces off the bumpers and eventually drops into the black hole. Many seem to approach life as if it were a game, the objective of which is to come out with the most points or stuff (the one with the most toys wins!). They maneuver and posture and try to get the advantage over others, who are regarded as opponents. Is life more than just the thrill of playing a game? Is there a teleological purpose, objective, or end-result (direction or destiny) that provides an answer to "WHY am I?"

Humanistic answers for the purpose of our being (*raison d'etre*) abound: ...to become a better me ...to develop one's personality in self-actualization ... to live happy ...to make the world a better place ...to leave a legacy ...to be a change-agent ...to find something to justify suffering ...to live passionately in the present moment, *carpe diem* ...to achieve a higher level of consciousness ...to connect with others relationally;...to enjoy the human freedom to be anything you want to be ...to prepare for the next step of enlightenment or *metalife* ...to give yourself away in service to others;...to commit oneself to an ideal ... to be all you can be ...to help others through the absurdity of life.

The Westminster Confession states, "The chief end of man is to glorify God and enjoy Him forever." Scripture verifies that we "are created for His glory" (cf. Isa. 43:7; Rev. 4:11). Paul wrote that we are "created in Christ Jesus for good works which God prepared beforehand that we should walk in them" (Eph. 2:10). The "good works" for which we are purposed and equipped by the grace of God in Jesus Christ (Heb. 13:21) to bring glory to our Creator are always the derived expression of His character. Jesus explained that the essence of our existence is encompassed in "Love God, and love your neighbor as yourself" (Mk. 12:30,31).

CONTAINERS NEVER BECOMES THE CONTENTS

The wine doesn't become the glass into which it is poured; the coffee doesn't become the cup in which it is contained; the beer doesn't become the mug or the stein from which you drink it. The occupants never become the house they live in. Yes, this can become semantically confusing when we explain: the residents never become the residence; those who abide in the abode never become the abode in which they abide. But when we speak in figurative or spiritual terms, people have sometimes mistakenly equated the container with the contents, or *vice-versa*, and have spoken of becoming Christ in their form.

Just because Christ has come to live in us as Christ-ones does not mean that we become Christ. Just as the container never becomes the contents, the Christian in whom Christ lives never becomes Christ. But this becomes confusing when we speak of "union with Christ," and quote I Cor. 6:17 - "he who is joined to the Lord is one spirit with Him." This is a relational "one spirit" union, rather than an essential union of equivalence. Spirit-union and Spirit-identity as "Christ-ones" does not mean that we become Christ, any more than the "one flesh" union of marriage signifies that the husband becomes the wife, or the wife becomes the husband.

When the living Christ dwells within the spirit of a Christ-one (Rom. 8:9,16) as their spiritual life, even their "all in all" (Eph. 1:23), there is still a distinction between the indwelling Spirit of Christ (the contents) and the receptive individual in whom He lives (the container). Galatians 2:20 explains that "my old spiritual identity has been crucified, and Christ (the contents) now lives in me (the container); and the life that I (the container) now live, I live by faith in the Son of God (the contents) who loved me and gave Himself for me." The distinction between container and contents always remains, even as we Christ-ones allow Christ to re-present Himself in us, or even as us.

AUGUST 1

GOD GIVES – HUMANS RECEIVE

God is the Creator, Redeemer and Sustainer. God is Triune as the Father, Son, and Holy Spirit; three persons in one Being. God is His own center of reference and the source of all things that are other than Him. God is not self-created; God has always existed as Who He is, the eternal God, unchangeable in His essential Being, "the same yesterday, today, and forever." God does what He does, because He is Who He is, never contingent but always independent of all others. God's ontological dynamic of operation is centrifugal – always moving out from the center point in Himself. What is the best word to express this constant and eternal givingness of God, giving Himself to others via His character of Love? We call it GRACE, a distinctively Christian concept – God doing what God does because He is Who He is, and He does what He does via His Son, Jesus Christ (cf. Jn. 1:17).

Since God is the Giver of all good things (James 1:17), giving "out of" (Greek *ek*) Himself, the receivers of God's givingness are the derivative human creatures that He created. Human beings are not independent creatures that function out of their own being but are functionally derivative and dependent on one spirit-source or the other (God or Satan). God did not create "little gods" called human beings who could "do their own thing," as the prevailing anti-theistic philosophy of humanism maintains. In response to God's givingness, human creatures are receivers; and the biblical word for this receptivity of God's activity of grace is FAITH. William Barclay noted, "the first element in faith is what we can only call receptivity" (*Mind of Christ*).

"For by *grace* we have been saved through *faith*" (Eph. 2:8). "We have access by *faith* into this *grace* wherein we stand" (Rom. 5:2). Faith receives from God's grace and says, "thank you" (Greek *eucharisteo*; *eu* = good; *charis* = grace); faith recognizes the eucharistic "good grace" of God for all we receive.

THE RESOLUTE RESOLVE OF RELIGION

Consider this paraphrase of I Corinthians 13:13 – "We constantly abide in faithful endurance, resolute hope, and the determination to love others, but the greatest of these is our loyal love for others." Most religious people will not detect a problem with that revision, because they have been taught by religion to engage in the determined and unwavering resolve to perform in accord with God's expectations. Eustace Haydon, religious historian and a leader in the humanist movement in Canada penned these words: "Religion is the resolute following of the star of hope through the triumphs and tragedies of time." He's right!

Four key words in that rewrite of the final verse of Paul's great chapter on love should stick out as "red flags" in the mind of every Christian who understands God's grace in Jesus Christ. Those four words (in reverse order) are: loyal, determination, resolute, and endurance. They all point to human effort, the "works" and striving performance of men to please a demanding God. Religion has denigrated and diminished the meaning of the basic Christian words: Faith is more than believing the right things; Hope is more than optimism for positive outcomes; Love is more than mere sentiment of concern. Rather, grace is based on God's faithfulness to act in accord with His own Being and character. Faith is our human receptivity of God's activity of grace. Hope is the confident expectation of receptive believers that God will eternally act out of His Being of Love to save others from their own self-destruction.

The good news of the gospel is not encouragement to hold on with grit and determination to what you believe within a changing culture and an anxious age. Grace advises, "He who began a good work in you will perfect it until the day of Christ Jesus" (Phil. 1:6). Instead of "the resolute resolve of religion," we look to the generous grace of God in Jesus Christ.

AUGUST 3

MANIFESTING JESUS WHEN CAUGHT OFF GUARD

I have observed good waiters or waitresses who have learned to balance plates of food and multiple drinks while moving through a crowd without dropping or spilling anything. That is not to say, that it is not still possible that someone might move abruptly, bump into them, and cause them to dump the entire platter they are carrying to the customer. A similar situation occurs in the daily lives of Christ-ones as we are attempting to balance the various response-abilities of life and are abruptly surprised by a trial that might pierce our status-quo, and we have no time to plan or think through our reaction to such (perhaps putting on a "show of religiosity" to maintain a public persona).

When we get "bumped," there is a tendency to spill out what we are full of; and it is not always a pretty scene. What spills out when we are disturbed, agitated, or perturbed is simply what is within. If there is dirty water in the container, then it is dirty water that spills out; if there is clean water in the container, then it is clean water that spills out. Is this what Jesus was referring to when He said, "From within, out of the heart of men, proceed evil thoughts, fornications, thefts, murders, adulteries, deeds of coveting and wickedness, as well as deceit, sensuality, envy, slander, pride *and* foolishness. All these evil things proceed from within and defile the man" (Mk. 7:21-23).

Why are such attitudes and characteristics still within a Christ-one? The fleshly patterns of selfishness and sinfulness remain in the desires of our soul, and by such the tempter attempts to counter the work of the Spirit of Christ within our spirit. "The flesh sets its desire against the Spirit, and the Spirit against the flesh; for these are in opposition to one another, so that you may not do the things that you please" (Gal. 5:17), i.e., the things that Christ would desire to do in and through you. By God's grace, we allow the living Lord Jesus to manifest Himself in our behavior.

SHOOTING SACRED COWS

Moses was most annoyed and unhappy with the Israelite people for constructing a "golden calf" during the time while he was on the mountain with God to receive the tablets of the old covenant Law (Exod. 32). He reacted with vehement anger, throwing the tablets down and smashing them to smithereens. God revealed to Moses that the Israelite nation was indeed an obstinate group of people; but, in accord with Moses' plea for mercy, He was not going to annihilate them for their idolatry. However, He would refrain from personally leading them into the Promised Land, to be led instead by an angel of the Lord.

I can certainly relate to Moses' intolerance and disdain for idolatrous formulations. Though I have not encountered a golden calf made of ornaments of gold, I have certainly dealt with the thought-gods of ideological idols, where man-made religious thought has constructed doctrines and theological creeds into misrepresentative descriptions of God and His Son, Jesus Christ. I didn't sign up for the task of exposing the idols of fallacious presuppositions; but my friend, Burt Rosenburg, has pointed out that people need to know what ain't, in order to know what IS. It is helpful for people to understand why the false is false, in order to fully comprehend the singular Truth in Jesus Christ.

Famed American artist, James E. Seward, drew a line-drawing cartoon with a number of cows standing in a pasture, each of which had holes shot through them. The distraught farmer/rancher was lamenting what had happened to his cattle; and his friend explained, "Someone has shot holes in your sacred cows." In the upper left-hand corner of the drawing was a caricature of a fellow with a smoking musket, and Jim Seward identified that figure as Jim Fowler. It is my only claim to fame as an iconoclast with a ministry of idol-smashing – eliminating the "what ain'ts" in order to emphasize the "what IS" of Jesus Christ.

AUGUST 5

WHO DO YOU THINK YOU ARE?

It may have been a parent, a teacher, a coach, or someone else in a place of authority that questioned, "Who do you think you are?" as they found you in a place where you had no right to be. "What gives you the right or authority to be doing what you are doing?" Many of the times when these questions are asked, the person is simply showing off, presuming or pretending to take a position or place of importance that it was not his or herplace to assume. The one acting out in this manner often exhibits a sense of arrogance or presumption, wanting people to "look at me," as they take center-stage or put themselves on the pedestal.

On a more serious note, when Christians are asked, "Who do you think you are? How would you explain your new spiritual condition as a Christian?" they often assume a false-humility that responds, "I am just a sinner saved by grace." Such an answer certainly fails to present a positive explanation of the magnificent spiritual transformation that has occurred in every Christian. Would it not be more appropriate to answer such questions by answering, "I am a saint endowed with everything God has to give in His Son, Jesus Christ, to the extent that I am a partaker of the divine nature (II Pet. 1:4), and I am known as a Christ-one"?

The real issue is not a matter of "who you think you are," but "who does God say you are" when you have been "joined in one spirit with the Lord Jesus Christ" (I Cor. 6:17) and have become "a new creature in Christ" (II Cor. 5:17). The presence of the Triune God – Father, Son and Holy Spirit – dwelling in the spirit of a Christ-one allows the very character of God to be applied to who we are. The Christ-one is identified as righteous, holy and perfect, not because we are essentially, inherently or intrinsically such *a se* (in ourselves) as only God is. Ours is a derived identity based on the character of the spiritual indwelling of the divine nature of the three persons of the Trinity.

GOD CALLING

Some people answer their phones with the question, "Who's calling?" In that way, they immediately know who they are communicating and conversing with on the other end of the line. Would you be surprised if the voice on the other end of the phone were to say, "God calling"? It is not likely that we will get an audible telephone call from God, but God has many ways of making Himself known to us and expressing His desire to commune and communicate with us. Jesus said, "My sheep hear My voice" (Jn. 10:16,27). There is a spiritual connection whereby the Spirit causes us to hear the voice of God in Christ.

This ability to hear from and speak with God is not empirically explicable or explainable. Nor, is it the same process for every child of God. Every Christian seems to have his or her unique communicative connection, our own "hot-line" with God. Sometimes, we might have a persistent and niggling sense within our mind, spirit, heart, or emotions that God is attempting to get our attention. We have an inner sense that God is calling us *about* something or *to* something, and we are aware that we need to "listen up" to the revelation that He wants to share with us. Be advised that this message is not for everyone everywhere, or God would have used a megaphone rather than your private line.

When God is calling, bear in mind that He is not usually calling us to a task. God has the means to take care of His own matters; it is called "grace." He may be nudging us to participate in a particular endeavor, but we will only be His instrument and vehicle through which He works by His Spirit to minister to others. Nor is the subject of God's calling usually a call to trials, sufferings or heartaches. The "ruler of this world" is usually God's instrument to orchestrate those. God is not calling us to anything other than Himself, to be engaged in an ever more intimate relationship with the Father, Son and Holy Spirit.

AUGUST 7

OVER-EMPHASIS ON IDENTITY

There are numerous Christian ministries today focusing on the Christian's "identity." These groups have various ideas and distinctives about the ideological formulations that might comprise one's Christian identity. Those who attempt to find their identity in being "a Christian," especially within a particular denominational or theological venue, risk having an "identity crisis" if they cross the borders of denominational membership. Our deepest sense of identity is not in being a Methodist, Baptist, Episcopalian or Presbyterian, but in being a Christ-one whose identity is found in spirit-union with Jesus Christ.

There seems to be an over-emphasis in some religious circles on finding and determining one's identity, with the subsequent suggestion that in knowing one's identity the individual will then have a greater knowledge-power to behave like who they have identified themselves to be. Christian groups that focus on a Christian's identity must be cautious of orienting and directing their followers to undue self-concern about their own personal identity. Finding oneself or one's identity is not the focus of the Christian life. In fact, undue concern about one's identity can becomes a subtle egocentric and idolatrous concern.

The issue should not be "who I am" but "who He is in me." Introspective analysis of who I am creates a focus on myself, on "my identity," when our focus should be on Jesus. A proper sense of identity is only established in union with a spiritual source who resides in the very core of our being, in our spirit, and derived from His presence and character in us. Satan will tempt us to find our identity elsewhere than in Christ – in what we do, in who we associate with, in our talents and abilities, in our accomplishments, even in our spiritual progress in discipleship or maturity. We must let our identity be settled in spiritual union with Christ, and the focal point of our proclamation must be HIM.

A PERSONAL RELATIONSHIP WITH JESUS

Genuine Christians will often explain that "Christianity is not a religion but a personal relationship with Jesus Christ." Such a comment requires additional explanation. You see, I am related to my second cousin, twice removed, as determined by Ancestry.com using DNA markers. Do I know that person? No. I may be biologically related to this unknown person, but there is no personal relationship that allows for personal interaction or involvement. A genuine, personal, and spiritual relationship with the risen and living Lord Jesus is not merely a legal relationship of natural commonality of belief or background.

In a personal spiritual relationship with the living Lord Jesus there is inevitable interactive intimacy. Understanding oneself and defining oneself as one "beloved by Jesus" (as the apostle John did – Jn. 13:23; 19:26; 20:2; 21:7,20) indicates that we have begun to understand the reality of a genuine, personal relationship with Jesus. It is far more than just the head-knowledge information that we have a new spiritual identity as a "new creature" (II Cor. 5:17) in Christ. We know that we are "God's beloved," that He regards us as "a pearl of great price" (Matt. 13:46), worthy of expending everything He had to give His own Son, Jesus, to pay the price for personal relationship with us. We know deep within our hearts that we are secure in His love and are able to trust Him for every circumstance we might encounter. His grace is our sufficiency (cf. II Cor. 12:9).

"How do you know for sure that you have a personal relationship with Jesus?" some might ask – by the Spirit (cf. I Cor. 15:45), the living Lord Jesus dwells within our spirit (cf. Rom. 8:9) and has become our Life (cf. Col. 3:4). "For me to live is Christ" (Phil. 1:6), living in spiritual union with me (cf. I Cor. 6:17). "The Spirit *of Christ within us* bears witness with our spirit that we have become children of God" (Rom. 8:16).

AUGUST 9

A BALANCE OF IDEOLOGICAL CONCERNS

If you haven't noticed, there is still a polarization of outlook and opinion among the persons in our nation. The election of new government officials in the nation, states, and cities did not resolve the different paradigms of thought. That's okay. Absolute agreement would be terribly boring and would not allow for the clashing process where "iron sharpens iron" (Prov. 27:17) as we interact and debate our ideas and beliefs in order to clarify where we stand. When we sort out our thoughts in a civil manner, then, we can either integrate our thoughts in some form of compromise or decide to agree to disagree agreeably.

The continued ideological conflict of an "us versus them" standoff will continue to produce suspicions and conspiracy theories that will tear apart the fabric of our nation and churches. We must learn to get along in unity within our national union without demanding uniformity of opinion and ideology. You are free to think this, and I am free to think that. Westerners, in particular Americans, have tended to think in either/or, bi-polar, dichotomous categories of right and wrong, with strong aversion to the tensioned balance of dialectic thinking wherein one can appreciate the balanced positions of both/and.

In the U.S.A. at the present time we have a dichotomy of "this or that" thinking, polarized in an "us-vs.-them" conflict, which, if we are not careful, could be pushed to the extreme of an ideological civil war. The polarized political extremes in our country at the present time might be cast in the man-made -isms of socialism versus nationalism. What an unfortunate polarity. Those charged with advocating socialism are not averse to national pride in their country. Those charged with nationalism are not averse to the social programs that benefit those in need. How do we develop a balanced understanding of social concern and national distinction that quenches the extremist flames?

THE ANOMALY OF CHRISTIANITY

Everything about Christianity, the Christ-life, is absolutely antithetical to the world's ways – the principles by which the world-system operates. In fact, Christianity does not operate on the basis of principles but out of the vital reality of the Person of Jesus Christ. The world, i.e. the system of pragmatic productivity that expediently promotes the maximum performance of people via the most effective techniques and procedures to achieve a utopian dream of human betterment is on a totally different wave-length than those who are tuned in to what God is doing in His Son Jesus Christ by the power of His Spirit.

The word "anomaly" is derived from two Greek words; *an* = no, not; *homos* = same and means that something does not correspond; i.e., there is an incongruity, deviation, irregularity, peculiarity, or contrariety between the ideas being considered. They do not fit together because they are not the same. To attempt to make them coincide is like trying to fit a square peg in a round hole. "For My thoughts are not your thoughts, nor are your ways My ways," declares the Lord. For *as* the heavens are higher than the earth, So are My ways higher than your ways And My thoughts than your thoughts" (Isa. 55:8,9). "His ways are past finding out" (Rom. 11:33).

That is why Jesus was such a misunderstood misfit during His earthly ministry. He operated on a totally different *modus operandi* than the religious world around Him. He did not fit the expectations of the Jewish religion for a militaristic Messiah. He could not accept the Roman elevation of Caesar as King. The world and its religion continues to fail to understand Jesus, for He is counter-intuitive and counter-productive to all the principles of their endeavors. The advent of Jesus required a new creation, a new kingdom, a new spirit, a new dynamic whereby the Spirit of Christ functions within His Christ-ones.

AUGUST 11

CHRISTIAN GROUP DYNAMICS

I have observed many Christian gatherings disintegrate over time, because they lacked the boldness to declare the objectives of their group and their intention to stay with the goal at hand – to know Jesus. With humble acceptance, they eagerly invite any newcomer into participation with their group, but there are occasions when the person(s) who joins them is not genuinely interested in the gospel of Jesus Christ. Some people come with an agenda, whether political, ideological, or theological; and their objective is to usurp the leadership and direction of the group by engaging in argumentation and disruption.

How do we handle such a situation? Do we elect a "sergeant at arms" to keep the meeting on track? Do we hire a "bouncer" to boot the disrupter out the door? So often these intruders do not have any genuine desire to know the truth and are unwilling to submit to Jesus as their Lord in an intimate personal relationship. They want to argue about the peripherals of insignificant data and chase rabbits into dead-end holes of thought. They are antagonists who qualify as "antichrists" (I Jn. 2:18; 4:3), engaging in the "deeds of the flesh" which Paul identified as "enmities, strife, jealousy, disputes, dissension, factions" (Gal. 5:19).

Most of Paul's epistles were written to church groups embroiled in just such problematic situations where interlopers had crashed the gates to engage in polemic disputation. These "wolves in sheep's clothing" permeate and penetrate Christian gatherings to confuse those who genuinely want to know Jesus in an ever-deeper way. They disrupt the Christian gathering by asking a plethora of irrelevant questions, contending with any legitimate answers those in the group might attempt to provide. These adamant unbelievers should be met with a clear explanation: "If you want to talk about JESUS, this gathering will be continued as an opportunity to do so.

AUGUST 12

THE WORD OF GOD DIVIDES

The title of this article is taken from Paul's words in Hebrews 4:13 – "For the word of God is living and active and sharper than any two-edged sword, and piercing as far as the dividing of soul and spirit, of both joints and marrow, and able to judge the thoughts and intentions of the heart." The first issue of consideration is the meaning of the phrase "the word of God." The apostle John explained that "In the beginning was the Word and the Word was with God, and the Word was God" (Jn. 1:1). "The Word became flesh and dwelt among us" (Jn. 1:14). The Word (Greek *logos*) clearly refers to the Son of God who was incarnated in the flesh as a human being.

Throughout the new covenant literature, consistency of exegesis would dictate that the phrase "word of God" should primarily be understood in reference to the living Word of God in Jesus Christ, the personal revelation of the Triune God. We are quite aware that the Christian religion has primarily used the phrase "the word of God" in reference to the Bible, the inspired scriptures in book-form. For many, the emphasis has long been on how human minds are to "rightly divide the word of truth" (II Tim. 2:15) in order to be "unashamed workmen of God." This places the emphasis on what man does, rather than what God does.

Back to Hebrews four: "The word of God (the living Lord Jesus) is living and active, and pierces as deep as the dividing of soul and spirit ... able to determine the thoughts and intents of the heart." The deepest intents of my heart in the spiritual core of my being are to be a Christ-one who manifests the character of God. But there are competing and conflicting thoughts in the heart of my soul that are selfishly and sinfully patterned to do it my way in the "flesh." The living "word of God," Jesus within, divides and separates the spiritual intents from the soul-thoughts to clarify the faith-choices we face moment-by-moment.

AUGUST 13

GOD-GIVEN HUMAN DESIRES

God has given every human being a full set of God-given human desires. There is nothing wrong with those desires. They are simply conduits through which spiritual character (derived out of God or Satan) flows through and is developed into personality patterns. Initially, because all humans commence life (thanks to Adam - Rom. 5:17) "dead in trespasses and sins" (Eph. 5:1), we draw from "the spirit that works in the sons of disobedience" (Eph. 2:2), "taken captive by him to do his will" (II Tim. 2:26). In that process, Satan's character of selfishness and sinfulness is uniquely patterned into each person's desires in bundled patterns called "the flesh" (Gal. 5:16,17; Eph. 2:3).

Our desires are not pesky tendencies, designed to trip us up or tempt us. But when patterned in selfish and sinful ways by Satan's character, we might indulge them in sinful behaviors, or seek to deny that we have such desires (God-given or Satan tainted). When an individual becomes a Christ-one, "a new creature in Christ," the old spiritual condition has passed away, and behold everything about our spiritual condition has become new (II Cor. 5:17); but that does not imply that we no longer have our flesh-patterns in our soul that wage war against the desire of the Spirit of Christ in our spirit (Gal. 5:16,17).

Some Christians mistakenly believe that spiritual regeneration should eliminate all of our flesh-patterns, or that the maturity of sanctification will dissolve all our selfish and sinful tendencies. Not so! We will never be able to cut Gal. 5:16 out of our Bibles – it will remain true. But as the grace of God in Christ manifests His character through our desires, they can be transformed and repatterned into Spirit-filled desires. Sam Storms writes, "Grace is the work of the Holy Spirit in transforming our desires so that knowing Jesus becomes sweeter than illicit sex, sweeter than money and what it can buy, sweeter than every fruitless joy."

SEEING JESUS IN OUR SUFFERINGS

To live is to experience pain and suffering. This is an inevitable part of post-fall human life here on earth. As Christians, we have not yet arrived at our final destiny in heaven, where life is absent of trials, tears, pain, and suffering (Rev. 21:4). The present pain and suffering might be physical, mental and emotional, or social and relational. The wounds often run deep and may be short-term or chronic. Paul's "thorn in the flesh" (II Cor. 12:8,9) appears to have been long-term chronic suffering; and, despite his plea for God's deliverance, he had to wait until God's grace in Jesus proved sufficient in the midst of the suffering ordeal.

How do Christians react and respond to pain and suffering? Like all other human beings, the pain is not pleasant. We want to be delivered from it; but, when relief does not soon come, many have attempted to blame God for their woes; why did God allow this? Since that is no solution, some people try to escape and run away from the problems. Some seek others who will join them in a pity-party. Some try to analyze and figure out the problem, asking "What is God trying to teach me in this situation?" Some try to hide behind their problem, or even to find their identity in their problem by allowing the situation to define them.

When we refer to "seeing Jesus in our suffering," we speak not of objective abstraction but the subjective awareness that we are Christ's beloved Christ-ones, inseparable in our union with Him; therefore, He is always with us in our painful sufferings. We should not seek to slither out of our situations but wait until we sense the presence of the living Lord Jesus experiencing our pain with us and walking through it by His grace sufficiency in such a way that He is glorified (II Cor. 4:17), while people around us are asking, "How did she do that?" Afterward, with 20/20 hindsight, we may (or may not) begin to get a glimpse of any objectives that God had for walking with us through suffering.

AUGUST 15

THE WAY, THE TRUTH, THE LIFE

Jesus did not come to answer the questions of life; He came to BE the answer. Jesus did not come to point us to the way or to give us directions to the way to live; He IS the Way. Jesus did not come to teach us the truths of reality; He came to BE the True reality for mankind. Jesus did not come to outline the propositions of proper doctrine but to BE the Divine Person who encompasses all that God is. Jesus did not come to tell us how to live; He came to BE the very spiritual life that man requires to be man as God intended, the Life of God in man. Have you noticed how religion seeks to cast Jesus as an intermediary to what God has for us, rather that the reality of all that God IS to us? Religion always portrays Jesus as less than He is – just a stepping stone to the goal, so the devotees can strive to arrive at the goal.

God identified Himself to Moses from the burning bush, saying, "I AM that I AM." I AM the very Being and Action of the One true God. I AM the essence and function of Jehovah God. I AM the ontological dynamic of the One true God. As the fulfillment of the new covenant promises, Jesus repeatedly uses the *ego eimi* phrase, the "I AM" in identification with how God identified Himself to Moses: "I am the Bread of Life" (John 6:35), "I am the Light of the World" (John 8:12), "I am the Door" (John 10:9), "I am the Good Shepherd" (John 10:11,14), "I am the Resurrection and the Life" (John 11:25), "I am the Way and the Truth and the Life" (John 14:6), "I am the Vine" (John 15:1,5). He uses the Greek predicate nominative verb form to identify Himself as THE ontological dynamic of the objects He is identifying Himself as.

Jesus is the ontological dynamic of the singular, trinitarian, monotheistic God. When Jesus identified Himself as the Way, the Truth, and the Life, He identified Himself as the modality, reality, and vitality of God in action doing what God does because He IS Who He IS. Jesus was saying, "I AM God in action."

REPENTING OF RELIGION

This is the title of a book written by Gregory A. Boyd and published in 2004. The author keys off of the thoughts of Dietrich Bonhoeffer who was murdered in a Nazi concentration camp in 1945. His major thesis is that Christians have failed to recognize the antithesis between the love of God and human judgment of others who do not think and act like themselves. Identifying such human judgment with "the tree of the knowledge of good and evil" in the garden of Eden, Boyd explains that man-made religion has engaged in judgment of alleged right thoughts and actions, rather than allowing the love of God to be manifested.

Repentance is a change of mind that leads to a change of action. The mind-set that Christians are meant to have is that they are derivative creatures, intended to derive the character of God from the indwelling life of Christ and to allow for the manifestation of that love unconditionally by the power of the Spirit. Religion is the forbidden tree – the tree whereby we open ourselves up to death. It is the tree that represents man's attempt to set himself up as his own center of reference, to attempt to be like God in making judgments about what is "good or evil," right or wrong, acceptable or not acceptable.

There is no doubt that people need to change their minds and change their active involvement in religion – particularly in the "good and evil" judgment that is inevitably involved in religion. Our attempts to judge people into good and bad categories will always be selfishly and sinfully oriented because they are satanically energized by "the spirit of this world" (I Cor. 2:12). Yes, religion is the devil's playground, and he is running rampant in the moralistic judgmentalism of religious people and organizations. It is time that we make clear distinction between religion and Christianity and repent of our tendency to judge others rather than love others.

AUGUST 17

MANIFESTATIONS OF SELFISM

The Declaration of Independence, written by Thomas Jefferson in 1776, reads, "We hold these truths to be self-evident, that all men are created equal, that they are endowed by their Creator with certain unalienable rights, that among these are life, liberty and the pursuit of happiness." The theistic emphasis of the Creator God and His intention that human beings might be personally related to Him and one another is implicitly implied. Human derivation from God was interrupted as soon as it was initiated, when mankind "in Adam" thought they could reject God's plan of derivativeness, and become "independent selves." It was a lie, fostered by the "father of lies" (Jn. 8:44); and humans, now estranged from God, were deriving from the satanic spiritual source of selfishness and sinfulness.

From that satanic source of selfishness, humans have continually developed systems of selfism – man-made systems of thought (-isms) that incorporate their self-serving sense of supremacy and privilege, claiming advantage to themselves and those like them and disadvantage to all others. Some examples of such selfism are racism, genderism, sexism, religionism, elitism, and intellectualism, to name just a few.

Racism, for example, is systemic in our society because selfism is systemic. Racism is when we give preference or advantage to one race over another, prejudicially judging and discriminating against other people with bigotry and bias based on the color of their skin or physical characteristics. All races are guilty of the selfism of racism (cf. "black lives matter," FUBU brand). Entering into an environment of intense racism (cf. "God's chosen people"), Jesus lived and died to redeem all humanity from their satanic selfism and to reinvest Himself as the Son of God into receptive individuals, who as Christ-ones might manifest His character of unconditional love to all other people.

IS EVERYTHING PREDETERMINED?

Philosophy and religion have long struggled with determining to what extent all events are predetermined by God or by some all-inclusive principle of action in the universe. The predominant conclusion in human thinking has been to accept some form of compatibilism, however nebulous, between causal determinism and human self-determination. But the modern winds of change in the human thought categories of philosophy and science are slowly turning toward some form of deterministic explanation for all that occurs in the universe and in the course of human social affairs at large.

Most Christians will assert that God is sovereign, but some interpret that to mean that God determines all events in advance and controls those events in the manner that He has determined, calling the process "divine predestination." Other Christians interpret God's sovereignty to mean that God reigns and rules in the kingdom that Jesus came to bring in Himself. God predetermined (Greek *prohorizo – pro* = pre; *horizo* = to establish limits or boundaries), i.e. pre-horizoned that Jesus would be the reference line to which all of His intentioned actions would relate, and all who are "in (*union with*) Christ" will enjoy the eternal life that is in Him alone (cf. I Jn. 5:12).

All forms of determinism or predeterminism tend to erode the importance of personal response-ability via freedom of choice. When human beings no longer believe they are free agents, they stop seeing themselves as culpable for their own decisions and actions, and all sense of morality suffers. Though humans derive character and energy for action from the spirit-source of either God or Satan, they are responsible for the volitional choice to determine the source to which they will be receptive. Pre-determinism becomes a blank-check for reversion to the primal (pre-regenerate) condition of satanic selfishness.

AUGUST 19

THE QUESTION OF FREE-WILL

The topic of "free-will" has been debated in Christian thought for centuries, often creating more heat than light. The problem has often been a lack of clear definition of the terms being used. For example, "free-will" and "freedom of choice" have often been used as synonyms. Freedom of choice is the volitional freedom of all human beings to make determinative choices in the will of their soul (*psuche*). Free-will has often been defined with an additional component that indicates that an individual has the free and unassisted ability to perform and implement their freely chosen determination in human action, i.e., "You are free to be and do whatever you choose to be and do."

To apply the above definition of free-will to human beings is the basic premise of humanism and its thesis of self-potential, leading Augustine to condemn Pelagius. God alone has full and absolute free-will as defined above; for He determines His own course of action (God's will) contextualized only by His own character, which He will never violate and "act out of character, for "it is impossible for God to lie" (Heb. 6:18). God, in His omnipotence, certainly has the inherent divine power to implement and enact the action that He has determined to do. He does what He does, because He is who He is.

Human beings have the freedom of choice to determine what they intend to do, but should they choose to act righteously they do not have the power to do so in their natural spiritual condition. "There is none righteous; no not one" (Rom. 3:10), because the spirit of iniquity dwells in the unregenerate (cf. Eph. 2:2). The freedom of choice to act in righteousness is only granted by God's grace in Jesus Christ, whereby the righteous presence of the Spirit of Christ in the spirit of the Christ-one (cf. Rom. 8:9) provides the dynamic provision to manifest the righteous fruit of the character of Jesus (cf. Phil. 1:11).

"MEANS OF GRACE"

Various streams of Christian theology have long referred to the "means of grace," identified as "the actions through which one receives God's grace." Included in those human actions are baptism, prayer, good works, etc.; but the primary means of receiving God's grace has been determined to be participation in the Eucharist,that in receiving the bread and the wine God's grace is administered to the participant. Foundational to such thinking is the conviction that the Church is the primary means of grace responsible for administering the sacraments, a concept first introduced by Irenaeus (A.D. 130-202), bishop of Lyons, France, who wrote, "Where the church is, there is the Spirit of God; and where the Spirit of God is, there is the church, and every kind of grace."

Religion sets itself up as the pipeline of God's grace. In so doing it attempts to take the place of Jesus, to serve as the conduit of what only the living Lord Jesus can be and accomplish. Coincidentally, religion seeks to make everything into a necessary performance action; something the adherent must DO – if you perform and participate in this act, you will receive God's blessing or grace.

Categorically and definitively: There is only one salvific "means of grace," and that is through the Person and work of the Lord Jesus Christ – not something we are or do, but who Jesus is and what He has done. The apostle John states this clearly: "Grace and truth were realized through Jesus Christ" (Jn. 1:17). The Greek verb used in this verse is *egeneto* which has its root in *genesis* meaning "to bring into being," to come to pass, to realize (cf. Jn. 1:14; I Cor. 15:45). Grace and truth (the divine dynamic and the divine reality) came into realization through (Greek *dia* = through, by means of) Jesus Christ. It seems the only legitimate conclusion is that Jesus alone is God's only "means of grace."

233

AUGUST 21

CHRISTIAN MINISTRY

Corrie Ten Boom was the youngest daughter of a Dutch watchmaker, and the Christian family worked with the resistance movement to protect Jewish people from the Nazis. After being reported to the Gestapo by a Dutch informant, the home was invaded. Corrie, her sister Betsie, and the father, Casper, were imprisoned in a German concentration camp. The Jews who were huddled in "the hiding place" were not found and were moved by other resistance workers to another location. Corrie was released in 1944, just 12 days after Betsie died, and was later advised her release was due to a clerical error.

After the war, Corrie traveled the world telling her story, as recorded in the book, *Tramp for the Lord*. Later, she settled in the United States and died in California in 1983. In the midst of her travels among American Christians, she made many observations about the state of American Christianity. One of my favorites is the comment about American Christians being so fascinated by eschatological theories of amillennialism, premillennialism, and postmillennialism. Her classic comment: "I think that all this speculation about the future coming of Jesus among American Christians is a preposterous idea."

Corrie also observed how Christians in America were engaged in "doing church" in calculated statistical categories and employing the business models of American productivity. She commented: "Trying to do the Lord's work in our own strength is the most confusing, exhausting, and tedious of all work. But when you are filled with the Holy Spirit (*the Spirit of Christ in your spirit – Rom. 8:9,16*), then the ministry of Jesus just flows out of you." She was so right. Christian ministry is the overflow of the life of Jesus into the lives of others. Paul wrote of his ministry, "I do not presume to speak of anything, except what Christ has accomplished through me" (Rom. 15:18).

HOW CAN A PERSON BE RIGHTEOUS?

The main theme of the Reformation was justification, aka righteousness. Luther and Calvin were reacting to the "works" performance righteousness of the Roman Catholic Church – "You do this and you will be regarded as righteous." They failed, however, to take the theme of righteousness out of the forensic and legal categories of consideration. The reformers regarded righteousness as a status, standing, or position of right standing before God, a juridical pronouncement or declaration of God, the Judge, regarding or imputing an individual as righteous (*dikaiosune*) when they profess belief in the historicity and effectiveness of the life, death, and resurrection of Jesus.

What the reformers failed to emphasize is the ontological reality of righteousness. God is righteous in Being (I Jn. 2:29; 3:7); righteousness is an essential attribute of His character. Jesus, the Son, is referred to as "the Righteous One" (Acts 3:14; 7:52; 22:14; I Jn. 2:1). Jesus is not just the One who brings an alien and detached righteous condition to humanity, but He is Righteous in Himself *(autodikaion)*, the ontological reality of divine Righteousness, who "makes one righteous" (Rom. 5:19; II Cor. 5:21) by the presence of His Spirit in our spirit (Rom. 8:9,16), forming a spiritual condition and identity of "righteous ones."

To be righteous in behavior is predicated on the fact that one has previously become righteous in spiritual condition by the presence of Jesus, the Righteous One. The living Lord Jesus manifests His righteous character in the Christ-one as we are receptive to such by faith. "In the gospel the righteousness of God is revealed from faith to faith; as it is written, 'the righteous man shall live by faith'" (Rom. 1:17). "He who practices righteousness is born of God in Christ" (I Jn. 2:29). "The peaceful fruit of righteousness comes through Jesus Christ" (Phil. 1:11; Heb. 12:11) as we participate in the kingdom of God (Rom. 14:17).

AUGUST 23

WHAT ABOUT THE CHURCH?

The word translated "church" in the New Testament is the Greek word *ecclesia*. There was little connotation in that original word to the entity(ies) and buildings called "church" in the modern world. *Ecclesia* referred to a "gathering, assembly, or congregation" of people for a common purpose (cf. Acts 7:28; 19:32). The early gatherings of Christ-ones inevitably developed structures of corporate leadership and polity. After the fourth century when Emperor Constantine I adopted Christianity as the official religion of the Roman Empire, the assembly of Christians was institutionalized into the Roman Catholic Church.

Perspectives of "church" were many and varied after the schism of Western and Eastern churches in A.D. 1054 and the Protestant Reformation of the 16th century. Each group tended to view themselves as "the one true Church," and idolatrous attribution of the Church as "the sum of all spiritual things" among some led to regarding the Church as equivalent to Christ. Biblical metaphors of the Church as the "Body of Christ" (I Cor. 12:27) and as the "Bride of Christ" (Rev. 21:9; Eph. 5:22-33) were interpreted as literal designations of particular corporate entities, even to the point of deifying such.

As early as the 4th century, Augustine differentiated between the visible church in corporate form and the invisible church as the spiritual "communion of the saints." The collective congregation of Christ-ones around the world comprised of individuals who have received the risen and living Lord Jesus into their spirit form the *ecclesia* of God in Christ. The unity of the Church is not in organizational structure, but in the common indwelling of Jesus' functionality according to divine spiritual giftedness whereby Christ-ones allow Jesus within to minister to one another and the world as they "forsake not their assembling together but encourage one another" in spiritual growth.

WORDS MATTER

Philosopher Ludwig Wittgenstein wrote, "Whereof we cannot speak, thereof we must remain silent." If we do not have the language to discuss something, then it is best to remain silent. This is similar to a hermeneutic principle which states, "Where the Bible speaks, we will speak. Where the Bible is silent, we will remain silent." Words and their meanings are important tools for human discussion. In the Council of Nicea (A.D. 325), Athanasius made the point that Jesus and the Father were *homoousion*, (*homo* = same; *ousia* = being) i.e. of the same divine being. Others wanted to use the word *homoiousion*, meaning "of similar being." Athanasius' word was written into the Nicene Creed of the Church. "Does it make one iota of difference?" asked some. Indeed, it does! The word *homoousion* is foundational to Christian understanding of the Trinity.

Words matter, but they are not meant to be used as weapons of argumentative warfare. Paul advised Timothy to "solemnly charge people in the presence of God not to wrangle about words, which is useless and leads to the ruin of the hearers" (II Tim. 2:14). In his previous letter to Timothy, Paul had warned about those who have "a morbid interest in controversial questions and disputes about words, out of which arise envy, strife, abusive language, evil suspicions" (I Tim. 6:4). Words can be important building blocks in constructing ideas and thoughts, but can also be used as destructive battering rams to destroy fellow believers and tear down the church rather than building it up. "Our instruction is love from a pure heart and a good conscience and a sincere faith. Some men, straying from these things, have turned aside to fruitless discussion" (I Tim. 1:5,6).

Mike Q. Daniel wrote this practical comment that fosters unity: "Maturity is not correcting others' semantics as much as leading in the truth. Wisdom is knowing the difference."

AUGUST 25

A MATTER OF TIME

Time is precisely calculated in the modern world. Time-pieces are synchronized in milliseconds by an atomic clock. The concept of time was not as mechanistic in Biblical times. The Greek language has three words for time: *hora, chronos,* and *kairos.*

Hora pertains to the cyclical nature of time, implying that there is a repetitive factor in time. An hour comes and goes; a day comes and goes; weeks, months, seasons, years, decades, centuries, millennia come and go, and another one starts. In the scriptures, *hora* is predominantly translated as "hour" (84 times), but such was not necessarily calculated as 60 seconds. It referred to a particular time in the cycles of time when an event occurred or was to occur. "My hour (*hora*) has not yet come" (Jn. 2:4), Jesus explained concerning the time of His death. In modern Greek, *hora* is the primary word for "time."

Chronos refers to the linear nature of time, allowing human beings to calculate the chronological progression of time in past, present and future categories. This allows us to determine when certain events occurred in history. Science calculates *chronos* into the milliseconds of what occurred in the "Big Bang" and the trajectory of spacecraft landing on Mars. The division of *chronos* time into B.C. and A.D. was miscalculated by historians, and it is now calculated that Jesus was likely born in 4-6 B.C.

Kairos is the moment or occasion when God breaks into human time. It may be an historical *kairos* occasion such as the incarnation of Jesus (Titus 1:3) or the redemptive death of Jesus (Rom. 5:6). But more often than not, the *kairos* moment is an experiential God-moment of divine revelation, the "now moment" when God breaks through to act in our lives. Initially, it may be at regeneration; but our sanctification comes via many "a-ha" moments of godly *kairos* when God reveals Himself to us.

AUGUST 26

PERSONAL INTIMACY WITH JESUS

Many are familiar with Oswald Chambers and his daily devotional book, *My Utmost for His Highest*, which was first published in 1924 by his widow, "Biddy" Chambers. Born on July 24, 1874, Oswald was a Scottish lad, the son of a Baptist preacher, who from his earliest years showed great interest in spiritual matters. He studied at the Dunoon Bible College near Glasgow, Scotland, and became a young preacher throughout Scotland; in London, England; and made a visit to Japan where he met Charles and Lettie Cowman (*Streams in the Desert*); and two visits to the United States. In 1915, at 41 years of age, he became the YMCA chaplain in Zeithoun, Cairo, Egypt, during World War I. He died Nov. 15, 1917, at age 43, of acute appendicitis.

Most of the volumes by Oswald Chambers available today were transcribed by his widow from shorthand notes taken of his preaching and teaching. Consider these words of Oswald Chambers: "The soul is in danger when knowledge of doctrine is adjudged to be of more importance than one's intimate touch with Jesus." O.C., as some affectionately refer to him, was not indicating that doctrine – scriptural teaching – is not important for Christians of every age but the mental knowledge of doctrine and dogma should not be prioritized as more important than one's personal and relational intimacy with the living Lord Jesus.

Didactic teaching of the doctrines of the Christian faith will always be foundational as we articulate the historical basis of Jesus' life, death, resurrection, ascension, and the reasoned explanation of the theological explanation of such. But unless our faith moves from our head to our heart and affects us in the inner core of our spirit in the realization of deep spiritual union between the Spirit of Christ and our human spirit (cf. Rom. 8:9,16), we have just a "believe-right" religion with a consequent "do-right" morality and fail to manifest the Christ-life.

AUGUST 27

CHRISTIANS AND MUSIC

Music has long been part of the worship experience of God's people. To participate in music doesn't require a trained musical voice. God knows the heart. The psalmist encourages us to "make a joyful noise unto the Lord" (Ps. 66:1; 95:1,2; 98:4,6; 100:1). The Greek word *psalmos* refers to making music using a stringed instrument, such as a harp or lyre. I find it interesting that the Old Testament, written in Hebrew, has Greek book titles: *genesis* (bring into being), *exodus* (the way out), *psalmos* (music with stringed instrument). Paul encouraged Christians to use "psalms, hymns, and spiritual songs" to express God's grace and make melody in one's heart (Eph. 5:19: Col. 3:16).

How tragic that styles of music have so often become points of bickering and contention among Christian people. Of course, we have personal preferences, but music in worship is not about us; rather it is a means of sharing the message of the gospel in a melodic and rhythmic manner. Music styles range from chants, liturgical expressions, classical music, hymns, praise songs, even rock and roll, jazz, rap, etc. Music is a medium to convey a message to others. It is far more than the mechanics of correct notes formed by one's human voice or an instrument. Musicality expresses God's beauty, gives God's grace, and effects God's joy.

In modern specifications of job descriptions, we refer to "music ministry." To minister via music is far more than a display of musical talent showcasing a person or group's musical ability. There must be personal spiritual maturity, wherein Jesus, the divine Giver living within a musician is allowed to give the gift of God's grace via the medium of musical conveyance. The divine givingness of music often has an emotional effect upon the listeners in the recognition of God's grace. This is true whether it is a human voice, an instrument, a singing bird, or the sounds of nature. They can produce joy, often accompanied by tears.

GOD IS INTERESTED ... IN YOU

...not in your sin, back then or now
...not in your failures
...not in how many lies you have told
...not in how many times you swore or cursed
...not in how many times you used His name in vain
...not in how many trysts you have experienced.
...not in how many partners you have had
...not in how many broken relationships you have had
...not in whose fault those severances were
...not in how many abortions you have had
...not in your morality issues
...not in your endeavors to please Him
...not in your litany of "do good" activities
...not in how many times you attended the church
...not in how many contributions you have given to the church
...not in how much time you have invested in helping others
...not in how much scripture you have memorized
...not in how many hours you have spent in prayer
...not in how many times you forgot to pray
...not in your knowledge of Christian doctrine
...not in your efforts at ministry

God is so interested in YOU, that He will pursue you to the ends of the earth to share His love with you. He is "The Hound of Heaven," and will do whatever it takes to draw you to Himself. He knows your highest good is to be filled with Himself by the presence of His Son, Jesus, and the power of His Holy Spirit. Nothing else will bring complete satisfaction to YOU, except Him. Nothing else will bring satisfaction to Him, but to see you filled with the fullness of His grace. God loves YOU so much and will be ecstatic when you surrender yourself to Him, that He will likely do back-flips throughout the universe in joyous celebration of your acceptance of a relationship of spiritual union with Him.

AUGUST 29

GRACE IS NOT A DIVINE WELFARE SYSTEM

I recall visiting with an older gentleman from Scotland. He attended a performance, "works" type of church; and he was a hard-working, proud, and self-sufficient man. What we call "government welfare" in the United States he referred to as "the dole," and he was adamant that he had no intention of ever "going on the dole"; i.e. being a "welfare recipient." The problem was that he viewed God's grace as equivalent with "going on the dole," and his pride forestalled him from accepting such. How sad when God's grace is viewed as the "divine welfare system," and one insists on attempting to work their way into God's favor.

God's grace is available through Jesus Christ (Jn. 1:17) and is the divine provision and empowerment for doing everything in the Christian life. Personal pride can prevent the reception of God's grace; but, in such a case, faith becomes equivalent with human "works," rather than the antithetical contrast to human works in "the receptivity of God's grace activity" in one's life. Such a false reversion of grace and faith is a pathetic perversion of the all-sufficient grace of God that relieves us from human performance on the religious treadmill of human performance to appease and please God and attempts to "pay God" for what has already been paid for in full by the "finished work" of Jesus (Jn.19:30).

The full and plenteous provision of God's grace is the privilege of every Christ-one in order to be and do all that God desires to be and do in our lives. The grace-privilege relieves us from the onus of continuous performance of trying to be and do what we falsely perceive to be God's expectation of us to be and do in accord with the obsolete standards of His law requirements. Oh, the joy and peace that is to be found in God's grace-provision in the living Lord Jesus Christ. Grace is not "going on the dole" but is the gracious and freely-given gift of God and His willing to be all and do all in the Christ-life – His all-sufficient grace (II Cor. 12:9).

FALSE PERCEPTION OF WHAT WE ARE TO DO

Many Christians seem to have a false perception that our relationship with God in Christ is primarily about what we are supposed to be doing *for God*, rather than all about what God has completely *done for us* in His Son, Jesus Christ, and what He desires to continue to do by His grace to provide everything necessary to live the Christ-life. This faulty perception leads inevitably to viewing the Christian life as a miserable burden of performance instead of the gracious provision and fulness of God's grace, whereby He does everything that needs doing to re-present the Christ-life through our behavior unto His glory.

Paul wrote that "we are to be confident of this, that He who began a good work in us will carry it on to completion until the day of Christ Jesus" (Phil. 1:6). "The one who calls you is faithful, and He will do it" (I Thess. 5:24). The good news of the gospel is that it is not what we do for God, but what He does in and through us. This is the message of divine grace, and it is the part of the gospel that is so often lacking in the teaching and preaching of religion in the churches of the twenty-first century. Instead, they develop program after program to keep Christians busy building the statistics in their institution.

Churchy busyness is another faulty perception of the activity in which Christians are meant to be involved. God's business on the other hand, is to act by His grace to manifest the life and character of His Son, the living Lord Jesus, who lives within every Christ-one, as a witness and testimony of His intention for all of humanity. His grace is via the empowering of the Holy Spirit within every Christ-one to accomplish His intent to redeem and restore every human being to the divine functioning within humanity. It is not what Christians are to be doing for God, but what God has already accomplished for humanity through the death and resurrection of His Son, Jesus Christ.

AUGUST 31

TEL EVANGELICA

An archaeologist and a paleontologist set out on an expedition to find the origins of Christianity. They commenced a "dig" in the Judean Hills north of Jerusalem and were actively scraping the dusty and crusty accretions from the objects they uncovered. They carefully scraped off the encrustations of religion that had become attached to Christianity over the centuries and millennia – the institutionalism, the authoritarianism, the rituals, the moralism, and the carefully crafted belief-systems. Imagine their surprise when they discovered that beneath all the accretions was not a static object of antiquity as they expected.

They discovered that the core of Christianity is a dynamic, living person, Jesus Christ, who after His resurrection from the dead (I Cor. 15:1-7), made Himself available as the "living Spirit" (I Cor. 15:45), the Spirit of life (Rom. 8:2,10,11), to indwell all believers who became Christ-ones. They discovered that Christianity is the living Christ. Jesus is alive and well on planet earth! When their findings were published in the *BAR* (the *Biblical Archaeology Review* journal), the leadership of the institutional churches were in a panic, fearing that such exposure would put them out of business. If the church is indeed such a hoax, it deserves to be deserted and to die the death of all dinosaurs.

Tel Evangelica became the foremost archaeological discovery known to man in human history. But far more important was that the living reality of the Christian gospel was no longer the best-kept secret of religion; and the mystery (once concealed, now revealed) of the living Christ was now being proclaimed, so that mankind throughout the world could be enlivened by His life. "if anyone does not have the Spirit of Christ, they do not belong to Christ" (Rom. 8:9). "Whoever has the Son has life; whoever does not have the Son of God does not have life" (I John 5:12). Jesus said to His disciples, "I am the Life" (Jn.14:6).

MEETING JESUS IN OUR SUFFERINGS

It is when we are in the midst of trials and tribulations that we are most apt to think that we are trudging through our difficulties all by ourselves without any assistance, having to endure our problems as "independent selves" relying on our own self-sufficient potentiality, trying to hack through the entanglements. But in those suffering situations, we often encounter Jesus, "Fancy meeting you here," we might remark. "I thought you were up in heaven, sitting at the right hand of God the Father, immune from earthly suffering" "You know better than that," He might say. "You know that I am living within you, as your Life. Anywhere you are, I AM. Anywhere you go, I AM there. Any time you are suffering, I AM suffering within you. You cannot be where I am not, and you cannot experience anything but that I AM experiencing that thing with you and within you and as you."

What a blessed fellowship we have with Jesus in the midst of our sufferings. "Blessed are they that mourn" (Matt. 5: 4), Jesus explained. The grace of God is especially gloriously sufficient (cf. II Cor. 12:9) when He arrives into our suffering situation in a personal way. Yes, grace is a Person, the 3-in-1 Persons of Father, Son, and Holy Spirit, who are particularly desirous of meeting us when we need Him the most, when we are hurting, helpless and hopeless, and prone to forget His presence, empowering and energizing. When we are frail and weak, thinking we are all alone, then we are most receptive to recognizing His strength right in the midst of the suffering situation (II Cor. 12:10).

It would be advantageous if we would but learn that whenever we are in a logjam of painful suffering, we should just sit down, rest, and wait for the presence of the Jesus of all comfort to meet us personally in our suffering situation and become our all-sufficient way through – not way out, but way through.

245

SEPTEMBER 2

WHAT UNBELIEVERS WANT FROM CHRISTIANS?

When asked this question, many people answered, "love." Others answered, "truth," or "integrity," or "empathy." The Barna Group, a research and opinion poll agency, conducted a survey and found that 62% of non-Christians answered the question of what they wanted from Christians by indicating they wanted "a person who will listen without judgment." This is a sad indictment upon contemporary Christian people that they should be perceived as critical, judgmental or condemnatory, rather than people of relational grace, willing to meet a person where they are, and to listen to their individual "felt needs" and concerns.

Some Christians need to learn that a major part of human conversation is listening, not just verbalizing one's opinion. To really listen to another person is to connect with them relationally, desiring to hear what they have to say – more than merely a pause from verbal speaking until you can interject into the conversation what you think is important to convey. "Let every man be swift to hear, slow to speak," wrote James, the Lord's brother (James 1:19). It is far more important to listen and to hear what is on another person's mind than to be heard, even if what you have to say is the truth of the gospel.

What non-Christians need most, of course, from Christians is Jesus – His life and character. Jesus knew how to interact with unbelievers with the grace of connecting with a person by listening prior to speaking any words of truth. Whether it was the woman at the well in Samaria or the woman taken in adultery and ignominiously dragged before Jesus in Jerusalem, Jesus did not start with critical preaching, but by meeting the person in the situation where they found themselves and graciously allowing the conversation to turn toward their real needs. By learning from the Master Teacher, we can learn what it means to listen to others without judgment.

"BY NATURE, CHILDREN OF WRATH"

Paul wrote to the Ephesians, explaining that they "were born in trespasses and sins" (Eph. 2:1,5) and "were by nature, children of wrath" (Eph. 2:3), functioning "according to the prince of the power of the air, of the spirit that is now energizing in (Greek - *energeo en*) the sons of disobedience" (Eph. 2:2). This is the initial spiritual condition of every human person. The "spirit energizing" in the sons of fallen Adam (cf. I Cor. 15:22) is the diabolic spirit manifesting his character of selfishness, sinfulness, and wrath – certainly not the spiritual character of the God of love intended to be exhibited in mankind for the purpose of His own glory.

Brad Jersak explained that "wrath" had become a Jewish synonym for Satan, Hades, or "the kingdom of darkness" in first-century Jewish thought (*CWR*). This certainly makes consistent sense within the context of Eph. 2:1-3. Satan, the Evil One, the one with the character of wrath toward God, the spirit of the antichrist (I Jn. 4:3), is operative in fallen, unregenerate mankind, because all human beings derive spiritual nature, identity and character from either God or Satan. There is no third humanistic alternative.

Christ-ones, on the other hand, have been "rescued from the domain of darkness" (Col. 1:13) and have experienced the radical spiritual transfer and transformation from "the nature of wrath" to being "participants in the divine nature" (II Pet. 1:4), and thereby "sons of God through faith in Christ Jesus" (Gal. 3:26), transferred into the kingdom of God's beloved Son" (Col. 1:13) wherein God is energizing in (Greek – *energeo en*) us both to will and to work for His good pleasure (Phil. 2:13). We all began life on earth "by nature children of wrath" (Satan); but, in union with Christ we are "by nature children of God" with the Spirit of Christ energizing within us.

SEPTEMBER 4

"THE SPIRIT OF THE ANTICHRIST"

Speculations about the identity of the "antichrist" have been many and varied throughout the history of Christian thought. The apostle John indicated that "the spirit of the antichrist" (I Jn. 4:3) was already present and active during the first century in the midst of the false teachers of Asia Minor. John did not attempt to identify a particular historical personage as the "Antichrist" but explained that anyone who does not confess (agree with God) that Jesus has come from God as God should be identified as deriving from "the spirit of the antichrist." Anyone who is against Jesus Christ, His life, character, and values, is operating and expressing "the spirit of the antichrist."

I overheard a conversation the other day between two people strategizing to become politically involved in their communities with the express intent to quench the advocacy of Christian thought and the Christian values involved therein. As I listened, I was aware that the ideology they espoused and sought to propagate was "the spirit of the antichrist." Antichrist is not merely a concept or expected evil person projected into eschatological speculation, but is the spirit of our age as Satan is "alive and well" and operative in world affairs and thinking in our age and every age. Christians encounter anti-Christ every day.

As the world plays out in history, with "the ruler of this world" (Jn. 12:31; 16:11), Satan, the devil, the Evil One, the antichrist, advocating his anti-Christian ideology in all of the world formats (political, educational, religious etc.), we will see more and more clearly the antithesis of the world and those identified as Christ-ones in the kingdom of Christ. We should not be fearful of, or alarmed at, this ideological and spiritual conflict – just aware that this will play out until Jesus Christ overcomes in victory and has put all His enemies under His feet (I Cor. 15:25). "Greater is He who is in you, than he who is in the world" (I Jn. 4:4).

CHRIST IN ME, AS ME

Many identify themselves as Christians, i.e. as Christ-ones; but that can be no different than saying you share a family surname with a relative that you have never met, who may live in a different country, even a different period of time. To say "Christ is my life" (Col. 3:4) is more than saying Jesus' life lives in me; it is to say that one is receptive to allow the indwelling Christ to manifest His life and character in our behavior – in me, through me, as me. Paul explained, "For me to live is Christ," (Phil. 1:6), meaning that there is no accounting or explanation for me apart from the fact that Jesus is manifesting Himself through me, as me.

Jesus "in me" and "through me" is equivalent to "as me"; i.e., "in me" + "through me" = "as me." In using the phrase "Christ as me," this is not to say that I am Christ, essentially, inherently or intrinsically. The phrase "Christ in me" evidences the distinction between Christ and me. The Christ "in me" expresses Himself "as me"; and what is visible to others is me behaving with the character of Christ, who is my Life. Paul wrote to the Corinthians explaining, "You are a letter of Christ, cared for by us, written not with ink but with the Spirit of the living God, not on tablets of stone but on tablets of human hearts" (II Cor. 3:3). Christians are the epistles of Christ for the world to read and see.

In the expression and manifestation of the character of Jesus in our behavior, we re-present the living Jesus to the world around us. We may be the only manifestation of Jesus that another person may ever see. When people see us with physical vision, they may be unaware that the spiritual reality they are seeing is really "Jesus in us, as us." Without spiritual under-standing, they may not recognize the "me" they see is really the life and character of Jesus expressed "in me, through me, as me"; but they will nonetheless have seen Jesus, and the Spirit of God will use such manifestation to the glory of God.

SEPTEMBER 6

RELIGIOUS SOLICITORS COME TO YOUR DOOR

Some people get very agitated when religious solicitors come to their door. Perhaps these solicitors are religious hucksters, "peddling the word of God" (2 Cor. 2:17) – not real prophets, but only in it for the profit. Perhaps the person who answers the knock on the door has been advised that 2 Jn. 10 indicates that "false-teachers should not be received into their house" and interpret that to mean that they should "tell them to get lost; never come back" and slam the door in their face. Does that sound like the gracious attitude of Jesus Christ to you? Perhaps John meant that they should not be received into one's home like a brother or sister in Christ to fellowship around what you have in common.

Wanting to express the gracious kindness of Jesus, I am willing to engage the religious solicitors in conversation, but am not willing to engage in any argumentation about their belief-system. If they want to ask questions, I set the parameters of the conversation in advance by explaining that for every question they ask, I request the equity of asking a question of them as well. My first question is always, "Where is Jesus right now?" A common answer is, "He is seated at the right hand of the Father." I affirm that their answer is correct, as far as it goes; but the transcendence of the risen Jesus must also be balanced with the immanence of Jesus. In 2 Corinthians 13:5, Paul asks, "Do you not recognize that Jesus Christ is in you, unless you believed in vain?"

Seldom do the religious solicitors know how to deal with Paul's question, because religion seldom knows anything about the risen, living, and indwelling Spirit of Jesus Christ in the spirits of receptive believers. This provides an opportunity to share the gospel with the visitors; but they will often want to change the subject by employing their proof-texts or choose to terminate the conversation.

NOT WHAT YOU KNOW, BUT WHO YOU KNOW

Many Christians have long thought that Christianity was a matter of what you know and what you believe and what you are committed to. They have thought of Christianity as a corpus of information, the dogma and doctrines of the church. But did Jesus come to bring another belief-system? Belief-systems are a dime a dozen. They proliferate in the world-system, as the tendency of natural man is to define himself by his belief-system. Jesus did not say, "I came that you might know what to believe." He said, "I came that you might have life, and have it more abundantly" (Jn. 10:10). "I am the Life" (Jn. 14:6).

Knowing facts is far different from knowing a person personally and relationally. Knowledge of information tends to puff one up with pride (I Cor. 8:1). Knowing Jesus and becoming one with His character will always lead to humility (Phil 2:3,4). The contemporary church is full of human information processors constantly at odds with one another and arguing over the small-print of doctrinal issues. Sadly, that does not facilitate a living corporate Body of Christ wherein the character of the life of Jesus within Christ-ones is interacting to re-present Jesus in the world where we presently reside.

What one knows and what one believes and what one is committed to is but sterile data. Knowing Jesus as one's life is the ever-sufficient dynamic of living truth and reality as He serves as the way to functional social human interaction – to life as God intended. The life of Jesus is love-life that counteracts the natural selfishness and me-ism of fallen human beings. The assembly of Christ-ones was never intended to be a think-tank of doctrinal ideology, but a community of love wherein Christians are reveling in the common-union that they have in the risen and living Jesus and presenting a collective unity of love that is unique in a world of discordant beliefs and commitments.

SEPTEMBER 8

JESUS' DENUNCIATION OF RELIGIOUS LEADERS

I recall my mother saying time and again: "If you don't have something nice to say, don't say anything at all." That is a valid premise for curbing our outspoken, and often selfishly biased opinions of those with whom we might dislike or disagree. Jesus, however, was not voicing selfish and biased opinions when He repeatedly denounced the religious leaders of His day (usually the scribes and Pharisees), nor did He use delicate language that would not offend the ears of those He was indicting. The epithets He used were often colorful analogies that exposed the religious false teachers as self-serving and deceiving counterfeits.

Jesus didn't "pull any punches" when it came to denouncing the religionists. He knew full well they were "hypocrites" who did not practice what they preached. Their religion was based on external image, on a veneer of godliness, while internally they were full of greed and wickedness. They were greedy, self-indulgent, and full of vain glory. They were white-washed tombs, full of death and devoid of life. They were wolves in sheep clothing, extracting money from people and burdening people with meaningless, insignificant performances of the law. They were deceitful workers, masquerading as "men of God" when in reality they were "blind guides" who abused their alleged authority as those closest to God and trafficked on the guilt-induced generosity of sincere people.

Even beyond that, Jesus used more direct name-calling for the religious leaders. He called them "snakes," a "den of vipers." He accused them of being "murderers of righteous people" for having killed the prophets of old. Then, He was so audacious as to call them "children of hell," challenging their proud contention that they were "children of Abraham" by indicating that they were "of their father, the devil." Jesus knew full well the spiritual source of religion. Is it any different today?

THE "REPRESSED MEMORIES" FALLACY

In the late 1980s and early 90s, there was a movement among psychotherapists to posit the phenomenon of "repressed memories" to attempt to explain past causes for a person's personal problems. Since the counselee-client could not recall past incidents in their life to account for present feelings and thoughts, they were alleged to have "stuffed" problematic traumatic experiences deep in their subconscious; and the job of the psychotherapist was to recover those terrible memories or alternatively to concoct connections to the disassociated memories to provide psychological explanation for such.

The daughter of a dedicated missionary friend was having personal problems as a young adult and went to see a counsellor to seek help. The psychotherapist advised her that she had "repressed memories" of sexual abuse by her father. While there was no credible evidence for such, the family was devasted by such accusations, causing fractured relationships between father and daughter, husband and wife, and ministerial colleagues. The daughter eventually realized that she had been duped into believing such a false scenario, reconciled with her father, and went on to serve in missions with her father.

My point? We should not be so quick to think that humanistic psychology has all the procedures and answers for our human problems. Yes. there are trained Christian persons who are "competent to counsel" (Rom. 15:14) by the leading of the Spirit, but they must beware of novel procedures. The "repressed memories" movement was ultimately debunked by the psychological community as dangerous and fraudulent, and testimony of such was deemed inadmissible by the legal system. The "father of lies" (Jn. 8:44) is continually at work to destroy people's lives and their communities, and we should seek counsel from Christ-ones who draw from God's counsel.

253

SEPTEMBER 10

NO THIRD ALTERNATIVE

We have all likely heard Christian speakers asking us to consider whether a particular action is sourced from Satan, or God, or man. The fallacy of such questioning is the introduction of the third alternative. When there is a dividing line, one can only be on one side or the other. There are only two diametrically opposed spiritual sources for human behavior. Even songwriter - singer, Bob Dylan, understood this in the refrain of his popular song:

> *But you're gonna have to serve somebody, yes indeed,*
> *You're gonna have to serve somebody.*
> *Well, it may be the devil or it may be the Lord,*
> *But you're gonna have to serve somebody.*

The most important premise to be taken from that song is the denial of a "third alternative," the fallacy of a human source for spiritual character or power – that we can be our own master, and "run our own show." The humanistic premise of being an "independent self" was first introduced in the Garden, with the suggestion "You will be like God." It was a lie from the "father of lies" (Jn. 8:44) and remains so to this day despite its popular acceptance in humanistic thought today.

Spiritual source is an either/or option – either Satan or God – either Satan and his character of evil, selfishness and sin; or God and His character of righteousness, as revealed and made available in the Son. The unregenerate are actuated by "the spirit working in the sons of disobedience" (Eph. 2:2) and "held captive by him to do his will" (II Tim. 2:26), thus "deriving their sin out of the devil" (I Jn. 3:8). Christians have accepted a spiritual exchange (Acts 26:18) and are indwelt by "the spirit of Christ" (Rom. 8:9), deriving from the divine source "to will and to work for His good pleasure" (Phil. 2:13).

254

HEAVEN OR HELL

Since there are two antithetical spiritual sources from which human beings are spiritually united and derive character (God or Satan), and these two spirit-personages are linked to two contrasting destinies – heaven and hell – it is in accord with spiritual reason and the revelation of God to posit that the destinies of all mankind will be either heaven or hell. Heaven is the eternal presence of God (cf. Acts 17:24; II Cor. 5:1). Hell is the extended presence of evil "prepared for the devil and his cohorts" (Matt. 25:41). Both destinies are the perpetuity and extension of the spiritual connection one has freely accepted.

Religion has identified heaven and hell as places of reward and punishment for human performance and behavior, but they are better viewed as the continuation of our chosen spiritual affiliation and union. It is not that we are expecting anything better or worse than what we already have and are familiar with in this present life. The primary change at physical death will be the context in which our spiritual bonding and activity transpires. Since spirit-beings are trans-locative and trans-temporal, the change of place and time in the extension of heaven and hell is consistent with spiritual reality in general.

When we think of heaven and hell, it is not a matter of choosing a travel destination – whether you want to go to Paris or Calcutta – it is a matter of a choice between the spiritual beings who are sources of character and energy in human lives. The choice is between the default "spirit that works in the sons of disobedience" (Eph. 2:2) or the Spirit of the living Lord Jesus (Rom. 8:9) who offers to give His eternal life to us (Jn. 3:16; 10:10), having already taken our deserved death for sin. So, what we are considering in this distinction between heaven or hell is really what might be termed "the taxonomy of spiritual reality" between God or Satan and their eventual spiritual destinies.

SEPTEMBER 12

SEEKING CHRISTIAN FELLOWSHIP

After our recent move from California to Texas, and now that the global pandemic seems to be lessening in severity, we have been attending and observing different Christian fellowships where we might find a spiritual family to identify with. We are not real concerned with the denominational "brand" on the front door, but we are desirous that the people be Christ-ones who want Jesus to function as their life and are willing to genuinely open up and discuss how the living Lord Jesus affects their lives on a day-to-day basis. We do not want a religious group who are monotonously going through the motions of obliged duty.

We are saddened to report that many groups seem to be devoid of the vitality of Christ's life. My wife and I walk away from these gatherings, saying to each other, "Where's the joy?" Love and joy are to be an evident characteristic of people who are experiencing the Christ-life. That is why Paul began his explanation of the "fruit of the Spirit" (Gal. 5:22) by explaining that such is characterized by "love and joy....". In some fellowships, even friendliness is hard to come by. One religious group seemed so fearful that they might violate the church teaching; they all appeared to have been sucking on a dill-pickle, and didn't even want to make eye-contact with a visitor.

Needless to say, we are still looking for the group of people we might enjoy fellowship with. We want to be where God wants us, and that may be in a group that does not articulate the gospel in the same manner that we do and may use different patterns of worship than we are familiar with. In that case, we have an opportunity to share what God has worked into our lives in the understanding of "Christ in you" (Col. 1:27) as our life (Col. 3:4), and our fellowship becomes a ministry opportunity, a mission field. We look forward to the Spirit's leading us to a fellowship where we "fit" and can allow Jesus to serve others through us.

SEPTEMBER 13

YOUR AWARENESS OF GOD IS TOO SMALL

Your god is only as big as your slightest irritation. For when, in the slightest irritation with what is transpiring in life you forget that God is in control, that God is sovereign, that God seeks your highest good in the midst of all things, then you have allowed the irritation to loom larger than your God. Can it be true that your awareness of God's peace and sufficiency can be overcome by a mosquito? ... by a knot that you cannot untie in your fishing line? ... by an apparatus that fails to function as you expect it to function when needed? ...or by your own inability to do what you think you should be able to do?

When an object or an action becomes irritating to us, it usually indicates that we are operating in the "flesh" (Gal. 5:16-21), rather than by allowing the Spirit of Christ to respond as us. It indicates that our selfishness is reacting to something that is not going as we wanted it to or hoped and expected that it would. The smallest disruptions of the status quo of our well-being can become niggling annoyances wherein we fail to rest in the sufficiency and provision given to us by the presence of the living Lord Jesus. We fail to let Him respond as us, even it if is merely to endure and overlook the irritation.

Theologically, we may be able to list and articulate the attributes of God; but our practical theology that allows our God to act in and through us in the difficult situations of life may be quenched by our lack of trusting and reliant faith. Our awareness of God – His presence and power and ever-present desire to be our sufficiency may lag behind our reasoned understanding of God's ability. This breakdown always comes back to faith – our availability to His ability, our surrender to His sufficiency, our receptivity of His activity. God is always willing to be everything we need, but we can certainly forestall His action by our limited awareness of all He is willing to be and do.

SEPTEMBER 14

INTERPERSONAL DISCUSSION

In the midst of a discussion with a friend the other day, I realized that the two of us came into the discussion with different frameworks of thought. It was soon apparent that she thought that any discussion where there was a difference of opinion was a contest or a conflict (an argumentative battle) to determine who was right and who was wrong. With her perspective of a discussion being a contest that necessarily involved anger against the person holding the opposing opinion, the purpose of such was to determine who would win and who would lose. Since she had a personality that disliked conflict, she tried to avoid all discussion and live in her self-insulated opinion bubble.

I view a discussion as an opportunity to understand the opinion of another, with the willingness to agree to disagree if necessary. I have been in many philosophical and theological discussion groups where participants' opinions were voiced with heated passion, even yelling and the pounding of fists on the table. They were not opponents to be conquered, but persons with differing opinions; and it was interesting to see how adamantly they expressed and defended their position. But in the end, we learned from one another and agreed to disagree about our different perspectives on the topic at hand.

Those who have engaged in forensic debate in school, having to argue and defend both sides of a position, seem to have a healthier understanding of interpersonal discussion. Life in the human community involves many inevitable opportunities for such discussion. Those who have been involved in politics, church boards, or booster clubs have observed such discussion. Scripture indicates that Christ-ones should always "be ready to give a defense for the hope that is in you" (I Pet. 3:15), but the temper of the discussion should always involve "love and understanding" (Col. 2:2).

DECIDING WHEN TO TAKE A STAND

On occasion, we are all put into situations wherein we are called upon to make a choice whether the issue at hand is worth taking a stand on or whether we should just back off, let it go, and keep our mouth shut. Parents are often confronted with situations involving their children (especially teenagers) when they have to "pick their battles." I am thinking of such issues as tattoos, body piercings and jewelry, hair color, clothing styles, etc., most of which are but temporary whims; but other issues such as offensive behavior or illegal actions must be dealt with, and we must consider how to do so in a loving manner.

There are also issues of political opinion and social morality where we may have to decide whether we are to "take a stand" publicly, or let the issue slide in our interactions. Many of us have LGBTQ friends. We may not agree with their choices, but they are still human friends with pains and problems. Sometimes we have to determine that people are more important than issues, that relationships are more important than being right. It is possible to disagree with another person's behavior without expressing any confrontational indictment upon such – to just express love without expressing any words or opinions.

As we negotiate life in the twenty-first century with its ever-increasing alternative options, we will likely be faced with numerous decisions of whether we should "take a stand" and make an issue of the situation. These are individual decisions; there is no "cut and dried" procedural and formularized propriety standards. If one is not part of the problem or the solution, perhaps it is advisable to be quiet and not attempt to engage. A Christ-one should allow the "mind of Christ" to prompt them to act with the "wisdom of Christ, which will necessarily cause them to act with the "love of Christ," which seeks the highest good of the other person without trying to change them.

SEPTEMBER 16

UNDERSTANDING

The scriptures have much to say about our need to have "understanding" of spiritual things. The nation of Israel, as a whole, was referred to as "a people without understanding" of what God was doing in their midst and failing to understand the comprehensive plan of God in the fulfillment of the Abrahamic promises and the extension of such beyond themselves. Spiritually unregenerate people, non-Christians in general, are without spiritual understanding (cf. I Cor. 2:14; Eph. 4:18; Rom. 1:31). But spiritually regenerate Christ-ones can also lack understanding of the will of God" (Eph. 5:17; II Tim. 2:7) and spiritual things (*pneumatikoi*) in general.

There are certain personalities with a natural propensity to want to get everything figured out, to understand the logical facts of any topic, and to develop a rationalistic explanation. I confess, I have been one of them. But spiritual understanding is not just comprehending with our mental faculties; it is not cognitive and nouthetic ("with the mind," Greek *nous*) knowledge where our mind grasps a thought with cerebral and epistemological reasoning. Spiritual understanding requires the spiritual "mind of Christ" (I Cor. 2:16), made available by the Spirit of Christ (Rom. 8:9) whereby we can spiritually appraise the things of God.

When examining my natural life-long quest to "understand all things," and in particular the theological intricacies of dogma and doctrine that intrigued me, the thought came to me (yes, a personal revelation) that "to understand" is "to stand under" the Lordship of the living Lord Jesus and allow the Spirit-teacher to grant me spiritual understanding of that which He wants me to know on a level that goes beyond head-knowledge. It became apparent to me that spiritual understanding is closely allied with personal surrender and submission and the willingness to allow the living God to direct my thoughts and actions.

WHAT YOU VALUE IS WHAT YOU WORSHIP

Worship is not simply a matter of corporate excitement. It is possible to worship the idolatrous god of excitement, rather than God who has revealed Himself in Jesus Christ. Gathering together, clapping, swaying, jumping up and down (what one writer referred to as "pogo-sticking for Jesus"), and singing repetitive syllables and phrases can be merely a sociological experience, devoid of the deeper meaning of true worship. We want to engage in genuine spiritual worship. The English word "worship" is derived etymologically from the Old English word *weorþscipe*, meaning to ascribe worth-ship or veneration towards an object or person. Christian worship is expressing the worth-ship of Jesus in our lives. If He is the "all in all" of our lives, then worship becomes the comprehensive directional purpose of our lives as Christ-ones. All of life is worship!

The words of Mike Q. Daniel are instructive: "Worship is simply extolling the virtue of what we value the most. The question is not if, but what will we worship." We all have objects or activities that mean something and are important to us; they have value and worth to us, and it is these that we pay attention to and focus on and in one way or another we worship. But as Christ-ones, identified in union with the living Lord Jesus, our spirit indwelt by the Spirit of Christ (Rom. 8:9), we want to engage in spiritual worship (Jn. 4:24) wherein the Spirit prompts and guides us through the worship of God in Christ (cf. Rom. 8:26).

Every moment of life can be and should be a time of worship for a Christ-one. Our *raison d'etre* is to manifest the life of Jesus Christ in our behavior and to glorify and worship God in so doing. Ours is a life-long worship that extols the worthy character of God in all that we are and do – even in the common and mundane actions of normal life – in our family life, in our recreational life, in our working life, even in our times of goofing off.

SEPTEMBER 18

SELF-PROMOTING MINISTERS

No doubt you have noticed the self-promoting ministers who splash their own faces in public print ads, video clips, and vodcasts on public media every day. It's time that someone stood up and explained to them, "It's not about you, it's about the Lord Jesus Christ. Why do you insist on putting your human image before the public in everything you do?" It does not matter what Pastor so and so, or Reverend so and so, or Evangelist so and so looks like (whether photogenic or not); that is not the issue. The people in Jesus day came saying, "We would see Jesus," and that remains what the people need to see and hear today.

Many ministers sincerely want to share the message of Jesus Christ, but what viewers see is the face of the one delivering the message. It has been said that "a picture is worth a thousand words" (and a video perhaps more than that;, and, if that is the case, then those who post their own faces day after day are indicating that they are a thousand times more important than Jesus, the One they allegedly seek to share. Self-promoting ministers have bought into the media hype that the viewing public wants to see a personal presentation of the product being offered, but the product being offered is not the minister.

Those attempting to share the gospel of Jesus Christ and all that He brings to mankind in Himself do admittedly have a difficult and unenviable task. Spiritual truths are difficult to share with those "who do not understand spiritual things" (I Cor. 2:14). But Paul cautioned against those who are merely "hawking or peddling the word of God (II Cor. 2:17) and went on to refer to those "who seek to commend or promote themselves." Those who would be ministers of the gospel must make every effort to avoid promoting themselves (as is the practice of the world around us) and make sure that their message is singularly focused on the Person and work of the Lord Jesus Christ.

DO YOU TALK WITH JESUS?

A bewildered non-Christian, who "did not understand spiritual things" (I Cor. 2:14), asked her Christian friend, "Do you really talk with Jesus?" This phenomenon is entirely foreign to the mind of the "natural man" who cannot understand spiritual things, and it is viewed somewhat akin to hallucinatory self-conversations with an imaginary friend by a person who is a little "tetched" or "wacky." It is because Christians understand the Easter event of the resurrection of Jesus from the dead to mean that Jesus is just as alive today as He was two thousand years ago, but He is now alive in Spirit-form (I Cor. 15:45), allowing us to have personal spiritual relationship and conversation with Jesus, that we use this kind of language.

Most Christians would reply in the affirmative that they do "talk with Jesus," believing that the risen and living Lord Jesus, as God, is ever-present and available for conversation (though it may not necessarily be with audible words); and such conversation is more understandable to the non-Christian when couched in the awareness of conversational prayer. Even the concept of a "personal relationship" with Jesus is foreign to an unregenerate person who does not have any understanding of Jesus' ongoing life after being raised from the dead in the resurrection and His availability to personally engage us.

In order to explain the meaning of the Christ-life with others, we should be praying that "the eyes of their heart might be enlightened" to grasp a reality beyond their natural understanding; and this is a work that only the Spirit of God can accomplish. When the Spirit has prepared a person in this manner, then the most effective witness is to simply share with friends the personal testimony of what the living Lord Jesus has done and is doing in our lives. It will take some thought-adjustment for them to grasp what we are sharing with them.

SEPTEMBER 20

"IN HIS TIME"

We live in a very time-conscious culture with precise schedules and tightly-planned orchestration of our time. The children have to be here and there for their activities. Our spouses may have different schedules than our own. Regulating the timing can become very frenetic as we sort out our priorities. In that context, Diane Ball wrote the words to the song, *In His Time*, a fairly recent (1978) chorus based on Ecclesiastes 3:11, "God made everything beautiful (suitable, appropriate, right, fitting) in His time." She thought she was going to be late to a planned meeting, due to a change in her husband's responsibilities; but circumstances worked out that she arrived "in His time."

"Lord, please show me every day, as You're teaching me Your way, that You do just what You say, in Your time." We have such a tendency to seek to run our own lives in accord with our own projected timing, but we must learn to trust God's timing for the events of our lives. This is difficult for those of us who want to control the joy-stick of our own lives. We must "let go, and let God" control the daily details of our busy lives. This is certainly in accord with our "resting in Christ" from our own self-sufficiency, in order to recognize that God's ways and God's timing is always right for what He wants to do in our lives.

One young girl, a product of our self-centered humanistic culture, admitted that when she first heard this song, she thought it meant, "Be patient, and wait long enough, and God will make things turn out the way you want them to turn out – in His time." That is obviously not the message that we are to take from this song. It is not "our way, when God allows us to have our way." Rather, it is about God's way in God's time and our surrendering to God's sovereign orchestration of all things in a way that brings glory to Himself and "causes all things to work together for good, for those who love Him, and are called by Him" (Rom. 8:28).

264

"WHAT A FRIEND WE HAVE IN JESUS"

Most are familiar with the hymn, "What a Friend We Have in Jesus." It was written in 1855 by Joseph M. Scriven as a poem for his mother, who was living in Ireland, while he was in Canada. The popular tune to the hymn was composed by Charles Converse in 1868. Some have thought the words of the hymn evidence an over-familiarity with Jesus, in similar fashion as "Jesus is my bro, or Jesus is my bud." Others have thought the reference to Jesus as "friend" to be too weak and disrespectful. One must admit, however, that the words convey the sense of relational empathy and intimacy with the living Lord Jesus.

Jesus often referred to people as "friend" (Lk. 5:20; 12:4; Jn. 15:14). Abraham was called "the friend of God" (James 2:23). James explained that the choice had to be made between being "friends of the world" or "friends of God" (James 4:4).

The phenomena of being "a friend" has been somewhat diluted by the social media application of Facebook, where "a friend" has become someone who wants to be on your list of persons who can view your daily posts. Such a person may not even be an acquaintance but has found your name on someone else's "friend list," and wants to be on your list as well. Add to that the fact that many who accept another's "friendship" on Facebook immediately hit the "do not follow" button; so they never see what the other person posts every day. We might ask, "What kind of a 'friend' is that?"

There is a sense in which Jesus is "closer than a friend" (Prov. 18:24) for those who are Christ-ones. A friend can be viewed as detached; but, for the Christ-one who has an internal spiritual oneness with the Spirit of Jesus (cf. I Cor. 6:17), Jesus becomes the essential basis of who we are "in Christ," the basis of our spiritual identity.

SEPTEMBER 22

MENTORSHIP

In recent decades in the Western Church, especially in North America, there has been an emphasis on "discipleship" as a means of teaching Christians the fundamentals of their faith and preparing them to "disciple" others for the same reasons. Jesus did commission His disciples saying, "As you are going in the world, make disciples, by baptizing and teaching them…" (Matt.28:19,20); but I am wondering whether the process we are trying to achieve might better be called "mentorship," rather than the formulaic procedures being termed "discipleship" by the religious instructional institution of the modern church.

Discipleship suggests more of a teacher–learner dynamic, whereas mentorship suggests more of a respected friend–observer dynamic wherein the mentor lives out the Christ-life by simply being who he is "in Christ" and is available to explain why he does what he does, and to answer any questions as they arise. Mentorship is more of a Spirit-led friendship.

Some have wondered who the mentors were that affected the thought and practice of Jim Fowler. My first mentor was the pastor of my youth, Kenneth Cable, who planted within me the desire to serve in Christian ministry. He referred to me as his "first Timothy." I would list T.F. Torrance as an educational mentor. Authorial mentors would include Soren Kierkegaard, Karl Barth, and Jacques Ellul. Pastoral mentors would include Vernon Whitmore, Harry Jennings, and Frank Miller. More important than the academic mentors are the spiritual mentors: W. Ian Thomas, who introduced me to the reality of "Christ in you," and Norman P. Grubb who introduced me to the reality of "union with Christ." I will forever be grateful to these men who were instrumental in the formulation of my thinking and the outliving of the practical Christ-life.

"HOW DO YOU KNOW YOU KNOW JESUS?"

She was an older lady when she asked these questions. "How do you know you have a personal relationship with Jesus? How do you know that you know Jesus? How are you so sure that the spiritual things you talk about are really true?" They were sincere questions. How did I answer?

In order to swim, one must entrust themselves to the water. You have to jump in! You have to give yourself up to the buoyancy of the water, to surrender, to submit, to yield oneself to the water. Otherwise, you will never know you can swim. In like manner, one has to give oneself up to the Spirit of God, to surrender, to submit, to yield to the Spirit in a "leap of faith." As He envelops you in His love, "the Spirit bears witness with your spirit that you are a child of God" (Rom. 8:16). It is not merely an acceptance of empirical facts. It is a surrender of the control of one's entire life to the Lordship of Jesus.

"It's like this, Mom (yes, she was my mother), "How do I know that you are my mother and my father is my father after watching you both invest your lives in making me a constructive citizen of society? I know you are my mother, and no one could persuade me otherwise. I was born that way, and I have no doubt. In like manner, Jesus invested His life for the restoration of my humanity. He paid the price (I Cor. 6:20) that I might be "born anew" into the family of God, and no one can dissuade me from that personal knowing of Jesus. I have given my life to Him and that spiritual bond of union is so personal that I converse with Jesus just like I am conversing with you right now."

One cannot have a more important conversation with their birth-mother than I had that morning, sharing with her of the spiritual new birth and how she could become a "new creature in Christ" (II Cor. 5:17) and have assurance of knowing Jesus.

SEPTEMBER 24

"THE LOVE OF GOD"

Many Christ-ones enjoy singing the hymn about the "Love of God" by Frederick M. Lehman. Lehman first wrote the words of the first two stanzas; and years later after hearing a preacher quote the words of a poem written by Rabbi Meir ben Isaac Nehori (1020-1096), he added the third stanza incorporating the thoughts of the rabbi. The familiar tune was composed by Lehman himself, and the hymn was first published in 1917 by the Nazarene Publishing House which Mr. Lehman helped to establish.

The love of God is greater far, than tongue or pen can ever tell.

It goes beyond the highest star, and reaches to the lowest hell;

The guilty pair, bowed down with care, God gave His Son to win;

His erring child He reconciled, and pardoned from his sin.

Could we with ink the ocean fill, and were the skies of parchment made,

Were every stalk on earth a quill, and every man a scribe by trade,

To write the love of God above, would drain the ocean dry.

Nor could the scroll contain the whole, though stretched from sky to sky.

The all-encompassing love of God is immeasurable. "When His love for mankind appeared, He saved us, not on the basis of deeds which we have done in righteousness, but according to His mercy" (Titus 3:4). "Because of His great love with which He loved us, He made us alive together with Christ" (Eph. 2:4). "Nothing will be able to separate us from the love of God, which is in Christ Jesus our Lord" (Rom. 8:39). "The love of God has been poured out within our hearts through the Holy Spirit who was given to us" (Rom. 5:5), and by this provision we can manifest the love-life of Jesus in our daily behavior.

WHEN A CHRIST-ONE THINKS ...

... she has a deceitfully wicked heart, she will keep asking for forgiveness.
... Christ has forgiven her and given her a new heart, she will praise Him.

... he is still a sinner, he will focus on his sins.
... Jesus nailed all his sins to the cross, he will focus on Jesus.

... she is unholy, she will keep striving for an ideal of external holiness.
... the Holy One lives within her, she can allow Him to express holiness.

... he is less than God desires, he will perform to please God.
... he is complete in Christ, he will rest in Christ's finished work.

... God is detached, distant and far away, she will long to be nearer to God.
... she is joined to the Lord, she can be confident she will never be separated.

... he has two natures, he will approach life with a divided, schizophrenic mind.
... he has the divine nature, he allows God's nature and character to be expressed.

... she should be keeping the Law, her mind-set will be focused on performance.
... Christ was the end of the Law, she will live by the provision of God's grace.

"AS A MAN THINKS, SO HE WILL ACT" (Prov. 23:7)

SEPTEMBER 26

THE KOINONIA ECCLESIA

The fuzzy parameters of what we call "Church" in the English-speaking Western world need to be clarified. Though many decry what they call "the institutional Church," it must be admitted that Jesus did institute a social institution to be constituted of a community of Christ-ones in interactive commonality who would embody Him after His brief earthly mission. His words of institution were, "Upon this rock (of common faith in Me), I will build My *ecclesia*" (Matt. 16:18). The fellowship gathering of Christ-ones in whom the risen Jesus lives has continued to grow and expand, and is alive and well on planet earth today.

Though Jesus did establish a social institution of a community of Christ-ones, this was not necessarily intended to be a legal corporation or institution, as the "Church" has become in modern times. The *ecclesia* was certainly not intended to be a political action-group of so-called "Evangelicals" attempting to influence cultural values or mold national policies. The *ecclesia* is a dynamic and collective spiritual abstraction comprised of the living reality of the eternally living Jesus functioning in Christ-ones who are constantly receptive to His being their life, together forming a corporate expression of the life of Jesus on earth today.

The *koinonia ecclesia* is the community of Christ-ones who necessarily "love one another" (Jn. 13:34,35; 15:12,16; Rom. 13:8; Gal. 5:13; Eph. 4:2). Since Jesus lives in each Christ-one as the God of love (I Jn. 4:8,16), He, through each Christ-one, will necessarily love every other Christ-one in whom He lives. When we gather in *ecclesia* fellowship of the commonality of Jesus, we will encourage one another (Heb. 3:13; 10:25) to maintain the receptive faith that allows the life of Jesus to be expressed in an ever-hostile world. Those who might be gathering for selfish purposes ("to get something out of it") might better stay at home and cry in their own beer.

270

CHRISTIANS ARE MEANT TO BE ECCENTRIC

First, it might be helpful to consider the meaning of "eccentric." The word is etymologically sourced in two Greek words: *ek* = "out of"; *kentron* = "center." Linguistically, it has come to mean "odd, irregular, different, out of the ordinary, even to the point of peculiar." In the King James Bible there are two references to Christians being a "peculiar people" (Titus 2:14; I Pet. 2:9). This does not mean that Christians are to be "weird, freakish, or bizarre – kooks or crackpots – but it does mean that Christians will likely stand-out as different than those of the world around them in ways that are counter-intuitive and counter-cultural.

Christians will appear to be anomalous to the world. They just don't seem to fit, kind of like square pegs trying to fit in round holes. The ways of the world are diametrically opposite to the ways of God, and those who belong to God's community will be manifesting God's character; while those who follow "the ruler of this world" (Satan) will be manifesting selfish and sinful character, while engaging in fleshly and worldly manifestations of evil. Christians, while they are "in the world," are not "of the world" (Jn. 17:14-18); they do not draw from the world and its spirit-source in the Evil One. They are unconventional.

God created all human beings to be *ek-centric*, to derive and draw out of the spirit-source who resides in the spiritual center-core of our human being and function. The original intent was that God Himself – Father, Son, and Holy Spirit – should dwell in the human spirit and provide the divine resource and provision for all that mankind was meant to be and do. The sin of Adam and Eve in the Garden led humanity into the fallen spiritual state of being indwelt by "the spirit that dwells in the sons of disobedience" (Eph. 2:2) with the consequent dysfunction as they continue to draw from the spirit in their spirit, but now the Satanic spirit affects the activities of their souls and bodies.

SEPTEMBER 28

THE "ONE ANOTHER" COMMUNITY

Throughout the new covenant literature, we find repetitive references to activity that Christ-ones are meant to have towards "one another." These inculcations are to those in the new covenant community. But imperative inculcations for Christ-ones always come with the prior provision of the indicative sufficiency of the availability by God's grace in Jesus Christ. Following are some of the new covenant admonitions:

Pray for one another
Encourage one another
Be at peace with one another
Discussing with one another
Speaking to one another
Love one another
Give preference to one another
Greet one another
Devoted to one another
Building up one another
Same mind with one another
Accept one another
Admonish one another
Care for one another

Serve one another
Bear one another's burdens
Tolerance for one another
Speak truth to one another
Be kind to one another
Be subject to one another
Regard one another as
  more important
Forgive one another
Comfort one another
Build up one another
Hospitable to one another
Humble toward one another
Fellowship with one another

The "one another" phrase is actually the means of implementing and expediting the manifestation of the character of God's love in the new covenant community of God's people. Grace is the dynamic divine empowering, while "one another" is the means of implementation. Love always flows outward toward others, and is thus the exact opposite of selfishness which is directed inward for our own benefit. The "one another" phrase implies the dynamic movement of interchange from one to another. We exist for others; not for ourselves. We are the unique "one another community of the *ecclesia*."

"THOU ART THE POTTER; I AM THE CLAY"

The scriptures often use the metaphor of "the potter and the clay" in reference to God's desire to mold the lives of His people. In Isaiah 64:8 the prophet exclaims, "Now, O Lord, You are our Father. We are the clay, and You our potter." Using that analogy, Adelaid Addison Pollard (1862-1934) wrote the words of what has become a favorite hymn of many Christians. The first stanza begins, "Have Thine own way, Lord, Have Thine own way; Thou art the Potter, I am the clay." The hymn was first published in 1906, with the music composed by George Stebbins (1847-1945). The words are very meaningful:

(1) Have Thine own way, Lord,
Have Thine own way;
Thou art the Potter,
I am the clay.
Mold me and make me
After Thy will,
While I am waiting,
Yielded and still.

(4) Have Thine own way, Lord!
Have thine own way!
Hold o'er my being
Absolute sway.
Fill with Thy Spirit
till all shall see
Christ only, always,
Living in me!

The point of the metaphor of the Potter and the clay is that we, the People of God, are meant to submit and yield to the molding and conforming work of God, the divine Potter. We are to be pliable and malleable in order to allow the Lord to "have His own way" in conforming us "to the image of His Son" (Rom. 8:29) and "conforming us to the divine character of godliness" (I Tim. 6:3). Part of the process of allowing conformation to the character of God may involve our being "conformed to His death" (Phil. 3:10) and allowing for the termination of all character that does not conform to God's character. The objective of this conforming process is to be "conformed with the body of His glory" (Phil. 3:21) as the living Lord Jesus continues to eternally live within the Christ-one.

SEPTEMBER 30

"HE MUST BE, THEREFORE HE IS"

In my early years of exploring what I believed, I took a course in the "Philosophy of Religion." I wrote a thesis paper on epistemology (*epi* = upon; *histemi* = to stand) – how does a person know what he knows in order "to take a stand upon those truths?" My conclusion was that no person can really know absolute truth; but, based upon the various evidences they will take their stand. "Is God an absolute truth?" I asked rhetorically. My answer: There must be a benevolent creator behind this world that we live in; otherwise it is all chaos – every man doing what is right in his own eyes (cf. Deut. 12:8; Judg. 17:6;21:25; Prov. 14;12). He must be, therefore He is; I believe in God!

I didn't really believe in God. I simply believed in a logical conclusion about God. My god was a logical conclusion. Such a god of rationalistic logical conclusion was not very comforting. A few years later, I was introduced to the things of the Spirit (*pneumatikoi*), including God's creation of human beings comprised of "spirit, soul, and body" (cf. I Thess. 5:23), and the objective that the Spirit of God (Father, Son and Holy Spirit) was intended to dwell in the human spirit of man (cf. Rom. 8:9), restoring the Life of God to mankind and allowing "man to be man as God intended" when He originally created him.

I was spiritually regenerated! The very Son of God, Jesus, now lived within me (Gal. 2:20; Col. 1:27). The entire concept of "knowing" took on a new meaning – a relational knowing that went far beyond rationalistic epistemological knowing. Believing was more than logical reasoning but was now receiving the reality of God's being and character into my spirit. Logical conclusions were as far as epistemology could take me, but henceforth I could "grow in the grace and knowledge of our Lord and Savior Jesus Christ" (II Pet. 3:18), and what an exciting journey it has been, living as a "new creature in Christ."

OCTOBER 1

"MALE AND FEMALE, CREATED HE THEM"

Our English word "sex" is derived from the Latin *sexus,* meaning "to divide." The introduction of sex in God's creation was the bifurcation of the human race into two genders – "male and female created He them" (Gen. 1:27), with the divine intent that male and female would engage in coital copulation to reproduce additional male and female children (cf. Gen. 1:22,28) to replenish the human race. Biologically, there are only two sex-genders (male or female), and the rare aberrations to such (ex. intersexual, transsexual) are so statistically minimal as to be negligible in the discussion of biological sex-genders.

In the contemporary humanistic discussion, the biological issue of sex-genders has morphed into consideration of "gender-identity," a psychological, sociological and cultural phenomenon of mental, emotional and volitional dysphoria or dissatisfaction with one's sex-gender of birth, often leading to a transgender self-determination of one's gender-identity in accord with how one thinks, feels and wants to be. This ends up being a person "playing God" and saying to God, "I don't like the way You made me; I am going to pretend and present myself as my self-chosen gender-identity. I'll do it my way!"

God created us biologically as either male or female, having either X or Y chromosomes. Our responsibility as derivative creatures is to accept God's created order in accord with the genitalia with which we were birthed. We must not deny the way God made us. Though a person may have feelings and interests that align with the other sex-gender, they can (as many have done throughout history) continue to function in accord with the way they were formed in the womb of their mother (Ps. 139:13). God's spiritual intent is that the Spirit of Christ should live in our spirit (Rom. 8:9); "male and female are one in Christ Jesus" (Gal. 3:28), manifesting His character to His glory.

OCTOBER 2

WE CAN'T BE ANYTHING WE WANT TO BE

Despite the humanistic motto that the world is telling us every day, proclaiming that "you can be anything you want to be," I must be honest enough to tell you that it is a lie, straight from the pit of hell! You cannot be anything you want to be! Who do you think you are? God? Well, even God cannot be anything He wants to be. He is who He is – the same yesterday, today, and tomorrow. He is who He is and will always be who He is. God does what He does, because He is who He is. His actions will always be consistent with His unchanging character. He never acts "out of character," i.e., contrary to who He is.

The serpent in the Garden of Eden, Satan himself, was the first one to come up with the humanistic lie that "you can be whatever you want to be." Human beings were designed by the Creator God to be derivative beings, dependent on the power and character of God to be the human beings God designed them to be. Satan suggested to the original couple that such dependent derivativeness was tyranny and suggested they rebel against such an arrangement in order to be anything and everything they wanted to be. "You, too, can be like God" (Gen. 3:5) was the central axiom of his lie. God alone has inherent, independent character; humans always have derived dependent character.

The lie of humanistic potentiality to be and do anything that any individual sets their mind to be or do is so ingrained in the basic thought of our culture that some people are appalled that anyone should challenge the premise. Sports celebrities, educators at every level, social philosophers, psychological analysts, and even religious gurus – they are all encouraging the persistent self-effort of performance to achieve all you can be. The Christian gospel is counter-cultural to all such humanistic incentivizing, explaining that the dynamic grace of God made available in Jesus Christ is the means to be and do what God intends.

THE NECESSARY CHRISTIAN PARADIGM SHIFT

To become a Christ-one and function as the Christ-one we have become, requires a paradigm shift from the natural perspective of a "natural man" (I Cor. 2:14-16) to another unnatural and supernatural perspective of thinking. It is a paradigm shift from the humanistic thought that I am in control of my life, to the willingness to surrender the control of my life entirely to Another, i.e., to the living Lord Jesus Christ. That shift in control is what Soren Kierkegaard called "the Leap of Faith." It is a leap that many are unwilling to make for it involves a total surrender of our natural attempt at self-control in order to submit to the total control of One unseen.

The paradigm shift is from the false conception that I am an "independent-self," captain of my own ship, master of my own fate, in charge of my own life and able to be anything I can aspire to be, as well as solve my own problems, even save myself. The shift is to the opposite recognition that all created human beings are dependent creatures, dependent on a spiritual source (either Satan or God), and constantly deriving the character of their being and doing from one of those two metaphysical spiritual sources. There is no greater paradigm "leap" than to exercise the acquiescence and concession of perceived self-control in order to defer and submit to the Lord Jesus Christ.

It is very difficult for the "natural man," so thoroughly immersed in humanistic thought, to accept the reality of being a derivative man. Some have even declared, "Derivativeness is tyranny," because you are giving up your natural right to control your own life to derive from another (and that was likely the serpent's argument to Adam and Eve in the Garden). As dependent, derivative, and receptive creatures, human beings are not "gods unto themselves" but must submit and receive from either "the god of this world" (II Cor. 4:4) or "God Almighty" (Rev. 21:22).

OCTOBER 4

THE FATHERHOOD OF GOD

The "universal fatherhood of God" thesis is simply an assertion that God is the originator and source of everything that exists, including mankind in general. This requires no spiritual understanding whatsoever, just logical reasoning concerning an "intelligent designer" behind all that exists. A non-Christian theist, as was C.S. Lewis, could assent to "the universal fatherhood of God"; but he later, by his own admission, became a Christian, entering into a personal relationship with God the Father through the spiritual reception of the Son, Jesus Christ. Triune relationality evidences the spiritual Fatherhood of God.

So, the natural reasoning of the "universal fatherhood of God" is an extremely limited perspective – merely a baby-step toward the understanding of God as our spiritual Father. The loving Father, who because He has a Son, Jesus, draws us into a personal and intimate family of sons and daughters (cf. Heb. 2:10) who personally relate to Him as "Abba, Father" (Rom. 8:15; Gal. 4:6). By our spiritual birth (Jn. 3:1-6; I Pet. 1:3), we participate in the Family of God, wherein God is our loving Father in genuine relational intimacy. Since "like begets like" in spiritual parentage, as in biological parentage, we "are partakers of His divine nature" (II Pet. 1:4) by spiritual new birth.

The "spiritual Fatherhood of God" equips us to comprehend the spiritual things (cf. II Cor. 2:14-16) passed on by our spiritual Father. "As many as received Him, to them He gave the right to become children of God, even to those who believe in His name, who were born, not of blood, nor of the will of the flesh, nor of the will of man, but of God" (Jn. 1:12,13). Nicodemus did not understand such "spiritual things," as evidenced by his naturalistic gynecological comment about crawling back into his mother's womb (Jn. 3:4) in order to be "born again." He knew better, for Jesus said, "You must be born from above" (Jn. 3:3).

THE MYSTERIES OF GOD

Preachers, pastors, and Christian scholars often try to convince Christ-ones that there are simple answers for the great questions of Christian thought. To the contrary, there are not simple answers; and, to give that impression, ends up in glossing over and covering up the difficult issues. For the finite understanding of man to attempt to understand the infinite complexities of God and His ways, which are "past finding out" (Rom. 11:33), is impossible; and we have to admit and accept such. But to the extent that we can understand with our finite minds, we must attempt to do so and express such in human words.

We must understand that the mysteries of God and His actions in His Son, Jesus Christ, must remain just that – mysteries! Philosophy has long recognized that some of what we call knowledge is *apophatic*, i.e. we speak of what we do not know empirically. There are realities that are inexplicable, unexplainable, unknowable. Even science cannot explain how electricity works, much less why our mother loves us. Some things are not meant to be explained but are simply meant to be enjoyed. The first tenet of the Westminster Confession explains, "the chief end of man is to glorify God and enjoy Him forever."

Our knowledge of God must remain both *apophatic* (speaking of the mysteries we do not fully understand) and *cataphatic* (speaking of God in accord with His Self-revelation of Himself in His creation and specifically via His Son, Jesus Christ). "If you have seen Me, you have seen the Father" (Jn. 14:7,9), Jesus explained. We must avoid attempting to fit God into our finite comprehension, for we risk making a "god of our own under-standing," conformed and distorted like putty to our own criteria. We must also avoid simplistic explanations, like "all the answers are found in the Bible, and the preacher knows them all." We can know the unknowable mysteries via what God makes known.

OCTOBER 6

GOD WAS SATISFIED WITH JESUS' DEATH?

The Greek language had two words (*hilasterion* and *hilasmos*) which were used primarily to express how one was to satisfy the pagan gods. The wrathful and blood-thirsty gods needed to be appeased, pacified and placated in order to be satisfied and gratified with man's restitutional performance of sacrifice and recompense. These two words are used in the New Testament (Rom. 3:25; Heb. 2:17; I Jn. 2:2; 4:10). They are usually translated into English as "propitiation" or "expiation" and used to explain a theory of the atoning work that was accomplished in the death of Jesus Christ on the cross of Calvary.

Anselm (1033-1109) developed the "satisfaction theory of the atonement of Christ," explaining that Jesus' death satisfied God's subjective offense at the insult of sin. John Calvin (1509-1604), who was trained as a lawyer, developed the "penal substitution theory of the atonement of Christ," framing Jesus' death in legal and forensic terms, explaining that Jesus' death satisfied God's wrath upon sin by taking God's just penalty for the sin of all mankind vicariously and substitutionally, dying in the place of sinful humanity. This has been the predominant Protestant explanation for more than four hundred years.

Yes, God was dissatisfied with sin, contrary to His character. The triune God – Father, Son and Holy Spirit – in loving conjunction and complicity, determined to remedy the sin consequences and restore mankind. God was satisfied that the Son volunteered to empty Himself of all right to divine function and to become and function as a human being, living in faithful receptivity as the Perfect Man (Jn. 14:10). God was satisfied that this sinless, Perfect Man could be the perfect substitutional sacrifice for the sins of mankind. God was satisfied that Jesus voluntarily laid down His life in death, effecting the "one mind" of God's teleological intent to restore mankind to God-indwelt humanity.

CARPE DIEM

The first known use of the Latin phrase *Carpe Diem*, meaning "to pluck" or "seize the day," was in the Roman poet Horace's *Odes* (I.11), dating to 23 B.C. The idea, however, goes back into ancient literature, often corresponding with the ideas of the Greek philosopher, Epicurus (341-270 B.C.), focusing on present, personal pleasure (Greek *hedone*, thus "hedonism"). Robert Frost published a poem in English in 1938, entitled *Carpe Diem*, wherein a character called "Age" tells children, "Be happy, happy, happy; seize the day of pleasure." In the 1989 film, *Dead Poet's Society*, English teacher John Keating encourages his students, "*Carpe diem*. Seize the day, boys. Make your lives extraordinary."

From its inception, the phrase has usually been used in accord with such humanistic premises as "Make the best of today by being all you can be, for the betterment of yourself and the world around you." "Live for today; you may not get another." "Enjoy life while you can." "Enjoy the moment." A contemporary acrostic expression, "YOLO," means "you only live once," so seize the day. Social philosophers have used the phrase *carpe diem* as a means to counter the random spontaneity indicated in the popular "Just do it!" motto made famous by Nike.

A statement similar to the *carpe diem* phrase seems to be included in the Apostle Paul's epistle to the Christians in Ephesus. "Make the most of your time, because the days are evil" (Eph. 5:16). The Greek word for "time" that Paul used was *kairos*, referring to those times when God interjects Himself into our *chronos* time, making Himself and His will known to us. From a Christian perspective, then, we are to make the most of our time by being all that we are "in Christ Jesus" today, in accord with God's personal revelations to our lives. It is not a humanistic self-striving to be or do something, but living out of all that God has become by the Son and through the Spirit in us.

OCTOBER 8

PROVIDENTIAL ORDERING OF ALL EVENTS?

Beginning with the conviction that God is all-loving, all-knowing, and all-powerful, our human thought must proceed to the questions: "To what extent does God order and orchestrate all events among the world of mankind? Is God in charge and in control of all that occurs within His created order? Are all events divinely determined in advance?" Those who answer the latter two questions affirmatively often refer to their perspective as the Sovereign Providence of God, often implying that every action in the universe is predestined to occur and enacted in accord with God's divinely predetermined plan.

But the word "providence" does not necessarily indicate such absolute divine planning and implementation. Derived from two Latin words: *pro* = before, ahead; *videre* = to see, the word "providence" means seeing or being aware of what is to come, i.e. foresight or foreknowledge. The omniscient God can see what is yet to come but always acts consistently with how He created human beings to function as choosing creatures with freedom of choice. Finding and maintaining this balance between divine control and human acceptance constitutes a dialectic that is difficult for many humans to hold in tensioned balance.

A balanced understanding of "providence" must find the middle ground between the extremes of Pelagian humanism which diminishes the Lordship of God and Augustinian divine determinism which diminishes human freedom of choice. We must admit that everything that pertains to human salvation is initiated by God's grace. Nothing of the salvation of humans can be attributed to the free choice of man – man can in no way save himself. However, God created humanity with response-ability in the freedom of choice to God's grace, and that was not rendered inoperative by the sin of Adam. This dialectic of God's grace and human receptivity of faith is crucial to Christian thought.

OCTOBER 9

"RESIDENT BOSS"

In his classic book, *The Normal Christian Life* (chapter 10), Watchman Nee tells of a mechanic and his wife in China, whom he had introduced to Jesus during an extended retreat in the hills. "They were born again, and a new light and joy came into their lives, a real conversion," recounts Nee.

The man and his wife returned home. He was in the habit of drinking wine with his meals during the cold winter months, and he would often do so in excess. As winter began to settle in, the wine was brought to the table; but that day, his custom to give thanks to God for the food was met with speechlessness. He was bewildered as to why he could not pray, and he and his wife searched the Scriptures in vain to ascertain whether God's word would shed any light on the matter. As new believers, they did not know the Bible very well; and they would not be able to consult with Watchman Nee for a few months. They decided that they would drink their wine for now but would refer the matter to Nee the next time they saw him. Yet, remarkably, no prayer could flow out of the man's mouth. When the man finally met with Watchman Nee and told his story, he said, "*Resident Boss* would not let me have that drink!" He was referring to the spiritual indwelling control of the living Lord Jesus Christ.)

Christians often fall into the trap of living according to principles and precepts of right-versus-wrong external behavior. They may even ask themselves, "What would Jesus do?" That question, however, implies that Jesus is not present. But, in fact, Jesus is living in the spirit of all Christ-ones; and He has set up His throne as Lord in our hearts. Have we consulted with the *Resident Boss*? He's a real living Person, and He wants to be expressed through us. One word or prompting from Him can change everything! If He says "No," it doesn't matter how right or good or reasonable or expedient it is, God has revealed His word for you!

OCTOBER 10

MOTION REQUIRES A SOURCE OF GENERATION

When I was in high school, I took a science course in physics. I dropped out after a few weeks. The teacher knew his subject but didn't know how to teach, i.e., to convey the subject so others could understand. (Some people think that is my problem also!) The subject at hand in this article is an attempt to transition from the physics of motion-generation to the recognition of spirit-motion generation. There is no spontaneous self-generated human motion or existence "out of nothing," not in the physical or spiritual realms. Dynamic motion must have a source of dynamic generation outside and other than the object itself.

The single example of Self-generated and perpetuated motion is God. God *does* what He *does*, because He *is* who He *is*. All that God does He does *ek autos* = out of Himself. God is the Creator, and His creative activity is *ek autos*. He did not create *ex nihilo* (out of nothing), as theology has speculated, but *ek autos* (out of Himself). Paul wrote to the Christians in Rome, "For from (Greek *ek* = out of) Him (God)...are all things." To the Corinthians Christians, he wrote, "There is one God, the Father, from (*ek* = out of) Whom are all things" (I Cor. 8:6). This is not spontaneous generation "out of nothing," but divinely generated creation.

This is simply the theological expression of Einstein's physical theory of relativity, $E=MC^2$. All of the energy that supplies the motion/action of created beings is relative to a spiritual energy source beyond the creature itself, i.e. derived out of Satan or God. Science explains, and spiritual experience reveals, that everything in the cosmos is in dynamic motion, from the protons, neutrons, electrons inside every atom to the spiritual action of Father, Son, and Holy Spirit operative throughout the universe. The tragedy is that religion, the tangible counterfeit of spiritual reality, treats everything from a static perspective, failing to recognize that motion must have a divine generative source.

OCTOBER 11

HUMAN BEING AND FUNCTION IS DERIVED

One of the greatest neglects in the history of Christian thought is the topic of biblical anthropology, i.e. how did God constitute human creatures, and intend mankind to function? Subsequently, how did the dysfunctionality of man occur? To develop a foundation for such, we need to consider the exigency of mankind. "Exigency" comes from two Latin words: *ex* = out of; *agere* = to set in motion – that which is required for human beings to be set in motion, since they are not self-generating. Consideration of the source-impetus out of which mankind is set in motion sets a philosophical foundation to our theology.

God did not create "little gods" (despite the Greek conception of a pantheon of gods who were alleged to anthropomorphically copulate and create "other gods"). In the decalogue (ten commandments), God explained, "You shall have no other gods before Me." The prophet Jeremiah declared, "There is none like You" (Jere. 10:7). Human beings are not "little gods" (despite the humanistic premise that posits that humans are a generating source unto themselves). Human beings are not self-generating beings, as only God is eternally and perpetually self-generating. God did not create lesser self-generating automatons.

Since human beings are not self-generating, they must be derivative, deriving their source of being and action from outside of themselves, out of another, from a spirit-source, either God or Satan. Human beings are creatively derived from the Creator God and intended to be functionally derivative from the Sustainer-Creator God. This distinctive thesis of mankind being derivative creatures, requiring the presence and function of the Creator God within the creature in order to function as intended is the key to understanding Christian anthropology. It is the only real antithesis and antidote to the prevailing humanistic philosophy that pervades human thought and culture in our day.

OCTOBER 12

A REMADE MAN

Why is it so difficult for modern males to be open to the gospel of Jesus Christ? (I don't think it is any different in the twenty-first century than it has been for the millennia of the past.) So many men pride themselves on being "a self-made man" (ex. President Nixon). Having endured hardships of war, the trials of life and fought through the jungle of life, the masculine gender has a particularly difficult time overcoming the humanistic conclusion that "I am a survivor; I am a "self-made man." They are not inclined to give up on what they think they have earned in exchange for a free unknown gift of becoming a "new man".

In light of such, many men are not interested in becoming a "remade man." "I fought to make myself what I am; I survived all that was thrown at me, and I am not interested in giving that all up to be completely remade, renewed, made new." "I am not sure I want to be a 'remade man'; for to do so, I would have to give up on (repudiate? die to?) the 'self-made man' that I am." "I would have to exchange my identity." "I would have to start over on who I consider myself to be." "I am not sure I want to take on another remodeling project." They do not understand that what they are being offered is not a performance rebuilding or reconstruction project of self-improvement.

To surrender, to release control, to submit is a decision that is very difficult for the male mind, the male ego to consider. There is a sense in which he feels like he is giving up everything. Like all human beings in our performance-oriented culture, the grace of God is foreign to natural understanding. They do not understand that grace is what God does, not what we do – no self-performance involved. On the basis of the "finished work" (Jn. 19:30) that God has already completed in the death of His Son on the cross, God has done and will do everything necessary to make us a "new creature" (II Cor. 5:17) and perfect us as such (Phil. 1:6).

"FOR BETTER OR FOR WORSE"

When we get married, whether younger or older, we are committing ourselves to a blind bind. There is so much about the other person that we are not aware of, that we do not know. We are, for the most part, unaware of the many possible problems that may be lurking within that partner. We commit ourselves to take this person as our lifetime mate, "for better or for worse." Does their family have a history of physical, neurological, mental or emotional problems? We do not know the extent of the fleshly patterns of selfishness and sinfulness that have been contoured in the desires of the soul of this potential partner.

Is there a noticeable humanistic or narcissistic quest in the family for money, power, or prestige? Is there a propensity to any form of addiction (alcohol, drugs, medicines, material acquisition)? What are the values and priorities of the family with which we are connecting? The sins of the father (and mother) are often passed on to the third or fourth generations (Exod. 20:5; 34:7; Numb. 14:18). With all of these uncertain variables, it is a wonder that any marriage remains intact for more than five years – only by the grace of God – because the "worse" often reveals itself in that amount of time.

The best hope for a human marriage comes when both persons (male and female) have a commonality of spiritual reception and have exchanged the satanic spirit for the Spirit of Christ within their human spirit (Acts 26:18; Col. 1:13). Otherwise, they are "unequally yoked" (II Cor. 6:14) spiritually. One has to consider whether this would-be partner understands the difference between religion and being a Christ-one. Is their faith more than skin-deep – more than just a religious veneer of mental assent and emotional sensation? To what extent are they allowing the indwelling Christ to be the central reality of their life and manifesting His character in their behavior?

OCTOBER 14

FATHER GOD IS SO FAITHFUL

It will soon be fifty (50) years since God was so gracious as to reveal His spiritual realities to me in October, 1973. As an arrogant P.A. (pompous ass), who thought he knew everything (and really knew nothing), God, working through an Assembly of God pastor, with a Baptist pastor and Nazarene pastor alongside, explained spiritual regeneration with a haughty younger pastor who thought that the rite of water baptism was all that was necessary. My eyes of spiritual enlightenment were opened as I knelt in the pastor's study and opened myself in availability to everything that God might have for me in Jesus.

I have not wavered from what God so faithfully taught me by His Spirit in the ensuing years. The message of "Christ in me" (Gal.2:20; Col. 1:27), learned primarily through W. Ian Thomas and the correlative message of "Christ as my Life," learned primarily through the teaching of Norman P. Grubb, have remained the spiritual foundation of reality for me through those almost fifty years. Father God has been so faithful to allow His Spirit to teach me the lessons of the inspired scriptures, but more importantly the intimacies of "knowing Jesus" in spiritual union and allowing the living Jesus to manifest His life "as me."

I look back at what God has taught me and been doing in my life, using the teaching notes and the written materials developed in those years, and I stand amazed at the faithfulness of God in directing my thinking and my steps. With only a few slight missteps into questionable thinking and practice, I have been kept on course by the guidance of the Spirit and the grace of God. I stand in awe at how God has faithfully and consistently formed my life and my thought and has been conforming me to Himself to express divine character in my behavior to His glory (Isa. 43:7). Anything that might be called "my faithfulness" in this process is ultimately the expression of "His faithfulness."

FROM THE INSIDE OUT

Many people do not seem to be aware of the centrifugality of human behavior. The word comes from two Latin words: *centrum* = center; *fugus* = to flee, spread out; thus meaning "to spread out from the center." Combined with the Greek words: *ek* = out of; *kentron* = center, meaning "out of the center", we have the basic function of humanity – from *the inside out*. Paul indicates we are comprised of "spirit, soul, and body" (I Thess. 5:23); so, from the center spirit-core of our human function, we allow for the spiritual character of the spirit (God or Satan) indwelling our human spirit to radiate out into bodily behavior.

The world and its religion alternatively speculates that human behavior is to be regulated by external application of rules and regulations (morals and God's Law) imposed upon human beings. to be performed by human beings. These "do this" and "don't do that" admonishments are considered to be the basis of behavior modification. The problem with these is that there is no provision to implement the performance of these regulations other than human will-power and self-effort. Such means of behavior mobilization are notoriously inadequate and inefficient, usually culminating in personal failure.

Using the imagery of an artesian well where the water comes out from within the earth, the scriptures seem to explain that divinely intended human behavior functions from the inside out – "from one's innermost being shall flow rivers of living water" (Jn. 7:38). As life rolls out, the rotating motion from one's center point creates the centrifugal force that presses things outward from the center to the perimeter. From the spirit-source that dwells and operates within our human spirit – either Satan or God – the character of one or the other radiates out to the behavior of our soul and body. This centrifugal action, whereby we derive from one or the other, best describes human behavior.

OCTOBER 16

SCRIPTURE TRANSLATION

Translation of any book into another language is not an easy task. The grammar, the word order, and the meanings of different words must be considered. In the Jewish and Christian scriptures of Old and New Testaments, they must be translated from the original languages of Hebrew, Aramaic, and *koine* Greek; and the translator must have an adequate understanding of the original language. No original manuscripts are available, so the best manuscripts (usually the oldest) must be utilized. Older translations into English (ex. KJB) did not have access to the best manuscripts which were discovered at a later date.

"All scripture is inspired" (Greek *theopneustos* = God-breathed – II Tim. 3:16); so scripture translation is a sacred responsibility, and the accuracy of words and meaning from the source text must be maintained without inserting theological or ecclesiastical bias. Since translators are fallible human beings, most English translations have some bias – I do not know of any that do not. The plethora of modern English translations in the twentieth and twenty-first centuries includes many with gender, racial, and theological bias and causes many readers to be skeptical of the reliable accuracy of the translation they use.

There are two primary styles of English translations. Formal equivalence strives for precise translation of the words (ex. RSV, NASB, ESV), whereas functional equivalence seeks to present the general meaning of the text (ex. LB, NIV, Message). Whatever translation English readers choose to read, they must remember that the Bible must not be substituted for the living Word of the person of Jesus Christ (cf. Jn. 1:1,14). To do so is bibliolatry – idolatrous worship of the book. Christ-ones must also keep in mind that the Bible is the only book in the world that requires the reader to know the Author of the book in order to understand the real meaning of the text.

NOMINAL CHRISTIANS

Periodically, I hear people refer to "nominal Christians," meaning that some who call themselves "Christians" are "Christians in name only." Personally, I do not want to make such a judgment, because "God knows who are His" (II Tim. 2:19). A Christian is a Christ-one, one who has received the living Lord Jesus into their spirit by the receptivity of faith. This transaction is far more than assuming a label, title, or designation. It is a vital transformation whereby the "spirit of error" has been exchanged for "the spirit of truth" (I Jn. 4:6), and the presence of the Spirit of Christ (Rom. 8:9) makes one a Christ-one.

To become a Christ-one means far more than to assume a new name (Greek *nomos* = name). "If any person is in Christ, he is a new creature; old things have passed away, behold all things have become new" (II Cor. 5:17). In our initial spiritual state, we were an "old man" (Rom. 6:6; Eph. 4:22; Col.3:9); but, when we became a Christ-one, we became a "new man" (Eph. 4:24; Col. 3:10), part of a new creation (Gal. 6:16), and a "new humanity" (Eph. 2:15-NIV). The Christ-one has partaken of "newness of life" (Rom. 6:4) and "newness of spirit" (Rom. 7:6), whereby our human spirit has become indwelt by the Spirit of Christ.

The "new creature" Christ-one is a vital participant in the "new covenant" (Matt. 26:28; Lk. 22:20; II Cor. 3:6; Heb. 8:8; 9:15; 12:24), the fulfillment of all God's promises (II Cor. 1:20) that He intended to put into action in His Son, Jesus Christ. What a privilege to be a Christ-one, but it is far more than just a name or designation. Everything about our spiritual condition has become new. We are ontologically new (new in being) and are intended to be operationally new (new in behavior, as we allow the Christ-life to be manifested in all we think and do). There is no such thing as a "nominal Christian," for the living Lord Jesus must of necessity live out His life in every Christ-one.

OCTOBER 18

THE CHRISTIAN AND SUFFERING

Christians in the Western world have, for the most part, not had to deal with suffering (real life or death suffering) to the extent that Christians in other parts of the world have had to do. It is one thing to ponder suffering as an abstract topic of discussion or hear of suffering happening to others on the far side of the world; but, when it hits close to home in our own lives or in the lives of our loved ones, then the pain of such has to be absorbed and responded to. It is a natural human response to ask, "Why, Lord? Why did you allow this pain in my life?" Others may respond, "Why not you? Why should you be exempt?"

In his book, *A Grief Observed*, author C.S. Lewis, having experienced personal suffering, explained, "We were promised sufferings. They were part of the program. We were even told, 'Blessed are they that mourn,' and I accept it. I've got nothing that I hadn't bargained for. Of course, it is different when the thing happens to oneself, not to others, and in reality, not imagination." The reality of personal suffering is painful in the midst of such, but when viewed with 20/20 hindsight, many will comment, "It is the best thing that could have happened to me, for it forced me to reach out and draw near to God as my refuge."

French thinker, Simone Weil, wrote, "The extreme greatness of Christianity lies in the fact that it does not seek a supernatural remedy (to avoid or overcome) suffering, but a supernatural use for suffering." The apostle Paul certainly realized that his "thorn in the flesh" was an impetus to recognize that "the grace of God was sufficient" (II Cor. 12:9), for divine power is perfected in our weakness. If you are "in Christ" and Christ is "in you," where is Jesus when you are suffering? When He is your life, then He is right there in the midst of the suffering, feeling your pain and hurt, and willing to endure it with you and as you, providing you with His comfort and sufficiency.

CHRIST IS ALL IN ALL

Some groups of Christ-ones like to repetitively use the phrase, "Christ is all in all." What do they mean when they use the phrase, and is there any biblical justification for such? If not clarified, the phrase is subject to monistic and panentheistic implications. Swiss theologian, Karl Barth, emphasized a Christocentric theology; but there were some who charged him with Christomonism, a false-charge in the classic sense of denying the Trinity. Barth's theology was a corrective to the theological liberalism of the early twentieth century, seeking to emphasize how the God-man was central to the redemptive mission of God.

One of the mottoes of the Protestant Reformation was *solus Christus* (Christ alone, only), indicating that Jesus Christ alone is the "one mediator between God and man" (I Tim. 2:5). This is so integral to the gospel that it is not incorrect to indicate that "Christianity is Christ." The risen and living Lord Jesus is both Lord and Savior, as well as the very Life from which ever Christ-one operates. He is the dynamic of God's grace for everything that comprises Christianity, i.e. the Christ-life. "It is no longer I who lives, but Christ lives in me" (Gal. 2:20). "For me to live is Christ" (Phil. 1:21), wrote Paul. "Christ is my life" (Col. 3:4).

Writing to the Ephesian Christians, the apostle Paul referred to "the *ecclesia*, which is His Body, the fulness of Him that fills all in all" (Eph. 1:23). At least in the context of the corporate collective of the congregation of Christ-ones, the living Lord Jesus Christ is said to "fill all in all." The living Spirit of Jesus is the fulness of all that we are and all that we do in all Christ-ones. Jesus fills every spiritual need that Christ-ones will ever have. He is the entire identity of who we are "in Christ" and the full provision for the manifestation of His Christ-life. Thus, we have a clear and adequate biblical explanation of the declaration that "Christ is all in all" – He is all that all Christ-ones need.

OCTOBER 20

WHEN GOD IS GRACIOUS TO TAKE ME HOME

The psalmist indicates that a usual human lifespan is "threescore years and ten, and if by reason of strength fourscore years" (Ps. 90:10 – KJV). This has been statistically extended by means of modern medicine, but as a general rule it remains true. Since I am past the threescore and ten (seventy years of age), but not yet to the fourscore (eighty years of age), it is likely that I am in the twilight years of my lifespan here on earth. I am satisfied with the life that I have enjoyed in my physical spacesuit, but I am looking forward to that time when I can walk through the door into the eternal perpetuity of heavenly relationship with Jesus.

I am not so presumptuous as to attempt to implement that transition at my own timing and am quite willing to wait for God's perfect timing to call me home to Himself. "His ways are always right." (Hosea 14:9). I do not expect to receive anything other than what (or Who) I have already received in my receptivity of the life of the living Lord Jesus. To think that there is something additional to what we have in Jesus is to subtly indicate that Jesus is insufficient or not enough –and that I do not believe! The content of being united in "one spirit" with the life of Jesus will remain the same, but I expect the new context of a "new body-house" (II Cor. 5:1-4) in a perfect neighborhood.

How amazing it will be to experience the perfect Christ-life in an eternal location absent of all hindrances. While living on earth in our physical body, we have had to endure the constant temptation of the enemy (Satan), attempting to repeatedly lie to us by indicating that we are not who God says we are "in Christ. In our heavenly spiritual body there will be no residual soulical flesh patterns that war against the impulses of the Spirit (cf. Gal. 5:17). The apostle John explains that "there will no longer be any death; there will no longer be any mourning, or crying, or pain; those things have passed away" (Rev. 21:4).

OCTOBER 21

"PERFECT LOVE CASTS OUT FEAR"

This well-known phrase of the New Testament contained in
John's first epistle, chapter four, verse eighteen is commonly
misunderstood. The full verse reads, "There is no fear in love;
but *perfect love casts out fear,* because fear involves punishment,
and the one who fears is not perfected in love." The first question
that must be asked is what, or who, is "perfect love"? In the same
chapter, John twice indicates that "God is love" (I Jn. 4:8,16) and
explains that such perfect *agape* love expressed among Christ-
ones must be derived from God who is love. If a Christ-one is not
manifesting love, he is not united with God who is love.

Love is not an abstract commodity or sentiment. Love is always
an active expression of the character of God directed toward
others. The "perfect love" that God is, when expressed by Christ-
ones is always the love of God perfected in active manifestation
of God's love toward others. "The love of God was shed abroad in
our hearts by the Holy Spirit who was given to us" (Rom. 5:5)
when we were spiritually regenerated in new birth. Paul proceeds to explain that "the fruit of the Spirit is love..." (Gal. 5:16).
Agape love is not an attitude or sentiment that any human can
generate out of themselves. It is always an act of God.

Interestingly, John explains that "fear involves punishment." The
twice stated phrase that "God is love" implies that God is not a
punitive God imposing penalties for failure to act lovingly.
Punitive consequences are more likely the character of Satan:
"You're going to have to pay for your misdeeds and failure to
perform up to the love-standards. You better be afraid of those
consequences." That kind of satanic fear is cast aside when we
recognize that God's love is always derived from the God who is
love, who always desires to express His love through us by His
grace; and this is the sure certainty that God is working in and
through us when we allow God to express His love to others.

OCTOBER 22

"HE'S EVERYTHING TO ME"

Ralph Carmichael was a popular and prolific composer of Christian music during the twentieth century. He was the music director of Billy Graham's early films and composed several folk-rock musicals in the late 1960's. This song, "He's Everything to Me," was written in 1964 and expresses a great testimony:

> "In the stars His handiwork I see;
> On the wind He speaks with majesty;
> Though He ruleth over land and sea ... What is that to me?
> I will celebrate nativity, for it has a place in history.
> Sure, He came to set His people free ... What is that to me?
>
> 'Til by faith I met Him face to face,
> and I felt the wonder of His grace,
> Then I knew that He was more than just a God
> Who didn't care, that lived a way out there,
> And now He walks beside me day by day,
> Ever watching o'er me lest I stray,
> Helping me to find the narrow way.
> He's everything to me.

When Christ-ones come to the place where they can say, "Christ is everything to me," they truly recognize the Lordship of Jesus in total availability and receptivity. Jesus is everything I need and desire; everything that brings me joy (Jn. 15:11; 16:24; 17:11); everything that thrills my soul; everything that provides my greatest need; everything that makes me complete (Col. 1:28); everything that brings peaceful serenity (Phil. 4:7); everything of eternal consequence.

In Christ I am lacking nothing (James 1:4). What more could I want than Jesus? He is my redemption, my righteousness, and my sanctification (I Cor. 1:30). "He's everything to me!"

THE GREAT HUMAN DECEPTION

The Deceiver (Rev. 12:9), the "father of lies" (Jn. 8:44) has "blinded the minds of the unbelieving (II Cor. 4:4). The "natural man" (I Cor. 2:14) is deceived (Tit. 3:3), just as Eve was deceived by Satan (II Cor. 11:3), and the world of unregenerate persons are "lovers of self" (II Tim. 3:3), deceived by a natural, humanistic wisdom that is demonic (James 3:15), thinking that they are "independent selves," having ultimate control and power of what they think and do. It's a lie! They need to "come to their senses and escape from the snare of the devil, having been held captive by him to do his will" (II Tim. 2:26).

Far from being independent, these duped "slaves of sin" (Rom. 6:17) are indwelt by the diabolic "spirit that is now working in the sons of disobedience" (Eph. 2:2). Natural, disobedient humanity does not "sin because they are sinners" (the common theological explanation), but they engage in selfishness and sinfulness because they derive character from the Evil One. Yes, fallen humanity are designated with the spiritual identity of "sinners" (Rom. 5:19) because the source of sin and selfishness (Isa. 14:14) dwells within them; and, when they sin, they derive what they do from the devil (I Jn. 3:8).

It is time for those who call themselves "Christians" to give up the vestiges of humanistic thought, understand "the great human deception," and share the gospel message of genuine conversion "from the dominion of Satan to the dominion of God" (Acts 26:18). The need of fallen mankind is to be "rescued from the domain of darkness, and transferred to the kingdom of God's beloved Son, in whom we can have redemption, the forgiveness of sins" (Col. 1:13,14). Such a rethinking of Christian thought will require the acceptance of the biblical teaching of derivative humanity, recognizing that all behavioral manifestations must have a spiritual source in either Satan or God.

OCTOBER 24

EVANGELICAL HUMANISM

This phrase actually comprises an oxymoron; it is an intended incongruity of words that should never be conjoined because they have such disparity of meaning as to be antithetical one to the other. The fallacy of humanism began in the Garden of Eden when the serpent said to the original couple, "You will be like God, knowing good and evil" (Gen. 3:5). When human beings aspire to be like God, or think that they are the self-determiners of good and evil, these are the premises of humanism. The natural wisdom of the world of fallen mankind is the deceived thought of humanism that elevates man above God.

The basic thinking of what is now called "evangelicalism" is so infected with humanistic philosophical premises that it has veered away from true meaning of evangelical, i.e. the true and biblical gospel of the living Lord Jesus. "Evangelical" is derived from two Greek words, *eu* = good; *angellion* = message (*angellos* = messenger, often an angel). The "good message" of the gospel of the God-man, Jesus Christ, who lived the perfect life and died to redeem humanity from sin and restore humanity to inhabitation by God and derivation from God, has become so diluted by the antithetical thought of humanism as to become an incongruous corruption – evangelical humanism!

The need of the hour among the community of Christ-ones is to repudiate all of the premises of humanism, which are Satan's lies to elevate man over God and deceive mankind into believing that they are "independent selves" that function like God. In addition, the *ecclesia* community must rethink the uniqueness of the gospel message, understanding that created humanity derives all character and behavior from either the spirit-source of Satan or God, and the "good news" of the gospel message is that the risen and living Lord Jesus is available to indwell receptive persons and to live His Christ-life through them and as them.

WHO IS DOING THE DOING IN YOUR DOING?

The common natural thinking among mankind is that every human being has the inherent and intrinsic self-potential and ability to do whatever they desire and determine to do. That is why we hear the popular encouragement to give your best effort to succeed, because you can be and do whatever you set your mind to become and accomplish. This self-potential incentive is fueled by the humanistic premise that human creatures are independent beings who can self-initiate and self-generate their own activity by their own self-effort to be all they can be, follow their own dreams, and create their own utopian future.

In contrast to this popular inculcation, with its attendant mottoes to "do your own thing," "just do it!" is the divinely revealed explanation of human function, that we are derivative creatures who of necessity and design derive our being and doing from a spirit-source in either God or Satan. These contrasting spirit-sources will energize (cf. Phil. 2:13; Eph. 2:2) their character and activity in our human behavior resulting in either godliness (I Tim. 3:16; II Pet. 1:3) or sinfulness (Rom. 7:13). We may falsely think that we are doing our own doing, energizing our own activity, solving our own problems, and following our own dreams; but in reality we are deriving from another.

So, it is really not what we are doing, but what the spirit-source is doing in us, whether Satan or God. That does not mean that human beings are not responsible for their own behavior; it simply means that we are not responsible to be the source of our own activity. We are responsible to make the choice(s) of the spirit-source from which we will derive character in our behavior. Whereas the unregenerate person is a "slave to sin" (Rom 6:6,17), the Christ-one has chosen to receive the Spirit of Christ (Rom. 8:9) into his spirit and has a real freedom of choice whether he will derive his doing from God or Satan.

OCTOBER 26

EITHER/OR CONTRASTS

SPIRIT-SOURCE

God.. Satan

SPIRITUAL CONDITION

Redeemed ....Enslaved
Forgiven................................... Condemned
Reconciled................................... Alienated
Eternal Life .... Dead in trespasses and sins
Spiritual man .... Natural man

SPIRITUAL IDENTITY

Saints .... Sinners
In Christ.. In Adam
Child of God ....Child of the devil

FUNCTIONAL MOTIVATION

Spirit..Flesh

CHARACTER EXPRESSION

Holiness......................................Wickedness
Godliness ....Sinfulness
Righteousness......................Unrighteousness
Goodness ....Evil

FINAL DESTINY

Heaven....................................... Hell

WHAT'S YOUR MINDSET?

For many Christians, there are a variety of things that occupy their minds and attention to a greater extent than the living Lord Jesus. We live in a world where we are barraged with opportunities to turn our minds and attention to sensational events, new products, sports contests, politics, entertainment, etc. The apostle Paul wrote, "Set your minds on things above, not on the things that are on earth" (Col. 3:2). Spiritual concerns are of far more consequence than what is available and transpiring in the world-system that surrounds us. The things of eternal value take precedence over the temporal occurrences of the present.

In the world of humanistic psychology, there has been much emphasis recently on formulating one's mindset, because they think that the human mind is the ultimate determiner of life-outcomes. Differentiation has been made between a "fixed mindset" that is stagnant and believes that the person "can't do it" and "can't change"; whereas the alternative is designated as a "growth mindset," also known as "the mindset of success," that keeps reiterating to oneself that whatever you set your mind to you can achieve and accomplish to the betterment of yourself and the world around you.

For Christ-ones, we might advocate, as Paul seems to do, a "Christ mindset," taking into account all that He has become to us, and the provision of the Christ-life for all that He calls us to be and do. We are not advocating a constant Christ-consciousness whereby He is the only thing on our minds and we fail to pay attention to other people and the practical implications of how His life is to be manifested in our daily lives. The Christ-mindset is simply the constant underlying awareness of our identity "in Christ" as a Christ-one who is to be available in every situation to re-present His life in every situation that we find ourselves, and that always to the praise of God's glory.

OCTOBER 28

WHEN EVERYTHING WENT SOUTH!

The Christian gospel is about the redemption and restoration of mankind in Jesus Christ. But to fully understand what is rectified in Jesus, it is imperative to understand what went awry soon after God created humanity. Created as derivative creatures with freedom of choice, the original couple (male and female; Adam and Eve) were told the "tree of the knowledge of good and evil" was a forbidden tree, from which they were not to partake, for "in the day that you eat from it, you will certainly die" (Gen. 2:17). That was not a threat that a punitive God would impose a death penalty upon them, but it was a warning of consequences.

As the narrative is recorded, Eve saw that the fruit of the forbidden tree in the middle of the Garden of Eden looked delicious as healthy food and speculated that it could possibly make her wise; so she took some fruit and ate it and offered some to her husband, and he ate of it also (Gen. 3:6). One wit noted that the problem was not the apple on the tree, but the pair on the ground! As derivative and dependent creatures, they chose to be disobedient to God's directives, deliberately choosing not to depend on God, but to defy God. Thereby they sacrificed the perfect and total divine provision they had in the Garden. That's when everything went south and humanity went astray.

True to His promised warning, the two original human beings died spiritually on that very occasion. Still living physically and psychologically, they died spiritually. What does that mean? They began to derive their spiritual death condition from the antithetical spirit-source – "the one having the power of death, that is, the devil" (Heb. 2:14). Since all humanity was "in Adam, all died" (I Cor. 15:22); and, because of the one man's disobedience, "death spread to all men" (Rom. 5:12,17), "the spirit of death worked in the sons of disobedience" (Eph. 2:2), and all of humanity was "dead in trespasses and sins" (Eph. 2:1,5).

CHOICES

God created human beings as choosing creatures with freedom of choice. Human choices are extremely important, having both divine as well as human consequences. It is important to note that "freedom of choice" is not equivalent to "free-will." Free-will is a humanistic and Pelagian concept that humans not only have the power to self-determine their actions, but such is conjoined with the inherent power to implement those choices with a self-chosen character in the seeking of their own ends. Humans have freedom of choice, but not the self-generative power to create the outcomes of such choices (as only God does!).

Human life is comprised of human choices – choices of how we react and respond to the inevitable experiences of life. We are responsible for our choices, but not in the meritorious sense that we are doing something for God in those choices. Human responsibility is actually response-ability to respond to what God wants to do by His grace. We are always tempted to take selfish shortcuts in our choices: temptations to act via personal aspiration, personal gratification, and personal reputation (I Jn. 2:16); temptations to react to circumstances with fight, fright or flight (aggression, apprehension, or avoidance).

Many believers do not understand that faith is simply a choice. We have a choice to receive, to derive, to let God work on our behalf by His grace, to let Him work in His own way in accord with His own will. "His ways are not our ways" (Isa. 55:8,9), but "His ways are always right" (Hosea 14:9). "There is a way that seems right unto man, but the end thereof is death" (Prov. 14:12; 16:25). Faith is the choice to place our circumstances under His control. "He chooses best who leaves the choice to Him." This does not diminish the importance of human choice, but allows God to act in accord with His character of love that always seeks the highest good of created mankind.

OCTOBER 30

RE: REST, RELAX, RECEIVE

The context of religion always incorporates the impetus of the performance of human works, *i.e.* what humans are called upon to do to be right with God or the ecclesiastical authorities who are deemed to represent God. In contrast to such religious calls to action (remember that "religion" is derived from the Latin *religio* and *religare*, meaning "to bind" or "to tie" a person to rules and regulations or rituals of devotion), we will consider *re:* (Latin, "in the matter of," i.e. regarding, referring to, concerning, about) the intent of God that His people should rest, relax, and simply receive what He makes available by His grace.

Grace refers to what God does, not what we do. Grace has to do with what God has done and continues to do as He reveals Himself in His Son, Jesus Christ, and in the power of His Holy Spirit. Grace is God in action, doing what the Triune God does to reveal His nature and His character – doing what He does because He IS who He IS, the Great I AM! Out of His BEing, God is the active DOer (divine grace), and human creatures are intended to be the receivers (human choice of faith) of God's active grace. Thus, we can avoid the DOing of religion by resting and relaxing in faith, the receptivity of His activity.

The apostle Paul wrote, "God is at work in you, both to will and to work for His good pleasure" (Phil. 2:13). As we receive God's grace-function, resting and relaxing in His sufficiency, this does not imply that we are inactive, that we just sit on our duff in indolence, doing nothing but twiddling our thumbs. The "rest of faith" occurs in the midst of God's grace-activity, and we discover that we are busier than ever; but such is not the human striving of self-effort. It is the receiving of God's promised rest (cf. Matt. 11:28; Heb. 4:1-11) in the midst of God's activity of grace. Many Christ-ones need to relax from the rigor of religion and rest in the receptivity of faith.

THE RELEVANCE OF THE GOSPEL

The gospel of the living Lord Jesus Christ relates to every aspect of our physical lives, and is therefore relevant to everything in our life. However, if one does not understand the "good news" of the indwelling Spirit of Christ and how Jesus is to be our life, then the religious paradigm of performance alone is indeed irrelevant to our lives. It is no wonder, then, that so many are exiting the institutional church, explaining that it Is no longer relevant. To simply repeat Bible stories and seek to attach some form of moral application of the story to life today will not be regarded as relevant by a good portion of people in the 21st century.

I sympathize with the thousands of people who are leaving the institutional church. I have sat through countless meetings and services in the brick and mortar buildings called "churches," and listened to many sermons and homilies that never explained how the resurrected and living Jesus in every Christ-one can be relevant to our practical lives during the next week. I have listened to many a preacher who tried to be humorous, thinking that he was a comedic entertainer. Unless a pastor shares the relevance of Jesus (the gospel) to every facet of our lives then that pastor's religious talk is irrelevant.

The relevance of the gospel is realized by the awareness and acceptance of God's grace in Jesus Christ. In Jesus alone, we have been supplied with the grace-dynamic to meet every trial and every need in our lives. That is why Paul writes, "I can do all things through Christ who strengthens me" (Phil. 4:13). "It is no longer I who lives, but Christ lives in me" (Gal. 2:20). Jesus told His disciples, "Apart from Me, you can do nothing" (Jn. 15:5). The provision for all things in the Christ-life is Christ, and He is the relevant "good news" for every facet of our living "in the world, but not of the world" (Jn. 17:11,14). We must remain intimately united with Jesus (I Cor. 6:17), the ever-relevant gospel.

NOVEMBER 1

HIS TASK, DONE HIS WAY, IN HIS TIME

Those who have spent considerable time interacting with God, attempting to determine what He wants to do, how He wants to do it, and when He wants to do it, have often expressed how difficult it is to know God's will for a particular venture. When attempting to communicate with a Spirit-being whom we have never seen, yet nevertheless know in a personal manner, we come to the end of our natural resources of how we are to apprehend and comprehend what He might be trying to convey to us. Similar to the old cell phone commercials, we are wandering around asking, "Are you there? Are you there? Are you there?" thinking we have lost our connection.

The foundation of obedience in the new covenant of Jesus Christ is learning how to listen, despite our inability to clearly comprehend what God might be saying in the situation. The primary Greek word for "obedience" is *hupakouo* (Greek: *hupo* = under; *akouo* = to hear or listen) and has the meaning of "listening under God." It seems to be a common human tendency to speak our mind and share our opinions, rather than place much value on listening to the Other; but we press on nevertheless, often "getting ahead of God," and then impatiently looking back to see why God is lagging behind our endeavors.

A common human tendency is to approach a task attempting to have God grant His "stamp of approval" for what we have conceived and determined to do. We bring our agenda, our plans for implementation and our timetable for the completion of the project. We want God to "bless" what we have planned; and we seem to have little patience with God's failure to meet our deadlines. We need to stop our hectic endeavors and realize afresh that what we are seeking is "His task, done His way, in His time" – all accomplished unto His glory. May God be glorified as we attempt to be the vessels of His glory in what we do.

306

THE COSMIC BATTLE

There is a cosmic battle going on! Do we really know what we are up against? Do we really know what this battle is all about? Religion has long hammered on the pulpit explaining that we are battling against sin; but, to some, that word seems increasingly antiquated and devoid of contemporary meaning. Can "sin" be explained in terms that contemporary humanity can understand and relate to? Perhaps, in seeking new definition of the word "sin," we might simultaneously get our theology sorted out to explain that sin has been completely dealt with and overcome in the death of the Son, Jesus Christ, on the cross.

Every strategist knows that you need to know your antagonist, how he thinks, what is his objective, what resources does he have at his ability, what are his weaknesses and vulnerabilities, prior to engaging in conflict. The antagonists in this cosmic battle are God and Satan, each fully invested in their character of good and evil respectively. God's character of love (I Jn. 4:8,16) is selfless, unconditionally given via the Son, Jesus (Jn. 3:16), and poured out into the hearts of Christ-ones by the Holy Spirit (Rom. 5:5). Satan's antithetical character is selfishness (cf. Isa. 14:14), the self-concern of egocentricity.

The cosmic battle is between the selfishness of me-ism and the selflessness of God's love. It is a conflict of character. Such character indicates the essence or nature of the spirit-source that energizes the antithetical orientations – either "it's all about me," or "it's all about others." Is the orientation of our character centripetal (moving toward the center in oneself) or centrifugal (moving away from the center in oneself), toward others? That battle of character orientation is being played out in our individual souls, as well as in the universe of mankind at large. The cosmic battle was won when Jesus gave His life for others on the cross saying, "It is finished" (Jn. 19:30)!

NOVEMBER 3

DARTING INTO RABBIT HOLES

In risky and uncertain times, rabbits and many other small animals will choose to make a brief dash across an exposed field and then take cover by darting into a rabbit hole to hide. Human beings also take evasive action during uncertain times, but their metaphorical "rabbit hole" for taking cover and hiding is likely to be in illogical constructs of human thought, a psychological refuge to allay their fears wherein they convince themselves they are less liable to risk. The particular "rabbit hole" I want to note is the tendency of otherwise reasonable people to escape into often far-fetched conspiracy theories.

Conspiracy theories have been proffered ever since Satan suggested, to cover up his own intents, that God was holding back the truth of good and evil from mankind; but they have been proliferating and running rampant in recent years, as so many seek to explain the uncertainty in the world by elaborate theories of deception by powerful people and behind-the-scenes forces. Some people are particularly susceptible to these theoretical scenarios because of a paranoid fear of living in a hostile world with powerful and sinister forces working their malevolent and secretive purposes of deception. Others are drawn to conspiracy theories because they feed their pride of "being in the know" and having figured out explanations for threatening phenomena around them. Since these theories always involve invisible forces, the conspiracists are usually skeptical of the conclusions of science which demand observable criteria.

Christ-ones must recognize that this is a battle for their mind. All these unsettling peripheral "what-if" theories are smokescreens of distraction that keep us from settling our minds on Jesus Christ and "things above" (Col. 3:2). Since Jesus is our life and peace and strength and security, we must give up on "rabbit holes" and "mount up on wings like eagles" (Isa. 40:31).

WHAT AM I CONSCIOUS OF?

No one can answer this question but the person who asks it. Personal consciousness and awareness are individual, subjective phenomena. No other person can verify what I am conscious or aware of, for some would say "it's all in my head" or heart (wherever it is that human consciousness takes place). So, what I am writing of here is beyond the empirically verifiable.

To begin with, I am aware that I exist as a distinct living creature among many creatures of differing varieties. I have ontological creature-awareness of my existence on planet earth. Beyond that, I am aware of my self-awareness of being a distinct human being, responsible for considering my relations with other creatures. I have social awareness. My social awareness goes beyond other humans to include the Spirit-beings of Father, Son and Holy Spirit. This spirit-consciousness commenced when the Spirit of God in Christ entered into my spirit, and I began to "understand spiritual things" (I Cor. 2:14). As I grew in spirit-consciousness, I was pleased to experience heavenly-consciousness, being made aware of the perfect presence of God and of "seeing the unseen" (II Cor..4:18); aware of participating and belonging in a sphere of indescribable love, peace and beauty in union with God.

If asked to farther explain this heavenly-consciousness, I am immediately at a loss for words. I have referred to it as "the paradigm of the sublime." It is a personal and intimate embrace of God. Some have called it "the divine dance." Perhaps it is what Paul was referring to when he wrote of "being caught up into the third heaven" (II Cor. 12:2). In 1963, Bing Crosby sang a new Christmas song with the questions, "Do you see what I see; Do you hear what I hear?" The awareness and consciousness that any individual sees or hears is theirs and theirs alone, to share as they might care and attempt to do so.

NOVEMBER 5

ARE YOU A MEMBER?

Many have attended a local institutional church and have been badgered by the question, "Are you a member?" "Do you want to become a member?" If you should answer that you are not a "member" and do not wish to become a "member," you immediately become *persona non grata*, deemed to be a rebel and an outsider. By offering membership in their organization, they are offering you "a sense of belonging," as well as an opportunity to progress into leadership and responsibility. If you wish to belong to a "chain gang" and submit to the work-ethic they have established for their gang, you might give it a try. Be aware, however, that membership in such an organization implies a willingness to submit to the authority of, and be accountable to, the designated leaders as they attempt to control your thoughts and censor your actions. They are inevitably part of the "believe-right, do-right" religious enterprise.

A Christ-one who has submitted to Jesus Christ as Lord and been regenerated with the Spirit of Christ within his spirit (Rom. 8:9) knows that he is already a functional member (cf. I Cor. 12:12-27) of the Body of Christ (Rom. 12:5; I Cor. 12:12,27). If such a Christ-one is subsequently required to join an organization as a legal "member" in order to participate in the group, then the logical conclusion is that it is not sufficient to be an organic member of the Body of Christ based on spiritual regeneration alone. The equation then becomes: Jesus + church membership = acceptability (to God, or to the religious group?)

The leaders may charge that you seek to be in control of your own involvement in the local church? No, I just want the Lord Jesus Christ to be in control of my life and actions among His people, and not some intermediary priestly leaders. I do not seek institutional leadership, but I "do desire to grow in the grace and knowledge of my Lord and Savior, Jesus Christ" (II Pet. 3:18).

THE MANIFESTED LIFE

If the Christ-one fails to understand the indwelling life of the risen Lord Jesus within their spirit (cf. Rom. 8:9), they will be unable to understand that the Christian life is the manifested life of Jesus in their behavior. Some religious persons who thought that the Christian life is but a detached mental assent to the historical Jesus, a belief-system, questioned and challenged that Jesus, the very Son of God who lived two thousand years ago in Judea, could actually live today and be manifested, demonstrated, and made visible in Christian people today. They apparently missed the meaning of the resurrection of Jesus, and His subsequent expression by the Spirit (cf. I Cor. 15:45).

Jesus explained that "the one who practices the truth comes to the Light, so that his deeds may be *manifested* as having been wrought/worked by God" (Jn. 3:21). Paul wrote that "the life of Jesus is to be *manifested* in our body (II Cor. 4:10), in our mortal flesh (II Cor. 4:11). For the privilege of re-presenting Jesus today, we "thank God, who always leads us in triumph in Christ, and *manifests* through us the sweet aroma of the knowledge of Him (Jesus) in every place we go" (II Cor. 2:14). "Do you not recognize that Jesus Christ is in you?" Paul asks in the same letter, "unless you believed in vain" (II Cor. 13:5).

The Christ-life is the manifested life, the supplied life, the grace-life, the out-lived and re-presented-life of the living Lord Jesus. It is lived only by the ontological dynamic (Being of God in action) of the grace of God. We cannot live the Christian life by our own effort! Human action cannot reproduce the divine. Grace is the divinely energized life of the risen and living Lord Jesus operating in and through receptive Christ-ones to manifest Himself – His character and ministry. The Greek word for "manifest" is *phaneroo*, which means "to make visible," to exhibit by becoming the "express image" of the life of Jesus Christ.

NOVEMBER 7

THE POST-RESURRECTION-LIFE OF JESUS

Christian teaching has consistently explained that Jesus is the God-man, fully God and fully man. The Greek-speaking early Christians used the term *Theoanthropos* (*Theos* = God; *anthropos* = man). As the God-man, He functioned as "the one mediator between God and man, the man Christ Jesus" (I Tim. 2:5). There has not always been a balance in Christian thought between emphasis on Jesus' deity and humanity. After the Enlightenment questioned everything supernatural, Christian teachers began to emphasize the deity of Jesus in order to explain that Jesus of Nazareth was more than just a man. This was followed by the need to explain that Jesus functioned as a derivative man, having emptied Himself (Phil. 2:7) of the prerogative of functioning independently as God in becoming a human person that would identify with all mankind in temptation and death.

When Christians consider the resurrection of Jesus, many have viewed such as the utmost manifestation of His supernatural deity – He rose from the dead because He was divine. Others have so emphasized the physicality of Jesus' life, death and resurrection, they have failed to proceed to explain the purposed extension of the resurrection-life of Jesus in Christ-ones thereafter (cf. Rom. 8:29). The physical life, death and resurrection of Jesus was intended to be the precursor of Jesus' divine-spiritual life being "brought into being," i.e. birthed, in receptive individuals who thereby became Christ-ones.

What Christian religion today so often either misses or neglects is the ongoing reality of Jesus' spiritual life beyond the physical life of His human redemptive mission. The resurrection of Jesus was far more than an historical event of the past that capped off Jesus' earthly. It was the occasion when the restoration of God's divine life was made available to mankind by the resurrection-life of Jesus spiritually regenerated in Christ-ones.

INCONCEIVABLE

My neighbor and I were visiting in the front yard one day, and I mentioned that I was writing about the preexistent life of Jesus. He thought it inconceivable that I would assert that Jesus existed prior to His being born as a human being in Bethlehem. But, he was even more flummoxed that I would assert that Jesus, having been crucified and resurrected was alive today "living in me." Here was a fellow who claimed to be an active Christian in his church, and the truths of Jesus' eternal preexistence (Jn. 1:1,14) and eternal Spirit-presence (I Cor. 15:45) were totally foreign concepts to him. How can this be?

I fear that this man is not an anomaly among Christians in the various denominational structures of the Church today. Many Christians are abysmally ignorant of the basic historical and theological tenets of the Christian faith. Despite the Church at large celebrating the incarnation of Jesus at the Christmas holiday, and the resurrection of Jesus at the Easter holiday – the two major holidays in the Christian year – apparently the basic theological implications that surround these pivotal events of Jesus' life are not understood by many of the Christians sitting in the pews. Does this reveal a failure of our teaching?

Perhaps, like Vizzini, the character in *The Princess Bride* movie who repeatedly exclaimed "Inconceivable," many Christians are boggled by how God orchestrated sending His Son to become the God-man, as well as the startling revelation that the Son continues to live eternally as the life-giving Spirit. "The Lord is the Spirit" (II Cor. 3:17). Such an eternal perspective of the life of the Eternal Son, both pre- and post- his redemptive mission on earth, is indeed inconceivable by finite comprehension alone. Only by God's personal revelation to our understanding via the teaching of the indwelling Holy Spirit can we ever begin to grasp how the eternal occupies the temporal.

NOVEMBER 9

RELIGION

The English word "religion" is derived from the Latin word *religare*, which means "to bind or tie," usually to rules and regulations or rituals of devotion.

Religion is the sweatshop where those who seek to prove their prowess and bulk up their pride exert their best effort to their own disadvantage.

Religion is the devil's playground; an expression of Satan's world-system of pseudo-productivity and spirituality.

Religion is controlled and governed by "natural men," who often have no more spiritual understanding than a native in Timbuktu.

Religious "scholars" approach the Bible as a dead relic to be dissected like a long-extinct dodo bird to marvel at "how things used to be."

Religion is to the Christ-life, what "toilet water" is to expensive perfume – cheap imitation.

Religion is a "knock-off," a cheap counterfeit of the inimitable and incomparable reality of the life of Jesus Christ.

Religion specializes in building expensive mausoleums, called "churches," to house the dead and static corpses of those who died trying to orchestrate and manufacture what only the living Lord Jesus can manifest.

Religion is the attempted replacement of divine work by the effort of human manufacture.

To speak of "Christian religion" is actually an oxymoronic attempt to combine opposites that are incompatible.

Religion is always about "works" and performance, failing to understand that all performance was accomplished when Jesus said, "It is finished!" (Jn. 19:30)

Religion is like running on a treadmill, and thinking that you are actually getting somewhere.

JESUS OUTSIDE OF THE BOX

Many are searching for what is inside of the box. Think cereal boxes, Cracker Jacks boxes, Christmas gift boxes, etc. But Jesus will not fit in a box, and cannot be contained in any man-made boxes. Many have attempted to contain Jesus in their denominational boxes (Baptist, Methodist, Lutheran, etc.), or their theological boxes (Calvinistic, Arminian, Pentecostal, etc.), or their worship-style boxes (traditional classical, contemporary, modern, etc.), or their social-cultural boxes (social reform, political party objectives, environmental ideologies, etc.). All attempts to claim Him by containing Him have failed.

The dynamic life of the living Lord Jesus cannot be contained in any man-made boxes. When something living is forced into an air-tight box it usually dies. Once something is static and dead, it can then be placed in a box. Ex. a coffin-box can contain a corpse. Might we suggest that that the church-box has become a coffin-box containing the dead residue of religion? Jesus explained that the new wine of His life could not be put in old wine-skins, for the living action of fermentation would explode out of the old brittle wine-skins. Are you waiting for the explosion?

Jesus will always live outside of the box – outside of the institutional church-box, outside of the walls of our church buildings, even outside of the historical box where we have long attempted to contain Him. We must allow Jesus to break out of any thought-boxes we might try to place Him in. Jesus explained that the Spirit is like the wind, and it blows where it will (Jn. 3:8). When the Spirit of Christ (cf. Rom. 8:9) is living within the Christ-one, He cannot be confined, but will be manifested in power beyond our wildest imaginations. We must allow Him to be spontaneously unique in the expression of His character in and through us. When we do so, we must be ready for something different beyond the status-quo.

NOVEMBER 11

CHRISTIANITY IS RELATIONAL

A lesson that many of us have had to learn, and are continually learning, is that Christianity is not so much informational, as it is relational. There is a foundational base of historical and theological information, but the real dynamic of Christianity is interactively relational. This uniqueness of Christian faith is founded on the Trinitarian relationality of the Father, Son, and Holy Spirit. Their plurality in unity, creating a perfect harmony of loving community, draws the rest of the divinely created personal order into their relational oneness. We are invited to participate in the intimate personal relations of the Triune God.

Unlike any other religious faith in the world, the Son of God identified with humanity, becoming a human being (Phil. 2:7,8), to bring us into the inner circle of genuine relationship with the persons of the Triune God. "The one who is joined to the Lord is one spirit with Him" (I Cor. 6:17), as Christ-ones become "partakers of the divine nature" (II Pet. 1:4). In likeness to the plurality in unity of the Trinity, Christ-ones in the one Body of the *ecclesia* (Col. 1:18,24) are to allow the grace-empowering of God's divine action to create a functional relationality of unity in a community (common-unity) of shared love.

The *ecclesia* gatherings of the new covenant community are intended to be interactive expressions of multiplicity in unity. "When you assemble, each one has a psalm, has a teaching, has a revelation, has a tongue, has an interpretation. Let all things be done for edification" (I Cor. 14:26). Unfortunately, religion has allowed them to become didactic teaching lectures with a focus on learning informational doctrine and dogma, and seldom do they ever allow Christ-ones to open up and allow the living Spirit of Jesus within to minister to one another relationally. Jesus in each of us has something to impart to another, and the fellowship will be lubricated by God's *agape* love.

316

NEW COVENANT GIVING

The techniques by which pastors and Christian leaders attempt to milk and bilk money out of Christian people are an abominable blight upon the Christian faith. They cast God into the role of a needy beggar, wanting to amass ever greater sums to finance ever-bigger projects – a gross misrepresentation, since He is the Creator, sustainer and owner of all things. The manipulative, guilt-producing schemes employed by many modern religious hucksters are man-made ploys of greedy leaders to line their own pockets at the expense of sincere yet susceptible believers who are conned into thinking they are giving to God.

These schemes are nothing new. Religion has long encouraged the performance-based practices of purchasing indulgences, seed-faith offerings, tithing percentages, faith-promise giving, etc. But in the new covenant, when the living Lord Jesus is received into the human spirit by faith, the Divine Giver has come to live within us. Never again need we be deceived or conned by religious profiteers. In the new covenant there should never be compulsion to give by church leadership using incentivizing schemes. "Each is to do as he has purposed in his heart, not grudgingly or under compulsion, pressure or duty" (II Cor. 9:7).

This is the unique dynamic of new covenant giving. Christ-ones give because the Divine Giver lives within them. We should not give anything, unless and until we have the inner prompting of our indwelling Lord. Every activity within the new covenant Christ-life is to be prompted by the Spirit of Christ as He seeks to live out His life through us. Everything in the Christ-life is to be prompted and motivated by the impulse of the divine presence within. That is what new covenant grace is all about. We derive everything *ek Theos*, "out of God," and allow Him to do as He wills in every aspect of our lives, whether it be our giving, our forgiving, or the out-living of His life as us.

NOVEMBER 13

ALL OF HIM IN ALL OF ME IS ALL I NEED

The true completion and satisfaction of humanity is the fullness of the Lord and Savior Jesus Christ in the human spirit of a man, woman, boy or girl. Who could ask for anything more? This is the restoration of humanity to God's original intent in creating them. What was lost in the Fall when God's indwelling life was rejected for the pseudo-promise of the humanistic independence of allegedly "being like God" (Gen. 3:5), could only be restored by God's initiative of sending His only-begotten Son, and allowing Him (Jesus) to incur all the death consequences that occurred in Adam, that we might be restored with God's life.

Yes, all of the Triune God, Father, Son, and Holy Spirit, comes to live within the spirit-core-heart of every faith-receptive individual – the fullness of the Godhead. God never comes "in part" or "in a measure," for the Triune God cannot be subdivided or trisected. It's all or nothing! God only comes in His fulness. God wants you to have all that He is! "God is at work in you" (Phil. 2:12). "Jesus Christ is in you" (II Cor. 3:5). "the Spirit of God dwells in you" (Rom. 8:9). The entirety of the Triune God wants to occupy and control every facet of our being, "our spirit, and soul and body" (I Thess. 5:23,24). He will bring it to pass."

There is nothing more that mankind needs, than to be filled with the fullness of God. When we are spiritually filled by Father, Son, and Holy Spirit (cf. Eph. 5:19), and allowing the Lord of the universe to control every portion of our lives, we are complete (Col. 1:28; 2:10), and "lacking in nothing" (James 1:4). That is what it takes for man to be man as God intended man to be – Father, Son and Holy Spirit indwelling and functionally operative in the out-living of His divine life in and through us. By means of His redemptive work on our behalf, and His restoration of the divine life in the resurrection and Pentecostal out-pouring, we can say, "all of Him in all of us is all we need."

PEACE AND SERENITY IN SERVING OTHERS

We have all observed a two-year old child throwing a temper-tantrum. Unbridled selfishness, as they seek to get their own way, and do what they want to do. It's not a pretty sight! It often appears to be an exhibit of pure wrath and fury. How can anyone doubt Paul's words that "we all formerly walked according to the course of this world, according to the prince of the power of the air, the spirit that is now working in the sons of disobedience, and we were by nature children of wrath" (Eph. 2:2,3)? Parental training might teach a child to refrain from such antisocial acting out, but it takes more than parental training to invest a child with the desire to love and serve others.

Only by the receiving of the Spirit of the living Lord Jesus within our spirit do we participate in the spiritual exchange of being "rescued us from the domain of darkness, and transferred to the kingdom of His beloved Son" (Col. 1:15), "turned from the dominion of Satan to the dominion of God" (Acts 26:18). By that exchange, we transfer from being "slaves of sin" (Rom. 6:6,17,20) deriving the character of selfishness from Satan, to receiving the presence and character of God's love within us with the possibility of experiencing peace and serenity in deriving God's character in serving others. What a radical turn, from the me-ism of selfishness to loving and serving others.

Therein is the heart of the gospel, that such a spiritual transfer and transformation can be enacted by God's grace in Jesus Christ. Selfishness is ultimately unsatisfying. The divine character of loving and serving others brings a joy unspeakable, as we make others the focal point of our life, rather than ourselves. Love is always for others! Selfishness is centripetal (moving towards a center in ourselves), whereas love is centrifugal (moving out from a center in ourselves, that center being Jesus in our spirit).

NOVEMBER 15

CONDUITS OF THE CHRIST-LIFE

Conduits are not glamorous. Conduits do not get the attention. Think, for example, of how your furnace delivers heated air through the heating ducts. Seldom do you hear someone praising your heating ducts – they simply exclaim how pleasant and enjoyable the temperature seems to be in your home. Conduits do not make things happen; they simply allow the activity to flow through them. So, it is for Christians: we are not the generators that make the Christ-life happen. We are simply the ductwork, the pipeline, the channel, the conduits through which the indwelling Spirit of Christ is allowed to manifest His life.

If you are looking for something glamorous, with the praise for what you have done, you are digging in the rubbish pile of religion, rather than yielding yourself to the Christ-life. We can't; only He can do what He wants to do in manifesting Himself. "It is no longer I who lives, but Christ lives in me" (Gal. 2:20). "Not that we are adequate in ourselves to consider anything as coming from ourselves, but our adequacy is from (Greek *ek* = derived out of) God" (II Cor. 3:5). The Christ-life is "not of (*ek* = derived out of) ourselves, it is the gift of God" (Eph. 2:8). We are saved and preserved by God's grace, not by our works or effort.

EVERYTHING in the Christ-life is what He does, not what we do. Even our identity in Christ is what He is in us, not something we are in ourselves. We cannot manufacture character of any kind, for we are derivative creatures who are the conduits of the character of either Satan or God. The living Lord Jesus is the actuator of the Christ-life. He does all the doing that needs done in the Christian life. "God is at work in us, both to will and to work for His good pleasure" (Phil. 2:13) "the good works which He has prepared beforehand that we should walk in them" (Eph. 2:10). He is the Giver, the Forgiver, the Lover in us, and we simply delight in being conduits of His Christ-life.

STOP IT!

No doubt, we have all had times in our lives when someone has told us to "Stop it!" It may have been our father or mother telling us to stop pestering our siblings, or classmates telling us to stop teasing or harassing them, or a teacher telling us to refrain from doing what we've been told not to do. But how often have you been told to stop doing what the preacher has been telling you do in every sermon that he/she has preached Sunday after Sunday, maybe for years? Who would be so audacious as to contradict the preacher? None other than one who is writing to advocate God's grace instead of human performance.

Stop it! I mean it: Quit trying to live the Christian life. You cannot do it. It is an impossible life for any human person to pull off. The more you try by your own effort and works to behave like a Christian, the more ridiculously religious you appear – kind of like a silly mime trying to climb a staircase to heaven, or a goofy clown trying to lift himself up by his own bootstraps. All your efforts to live the Christian life are but clumsy attempts to do what only Christ can do, and no one, especially God, is at all impressed by what you are trying to do. Telling someone to live like Jesus is like asking them to engage in make-believe unreality.

Oh, the pantomime of exaggerated pretense exhibited by the religious people who have been giving it their best shot to live like Jesus. The sooner we stop the pretense, we can proceed beyond the hypocrisy of religious play-acting, and begin to understand that everything Christian can only be enacted by Christ. Forget the pious performance and begin to experience the reality of the living Lord Jesus living out His life and character in our behavior. The Christ-life can only be lived in the Christ-one when Christ Himself is allowed to manifest His life in the mortal flesh of our mortal bodies (II Cor. 4:10,11). Forget any idea that you can add to what He is doing – STOP IT!

NOVEMBER 17

CONSUMER OR MINISTER?

When the *ecclesia* assembles and gathers together as a congregation of Christ-ones, are we thinking about "what I can get out of this gathering" or "what can I bring and give to this gathering of my brothers and sisters in Christ"? Many come with a consumerist mindset of wanting to get fed, wanting to acquire another tidbit of doctrinal understanding, wanting to be affirmed that they have correctly formed their believe-right religious belief-system. Few seem to realize that they are a functional part of the Body of Christ, equipped with the spiritual giftedness of Jesus within to minister and serve others in the congregation.

Instruction about spiritual gifts has been grotesquely misunderstood and misrepresented in Christian teaching. Handing out questionnaires and survey forms exploring personal interests and preferences is not a valid way to determine spiritual giftedness. Spiritual gifts are not job descriptions of what one is to do and perform in the church – that is religion. When a Christ-one receives Jesus to live in them, Jesus comes complete with all of His ability to minister to others. Every Christ-one has every spiritual gift mentioned in the New Testament; they are all inherent in Jesus.

In like manner, in receiving Jesus we receive the entire cluster of the "fruit of the Spirit" (Gal. 5:22,23). Jesus comes complete with the entirety of His character, desirous of expressing such in our behavior. Though Jesus comes complete with His ability to minister to others via spiritual giftedness, our particular position and placement in a local gathering of the *ecclesia* will determine the need of the particular ministry that Jesus wants to employ through us in that place at that time. It may be teaching, helping, leading, etc. (cf. Rom. 12:5-8; I Cor. 12:27-30) We do not come to a consumer buffet, but to an array of ministry opportunities wherein we might love and serve others.

CONSTANTLY SURPRISED

God is a surprising God, full of surprises, and incapable of being stuffed into any conformity-box whereby we can predict what He will do next in our lives. God is spontaneous and unpredictable. Those who attempt to overemphasize the immutability or unchangeableness of God, often do just that – attempt to put God into a conformity-box of human expectations, or a box wherein they think they have the "ways of God" all figured out, and can thereby explain how God will do what He does in predictable ways. NO, God cannot be put into a straitjacket that explains with doctrinal confidence that "God will always do it this way!" We will always be surprised when God starts throwing curve-balls.

God is immutable and unchangeable in His character. His character never changes. He is the same yesterday, today, and forever (cf. Heb. 13:8). He will never cease to be righteous, mercy, and love. But His *modus operandi* (His mode of operation) will always be adaptable to the situation and the people He is dealing with. For example, He dealt with the nation of Israel one way in the old covenant, but He deals with Christ-ones in another way in the new covenant. Likewise, in the lives of Christ-ones, He deals with us individually – not randomly, but in the precise and unique way that we each need the most to reach His purposes.

We do not usually have a clue what God is going to do next in our lives. "God's ways are past finding out" (Rom. 11:33). But we can be sure that whatever He does will be for our highest good, to "bring us to maturity, to the whole measure of the fulness of Christ" (Eph. 4:13. To be "mature" does not indicate a final resting place. The Greek word for "mature" is *teleiosis*, which implies a process whereby we are brought to the present goal or objective that God has for us. When we cease to be surprised at what God is doing, it is likely that we have chosen to go our own way, and are no longer adaptable to His surprising ways.

NOVEMBER 19

BUMMER LAMBS

In God's wonderful world of nature there are often anomalies. For example, a mother ewe, with an innate instinct to care for her baby lambs, will quite often reject one of her young offspring, for no known reason. The rejected, abandoned and orphaned lamb does not understand why it is rejected, is quite disheartened, and will not survive if someone doesn't intervene on its behalf. Such rejected lambs are referred to as "bummer lambs." It is indeed a "bummer" to be rejected or forsaken by your own mother, unable to care for oneself, and reliant on a compassionate hand of assistance in order to survive such abandonment.

In the pastoral setting of a shepherd caring for a flock of sheep out in the hills, it would be the responsibility of the shepherd to notice a rejected lamb, and attempt to assist the lamb to survive. In a farm setting today, someone in the family will often attempt to feed and care for the "bummer lamb" until it can rejoin the flock. In this process, the lamb often becomes quite bonded to its rescuer, and will become the first one to respond to the shepherd's or farmer's voice when called. Some have developed entire flocks of "bummer lambs," and such a flock might be a pattern for Christ's *ecclesia* of Christ-ones.

Living, as we do, in a rejective world-system, there is a sense in which we have all become "bummer lambs." The Psalmist wrote, "Though my father and mother forsake (reject, abandon) me, the Lord will take me up (receive, accept, care for) me" (Ps. 27:10). We are all familiar with "The Lord is my Shepherd, I shall not want" (Ps. 23:1). Jesus said, "I am the Good Shepherd" (Jn. 10:11,14), and "My sheep hear My voice" (Jn. 10:27). Life here on earth can indeed be a "bummer" as "the ruler of this world" (Jn. 12:31; 14:30; 16:11) orchestrates his character of selfishness and rejection among mankind, but the living Lord Jesus is the deliverer who takes us up to become our Savior-Shepherd.

WHAT DOES JESUS HAVE TO DO WITH TULIPS?

As the Creator of all things, the Triune God, Father, Son, and Holy Spirit, was involved in bringing all things into being, including all varieties of flowers, the birds and bees that pollinate such botanicals, and everything necessary for their sustenance. This article, however, considers the acrostic of T.U.L.I.P., developed to represent the major points of Reformed or Calvinistic theology (often referred to as "five-point Calvinism").

Total Depravity – This refers to the total degradation and corruption of human function in all of humanity due to the original sin of the original couple in the Garden. This is a denial of human "freedom of choice" to any of God's grace activity.

Unconditional Election – Since human beings are unable to exercise any conditional mental, emotional or volitional response to God's action, God must unconditionally elect individuals to receive redemption and salvation, giving them the "gift of faith."

Limited Atonement – The redemptive and atoning action of Jesus Christ on the Cross is limited to those whom God has individually elected to be recipients of His grace. All other human beings are necessarily not divinely elected and cannot be saved.

Irresistible Grace – Those individuals elected by God to receive the benefits of God's grace in Jesus Christ and given the divine "gift of faith," are necessarily unable to resist God's grace-action and will respond in reception to the gospel of Jesus Christ.

Perseverance of the Saints – Apart from any condition of faith on the part of the "elect" who respond to the gospel, God's action will cause them to persevere in their status of "saints," and cause them to "grow in the grace and knowledge of their Lord Jesus."

What does Jesus have to do with such a theological T.U.L.I.P.? In this author's opinion, NOTHING, for this humanly devised theological system of Calvinistic thought has inadequate biblical base, and should not be considered as God's gospel of love.

NOVEMBER 21

WOW! – NO DOUBT

When I get down to the bedrock of my certainty and assurance, the inmost parameters of my thinking where I have no doubt of the veracity of where I have chosen to take my stand, and do not question the reality of where I have invested my life, my foremost certainty is that God is love (I Jn. 4:8,16), that God loves me unequivocally, and He has demonstrated His love toward me in the incarnation of His Son, Jesus (Jn. 3:16), who in turn "loved me and gave Himself for me" (Gal. 2:20) by submitting to death on a Roman cross to die a death He did not deserve in order to give me His resurrection-life which I did not deserve.

I did absolutely nothing to deserve or earn such divine love-life. It was made available to me solely by the initiative of God's grace, which included His invitation to me to participate in His very being, nature, and character, to be joined in spiritual union (I Cor. 6:17) with the loving triune God of the universe. God's love reached out to me in my helpless and hopeless condition of being an "enemy of God" (Rom. 5:10), enslaved to Satan and sin (II Tim 2:26), and subject to the death consequences of my sin (I Cor. 15:22). The living God (I Tim. 4:10) sent His Son who had life in Himself (Jn. 5:26) to be my life (Col. 3:4) as God intended.

The objective historical details of the life and Person of Jesus Christ have become the unquestioned subjective reality of God's loving grace to give Himself to me in His Son, who is my life (Jn. 14:6; I Jn. 5:12). "I love Him only because He first loved me" (I Jn. 4:19). My love for God in Christ is only a freely-chosen response to His love, which allows for an eternal love-relationship in spiritual union. The certainty and assurance of the eternality of my love-relationship with God in Christ by the Holy Spirit is predicated not on my faithfulness, but on the unfailing faith-fulness of God Himself (I Cor. 1:9; II Cor. 1:18). Thank God, for His unfailing faithful love and His drawing me into such love!

NOVEMBER 22

WHEN CHRIST-ONES MANIFEST SINFULNESS

I have noticed for many years that many Christians are quite concerned about their self-chosen manifestations of sinfulness. Yes, Christians do sin, and yes, they should be grieved by such. Christ-ones do misrepresent who they are "in Christ" by such sin. "If we say we have no sin, we are deceiving ourselves and the truth is not in us" (I Jn. 1:8,9), but "if we confess our sins (say the same thing that God says about our sins (Greek *homologeo*), He is faithful and just to forgive us our sins (to apply the forgiveness achieved in the death of Jesus on the cross for the sins of all mankind), and to cleanse from all unrighteousness."

A friend wrote, asking, "When I sin, I know it is not Christ expressing Himself in that sin, but is it an expression from my soul?" The first statement is certainly accurate: Jesus is the Perfect and Righteous One, and He is absolutely antithetical and incompatible with all sinful expression. He is without sin (II Cor. 5:21) and does not sin (I Jn. 5:28). We should also note that since Jesus gave His life for all the sins of all mankind, we can rest assured that all sins have been dealt with, and we should not unduly occupy our minds with sins, but focus on Jesus as our Savior, our Life, our Righteousness, our Perfection in order to manifest His life in our mortal bodies (II Cor. 4:10,11)

I want to ask Christians if they think that they, or their soul, is inherently sinful. All Reformed or Calvinistic theology answers affirmatively that humanity is degraded in sinfulness, perpetual "sinners" incapable of ever being changed (just "a sinner saved by grace"). If that be so, then a human being is an "independent self" drawing sinful character from their own soul-self. I don't believe that, for I believe that human beings are derivative creatures always deriving character from the spirit-source of either Satan or God. Sinful character expression is not derived from the "flesh" in our soul, but from the character of Satan.

327

NOVEMBER 23

GOD WILL SUPPLY ALL OUR NEEDS

Perhaps you are like me, affirming what Paul wrote, "my God will supply all your needs according to His riches in glory in Christ Jesus" (Phil. 4:19), but sometimes subjectively questioning and wondering if God will really provide everything I presently need. I can certainly identify with Jesus' band of early disciples whom Jesus chastised by saying, "O, ye of little faith" (Matt. 6:30; 8:26; 14:31; 16:8). They often seemed to lose the confident expectation of hope that Jesus would indeed supply everything they needed in every situation. They believed that He could, but in the midst of the situation (in the "crunch time," they questioned if He would do so.

"Sometimes I question and wonder if God will provide everything I need? I am not referring to everything I want, for I know that my wants and my needs are often two different things. I can state quite categorically that I am willing to receive (by faith) all provision for my needs from God, but do I confidently expect (hope) that He will provide as needed? "Lord, help Thou my unbelief!" (Mk. 9:24). Jesus told His disciples to "observe the birds of the air" and "the lilies of the field" (Matt. 6:26-33; they are not anxious about God's supply for their every need, but with expectant hope go about being what they were created to be.

I, on the other hand, often begin to question and fret about God's provision. Has He ever been unfaithful? No, but the tempter is always badgering me with temptations to doubt that He will do so this time. Just as the serpent in the Garden began with niggling questions put to the original couple causing them to doubt whether God was faithful and fair, or was holding back something they needed, I am tempted to doubt whether God is faithful to provide the needed ideas that He wants me to write about in the "daily readings" articles that I have been writing every morning for the past six years. I must trust His faithfulness.

NOVEMBER 24

ARE WE OVERLY-CONCERNED ABOUT FINANCES?

We all have to pay attention to whether we have adequate monetary means to pay for what is necessary to live, and to meet our obligations and responsibilities for family and others. The question is whether such financial matters unduly occupy our mind, attention, and concern. As Christ-ones, we live in a world that is preoccupied with mercenary, monetary and materialistic acquisition, and despite wanting to be counter-cultural, we are constantly tempted to be drawn into the consumeristic culture. We are constantly bombarded with "opportunities" for financial security and wealth management to prepare for the future.

Jesus advised His disciples to consider the "birds of the air" and "the lilies of the field" to see they are not worried about what they will have for tomorrow (Matt. 6:25-29). Just prior to telling them to observe such phenomena, Jesus clearly warned His disciples, "No man can serve two masters; You cannot serve God and mammon" (Matt. 6:19-24; Lk. 6:9-13). To this day in modern Hebrew the word mammon means "wealth." But in biblical times, Mammon was an idolatrous Syrian false god. Split-loyalties between the God revealed in Jesus and an idolatrous concern for material gods are not compatible.

Money and finances are a necessary medium of exchange in the world in which we live, but we must maintain a proper perspective and attitude toward such as we submit ourselves to God. (James 4:7). To desire, acquire and possess material things can produce an elixir of pleasure that is akin to feeling like a god in one's own empire of material wealth. Money can be used as a power to control and leverage others; but Satan can use it to control us. Paul told Timothy, "the love of money (not money itself) is the root of all kinds of evil" (I Tim. 6:10). We must not be unduly concerned about money and wealth. Are we able to sit back in contented ambivalence about our assets?

NOVEMBER 25

FREE TO LIVE IN MARRIAGE UNION WITH CHRIST

Paul draws an interesting analogy in Romans 7:1-6. The marriage union is only valid until the other person dies. That's why we pledge our faithfulness to another in marriage, "until death do us part." If a wife were to have a sexual tryst with another man while still married to her husband, it would be considered adultery. But if the husband dies, she is free to marry another man. Paul draws the picture of a woman who is married to Mr. Law, an abusive taskmaster, but that terrible marriage was terminated when Mr. Law died at the crucifixion of Jesus on the cross. The woman (all of us) is now free to be joined in marriage union with Jesus (cf. I Cor. 6:17) and free to live in grace.

Let's expand the analogy a little farther than Paul does. What if, Mrs. Christ-one, previously married to Mr. Law, for some reason decides that the grace-life is too liberating and decides she prefers the strict parameters of performance – that way there's no questioning where one stands – in performance obedience or disobedience. She wants to sneak back into the bedroom with Mr. Law. But remember, Mr. Law expired, died, and became deceased at the cross, so any attempt to "hook up" with Mr. Law would be to engage in necrophilia (Greek *necros* = corpse; *phileo* = to love), making love to a dead corpse – macabre indeed!

It is a strange speculation that we are engaged in, but it occurs over and over again in the lives of Christ-ones. Why is it that Christians seem to continually want to revert back to legalistic religion? Non-Jewish Christians were never married to Mr. Law in the first place, but they mistakenly thought they were yoked to the Law. When, as Christ-ones, they want to structure the Christian life in terms of ethical rules and regulations, they inadvertently commit spiritual adultery. How so? To dilly-dally with the devil and his techniques of performance is to commit adultery against the One to whom we are joined spiritually.

WE BELIEVE UNTO RIGHTEOUSNESS

Many have not understood the difference between the intrinsic divine character of righteousness in the Father, Son, and Holy Spirit, as differentiated from the moralistic acts of human beings behaving rightly in accord with the acceptable standards of right and wrong behavior in various religious codifications of alleged "righteous behavior" by man's best effort to perform. God alone is Righteous. There is none righteous as God is righteous. What God is, only God is. "Your righteousness, O God, reaches to the heavens…who is like You? (Ps. 71:19). "There is no other. A righteous God and a Savior" (Isa. 45:21). Jesus, the Son of God, revealed God, and is "the Righteous One" (Acts 3:14; 7:52; 22:14).

Paul explained to the Roman Christians that "man believes unto righteousness" (Rom. 10:10). To believe is to receive, and we receive "the Righteous One" (the living Jesus) into our spirit, and "become the righteousness of God in (union with) Him" (II Cor. 5:21). Ours is a derived (not just declared) righteousness effected by the grace-action of the Righteous God (Rom. 5:17,21), and available to all who believe. "The righteousness of God through faith in Jesus Christ is for all who believe" (Rom. 3:22; Heb. 11:7).

Note that Paul does not write, "man *behaves* unto righteousness." The cumulative effect of our so-called righteous deeds does not make us righteous. Paul categorically denies that anyone can "*behave* unto righteousness." Earlier he wrote, "Christ is the end of all law-performance unto righteousness for everyone who believes" (Rom. 10:4). "God credits righteousness apart from works' (Rom. 4:6). To the Galatian Christians, he wrote, "If righteousness comes through the Law, then Christ died needlessly" (Gal. 2:21). If our performance behavior could make us right with God and righteous, then Jesus and His death for us on the cross was superfluous and totally unnecessary. God forbid! We believe/receive Jesus unto righteousness.

NOVEMBER 27

PAUL'S INDELICATE ARGUMENT

Nothing seems to have made Paul's blood boil and infuriated his sense of righteous indignation more than religionists coming into the churches where he had introduced the gospel of grace in Jesus Christ, attempting to advise the new Christians that they needed something more than God's grace in Jesus. This occurred time and again as Jewish Christians, known as Judaizers, arrived and told the new Christians that grace was too easy, and they needed to perform certain portions of the old covenant Law in order to really be right with God. It was a message with a false equation: Jesus + <u>something else</u> = salvation.

The primary "something else" advocated by the Judaizers for the new Christians in Galatia was the need for all males to be physically circumcised, for this was the sign that marked all true Jews as "the people of God" (Gen. 17:10-27). Though Paul himself was a Jew, he would have none of it! If the risen and living Lord Jesus was not sufficient for everything that God intended to do in restoring mankind by His grace, then the gospel was not "good news." In Galatians chapter five, Paul makes his argument against the addition of circumcision as a required condition of being a male Christ-one. He does not hold back!

Paul wanted the new Galatian Christians to experience the freedom of living in God's grace. "It was for freedom that Christ set us free" (Gal. 5:1), Paul begins. "In Christ Jesus neither circumcision or uncircumcision means anything, *but the issue is our faith-receptivity to God's grace allowing God's character of love to be worked out*" (Gal. 5:5). "You were called to freedom, brethren; do not turn your freedom into an opportunity for the flesh, but through love serve one another" (Gal. 5:13). Paul is saying, "As for those who are so knife-happy in their perform-ance inculcations, I could wish that the knife would slip and they might mutilate themselves (5:12) and cut off the entire organ.

NOVEMBER 28

THE DOUBLE HELIX OF INTERIORITY

Most of us are sufficiently educated in basic science information to know that human DNA (Deoxyribonucleic acid) is constructed of a double helix of two strands of molecules coiled in opposite directions around a common core. This molecular structure in the form of a double helix contains the unique genetic information that identifies every human individual and all living creatures. Using that double helix structure, I am suggesting that there is a comparable spiritual double helix of interiority that allows us to understand the unique relationship that a Christ-one has with the living Lord Jesus Christ.

This double helix of interiority, in like manner, has two strands coiled and intertwined around a common core. The common core is Jesus Christ. The two strands of information are the biblical statements that every Christ-one is "in Christ," and the living Spirit of Christ is "in every Christ-one." What does it mean to be "in Christ"? We must go beyond the spatial and locative categories of mechanical thought to consider our being "in spiritual union with the living Christ." "He who is joined to the Lord is one spirit with Him" (I Cor. 6:17). The Christ-one partakes of the divine nature (II Pet. 1:4); the Spirit of Christ becoming the energy in our human spirit at the core of our being.

The other strand of our spiritual double helix is to recognize that the living Lord Jesus Christ is in us, dwelling in our spirit. "Do you not recognize that Jesus Christ is in you," Paul asks the Corinthians, "unless you believed in vain" (II Cor. 13:5). This is basic spiritual information. "It is no longer I who lives, but Christ lives in me," Paul explained in Gal. 2:20. "If any person does not have the Spirit of Christ, he is none of His" (Rom. 8:9), Paul told the Roman Christians – that is to say that if the Spirit of Christ does not dwell in the spirit of an individual, then that person cannot be considered a Christ-one – bottom-line information!

NOVEMBER 29

"WORKING ON THE CHAIN GANG"

Sam Cooke and his brother Charles saw a group of prisoners working on a chain gang in the South. They wrote the song "Chain Gang," released in 1960, and the song went to #2 on the Billboard charts. Later it was sung by Otis Redding, Jackie Wilson, Count Basie, Jim Croce and others. The lyrics go like this:

> *Ho, Ha ...Well, don't you know...*
> That's the sound of the men...Working on the chain, ...gang.
> That's the sound of the men...Working on the chain, ...gang.

May I be so presumptuous as to suggest that similar lyrics and tunes might be heard from many church buildings every week. Many Christians do not understand or appreciate the freedom of God's grace that they have received in Jesus Christ. They would rather go back to the law-based drudgery of performance slavery than to be response-able to navigate the freedom of God's grace. Many do revert to the pre-set parameters of legalistic religion where the "thou shalts" and the "thou shalt nots" are carefully delineated and the punishments of the master/pastor in charge are meted out with regularity.

In his epistle to the Galatian Christians, Paul warned them about those who would attempt to persuade them to diminish the sufficiency of God's grace in Jesus Christ, and steer them toward the performance requirements of the Law. "It was for freedom that Christ set us free; therefore, keep standing firm and do not be subject again to a yoke of slavery" (Gal. 5:1). "You were called to freedom, brethren; only *do* not turn your freedom into an opportunity for the flesh" (Gal. 5:13). The chain gang of religious legalism is a poor exchange for the freedom of God's grace. The grunting and the groaning of laborious exertion of hard work is certainly not a pleasant sound compared to the joyful praise of God's all-sufficient grace.

GOD'S WORKMANSHIP

For many Christ-ones, Ephesians 2:10 is one of many overlooked verses, coming, as it does, immediately after the two famous verses of Ephesians 2:8,9 – "For by grace you have been saved through faith; and that not of yourselves, it is the gift of God; not as a result of works, so that no one may boast." Paul continues, "For we are His workmanship, created in Christ Jesus for good works, which God prepared beforehand so that we would walk in them" (Eph. 2;10). God's salvation necessarily leads to God's workmanship. There is a purpose to our being saved, and it is much more than cloud-surfing through the heavenlies

A basic truth that every Christ-one needs to understand is that everything of importance is what God's does; not what man does. God always takes the initiative of grace to redeem and save us, as well as to set us up as His workmanship to manifest His character and His ministry work unto His glory. All of this comes into being "in Christ Jesus," both in the historical work of Jesus dying on the cross, as well as the spiritual efficacy of our being joined in spiritual union with the Spirit of Christ (cf. I Cor. 6:17). His indwelling presence is the grace-dynamic necessary to derive and manifest His "good works," which God prepared beforehand that we should walk in them."

"In Jesus Christ," we are predestined to manifest the particular "good works" which God has prepared us to work out (cf. Phil. 2:12,13). God has "equipped us in every good thing to do His will, working in us that which is pleasing in His sight, through Jesus Christ, to whom be the glory forever and ever" (Heb. 13:20,21). Who is doing the working? Religion advises us that we must do the working. The gospel advises us that "God is at work in us, both to will and to work for His good pleasure" (Phil. 2:13), while we are the derivative creatures who are to faithfully receive His grace-action of His "good works" – His workmanship!

DECEMBER 1

"MUCH MORE"

"For if while we were enemies we were reconciled to God through the death of His Son, **much more**, having been reconciled, we shall be saved by His life (Rom. 5:10). We once were enemies of God, conjoined to "the spirit that works in the sons of disobedience" (Eph. 2:2), but while in that state of spiritual death (Rom. 5:1), we were made alive in Christ and reconciled to God based on the death of His Son, Jesus Christ, on the cross of Calvary, appropriated by our faith-acceptance of His sacrifice. Having become Christ-ones via our reception of Jesus, Paul adds a "much more" to his recitation of the gospel.

Paul does NOT mean that there is something more than the Person and work of Jesus that is necessary for our salvation. The gospel is always JESUS + nothing! *Solus Christus* (Christ alone) was the Reformation motto. Paul is saying, "Even more than the historical events, what's more, it follows then that the rest of the gospel (cf. Dan Stone) is also true, that *The Saving Life of Christ* (cf. W. Ian Thomas) is the vibrant and vital life of the risen Lord Jesus by which He continues the salvation process of living out His resurrection-life in His people, the Christ-ones, continuing to re-present His Christ-life in Christ-ones today.

There is "much more" to the gospel story than the abridged version we hear from the pulpits of the churches in America each Sunday. It is the "much more" of Jesus' continuing "saving life." The "good news" of the gospel is "much more" than a historical transaction event of 2000 years ago. The life, death and resurrection of Jesus was not simply a transaction to dispense a ticket to heaven after death to those who assent to the historicity of those events. "Much more," the resurrection life of Jesus dwells within and is active in every Christ-one. His life did not end at the cross, nor at the ascension; we are continually "made safe" by His manifested life in our behavior.

DECEMBER 2

IMPERATIVES BASED ON INDICATIVES

Let us define our terms, lest we have forgotten some of our grammar training from yesteryear. An imperative is a verb form expressing a command with an authoritative obligation to respond. For example, the teacher may have said, "Pay attention!" It is implied that the one so commanded is able to respond to the order. An indicative is a verb in the indicative mood that indicates a statement of fact. The indicative fact is: the students of the aforementioned teacher have the intelligence and ability to respond to the teacher's command, and are therefore responsible to obey what she has commanded.

The new covenant literature of what we call *The New Testament* contains over one thousand imperative verbs, implying that the readers are responsible to respond in obedience to what is commanded. An example of such an imperative command is Jesus' call to "Love one another" (Jn. 13:34; 15:12,17). If, in the new covenant, we are no longer called upon to attempt to perform in obedience to the imperatives of law and performance expectations, but to rely on God's grace to implement the activity expected, how do we explain these imperatives? We note that there are many indicative statements that explain the provision by which we carry out the imperatives by God's grace. For example: "The love of God has been shed abroad in our hearts through the Holy Spirit who was given to us" (Romans 5:5). "The fruit of the Spirit is love..." (Gal. 5:22).

Jesus does not call us to do anything, but what He has already given us everything in Himself in order to perform what we He has asked us to do. Jesus is the dynamic of His own demands. The grace of God in Jesus Christ by His Spirit comprises the empowering by which everything in the Christian life is accomplished to the glory of God. "Apart from Me, you can do nothing," Jesus told His disciples.

DECEMBER 3

WEIGHING THE BALANCE

To avoid extremism, we must weigh the balance in every category of thought. This often involves finding the tensioned balance in a both/and dialectic. The new covenant literature often brings together the concepts of both truth and love. "Speaking the truth in love, we are to grow up in all aspects into Him who is the head, even Christ" (Eph. 4:15). "Since you have in obedience to the truth purified your souls for a sincere love of the brethren, fervently love one another from the heart" (I Pet. 1:22). Both truth and love are important realities that find their essence in the Person of our Lord Jesus Christ.

Truth	Love
Correctness	Compassion
Rightness	Relational
Accurate	Accepting
Information	Empathy
Doctrine	Diversity
Facticity	Felicity

If we push the left column too far to the left, and neglect the right column of love, we end up with a fundamentalism that thinks they have the truth of God and His ways all figured out. If we push the right column too far to the right and neglect the left column of truth, we end up with a sentimental liberalism that has no concern for the conservation of truth. Neither of these alternatives is satisfactory. It is important that we find the balance that Paul was referring to when he wrote of "speaking the truth in love" (Eph. 4:15), and Peter was writing of, "You have in obedience to the truth purified your souls for a sincere love of the brethren" (I Pet. 1:22). Jesus always expresses Himself as both truth and love in balance, and we are obliged to consider the balance as we allow Him to manifest His character of Truth (Jn. 14:6) and Love (Eph. 3:19) in our behavior.

WHAT DOES IT MEAN TO BE "BORN AGAIN"?

Periodically, one needs to go "back to the basics" of spiritual realities (*pneumatikoi*). (Television programming might call these "re-runs"). The phrase "born again" is a metaphor used to refer to the spiritual reality of humans being re-lifed with the divine life of God (Father, Son, and Holy Spirit). That divine life was forfeited when humanity, in Adam, chose to defy God, and as God explained (Gen. 2:17) was subject to death (cf. Heb. 2:14). The Son of God who became human flesh (Jn. 1:14) in Jesus, willing endured death on a cross (Phil. 2:8), to take the death that mankind deserved upon Himself, in order to make divine life available again to receptive mankind.

The Greek word for "born again" is *anagenao* (I Pet. 1:3), derived from the word *genesis* meaning "to bring into being" (title of first book in Bible). Humans can be "brought into being again" spiritually by receiving the Spirit of Jesus Christ into their human spirit. Jesus said to Nicodemus, "You must be born from above" (Jn. 3:5), born not only physically, but "of the Spirit" (Jn. 3:6). Not understanding spiritual things (I Cor. 2:14), Nicodemus caricatured such an idea as having to crawl back into his mother's womb to be reborn. Jesus explained that the mystery of spiritual new birth is like the origins of the blowing wind.

The theological word used to explain "born again" is "regeneration" (cf. Titus 3:5 – *palingenesia*). This integral biblical concept has been much maligned in recent years. Those claiming to be "born again" Christ-ones have often not manifested the Christ-life in their subsequent behavior. Critics have spoken derisively of "born-aginners" being hypocritical. Even Christians have contributed to the misuse of the phrase by referring to a new translation of the Bible as "the Bible has been born again." There must be consistent integrity if we want to avoid negative and denigrating comments about the phrase "born again."

DECEMBER 5

WHAT DOES IT MEAN TO BE A CHRISTIAN?

Another reading in the "back to basics" series. With the abuse, overuse and misuse of the term "Christian," it is important to take another look at what it means to be a Christian from a biblical perspective. In the book of Acts, Luke explained that "the disciples were first called Christians in Antioch" (Acts 11:26). Some have speculated that it might originally have been used in a pejorative sense (we don't know for sure!). It obviously referred to those who were identified with Jesus Christ, and thus indicated a Christ-one, which is my preferred term for speaking of a Christian, to avoid the contemporary ambiguity of the commonly used term of "Christian."

Notice that those in Antioch were already disciples when they were first called "Christians." Today, religion has reversed the process by seeking to make all Christians into a specified form of "disciples" via the process of discipleship. Religion has it backwards again! We might also note that "Christian" is never used as an adjective in scripture (only as a noun), but is most popularly used as an adjective in contemporary English. We speak of a Christian plumber, a Christian politician, a Christian pastor, a Christian celebrity, a Christian church-member, a Christian theologian, etc. What do we mean by all of this?

From a biblical perspective, one who is called a "Christian" is a Christ-one, meaning that the Spirit of the living Christ has come to dwell in the human spirit of a receptive individual (cf. Rom. 8:9,16), with the intent to live out His life in that person's life and character. This might be called the bottom-line of what it means to be a Christian, and unfortunately many who call themselves "Christian" do not understand that. Theologically, it might be said that a Christian is one who has "Christ-in-one," and the resultant term of Christianity should be understood as "Christ-in-you-ity," with the Christ-life lived out as our behavior.

BAPTIZED IN THE SPIRIT

The concept of being "baptized in the Spirit" is more commonly referred to in some holiness and Pentecostal portions of the *ecclesia* than in others. What does it mean to be "baptized in the Spirit"? We can begin by saying it is not necessarily an esoteric or ecstatic event or experience subsequent to one's becoming a Christian in spiritual regeneration. But in the theology of some Christian groups it is considered to be a "second work of grace" after one has experienced spiritual new birth, and often to be accompanied by ecstatic experiences, sometimes in the context of entire sanctification or speaking in tongues.

John the Baptist mentioned that though he baptized in water, there was one coming after him (referring to Jesus) who would "baptize in (by, with – the Greek preposition can mean all of these) the Holy Spirit (Matt. 3:11; Mk. 1:8; Lk. 3:16; Jn. 1:33). Jesus referred to this just prior to His ascension (Acts 1:5). Peter referenced the same reality when the Spirit came upon the Gentiles (Acts 11:16). So, the phenomenon of being baptized in (by, with) the Holy Spirit was not an unexpected or unknown reality by the earliest Christians, especially after what occurred on Pentecost (Acts 2:1-13).

But, it is Paul's reference to all Christians, "whether Jews or Greeks, whether slaves or free," having been "baptized by one Spirit into one body, and made to drink of one Spirit" (I Cor. 12:13) that seems to give us the most inclusive mention of "baptism in, by, with the Holy Spirit." To be baptized in the Spirit is to be overwhelmed by or with the Holy Spirit. It was at our spiritual regeneration that every Christian's spirit was overwhelmed by the Holy Spirit. When we received the Spirit of Christ (Rom. 8:9) in spiritual regeneration we were at that time made part of the Body of Christ, the *ecclesia*, the community of Christ-ones in whom the living Christ lives and is manifested.

DECEMBER 7

ARE YOU RIGHTEOUS, HOLY AND BLAMELESS?

It is interesting to stand before a group of Christian people, and begin by asking, "How many of you are righteous? How many of you are holy? How many of you are blameless? How many of you are perfect?" There are usually a few persons with the spiritual audacity to raise their hand. I follow that with the next question, "If I were to ask your spouse, would he/she agree and verify that you are what you say you are? These questions do not refer to a person's behavior. They refer to a person's spiritual identity in Christ. Personal behavioral actions do not establish one's spiritual identity, though identity should play out in behavior.

A Christ-one is made righteous (Rom. 5:18,19; II Cor. 5:21), not as an essential or intrinsic characteristic (only God is), but because of the presence of Jesus, the Righteous One (Acts 3:14; 7:52; 22:14), in our spirit bringing the derived spiritual identity of a "righteous one" (Heb.12:23). Likewise, Jesus, the Holy One (Acts 3:14;) dwelling within us, brings with His presence the spiritual identity of a holy one (Col. 3:12; I Jn. 2:20). In the same manner, Christians are "blameless" (Col. 1:22) by the presence of Jesus, the "sinless one" (II Cor. 5:21; Heb. 4:15), and "perfect" (Phil. 3:15; by the presence of the Perfect One (Heb. 7:28).

The willingness to accept these seemingly outlandish designations of spiritual identity by faith is important for a Christ-one to confess and concur with in order to behave in accordance with who we have become spiritually. As stated previously, these are not inherent, intrinsic or essential character traits; they are not something we are in ourselves, and not attributed to us based on our behavioral performance. These character attributes are only derived from Another, from the presence of the risen and living Jesus dwelling within our spirit, and by His presence bringing us a spiritual identity of what and who He is. That is why we are designated as Christ-ones.

DECEMBER 8

OUR POINT OF REFERENCE

The artist set her canvas on the easel. She drew a horizon line and a point of reference (maybe more than one) to which every object in the picture will be arranged and aligned, giving perspective to the work. In our personal lives, every person has to determine an ultimate point of reference to which everything else in their thinking and life relates to and is oriented. For many people the point of reference is themselves. Everything relates to me, and my thoughts and opinions and desires and inclinations. If it doesn't serve what I perceive to be my good, then it is dispensable and easily dismissed. I am my own center of reference. This is the natural, humanistic point of reference.

When we are spiritually regenerated, our point of reference changes. The exchange of spiritual condition, from Satan to God, must necessarily lead to a change in our point of reference. The character of sin and selfishness, which is the character of Satan, has been exchanged for the character of righteous, the character of love (cf. Gal. 5:22,23), the presence and character of the Living Lord Jesus. In regeneration we die (cf. Gal. 2:20; Col. 3:3) to the humanistic orientation of placing ourselves as the center-point of reference, and Jesus and His love for others becomes our point of reference – a new perspective for everything.

This is why Paul writes, "Do nothing from selfishness or empty conceit, but with humility of mind regard one another as more important than yourselves; do not merely look out for your own personal interests, but also for the interests of others. Have this attitude in yourselves which was also in Christ Jesus" (Phil. 2:3,4). Is Jesus your point of reference? Is everything in your life evaluated in reference to the life and character of Jesus? Is He the living reality that gives perspective to all your thoughts and actions, and more particularly your love and concern for others? This should be the reality of every Christ-one.

DECEMBER 9

DRAW NEAR

My wife acquired an iRobot Roomba sweeper that randomly bumps into the walls and furniture, changes direction, and sweeps the floor. It has an electronic sensor that guides it back to the dock where it recharges. In similitude, the Christ-one seems to have a spiritual sensor that needs to "dock" in personal intimacy with God. "Let us draw near with a true heart in full awareness of faith" (Heb. 10:22), is a call to such intimacy. Older Christian writers called it "intercourse with God." A phonetic expansion of the word "intimacy" suggests that it means "into me see," a time when we can see into the heart of God, and God can see into our hearts also (Heb. 4:12,13).

Again, in Hebrews 4:16, Paul wrote, "Let us draw near with confidence to the throne of grace, so that we may receive mercy and find grace to help in time of need." When Jesus told His disciples, "I go to prepare a place for you" (Jn. 14:2,3), it may mean that He was going via His death, resurrection and ascension to prepare a place for them "near to the heart of God". It would be a place of personal intimacy where Christ-ones who have a "one spirit" union (I Cor. 6:17) with God in Christ could "draw near" and find refuge and the oneness of intimacy with the triune God in comforting peace and assurance.

The popular hymn, "Near to the Heart of God" was written by Cleland Boyd McAfee in 1903. The words are comforting, "There is a place of quiet rest, near to the heart of God... There is a place of comfort sweet, near to the heart of God .... There is a place of full release, near to the heart of God..." Earlier, in 1841, Sarah Flower Adams had written the words to the hymn, "Nearer My God to Thee." The human heart or spirit was intended to be filled with the presence of God, and to "draw near" in intimacy with God, to find its place of "docking" or connection in the continuing communion of personal prayer and worship.

DECEMBER 10

AT CALVARY"

Many Christ-ones have identified with and enjoyed the words and music of the hymn, "At Calvary," the lyrics of which were written by William R. Newell in the early 1900s.

> Oh, the love that drew salvation's plan!
> Oh, the grace that brought it down to man!
> Oh, the mighty gulf that God did span!
> At Calvary! (4th stanza)

> Mercy, there was great and grace was free;
> Pardon, there was multiplied to me;
> There my burdened soul found liberty
> At Calvary! (chorus)

Many have indeed found liberty when they were first regenerated, a true spiritual liberty, emancipated from Satan's control (Acts 26:18; Col. 1:13,14). But on an existential and experiential level their awareness of liberty was short-lived. They did not know how free they really were – that they were free from guilt and condemnation, and were no longer "slaves to sin" (Rom. 6:6-20). Conversely, they did not understand their new spiritual identity and the provision of grace that was theirs by the indwelling presence of the risen and living Lord Jesus.

The hymn has an interesting background. William (Bill) Newell was a troubled young man. His father, a pastor in Ohio, wrote a letter requesting that his son be might be accepted to attend Moody Bible Institute. The president of the school, R.A. Torrey, rejected the request, but after repeated pleas from the father, agreed to accept Bill Newell as a provisional student. Later, Bill was joyously regenerated, and eventually became a faculty member at MBI. He wrote the lyrics to this song early in the twentieth century, and D.B. Towner, composed the music.

DECEMBER 11

LIVING BY LAW = WALKING AFTER THE FLESH

Why is it that so many Christians seem to think that keeping the Ten Commandments and living by performance of the Law is the means by which they are going to advance in walking by the Spirit? Absolutely NOT! "If I just do this, and don't do that, I will be walking by the Spirit." NO! It is an old fallacy to think that by keeping the negatives and abiding by the prohibitions, one will thereby be participating in the positive of God's character and action. Not so! The "dos" and the "don'ts" are simply the performances of human effort, thinking that thereby God will be pleased and appeased, and express His "atta-boy" praise.

In the fifth chapter of his epistle to the Galatians, Paul addresses this fallacy of thinking that "living by the Law" enhances one's spirituality. Circumcision and law-keeping of any kind are so detrimental that if one so engages, "Christ is of no benefit to you" (5:2). If you are attached to law-keeping, thinking that you are justified by doing good and keeping the rules, then you are severed from Christ (5:4). It is law or grace, flesh or Spirit, but never an admixture of the two. They are antithetical the one to the other. You can't have both together. "If you are led by the Spirit, you are not under the Law" (5:18), Paul explains.

Some people have a dyslexic understanding of Galatians 5:16. They think it says, "Do not carry out the desire of the flesh, and you will be walking by the Spirit." Backwards! The positive of God's grace always swallows up the negative. "Walk by the Spirit, and you will not carry out the desire of the flesh" (5:16). Performance of rule-keeping in any form is legalistic self-effort which is always engagement of the flesh. Participating in religious exercises and disciplines is fleshly performance-effort. Such performance and participation is to be contrasted with "walking in the Spirit," which is always enacted by the grace-dynamic of God in Christ without any human supplementation.

DECEMBER 12

ATTITUDE TOWARD RELIGION

I have been asked, "Are you bitter at what Christian religion has done in your life?" Not really, but I am appalled at how religion has counterfeited, misrepresented and prostituted the truth of the gospel of Jesus Christ. I do not hesitate to say that I hate religion, because I believe that God hates religion (cf. Isa. 1:14), and I want to hate what He hates. The experience of religion was necessary to provide the contrast with the genuine reality God has made available in Jesus Christ. God used religion to develop a sense of discernment between the counterfeit and the genuine reality of the life of Jesus Christ.

I have said in the past, "You can take all the religion in the world and throw it into the deep blue sea." The problem comes in that this would be similar to trying to pick the tares (cheat) out of the wheat (cf. Matt. 13:25-40). They are difficult to separate, since they use the same terms and vocabulary. Religionists are often deceived into thinking they are participating in the reality of Christ-life, when in reality they are simply going through the performance-motions of religious exercises. It takes revelation from the Spirit of God to realize and see the difference, and then to enjoy resting in God's grace provision of Jesus.

Knowing that the "ruler of this world" (Jn. 12:31; 14:30; 16:11) is the one promoting and energizing all religion, and all the fleshly efforts to perform the religious exercises, I am sure that I will grieve until the day I die that so many people have been deceived and duped into keeping the Law and working for Jesus instead of participating in God's grace. Religion is the antithesis to all that God desires for mankind, and always keeps persons frustrated that they are never able to do enough to meet the demands. The truth of the matter is that Jesus is the dynamic of all God's demands, and God's grace-dynamic will never wear you out, but will allow one to rest in His sufficiency.

347

DECEMBER 13

UNEXPECTED REVELATION

God has ways to get our attention beyond anything we could even imagine. "His ways are past finding out" (Rom. 11:33). Many of us are quite hard-headed, and slow to recognize that the Spirit of God is attempting to speak through to our spirit. But when God wants to grant us a revelation of Himself and what He wants to do, He has innumerable ways and means to do so. The last thing on Saul's mind on the road to Damascus, as he made his way to persecute and prosecute Christians was that a flash of light from heaven would strike him down, and a voice would ask from heaven, "Saul, Saul, why are you persecuting Me?" and then identify Himself as the risen Lord Jesus (Acts 9:1-6).

Many Christ-ones have testified of receiving such unexpected visits and revelations, sometimes in dreams and visions, and sometimes via many other means (driving down the road, reading a book, sitting on the beach or on a mountain summit, or in the midst of a mundane moment). The triune God of Father, Son and Holy Spirit can breakthrough with a Spirit-burst of insight, joy, brilliance or fullness. These awe-inspiring visitations are "beyond what we could ask or think" (Eph. 3:20), beyond our wildest imagination or dreams. They are God-moments, when we exclaim, "Oh my!" or "Oh, I see!"

The more philosophical among us might call our experience an "existential moment" in the "experiential now." The theological inclined might call it an "incarnational breakthrough," wherein "heaven came down and glory filled my soul." In the *koine* Greek of the new covenant literature, such an event might be called a *kairos* breakthrough, wherein the eternal God revealed himself in our temporal time. Whatever we call such an experience, we are usually quite aware that we have been visited by God, and are sometimes left with attempting to figure out what the purpose of that visitation was all about.

HOSEA AND THE HO'

The message of Hosea is a real-life lived-out parable. The Lord asked Hosea, the prophet, to marry a street-walker; yes, a whore (ho'), a harlot, a hooker, a call-girl, a lady of the night, a prostitute. The purpose of such a request was to provide a living illustration that the faithful God, Jehovah, was joined to an unfaithful people, the nation of Israel. So, in obedience, Hosea found a lady of ill-repute named Gomer, married her, and loved her as his wife. The name Hosea, by the way, means "salvation" in the Hebrew language. Hosea's wife did not have a pattern of faithfulness, and kept running off to engage in the world's oldest profession of harlotry, being paid for sexual services.

When Gomer stayed home, she and Hosea had three children. The names of the children were symbolic in accord with what the life and marriage of Hosea was meant to illustrate. The first child, a son, was named Jezreel after a valley and city that had been devastated by war and pillaging, a disaster. The second child, a girl, was named *Lo-ruhamah*, meaning "no mercy" or "not loved." The third child, another son, was named *Lo-ammi*, meaning "not my people." On several occasions in the new covenant literature, there are veiled references to how "in (union with) Christ," the Gentile people who were "not My people" are now "My people" (Rom. 9:25,26; Heb. 8:10; I Peter 2:10), beloved and joined to God (cf. I Cor. 6:17).

The primary message depicted in Hosea is that God is faithful, even though His people are unfaithful. Despite anything we have done, continue to do, or will ever do, God loves us without measure and unconditionally, forgives us repeatedly, and keeps attempting to draw us back into the intimate personal relationship for which He created us in the first place. Can you think of a more graphic picture of "salvation" than Hosea's love and forgiveness of his unfaithful wife?

DECEMBER 15

THE PRESENT LIFE OF JESUS

Many Christ-ones have a life they never live. They seem to think that the life they have been granted is a commodity to be utilized in the future when they get to heaven. Most Christ-ones recognize that to receive Jesus by faith is to receive eternal life, but they have not adequately recognized that the risen and living Lord Jesus is eternal life. The vital dynamic of eternal life is the grace of God working through the living Christ by the power of the Holy Spirit to manifest the character of the triune God in human behavior. Becoming a Christ-one is not the receipt of an eternal-life-pass that grants admission to heaven after we die.

"I am the life," Jesus explained to His disciples in John 14:6. "No one comes to the Father but through Me." "He who has the Son has the life; he who does not have the Son of God does not have the life. These things I have written to you that you may know that you have eternal life" (I Jn. 5:12,13). Jesus is eternal life, now and forever. The life that is Jesus is not something in addition to Jesus, or something that Jesus comes to pass on to us. It is His life that is meant to be lived out by Him through us unto the glory of God. Present tense eternal life is a reality some Christ-ones are not experiencing.

Many have received Jesus Christ with the assurance that their sins are forgiven and they are on their way to heaven. They have expressed their appreciation for all God has provided for them in the life and death of the Son, Jesus Christ. They sing of going to heaven and living in "Beulah land." The past is forgiven, the future is assured, but they're just hanging around and going to church in the present until the second coming. It is time that the church explains to Christ-ones that the purpose of the present is that they might live in the power of who Jesus is, that they may live by His life here and now, that by the receptivity of His activity, Jesus is to lived out through us today.

WHAT HAPPENS IN CHRISTIAN CONVERSION?

Many churches ... many Christians ... think they exist to count Christian conversions, to increase the number of persons identified as Christians. Yet, most do not seem to know what occurs in Christian conversion. It is certainly more than joining a church, or changing one's mind to assent to a different belief-system, or to an acceptable statement of faith. Conversion often involves repentance, a change of mind that leads to a change of action, but the change of action is not our performance, but a change of spiritual actuator source whereby another spirit-being occupies our human spirit to manifest his character.

One of the clearest statements of what constitutes Christian conversion was expressed by Paul before Agrippa at Caesarea Maritima: "to turn (convert) Gentiles from darkness to light, from the dominion (authority, kingdom, power, control) of Satan to God, that they might receive forgiveness of sins..." (Acts 26:18). "We have not received the spirit of this world, but the Spirit who is from God" (I Cor. 2:12). "He rescued us from the domain of darkness, and transferred us to the kingdom of His beloved Son, in whom we have redemption, the forgiveness of sins" (Col. 1:13,14). Christian conversion occurs when "the spirit that works in the sons of disobedience" (Eph. 2:2) is exchanged for the Spirit of Christ (Rom. 8:9) dwelling within and working in the human spirit of a faithfully receptive individual.

Such a spiritual exchange in the core of our being, in our human spirit, entails our being occupied by and living by the life of another spirit-source. As derivative human creatures, we all derive character from either Satan or God. In Christian conversion, we are re-lifed with the resurrection-life of the risen Lord Jesus (cf. II Cor. 13:5). That is why Christians often use the metaphor of being "born again" (Jn. 3:1-6; I Pet. 1;3) in a spiritual new birth to refer to Christian conversion.

DECEMBER 17

HOW DO WE KNOW WHAT WE KNOW?

Even prior to the primary Greek philosophers (Socrates, Plato, Aristotle), the theories of how we know what we know were debated. Such discussion of knowledge is called "epistemology," (Greek *epistemi* = knowledge; *logos* = words, logic, reason, study of). I was first introduced to the idea of tacit knowledge through the writings of Hungarian scientist, Michael Polanyi (d. 1976). Tacit knowledge is knowledge that is not totally explicable. We know how to swim or ride a bicycle, not because someone explained the physics of such motion in logical propositions, but because we have engaged in such experientially.

How do we know that we know Jesus? Paul explained that "the natural man does not understand spiritual things' (I Cor. 2:14), but those who are spiritual have "the mind of Christ" (I Cor. 2:16). How do those statements relate to the epistemological categories of explicit, implicit, and tacit knowledge? Explicit knowledge is framed in logical propositions that can be put into written data research. Implicit knowledge is evidenced in transferrable principles that transcend skill platforms. Tacit knowledge is gained from personal subjective experience whereby we "know that we know," despite being unable to explain such existential knowing in sentential terms.

Back to the question above: How do we know that we know Jesus? Some would say that such knowledge is pure subjectivity. The Danish philosopher, Soren Kierkegaard, said, "All truth is subjectivity." If Truth is a Person, as Jesus said, "I am the truth" (Jn. 14:6), then to receive the Spirit of Jesus is an inner reality, known only by the person who has done so. Is this an inexplicable tacit knowledge? We must go beyond the epistemic categories of knowing *what* or knowing *how*, to the spiritual relationality of "knowing Whom I have believed, and am persuaded that He is able" (II Tim. 1:12) to be all He is in me.

DECEMBER 18

RIGHTLY DIVIDING SOUL AND SPIRIT

Writing to the Christians in Jerusalem, Paul wrote, "The Word of God is sharper than a two-edged sword penetrating as far as the dividing of soul and spirit." (Heb. 4:12). Some Christians are not listening and recognizing that separation of soul and spirit. "If any person is in Christ, he is a new creature; old things have passed away, all things have become new" (II Cor. 5:17). This statement pertains to the things of the Spirit, but the Christ-one still has old "flesh" patterns of selfishness and sinfulness in the soul. The things of the spirit are accomplished and settled at regeneration, while the things of the soul are ongoing.

Christ-ones have the "mind of Christ" (I Cor. 2:16), a spirit-reality. yet, we are still involved in the "renewing of the mind" (Rom. 12:2) in our soul. We are "made perfect" (Heb. 12:23) in derived spiritual identity, but "not yet perfect" (Phil. 3:12) behaviorally. We "have been saved" (Eph. 2:8) spiritually, but are "being saved" (I Cor. 1:18) in our soul. We "have been sanctified" (Acts 26:18; I Cor. 1:12;), but are still engaged in the process of sanctification in soul and body. Sin has been dealt with and we have been forgiven spiritually in regeneration, but that does not mean that we no longer sin and need forgiveness experientially.

Overemphasis of spirit-reality can lead to a perverted sense of "finished" grace-rest that amounts to passive inactivity, while overemphasizing ongoing soul-responsibility can lead to religious performance. We must keep a balance, and see both sides of the dialectic. We do not want to fall in the ditch of triumphal perfectionism that advocates an "entire sanctification" of holiness and minimizes the ongoing choices of faith, whereby we allow the Holy Spirit to manifest the "fruit of the Spirit" (Gal. 5:22,23) and actively manifest the life of Jesus in the behavior of our mortal flesh (II Cor. 4:10,11). In failing to divide spirit and soul, some are developing a spiritual pride.

DECEMBER 19

THE WALKING WOUNDED?

Wounds, scars, trauma and maiming are not only inflicted on physical bodies, but also upon people's minds, emotions, and volitional function. This has been called "soul injury." Many humans suffer from the diabolic character of selfishness and sinfulness that others (perhaps parents, siblings, extended family, so-called friends, etc.) have inflicted upon them in the rejective actions of failing to love them, protect them, or even relate to them. Those who are suffering the psychological wounds of war or other trauma have been identified as having PTSD, but there are many suffering from social wounding.

Oftentimes these social wounds have resulted in prolonged and severe psychological personality disorders that are quite debilitating, especially to social relationships and personal growth. Such personality disorders can lead to various identifiable forms of mental illness. There is a sense in which we have all experienced some rejective psychological wounding because we are products of a rejective world-system of which Satan is "the ruler" (Jn. 14:30; 16:11). All human beings fit in the category of "the walking wounded" and require the Creator to deliver and restore them to functional humanity.

Christian thought believes that ultimate healing comes from the Healing One in the spirit-core of our being as the living Jesus, the "great physician" is invited to heal us from the inside out. From His presence in our spirit, His character can permeate into our thinking, emotions, and decision-making into our mind, emotion, and will, but this does not happen overnight, immediately – it takes time to reformulate our "desires" from fleshly desires to godly desires, to engage in the "renewing of the mind" (Rom. 12:2) whereby we develop "established attitudes" consistent with God's attitude, and can allow such to be implemented in healthy behavior based on the character of God.

RELATIONAL OR MECHANICAL?

Evangelical Christians like to talk about the necessity of having a "personal relationship with Jesus." But when they engage in discussion of what this personal relationship entails and how it is to be explained, they so often revert to mechanical and informational doctrinal terminology, instead of couching their theological thinking in relational categories of an eternal loving and merciful God inviting all people into His trinitarian fellowship. They tend to use terminology and vocabulary of a *Deus mechanica* wherein God's action is explained in linear logic syllogisms and arguments.

Mechanical thought patterns tend to explain that if this part does this, then this part will do that; if this be true then that will be true. If God is immutable and unchanging, then we can figure out the mechanics of the ways by which God works and employ them in ecclesiastical utilitarian processes. If we can determine that an individual is "saved" by going through certain motions or actions, then we can mechanically surmise that he will always be saved permanently with eternal security. If spiritual regeneration has occurred, then the soul is "heaven-ready" and need not be concerned with the process of sanctification and genuinely relational interactive fellowship with one another.

The historic Augustinian-Calvinistic theology that has been popular for centuries in Christian thought, with the TULIP acrostic by which it often explained, is without a doubt a *Theologica mechanica* that posits God with absolute sovereign actions that are imposed upon a corrupted humanity incapable of relational response. The gospel of Jesus Christ demands a *Theologica personalem* that involves relationality with the Personal Triune God and with one another in the context of God's unpredictable grace that will inevitably be consistent with His character and allow for authentic human relationships.

DECEMBER 21

"OH, CHRIST IS GIV'N"

Many of our popular Christmas songs, though familiar and melodic, do not share the gospel message of the coming of Jesus Christ to redeem from sin and restore God's life to sinful humanity. An old German folk song, "O Tannenbaum," (fir tree) from the 16th century, gradually became a Christmas carol in the 20th century, and we still sing it today as "Oh, Christmas Tree." I have taken the liberty to change the words, and sing it to the same tune, thereby providing a more gospel meaning.

Oh, Christ is giv'n, Oh, Christ is giv'n,
Of all God's gifts most gracious.
Oh, Christ is giv'n, Oh, Christ is giv'n,
Of all God's gifts most gracious.

He is the Word, giv'n by God's love,
Bringing life, from God above,
Oh, Christ is giv'n, Oh, Christ is giv'n,
Of all God's gifts most gracious.

He has to us brought light and life;
Peace within the constant strife,
Oh, Christ is giv'n, Oh, Christ is giv'n,
Of all God's gifts most gracious.

He is my life, my constant joy;
Nothing can this peace destroy,
Oh, Christ is giv'n, Oh, Christ is giv'n,
Of all God's gifts most gracious.

Expectant hope, forevermore;
Fear and sorrow – no nevermore.
Oh, Christ is giv'n, Oh, Christ is giv'n,
Of all God's gifts most gracious.

"OH, WHAT JOY IT IS TO SING"
(to the tune of Jingle Bells)

Dashing through our lives,
With too much on our minds,
This our joy deprives,
And our spirit binds.
But the gospel rings
Making spirits bright
What joy it is that Jesus brings,
A hopeful song tonight.

(Chorus) Oh, glory dwells; worship swells;
Jesus is the way.
Oh, what fun it is to sing
Of the grace we can't repay,
Oh, glory dwells; worship swells;
Jesus is the way.
Oh, what fun it is to sing
Of the grace we can't repay.

I sought to have some fun;
I thought I'd take control;
And soon the Evil One
Was tempting my poor soul;
His attitude was mean.
My downfall was his goal.
But Christ within did intervene;
His grace I must extol. (Chorus)

It was not long ago,
The story I must tell,
I thought I'd run the show,
And on my face I fell;
Forever full of grace,
My God His hand extended,
And lifted me from my disgrace;
The sin, it was transcended. (Chorus)

DECEMBER 23

"I WONDER AS I WANDER"

John Jacob Niles jotted down the words of an Appalachian folk song he heard performed by a young girl named Annie Morgan in North Carolina. After collecting several such songs, he published a songbook entitled, *Songs from the Hill Folks* in 1933. One of the songs in that collection was "I Wonder as I Wander."

> "I wonder as I wander out under the sky,
> How Jesus the Savior did come for to die.
> For poor ord'nry people like you and like I...
> I wonder as I wander out under the sky."

The phrase in the first stanza, "How Jesus the Savior did come for to die," caught my attention. Here we have the explicit theological conception that the Incarnation was the purposed precursor of the Crucifixion. The sentiment of the Bethlehem event with the birth of Jesus as a baby boy, is connected to the gruesome reality of the Calvary event where the Son of God dies, not for His own sin (II Cor. 5:21), but for the sins of all humanity (I Jn. 2:2). Jesus said, "The Son of Man did not come to be served, but to serve, and to give His life a ransom for many" (Matt. 20:28; Mk. 10:45).

The second stanza continues the biblical connections:

> "When Mary birthed Jesus 'twas in a cow's stall,
> With wise men and farmers and shepherds and all.
> But high from God's heaven a star's light did fall,
> And the promise of ages it then did recall."

In this verse, the Incarnation-birth of Jesus is connected back to "the promise of ages," the promises of God to Adam and Abraham (Genesis 3:15; 12-22), promising God's blessing on all nations of people. When Jesus said He "came to give His life a ransom for many," the "many" means "all people," the universal availability of the gospel. This is clarified and documented in I Tim. 2:6 where Paul wrote, "He gave Himself as a ransom for all."

DECEMBER 24

HARK THE HERALD ANGELS SING

Some Christmas carols are merely trite sentiments about the birth of Jesus, and the festivities of the Christmas season. But this carol is loaded with biblical and theological meaning. More than any other Christmas carol I am aware of, this carol ties together many of the theological components of the Christian gospel in a full-orbed expression of the gospel in music.

This carol was originally written by Charles Wesley and first published in 1739 by his brother, John Wesley. The lyrics were later adapted by fellow Methodist, George Whitefield, in 1754. The melody is by Felix Mendelssohn, adapted by William H. Cummings.

> Hark the herald angels sing "Glory to the newborn King!
> Peace on earth and mercy mild, God and sinners reconciled"
> Joyful, all ye nations rise; Join the triumph of the skies.
> With the angelic host proclaim: "Christ is born in Bethlehem"
>
> Christ by highest heav'n adored; Christ the everlasting Lord!
> Late in time behold Him come, Offspring of a Virgin's womb.
> Veiled in flesh the Godhead see, Hail the incarnate Deity**!**
> Pleased as man with man to dwell, Jesus, our Emmanuel.
>
> Hail the heav'n-born Prince of Peace! Hail the Son of Righteousness!
> Light and life to all He brings; Ris'n with healing in His wings.
> Mild He lays His glory by, Born that man no more may die;
> Born to raise the sons of earth; Born to give them second birth.

How appropriate that the birth of Jesus in the first stanza leads to the awareness of the God-man in the second stanza, and then to opportunity for the spiritual regeneration of all mankind in the third stanza. As poet Angelus Silesius (John Scheffler) wrote, "Though Christ a thousand times in Bethlehem be born, if He's not born in you, your soul is still forlorn."

DECEMBER 25

THE PURPOSE OF THE BIRTH OF JESUS

Many of our Christmas celebrations are focused on the sentimental trappings of the nativity of a newborn male child, born to Mary more than two millennia ago. The purpose and objective of the birth of Jesus are often obscured in such trite observances as "Happy Birthday Jesus" banners displayed in the Christmas season. Celebrating the birth of Jesus was not practiced among early Christians until the fourth century, when Constantine became the Roman emperor, declared Christianity as the official religion of the empire, and church leaders declared the date of Dec. 25 (winter solstice) as the Feast of the Nativity.

From the earliest celebration of the nativity of Jesus, the incarnational explanation of "the Word became flesh" (Jn. 1:14), recognized that Jesus was the promised Messiah, Emmanuel (God with us), the incarnated God-man (Greek – *theanthropos*), fully God and fully man. This was theologically clarified by the Council of Chalcedon (A.D. 451) as the hypostatic union of deity and humanity in the one person of Jesus Christ.

But we still ask, "What was the purpose of Jesus' birth?" The birth of Jesus is a prototype or type, of which the new birth of the Christian is the antitype or fulfillment. The physical birth of Jesus was the foreshadowing, the type, of God's intent for the restoration of humanity to be "man as God intended" via the spiritual "new birth" (regeneration) of receptive individuals who thus become Christ-ones, Christians. The resurrection of Jesus is also represented as a form of birth, as Jesus was the "firstborn from the dead" (Col. 1:18; Rev. 1:5), and Christians are "born again to a living hope through the resurrection of Jesus Christ from the dead" (I Pet. 1:3). Paul explained that Jesus was the "firstborn among many brothers and sisters" (Rom. 8:29), referring to all Christ-ones, who are also born out of death into spiritual life in likeness of Jesus' birth and resurrection.

A DYNAMIC UNDERSTANDING OF SALVATION

The words "salvation, and "being saved" are so misused in
contemporary Christian thought, that they are but a mangled
mess of muddy semantics. One would think that after two
millennia (two thousand years) of Christian thought, this most
basic Christian concept would be sufficiently clarified, but not so.
It is quite common to hear Christians speaking of a person who
"got saved" (this seems to be such unbiblical language – I do not
find such terminology in the New Testament.) Salvation is a
much broader term than the meaning given to it in much
evangelical vocabulary. It is not an equivalent to regeneration.

"Saved" does not refer to an event or an experience – such
thought quickly becomes static and mechanical. "Being saved"
occurs when an individual opens themselves up in availability
and receptivity of faith to enter into relational spiritual union (I
Cor. 6:17) with the divine and living Savior, Jesus Christ. It is
personal, vital salvation in union with the Savior. If not spiritually
united with the living Savior; if Christ is not one's Life, then it is
questionable whether such person participates in Christian
salvation, whether they are delivered from the natural Satanic
indwelling and actuation of unregenerate persons.

Salvation is the presence and activity of a Person. There is no
Christian spiritual salvation apart from the Savior, Jesus Christ.
Being saved must be personally and vitally linked to the Person
and function of the risen and living Savior, Jesus Christ. Salvation
is the vital and dynamic function of the living Savior in a
receptive individual's life. Yes, an individual responds to the
salvation God has made available in His Son, by faith, our
receptivity of His activity. But the human action of faith does not
leverage an obliged necessity on God's part to "make us safe"
(Greek sozo = to make safe, salvation) either in the present or in
the future. Salvation is always a dynamic personal relationship.

DECEMBER 27

WHEN CHRIST IS OUR LIFE

Jesus is more than simply an object of belief. Jesus is more than simply an identification tag indicating that a person has engaged in the correct activities to identify as a Christian. Jesus is more than an add-on in the life of a Christ-one. When Christ has become the very life of a Christ-one, then every factor of our mental life, emotional life, volitional life, and physical life is to be submitted to the Lordship of the indwelling Spirit of Christ. Jesus is not peripheral to our lives and activities, but is the central essence of who we are and what we do, and is intended to function as the centrifugal energizer of His own manifestation.

Many Christians seem to think that the objective of the Christian life is to properly and accurately represent the life and character of Jesus before others in all they say and do. Such a separated attitude and detached perspective is a performance trap! It is impossible for any Christian to "live like Jesus" or "act like Jesus." When we attempt to do so, we will inevitably misrepresent Jesus in sinfulness. As Christians, we are not called to do our best to represent Jesus, but we are called to allow Jesus to re-present His life and character in our physical, bodily behavioral function, and thus to "manifest Jesus" (II Cor. 4:10,11).

Let's go one step farther. Every action in the life of a Christ-one allowing the indwelling Lord Jesus Christ to be their life will serve as an act of worship. Every action of one who is allowing "Christ to be their life" (Col. 3:4) and to re-present Himself in them, as them, will necessarily express the worth-ship (worship) of the divine character of God in Christ. Thereby, we fulfill the purpose and objective of our creation as human beings, "created for His glory" (Isa. 43:7). Is Jesus your "all in all" (Eph. 1:23), and are you desirous that all that is done in your life should be done to the glory of God (I Cor. 10:31; I Pet. 4:11)? That is what it means for Christ to be our life.

JESUS IS ETERNAL LIFE

This is such a basic reality of the Christian gospel that I am always surprised when religion uses language indicating otherwise. The religious perspective regards eternal life as a static commodity separated and detached from the living Person of Jesus Christ. An article in a theological journal explained that "Jesus is the dispenser of salvation." No! Jesus is the divine Savior, and all forgiveness, salvation and eternal life is "in Him" – intrinsically united with His very Being and function. "God so loved the world that He gave His only begotten Son, that whoever believes into (Greek *eis* = into) Him shall have eternal life" (Jn. 3:16). Such "eternal life" is His life – the resurrection-life of Jesus.

Well, it happened again! I received a bulletin folder from the memorial service of a friend who had lived a full physical life and died at 97 years of age. We first met 52 years ago, so I knew her for over half of her long life. The bulletin, using traditional religious language, indicated that "she entered into physical life in 1924, and entered into eternal life on the day of her physical death in 2021." The buzzer went off in my brain – "Tilt!" She did not become a Christ-one on the day she died, for I knew that she had believed, i.e. received Jesus, decades previously, prior to my ever meeting her.

Eternal life is not a life-commodity that a person acquires and possesses after physical life is completed. Eternal life is the life we participate in when we receive Jesus Christ into our spirit by faith and become a Christ-one, a Christian. Jesus is eternal life! Physical life and eternal life exist simultaneously, concurrently, at the same time on two different planes. When physical life is terminated, eternal life continues in perpetuity, transferred into a spiritual, heavenly, immortal, and glorified body (I Cor. 15; II Cor. 5:1-5). Heaven is the continuation of the presence of the eternal life of Jesus.

DECEMBER 29

THE IMPOTENCY OF WILL-POWER

It is often assumed within the humanistic paradigm of thought that every individual has an inherent, independent "will-power" that allows them to self-determine what they want to do, and to self-dedicate themselves to the implementation of their self-determined choice. God did create human beings with "freedom of choice" which includes basic determination of our actions, but this is not equivalent to the alleged "free-will" of self-determination that includes an intrinsic "will-power" of self-implementation. "Decide to do it; now just do it!" Humans do not have that kind of god-like power.

Even the humanistic-based anonymity groups recognize the impotence and inability of such human will-power, admitting that in and of themselves they are powerless to overcome their addictive and compulsive behaviors, as well as recognizing the necessity of reaching out to "a power beyond oneself" to deal with such habituated behaviors. Despite misunderstanding the spirit-source of such self-sought power that is unable to overcome their self-destructive behaviors, it must be admitted that they explicitly deny the power of human will-power. That is one step beyond what most religion is willing to admit.

Implicit in all religious teaching is the supposition of a human will-power to effect and enact performance, whereby a person can implement and obey what the deity figure expects or demands of the adherent or worshipper. This is the failure of all religion, including evangelical Christian humanism, the failure to recognize the impotency of human will-power. If the Christian religion were to recognize this, they would cease to proclaim and encourage people to "be like Christ" and to "live the Christian life." Instead, they would honestly tell people "you can't live the Christian life; it's an impossible life; you can't do it! But the grace-dynamic of the life of Jesus provides the Spirit-power to do so.

THE TRIALS OF LIFE

Living in the world necessarily involves encountering various trials, problems and irritations. Stuff happens, and the stuff that occurs is not always pleasant. In the *koine* Greek of the New Testament, the word translated "trials" is *peirasmoi*, derived from *peiro* which meant "to pierce in order to examine." The verb form. *peirazo,* could mean "to test," "to try," or "to tempt." The *peirasmoi* trials are situations and circumstances that "pierce our status quo, "and by which we are *peirazoed*, tested, tried or tempted, in order to ascertain what kind of character will come from within in the midst of the trial.

Will we view the trial as an opportunity or an obstacle? Every trial will elicit some sort of reaction or response. In the midst of the trial we will be tempted by the Tempter to react with his selfish and sinful character in different forms of anger, fear, paranoia, escapism, etc. Every trial in the life of a Christ-one will also provide an opportunity to respond with God's character of love and acceptance by allowing the life and character of the indwelling Lord Jesus to re-present Himself.

When Jesus and His disciples were on the eastern side of the Sea of Galilee, a large crowd of inquisitive people had gathered to watch and listen to Jesus. They were quite a distance from their homes, and they began to get restless and hungry. Jesus asked Philip, "Where are we going to find bread to feed all these people?" (cf. Jn. 6:5-7). John indicates that Jesus asked Philip this question to *peirazo* (test, try, or tempt) him. Philip's response was, "Even if there were a grocery store near, we do not have sufficient funds to purchase food for everyone." Jesus proceeded to take the five barley loaves and two fish and multiplied them to feed the 5000 people present. He wanted Philip and the other disciples to realize that when He, Jesus, is present you have all you need in every *peirasmoi* circumstance or situation.

DECEMBER 31

ANNO DOMINI (A.D.)

We have come to the end of another year, and will proceed into the next year. The calculation for the numeration of our years was first proposed by Dionysius Exiguus (470-544), a Christian monk, in the year A.D. 525. His proposal was that we should count years from the year of the birth of Jesus Christ. Years prior to the birth of Christ were to be numbered backwards and identified as B.C., meaning "before Christ", whereas years following the birth of Christ were numbered sequentially forward, and identified as A.D., signifying *Anno Domini*, in Latin, meaning "in the year of our Lord."

This use of the Gregorian calendar with its B.C. and A.D. calculations has become the international standard. Since these designations have a distinctly Christian orientation, there were some objections to its use internationally. In the interest of religious neutrality, the academic community began to use B.C.E. (before the common era) and C.E. (common era) for the periods prior to the birth of Jesus and following the birth of Jesus. Such usage became particularly prominent in the latter part of the twentieth century in scientific journals. There has been some push-back against the change among Christians.

The fact that the original calculations of the year of Jesus' birth were inaccurate, and historians now believe that Jesus was born between 4 and 6 B.C., has also contributed to the willingness to accept more secular designations for the periods of time. There remains, however, the recognition that the incarnational advent of Jesus Christ is the central dividing point of human history. So, as we transition to the next numerical calculation of historical years, those among us who seek precision might want to add four to six years to the date, but general worldwide acceptance will follow the sequence and add one year to the *Anno Domini* (A.D.) or C.E. (common or Christian era).

Indices

Topical Index....................369

Scripture Index.................373

TOPICAL INDEX

Subject   **Pages**

Abraham.................................... 51,
Acting like a Christian.............. 113,
Alcohol..................................... 164,
Anno Domini............................. 366,
Anomaly 223,
Antichrist.................................. 248,
Apocalypse 134,
Attitude...................................... 25,
Autos.. 24,
Baptism..................................... 157,
Baptized in the Spirit.............. 341,
Belief... 193,
Better Christian 17,
Boasting.................................... 111,
Books... 20,
Born Again......................... 339,351,
Caboose 7,
Calvinism.................................. 325,
Carpe Diem.......................... 12,281,
Character............................. 25,168,
Choices.............................. 194,303,
Covenants 16,
Christ crucified........................... 63,
Christ in everything......35,75,293,
   296,318,320
Christ in you.........73,213,249,333,
Christ is life 97,212,320,336,
   350,362,363,
Christian................................... 340,
Christian thought 269,
Christology 101,
Church............................... 199,236,
Church membership................. 310,
Complaining............................... 68,
Conformity 184,
Conspiracy theories................. 308,
Couples 153,
Cross.............................57,81,345,
Cross-life 91,
Crucified with Christ................. 36,

Cruciformity......................56,71,76,
Data dissemination................... 140,
Death........................29,41,206,294,
Death, spiritual......................... 100,
Death of Jesus 86,186,280,
Democracy................................... 69,
Determinism 129,231,
Derivative man...........66,172,247,
   254,276,285,
Desertion.................................. 115,
Desires 226,
Dialectic 54,70,338,
Discipleship.............................. 266,
Discussion................................ 258,
Dying to self............................. 102,
Eastern religion........................ 144,
Ecclesia........................ 270,272,324
Eccentricity............................... 271,
Electromagnetism..................... 159,
Empathy................................... 148,
Emptiness................................. 155,
Epistemology 274,
Expectations........................ 2,184,
Expedience 183,204,
Facts.. 23,
Faith 193,205,214,
Faith, flexibility 49,
Fellowship................................. 256,
Finances.................................... 329,
Flesh......................... 127,216,346,
Freedom 5,14,44,45,50,107,
   332,
Free-will 129,232,
Gender....................................... 275,
Generative source 284,
Giving.. 317,
Glory 197,
God, attributes........................... 74,
God as helper 135
God, faithfulness 299,

God, fatherhood........................278,
God, hidden..................................3,
God's holiness.........................118,
God's Integrity.......................... 28,
God's Love 268,295,
God's Negative.......................... 70,
God's Sufficiency......................328,
God's Ways........ 161,182,306,322,
God's Workmanship..................335,
Good.. 79,80,
Grace.............. 44,109,145,177,179,
     181,191,192,205,214,233,242,
Group dynamics.........................224,
Guilt...166,
Heaven.......................................255,
Hell...255,
Historicism................................244,
Hosea...349,
Husbands...................................151,
Human consciousness.............309,
Human constitution.................. 94,
Human soul...............................353
Human spirit.............................353,
Humanism.........276,277,298,302,
Humility...................................... 66,
Hypotheticals............................163,
Ideas... 8,222
Imperatives...............................337,
In Christ....................................333,
Incarnation........313,356,357,358,
     359,360,
Inconveniences........................... 67,
Identity.................95,171,218,220,
Idolatry......................................211,
Imitation....................................148,
Independent Self........ 60,276,277,
Inside out................................ 6,289,
Intimacy........................... 239,344,
Irritation....................................257,
Jesus alone................................ 19,26,
Jesus in Himself...................... 21,24,
Jesus fills all in all...................... 27,
Jesus is everything.............35,105,
Judgmentalism........................... 15,

Kingdom....................................188,
Knowing Jesus............................ 38,
Knowledge.........................251,352,
Law.................................53,110,346,
Lie.................................59,297,302,
Like God....................................176,
Listening..................................... 98,
Looking forward.......................120,
Lordship of Jesus.....................283,
Loving others.........43,71,195319,,
Manifesting Jesus..............216,311,
Marriage...................................52,287,
Martyr......................................130,206,
Masturbation............................125,
Maundy Thursday...................... 85,
Men..286,
Mindfulness........................136,301,
Mind of Christ..........................136,
Ministry 92,234,262,322,
Music...250,
Mystery................................185,279
Narcissism 123,124,156,
New Year's resolutions.................1,
Nominalism........................198,291,
Obedience..................................121,
Oneness with Jesus..................116,
Ontological dynamic.................228,
Original sin................................ 32,
Overwhelmed............................157,
Pain.. 90,
Parents..2,
Patience...................................... 89,
Peace..126,
Perichoreisis.............................122,
Performance............. 117,128,133,
     154,158,200,243,299,321,
Permissibility............................183,
Personal relationship......221,241,
     263,267,316,355,
Perturbation..............................139,
Point of reference....................343,
Politics..................................81,82,
Prayer....................................88,165,
Preach Jesus.............................. 22,

370

Present 12,
Pride 84,
Proclamation 146,
Progress 10,
Promises 1,
Providence 108,282,
Purity 65,
Purpose 46,47,212,
Quantification 9,
Raised up with Jesus 87,
Raison d'etre 47,
Reason 203,
Receptivity 18,304,
Rejection 11,33,
Rejection of gospel 141,
Relevance 305
Religion 13,42,106,110,131,
       137,160,173,175,177,191,192,
       215,229,250,252,314,334,347,
Reponse-ability 207
Repressed memories 253,
Rest 30,304,
Resurrection 39,312,313,
Revelation 162,348,
Reversion 34,104,196,
Righteousness .. 150,235,331,342,
Sacred cows 217,
Salvation 361,
Satan 247,
Science 178,209,
Scripture interpretation 138,
Scripture translation 290,
Security 147,326,
Self-conscious 77,
Self-denial 78,

Selfishness 43,48,230,
Significance 200,
Sin 143,175,327,
Solus Christus 19,
Special interests 58,
Spirit taught 174,210,
Spiritual being 72,
Spiritual exchange ... 169,170,351,
Strength 55,
Submission 273,277,
Sufferings 40,227,245,292,
Taking a stand 259,
Thanksgiving 99,
Time 238,
Transparency 167,
Trials 365,
Truth 208,
Understanding 260,
Union with Christ 330,
Unity 96,
Vision 189,
Unbelievers 246,
Uselessness 83,
Via negativa 102,
Walk 190,
Wives 152,
Weakness 55,
Will-power 364,
Word of God 225,
Words 237,
World 31,51,119,
World-view 189,
Worship 37,261,
Writer 202

SCRIPTURAL INDEX

Text   **Pages**

Gen. 1:1-2:3 64,
Gen. 1:22 275,
Gen. 1:27 275,
Gen. 1:28 275,
Gen. 2:7 79,186,
Gen. 2:9 208,
Gen. 2:17 48,208,302,339,
Gen. 3:4,5 59,
Gen. 3:5 33,48,60,95,116,276,
    318,
Gen. 3:8 176,
Gen. 3:15 358,
Gen. 3:22 48,
Gen. 4:1 38,
Gen. 6:18 16,
Gen. 9:9 16,
Gen. 12-22 16,51,53,358,
Gen. 17:10-27 332,
Exod. 3;14 118,
Exod. 8:10 74,176,
Exod. 9:14 74,176,
Exod. 20:5 287,
Exod. 34;7 287,
Exod. 32 217,
Exod. 34:7 164,
Deut. 6:4 176,
Deut. 11:13 98,
Deut. 21:23 141,
Deut. 31:18 3,
Numb. 11 68,
Numb. 14:18 287,
II Chron. 6:41 .... 79.
I Kgs. 15:3 164,
I Sam. 17:47 115,
Esther 4:16 206,
Job 90,
Job 32:10 98,
Ps. 18:6 135,
Ps. 19:1 197,
Ps, 23:1 324,

Ps. 27:10 324,
Ps. 29:12 98,
Ps. 30:7 3,
Ps. 55:1 98,
Ps. 66:1 240,
Ps. 68:10 79,
Ps. 71:19 331,
Ps. 72:19 168,
Ps. 86:8 74,
Ps. 95:1,2 240,
Ps. 98:4,6 240,
Ps. 100:1 240,
Ps. 104:14 164,
Ps. 139:13 275,
Ps. 142:2 68,
Prov. 2:3,7 269,
Prov. 11:2 84,
Prov. 14:12 182,303,
Prov. 16:18 84,
Prov. 16:25 182,303,
Prov. 18:24 265,
Prov. 20:1 164,
Prov. 20:9 65,
Prov. 21:9 124,
Prov. 21:23 84,
Prov. 25:24 124,
Prov. 27:17 222,
Eccl. 3:7 15,
Eccl. 3;11 264
Eccl .5:5 1,
Isa. 1:14 347,
Isa. 6:5 1,
Isa. 14:14 33,47,297,307,
Isa. 40:2` 308,
Isa. 42:8 197,
Isa. 43:7 47,168,197,212,362,
Isa. 45:21 331,
Isa. 46:9 74,176,
Isa. 48;11 47,168,197,
Isa. 53:7 206,

Isa. 54:8 3,
Isa. 55:8,9............10,141,182,223, 303,
Isa. 59:2 3,
Isa. 64:8 49,
Jere. 10:7 285,
Ezek. 14:3...............................211,
Ezek. 18:31.............................. 72,
Ezek. 28:14.............................. 33,
Ezek. 36:31.............................. 72,
Ezek. 37:1-14...........................196,
Zech. 4:6 31,188,
Hab. 2:4..................................161,
Hosea.....................................349,
Hosea 14:9....................... 161,303,
Matt. 1:20 93,
Matt. 1:23 93,
Matt. 3:2 146,188,
Matt. 3:11...............................341,
Matt. 3:15...............................157,
Matt. 4:3 183,
Matt. 4:17...............................188,
Matt. 5:3 137,
Matt. 5:4 245,
Matt. 5:8 65,
Matt. 6:19-24 329,
Matt. 6:23-33 328,
Matt. 6:25-29 328,
Matt. 6:30...............................328,
Matt. 6:34............................... 61,
Matt. 7:1-5 105,
Matt. 7:3-5 131,
Matt. 7:12...............................195,
Matt. 7:16,20............................ 9,
Matt. 7:24-27 14,
Matt. 8:26...............................328,
Matt. 11:27 3,
Matt. 11:28 30,304,
Matt. 13:11 62,
Matt. 13:19 31,
Matt. 13:25-30........................347,
Matt. 13:38 31,
Matt. 13:46 221,
Matt. 14:31 328,

Matt. 15:36..............................99,
Matt. 16:8................................328,
Matt. 16:16..............................184,
Matt. 16:18..............................270,
Matt. 16:24............... 56,66,78,137,
Matt. 29:24.............................137,
Matt. 20:20-23 76,
Matt. 20:21,22......................... 81,
Matt. 20:28.............................358,
Matt. 22:29.............................138,
Matt. 22:30............................. 71,
Matt.25:41..............................255
Matt. 25:40................................3,
Matt. 25:45................................3,
Matt. 26:28.............................291,
Matt. 26:29............................. 64,
Matt. 26:53............................. 81,
Matt. 27:11............................. 81,
Matt. 27:37.............................184,
Matt. 27:45............................. 86,
Matt. 27:51............................. 86,
Matt. 28:19,20.........................266,
Mk. 1:8...................................341,
Mk. 1:19.................................157,
Mk. 7:21-23 216,
Mk. 8:6...................................99,
Mk. 9:24.............................78,328,
Mk. 10:18............................... 79,
Mk. 10:25...............................137,
Mk. 10:37............................... 81,
Mk. 10:45...............................358,
Mk. 12:30,31...........................212,
Mk. 13:11............................... 62,
Mk. 14:25............................... 64,
Lk. 2;14.................................126,
Lk. 3:16 157,341,
Lk. 5:20 265,
Lk. 6:9-14 329,
Lk. 6:31 195,
Lk. 6:42 15,
Lk. 9:2...................................146,
Lk. 9:23 41,74,
Lk 9:60 146,
Lk. 10:27................................195,

Lk. 12:4 265,
Lk. 12:12 174,
Lk. 14:18 120,
Lk. 15:26 184,
Lk. 17:7-11 83,
Lk. 177:21 188,
Lk. 18:19 79,
Lk. 18:25 137
Lk. 21:22 12,
Lk. 22:20 16,291,
Lk. 23;38 184,
Lk. 24:7 146,
Jn. 1:1 146,198,225,290,313,
Jn. 1:11,12 18,
Jn. 1:12,13 18,46,278,
Jn. 1:14 93,109,146,198,225,
233,290.313,360,
Jn. 1:16 155,
Jn. 1:17 5,24,44,106,109,
117,179,232,
Jn. 1:**33** **341**,
Jn. 2:4 238,
Jn. 3:1-6 73,278,351,
Jn. 3:3 278,
Jn. 3:3-6 93,
Jn. 3:4 278,
Jn. 3:5 339,
Jn. 3:6 339,
Jn. 3:7 46,
Jn. 3:8 208,
Jn. 3:16 2,33,46,57,119,187,
255,307,326,363,
Jn. 3:21 411,
Jn. 3:33 74,
Jn. 4:14 6,
Jn. 4:24 37,74,261,
Jn. 5:24 46,
Jn. 4:26 326,
Jn. 5:38,39 138,
Jn. 6:5-7 365,
Jn. 6:11 99,
Jn. 6:35 228,
Jn. 6:40 46,
Jn. 6:43 68,

Jn. 6:46 3,
Jn. 7:38 6,289,
Jn. 8:12 .... 190.228,
Jn. 8:19 101,
Jn. 8:28 93,
Jn. 8:32 5,
Jn. 8:36 5
Jn. 8:44 59,114,208,230,
253,254,297,
Jn. 10:3,4 201,
Jn. 10:9 228,
Jn. 10:17 121,
Jn. 10:10 57,69,251,255,
Jn. 10:11 134,228,324
Jn. 10:14 228,324,
Jn. 10:16 194,219,
Jn. 10:27 98,219,324,
Jn. 10:28 46,
Jn. 11:6 139,
Jn. 11:14 134,
Jn. 11:21 139,
Jn. 11:25 228,
Jn. 11:26 86,
Jn. 11:32 139,
Jn. 11:35 139,
Jn. 12:20,21 22,
Jn. 12:24 57,
Jn. 12:24-26 206,
Jn. 12:25 57,
Jn. 12:30 324,
Jn. 12:31 31,33,117,119,248,
347,
Jn. 13:23 .... `134,
Jn. 13:34,35 71,84,
Jn. 12:35 190,
Jn. 13:23 221,
Jn. 13:34 337,
Jn. 13:34,35 270,
Jn. 14:2,3 344,
Jn. 14:6 5,8,174,178,201,
208,228,244,251,326,350,352,
Jn. 14,7,9 3,101,168,279,
Jn. 14:7 139,
Jn. 14:10 93,206,280,

375

Jn. 14:16,17 135,
Jn, 14:18 210,
Jn. 14:26 135,138,210,
Jn. 14:27 126,
Jn. 14:30 33,324,347,354,
Jn. 15:1 228
Jn. 15:4 196,
Jn. 15:5 228,305,
Jn. 15:11 296,
Jn. 15:12 71,270,337,
Jn. 15;14 265
Jn. 15:16 270,
Jn. 15:17 71,337,
Jn. 16:7 135,
Jn. 16:8-11 203,
Jn. 16:11 31,33,106,117,119,
    248,324,347,354,
Jn. 16:13 169,
Jn. 16:24 296,
Jn. 16:33 67,
Jn. 17:4 93,
Jn. 17:11 296,
Jn. 17:11 305,
Jn. 17:14 .... 305.
Jn. 17:14-18 271,
Jn. 18:36 31,81,188,
Jn. 19:12-15 184,
Jn. 19:26 134,221,
Jn. 19:30 154,169,242,286,
    307,
Jn. 20:2 134,221,
Jn. 21:7 134,221
Jn. 21:20 221,
Acts 1:5 341,
Acts 1:8 130,
Acts 2:1-36 93,341,
Acts 2:18 32,
Acts 2:24 86,
Acts 2:27 176,
Acts 3:14 143,150,161,176,
    235,331,342,
Acts 4:29 29,
Acts 6:2 92,
Acts 7:28 236,

Acts 7:52 143,150,161,235,
    331,342,
Acts 9:1-6 348,
Acts 10:14 88,
Acts 11:16 157,341,
Acts 11:26 184,210,340,
Acts 13:35 176,
Acts 15:11 154,
Acts 16:7 169,
Acts 16:22-40 97,
Acts 16:31 46,
Acts 17:24 255,
Acts 19:26 211,
Acts 19:32 236,
Acts 22:14 143,150,161,235,
    331,342,
Acts 26:9-15 40,
Acts 26:18 25,43,46,76,170,
    254,287,297,319,345,351,353,
Rom. 1:4 39,87,
Rom. 1:5 121,
Rom. 1:7 176,
Rom. 1:16 46,201,
Rom. 1:17 161,235,
Rom. 1:31 260
Rom. 3:10 161,
Rom. 3:22 331,
Rom. 3:23 33,162,172,232,
Rom. 3:25 280,
Rom. 4:6 331,
Rom. 5:1-12 32,
Rom. 5:1 126,336,
Rom. 5:5 33,71,195,307,337,
Rom. 5:8 187,
Rom. 5:10 64,336,
Rom. 5:12 86,100,186,214,
    302,
Rom 5:12-21 205,
Rom. 5:15 181,
Rom. 5:17 150,188,226,302,
    331,
Rom. 5:18 150,181,342,
Rom. 5:19 43,60,72,95,150,
    171,235,297,342.

Rom. 5:21 100,186,331,
Rom. 6:2 41,
Rom. 6:4 87,190,291,
Rom. 6:6 .... 43,107,187,291,299, 319,
Rom. 6:6-20 345,
Rom. 6:8 78,
Rom. 6:10 41,186,
Rom. 6:11 187,
Rom. 6:14 110,
Rom. 6:16-20 43,
Rom. 6:17 107,297,299,319,
Rom. 6:23 46,100,
Rom. 6:20 107,319,
Rom. 6:23 186,
Rom. 7:1-7 34,330,
Rom. 7:4 39,110,
Rom. 7:6 291,
Rom. 7:13 .... 299.
Rom. 7:19 1,
Rom. 8:1 166,
Rom. 8:2 100,244,
Rom. 8:4 190,
Rom. 8:5 268,
Rom. 8:9 .... 4,18,46,72,73,94, 97,101,162,169,173,213,221, 232,235,244,254,255,260,299, 315,318,333,340,351,
Rom. 8:10 161,244,
Rom. 8:11 39,73,87,244,
Rom. 8:14 161,173,294,
Rom. 8:15 278,
Rom. 8:16 .... 46,93,138,173,213, 221,235,267,340,
Rom. 8:20-22 208,
Rom. 8:26 62,135,
Rom. 8:26,27 165,
Rom. 8:27 95,
Rom. 8:28 4,75,80,108,264,
Rom. 8:29 93,273,312,360,
Rom. 8:36 37,103,
Rom. 8:38,39 97,130,
Rom. 8:39 268
Rom. 9:25,26 349,

Rom. 10:4 110,196,331,
Rom. 11:8 169,
Rom. 11:33 .... 10,223,279.323, 348,
Rom. 11:36 62,186,
Rom. 12:2 91,104,353,
Rom. 12:5-8 322,
Rom. 13:8 71,270,
Rom. 13:9 71,
Rom. 14:17 126,235,
Rom. 15:1 78,
Rom. 15:14 253,
Rom. 15:18 83,128,187,234,
Rom. 16:15 176,
Rom. 16:25,26 185,
Rom. 16:26 121,138,
I Cor. 1:9 74,326,
I Cor. 1:12 353,
I Cor. 1:18 76,353,
I Cor. 1:20 51,
I Cor. 1:20-30 141,
I Cor. 1:22-25 63,
I Cor. 1:23 146,
I Cor. 1:24 76,
I Cor. 1:30 171,296,
I Cor. 2:7 141,
I Cor. 2:8 185,
I Cor. 2:12 .... 73,154,174,229, 351,
I Cor. 2:12,13 203,
I Cor. 2:13 174,
I Cor. 2:14 .... 13,36,73,123, 136,141,144,172,182,250,263, 309,339,352,
I Cor. 2:14-16 277,
I Cor. 2:16 8,136,260,352,353,
I Cor. 3:1 136,
I Cor. 4:11 41,
I Cor. 5:1 93,
I Cor. 5:15-19 34,
I Cor. 6:2 61,
I Cor. 6:9-11 171,
I Cor. 6:12 164,183,

I Cor. 6:17.............. 4,61,87,91,116, 122,130,213,218,221,265,305, 330,333,335,344,349,361,
I Cor. 6:20........................... 107,181,
I Cor. 7:23........................... 107,181,
I Cor. 8:1 251,
I Cor. 8:6 285,
I Cor. 10:2 157,
I Cor.10:23....................... 164,183,
I Cor. 10:31 362,
I Cor. 11:24............................... 99,
I Cor. 11:25................................ 16,
I Cor. 11:26...............................146,
I Cor. 12:12 168,310,
I Cor. 12:12-27 310,
I Cor. 12:13 157,341,
I Cor. 12:27 236,310,
I Cor. 12:27-30 322,
I Cor. 13:1-13.............151,152,153,
I Cor. 13:4................................. 89,
I Cor. 13:4,5...............................123,
I Cor. 13:11...............................111,
I Cor. 13:13...............................215,
I Cor. 14:26...............................316,
I Cor. 15 363,
I Cor 15:1-7 244,
I Cor. 15:11,12...........................146,
I Cor. 15:21...............................186,
I Cor. 15:22.................247,302,326,
I Cor. 15:25...............................248,
I Cor. 15:28................................ 27,
I Cor. 15:31...............................103,
I Cor. 15:39...............................127,
I Cor. 15:45........ 100,101,142,163, 184,198,210,221,233,244,263, 311,313,
I Cor. 15:54............................... 93,
I Cor. 15:57.........................93,102,
II Cor. 1:8-11.............................. 40,
II Cor. 1:18................................326,
II Cor. 1:20................................291,
II Cor. 1:20-22 28,
II Cor. 2:10-15 138,
II Cor. 2:24................................311,

II Cor. 2;14-16............................278,
II Cor. 2:17 250,262,
II Cor. 3:3.................................6,249,
II Cor. 3:5...........1,60,117,128,137, 142,182,318,320,
II Cor. 3:6................................291,
II Cor. 3:7................................. 93,
II Cor. 3:17 313,
II Cor. 4:4...........142,172,182,189, 277,297,
II Cor. 4:10,11 ......4,6,17,18,26,34, 38,42,66,94,95,103,113,187, 311,321,327,353,362,
II Cor. 4:12-16...........................197,
II Cor. 4;17................................227,
II Cor. 4:17,18 12,
II Cor. 4:18 309,
II Cor. 5:1..................................255,
II Cor. 5:1-5................................363,
II Cor. 5:7..................................190,
II Cor. 5:12 86,
II Cor. 5:14 50,
II Cor. 5:15 66,
II Cor. 5:17 .... 36,64,78,87,168, 169,208,218,221,226,267,286, 291,326,353,
II Cor. 5:21 .... 41,57,93,150, 161,171,235,327,331,342,
II Cor. 5:24 86,
II Cor. 6:2.................................... 64,
II Cor. 6:4...................................287,
II Cor. 9:7...................................317,
II Cor. 10:12...............................166,
II Cor. 10:13...........................74,90,
II Cor. 11:2 65,
II Cor. 11:3 297,
II Cor. 12:2 309,
II Cor. 12:7-10............................ 90,
II Cor. 12:8,9...............................227,
II Cor. 12:9 ....55,139,221,242, 245,292,
II Cor. 12:9,10 76,
II Cor. 12:10.............. 137,155,245,

II Cor. 13:5........4,73,128,250,311, 333,351,
Gal. 2:19...36,

Gal. 2:20............33,36,41,45,46,71, 73,86,103,187,198,201,213, 288,293,305,320,326,333,
Gal. 2:21.......................................331,
Gal. 2:26...60,
Gal. 3:1,2,3,...................................18,
Gal. 3:7..51,
Gal. 3:9......................................38,51,
Gal. 3:11.......................................161,
Gal. 3:14...18,
Gal. 3:16,17.....................................53
Gal. 3:28.......................................275,
Gal. 3:29...16,
Gal. 4:6.....................................73,278,
Gal. 4:8.......................................211,
Gal. 4:19...17,
Gal. 4:22-31....................................34,
Gal. 4:26.......................................115,
Gal. 5:1..............5,14,107,332,334,
Gal. 5:2.......................................346,
Gal. 5:4.......................................346,
Gal. 5:5.......................................332,
Gal. 5:12......................................332,
Gal. 5:13.................14,270,332,334,
Gal. 5:14...71,
Gal. 5:16....................190,226,346,
Gal. 5:16,17.........................127,226,
Gal. 5:16-21.................................257,
Gal. 5:17............104,127,154,216,
Gal. 5:17,18.........................102,110,
Gal. 5:18.......................................346,
Gal. 5:19-21..........................31,103,
Gal. 5:19.......................................224,
Gal. 5:22.................11,71,255,337,
Gal. 5:22,23.............4,6,9,14,31,39, 89,153,195,343
Gal. 6:7..62,
Gal. 6:14...57,
Gal. 6:15.......................................208,
Gal. 6:16..................................64,291,

Eph. 1:1...............................171,176,
Eph. 1:3...77,
Eph. 1:4...17,
Eph. 1:6...33,
Eph. 1:17......................................169,
Eph. 1:18..46,
Eph. 1:19,20...................................39,
Eph. 1:22,23...................................27,
Eph. 1:23.........21,27,135,213,203, 362,
Eph. 2:1........43,100,142,247,302,
Eph. 2:1-3....................................247,
Eph. 2:2............31,32,36,43,60,72, 94,95,100,116,169,171,205, 226,232,247,254,255,297,299, 302,319,336,351,
Eph. 2:3..............127,142,226,319,
Eph. 2:4.......................................268,
Eph. 2:5.................43,100,142,154, 247,302,
Eph. 2:5,6.......................................87,
Eph. 2:7.......................................196,
Eph. 2:8,9........................18,46,335,
Eph. 2:8..............154,182,214,320,
Eph. 2:10.................................212,335,
Eph. 2:11-22...................................96,
Eph. 2:15......................................291,
Eph. 2:19......................................171,
Eph. 3:4.......................................185,
Eph. 3:8.......................................196,
Eph. 3:9.......................................185,
Eph. 3:19.................................17,338,
Eph. 3:20......................................348,
Eph. 4:2.......................................270,
Eph. 4:10..27,
Eph. 4:12......................................176,
Eph. 4:13......................................323,
Eph. 4:15......................................338,
Eph. 4:18......................................260,
Eph. 4:22.................................87,291,
Eph. 4:23......................................104,
Eph. 4:24.............17,36,78,87,291,
Eph. 5:1.......................................226,
Eph. 5:10......................................240,

Eph. 5:16 281,
Eph. 5:17 260,
Eph. 5:19 318,
Eph. 5:22-33.................................236,
Eph. 5:27 176,
Eph. 6:12 106,
Eph. 6:13,14 199,
Eph. 6:15 126,
Phil. 1:6.........10,154,200,221,243,
    249,286,
Phil. 1:11 161,232,235,
Phil. 1:19 169,
Phil. 1:21 19,97,187,198,201,
    293,
Phil. 2:3,4 66,251,343,
Phil. 2:4..............................78,156,
Phil. 2:7...312,
Phil. 2:8..........................44,93,339,
Phil 2:12 318,335
Phil. 2:13 10,128,133,247,
    254,299,304,320,335,
Phil. 2:14,15 68,
Phil. 2:25 115,
Phil. 3:8..........................38,40,119,
Phil. 3:10 38,39,40,41,273,
Phil. 3:12 353,
Phil. 3:13 120,169,
Phil. 3:15 342
Phil. 4:13,14 196,
Phil. 4:13 305,
Phil. 3:15 17,
Phil. 3:20 188,
Phil. 3:21 273,
Phil. 4:5...164,
Phil. 4:6.. 99,
Phil. 4:7......................126,239,296,
Phil. 4:8.. 65,
Phil. 4:19 328,
Col. 1:4 130,
Col. 1:13,14...............170,345,351,
Col. 1:13.............................. 247,287,
Col. 1:13,25...................................297,
Col. 1:15...319,
Col. 1:18.............................. 316,360,

Col. 1:22 171,176,342,
Col. 1:24...................................40,316,
Col. 1:26...185,
Col. 1:26,27 73,
Col. 1:27 128,185,187,197,
    256,288,
Col. 1:28...................17,93296,318,
Col. 2:2............................... 185,258,
Col. 2:6.. 18,46,
Col. 2:10 78,93,318,
Col. 2:12 87,
Col. 2:15 86,106,115,119,
Col. 2:20 66,78,
Col. 2:20-23 106,
Col. 2:23...208,
Col. 3:1.. 87,
Col. 3:2...................... 196,301,308,
Col. 3:3.....................66,86,187,343,
Col. 3:4.........36,38,73,97,135,163,
    169,187,201,221,249,256,293,
    326,362,
Col. 3:5.. 26,
Col. 3:9...291,
Col. 3:10.................................36,291,
Col. 3:12...342,
Col. 3:16...240,
Col. 3:17.. 99,
Col. 4:3...185,
Phlmn. 1:2....................................115,
I Tim. 1:5,6..................................237,
I Tim. 2:5............................293,312,
I Tim. 2:6.......................................358,
I Tim. 3:3-8 164,
I Tim. 3:16..........................138,399,
I Tim. 4:10....................................326,
I Tim. 4:23....................................164,
I Tim. 6:3.......................................273
I Tim. 6:4.......................................237,
I Tim. 6:10....................................329,
II Tim. 1:7.....................................169,
II Tim. 1:12 352,
II Tim. 2:1.....................................158,
II Tim. 2:3.....................................115,
II Tim. 2:7.....................................260,

II Tim. 2:11 86,
II Tim. 2:14 237,
II Tim. 2:15 225,
II Tim. 2:16 171,
II Tim. 2:19 291,
II Tim. 2:26 107,116,226,254,
    297,326,
II Tim. 3:2 123,
II Tim. 3;3 197,
II Tim. 3:8-13 92,
I Thess. 1:5 44,
I Thess. 3:16 126,290,
I Thess. 5:11 80,
I Thess. 5:14 89
I Thess. 5:18 68,
I Thess. 5:23 72,94,126,289,
I Thess. 5:23,24 318,
I Thess. 5:24 154,243,
II Thess. 3:3 31,
Titus 1:2 .... 28.
Titus 1:3 238,
Titus 1:11,12 56,
Titus 1:15 65,
Titus 2:14 271,
Titus 3:3 297,
Titus 3:4 268,
Titus 3:4 339,
Heb. 1:3 168,
Heb. 2:10 278,
Heb. 2:14 .... 43,55,86,100,107.
    119,142,302,339,
Heb. 2:17 280,
Heb. 3:12,13 199,
Heb. 3:13 270,
Heb. 3:14 73,
Heb. 4:1-11 30,304,
Heb. 4:12 353,
Heb. 4:12,13 344,
Heb. 4:13 225,
Heb. 4:15 342
Heb. 4:16 135,344,
Heb. 6:5 79,
Heb. 6:18 28,232,
Heb. 7:28 342,

Heb. 8:8 291,
Heb. 8:10 16,110,349,
Heb. 8:12 134,
Heb. 8:13 16,
Heb. 9:5 134,
Heb. 9:15 16,291,
Heb. 9:27 29,
Heb. 10:16 110,
Heb. 10:22 344,
Heb. 10:25 270,
Heb. 10:29 169,
Heb. 10:38 161,
Heb. 11:2 42,
Heb. 11:7 332,
Heb. 12:2 42,
Heb. 12:11 235,
Heb. 12:22 115,
Heb. 12:23 342,353,
Heb. 12:24 291,
Heb. 12:29 74,
Heb. 13:8 .... 323m
Heb. 13:20 16,126,335,
Heb. 13:21 212,335,
James 1:4 296,318,
James 1:13 50,
James 1:19 98,246,
James 1:25 110,
James 1:26 15,
James 2:5 186,
James 2:8 110,
James 2:23 265,
James 3:2 15,
James 3:15 297,
James 4:4 265,
James 4:5 73,
James 4:6 84,
James 4:7 103,118,329,
James 4:8 46,
James 4:14 12,
James 5:9 68,
I Pet. 1:3 187,278,339,360,
I Pet. 1:11 169,
I Pet. 1:15,16 176
I Pet. 1:22 338,

I Pet. 2:9.................................92,271,
I Pet. 2:10.....................................349,
I Pet.2:24.......................................86,
I Pet. 3:14......................................40,
I Pet. 3:15.....................................258,
I Pet. 3:18.....................................187,
I Pet. 4:11.....................................362
I Pet. 5:5..84,
I Pet. 5:8.............................104,106,
II Pet. 1:3...................6,17,299,351,
II Pet. 1:4................60,93,116,122,
    168,218,247,278,316,333,
II Pet. 2:10.......................... 127,154,
II Pet. 2:18.......................... 127,154,
II Pet. 3:9..89,
II Pet. 3:15.....................................203,
II Pet. 3:17.....................................104,
II Pet. 3:18.................... 10,140,310,
I Jn. 1:5..74,
I Jn. 1:7...190,
I Jn. 1:8,9......................................327,
I Jn. 2:1...235,
I Jn. 2:2...290,
I Jn. 2:6...190.
I Jn. 2:16 84,
I Jn. 2:18.......................................224,
I Jn. 2:20 342,
I Jn. 2:29 235,
I Jn. 3:3...65,
I Jn. 3:7 150,235,
I Jn. 3:8.........31,60,72,86,100,115,
    119,143,171,254,207,

I Jn. 3:11..71
I Jn. 3:14..93,
I Jn. 4:3 169,224,247,
I Jn. 4:4 25,248,
I Jn. 4:6 144,169,208,291,
I Jn. 4:7 116,
I Jn. 4:10.................................71,290,
I Jn. 4:8,16 11,23,33,43,47,
    50,71,74,279,307,326,
I Jn. 4:11...71,
I Jn. 4:18..23,
I Jn. 4:19.......................................326,
I Jn. 5:4 102,
I Jn. 5:12.............178,201,231,244,
    326,350,
I Jn. 5:19.................................31,107,
I Jn. 5:20.......................................208,
I Jn. 5:28.......................................327,
III Jn. 1:11......................................79,
Rev. 1:5 360,
Rev. 3:29...46,
Rev. 4:10,11.................................197,
Rev. 4:11.......................................212,
Rev. 11:15.....................................188,
Rev. 12:9.......................................297,
Rev. 15:4.......................................176,
Rev. 19:19 115,
Rev. 20:10 107,
Rev. 21:1...12,
Rev. 21:4.......................................227,
Rev. 21:9.......................................236,
Rev. 21:22 277,

Made in the USA
Columbia, SC
11 November 2021